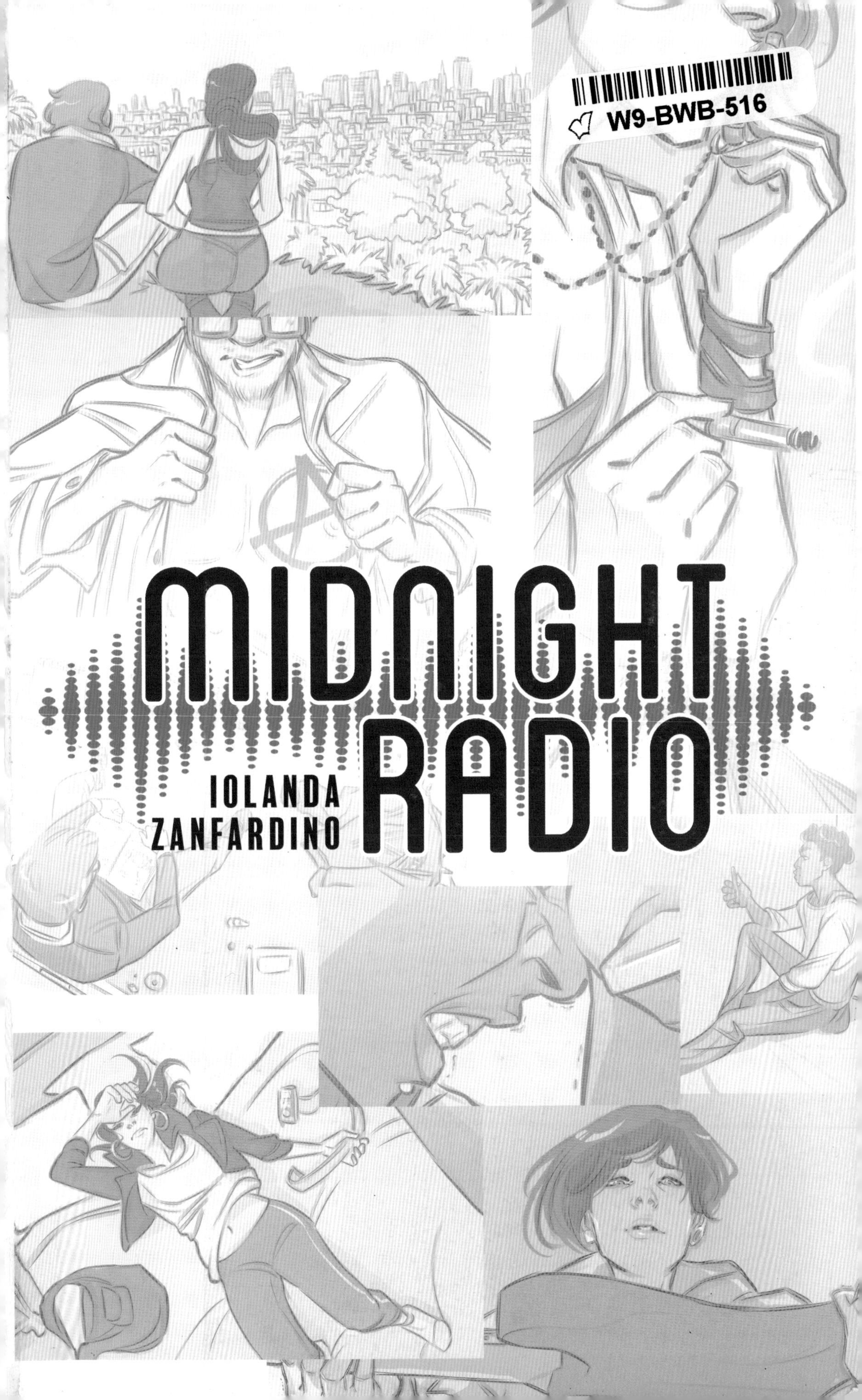

MIDNIGHT RADIO

IOLANDA ZANFARDINO

Written and illustrated
by
Iolanda Zanfardino

Editing and Layout by Mike Kennedy

LION
FORGE

ISBN: 978-1-942367-99-4
Library of Congress Control Number: 2018962458

10 9 8 7 6 5 4 3 2 1

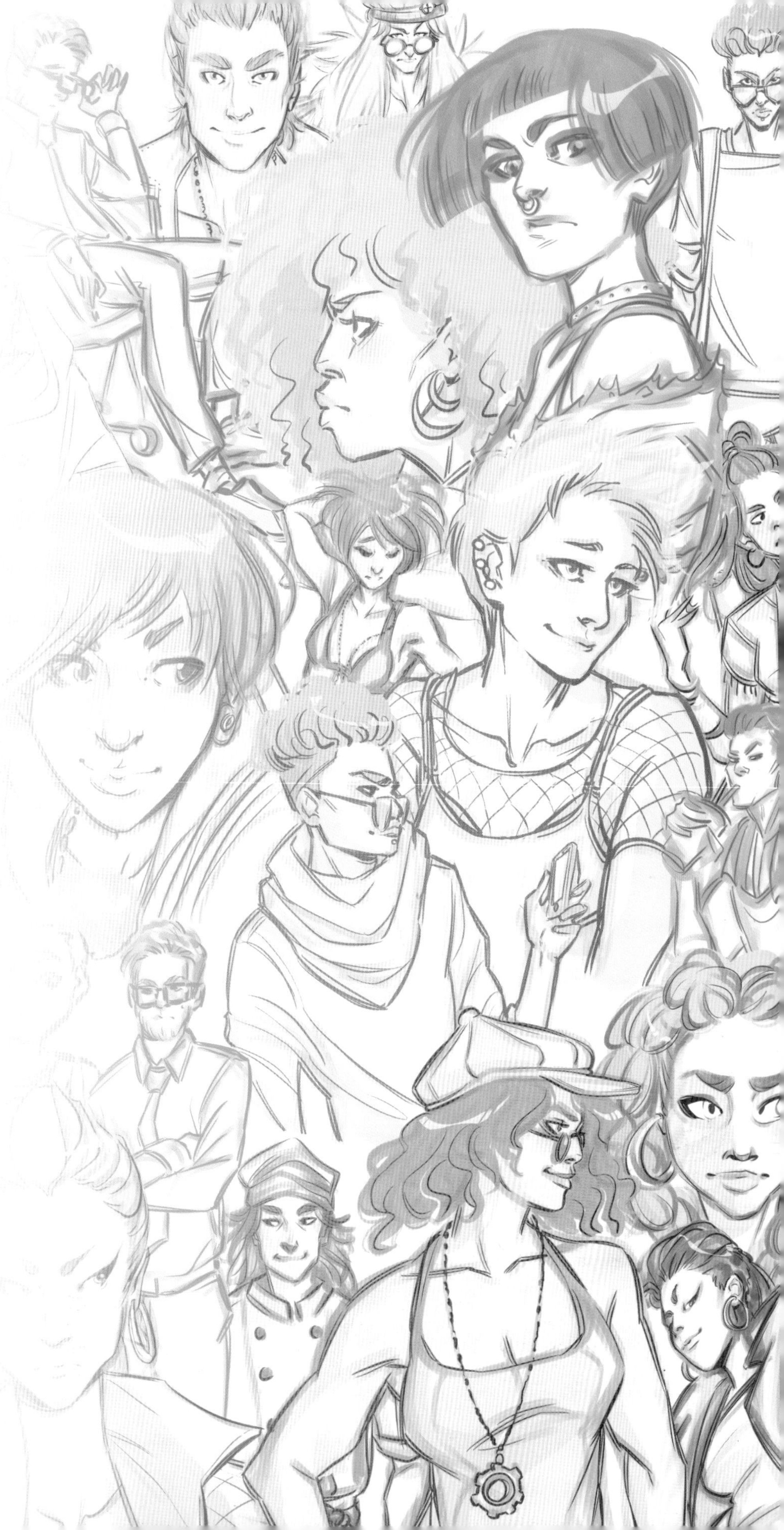

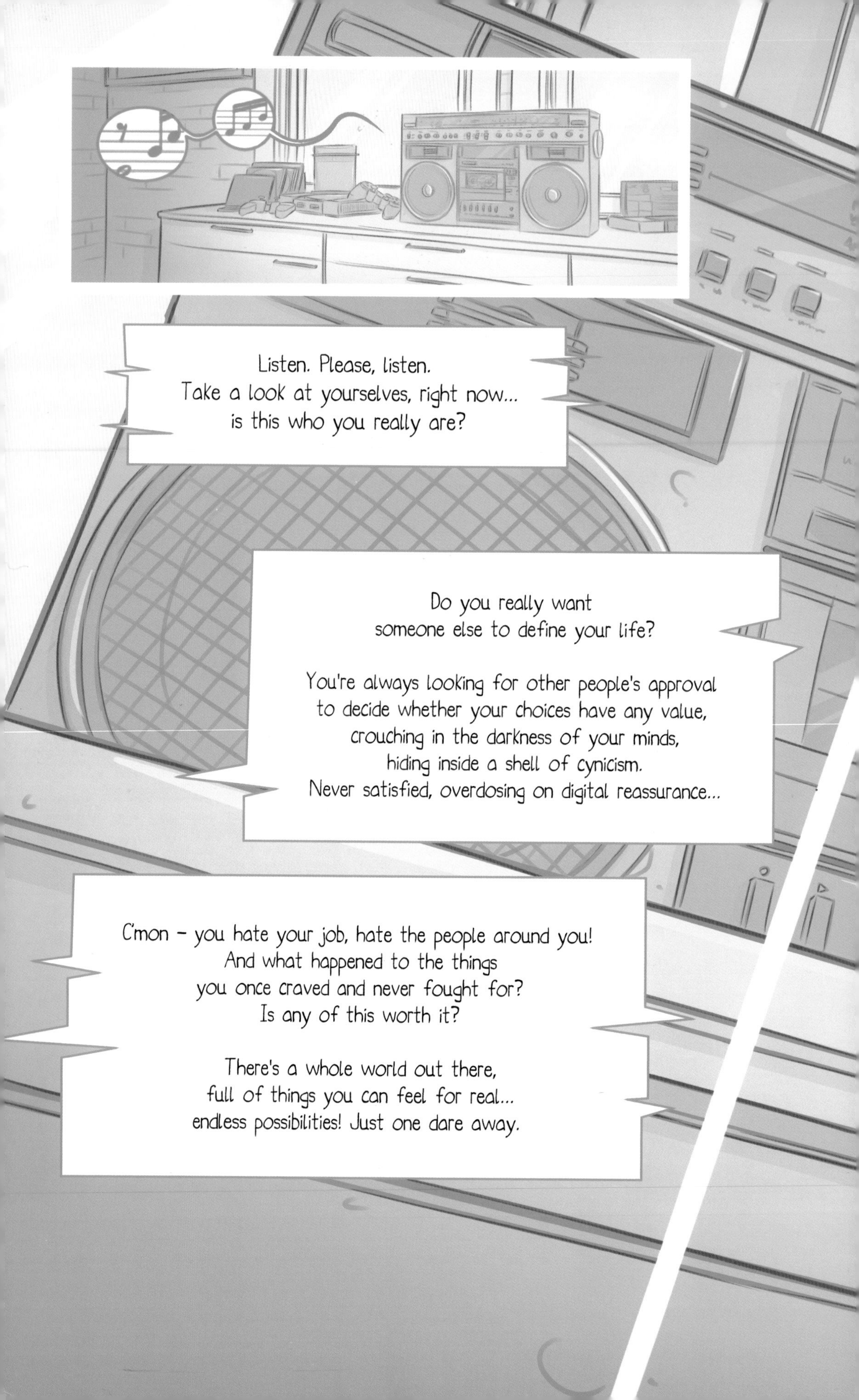
Listen. Please, listen.
Take a look at yourselves, right now...
is this who you really are?
Do you really want
someone else to define your life?
You're always looking for other people's approval
to decide whether your choices have any value,
crouching in the darkness of your minds,
hiding inside a shell of cynicism.
Never satisfied, overdosing on digital reassurance...
C'mon – you hate your job, hate the people around you!
And what happened to the things
you once craved and never fought for?
Is any of this worth it?
There's a whole world out there,
full of things you can feel for real...
endless possibilities! Just one dare away.

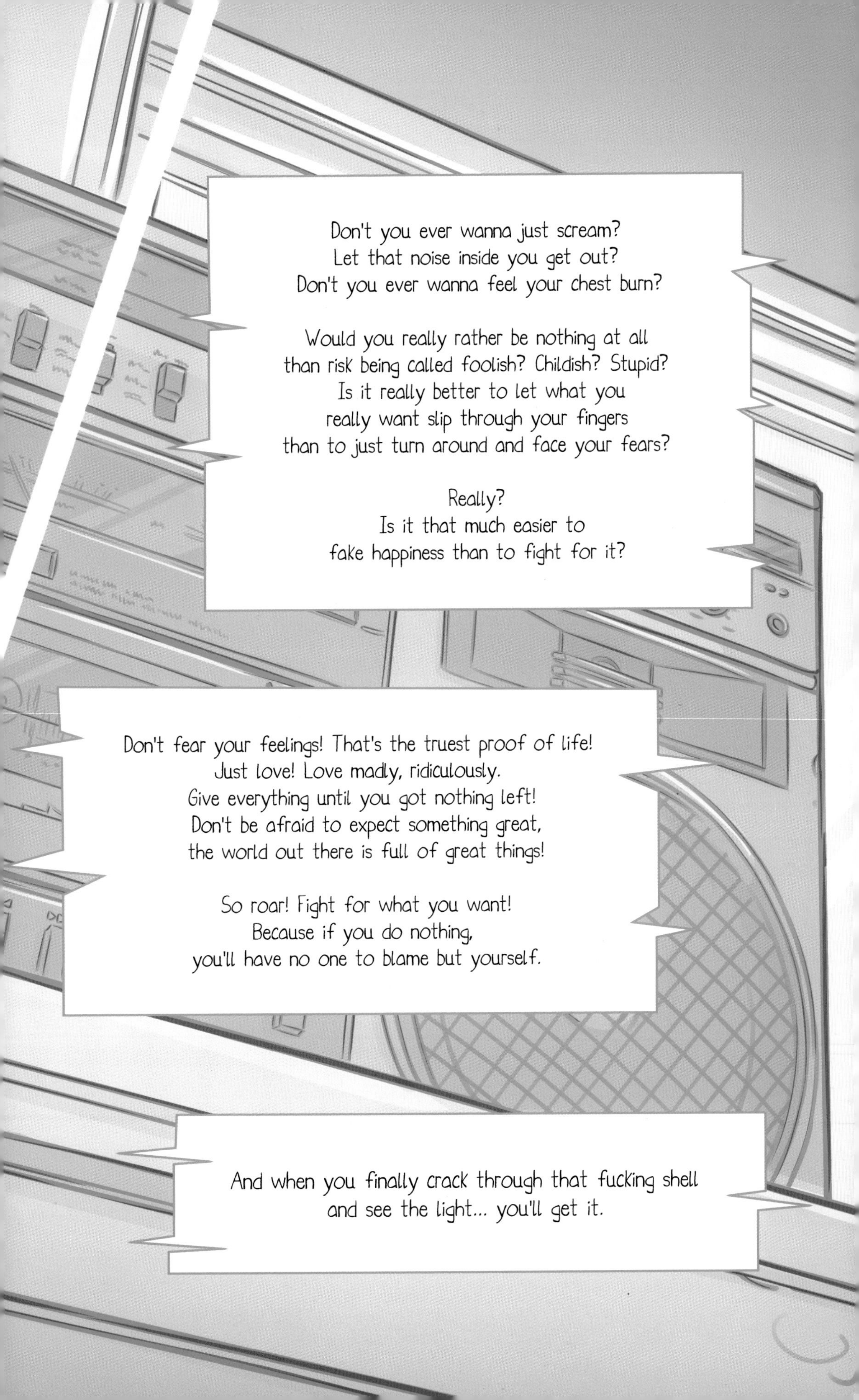
Don't you ever wanna just scream? Let that noise inside you get out? Don't you ever wanna feel your chest burn?
Would you really rather be nothing at all than risk being called foolish? Childish? Stupid? Is it really better to let what you really want slip through your fingers than to just turn around and face your fears?
Really? Is it that much easier to fake happiness than to fight for it?
Don't fear your feelings! That's the truest proof of life! Just love! Love madly, ridiculously. Give everything until you got nothing left! Don't be afraid to expect something great, the world out there is full of great things!
So roar! Fight for what you want! Because if you do nothing, you'll have no one to blame but yourself.
And when you finally crack through that fucking shell and see the light... you'll get it.

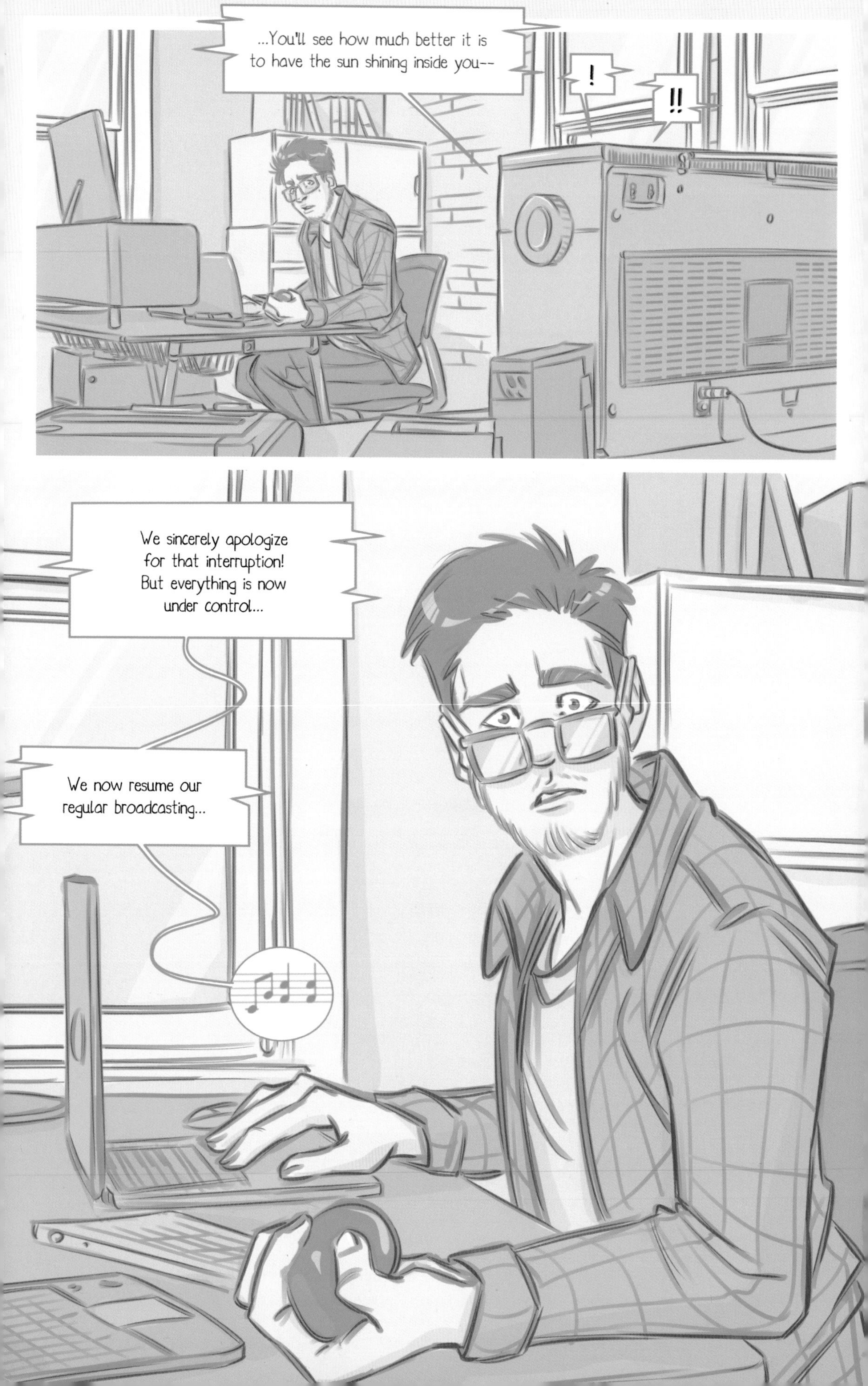
...You'll see how much better it is to have the sun shining inside you--
!
!!
We sincerely apologize for that interruption! But everything is now under control...
We now resume our regular broadcasting...

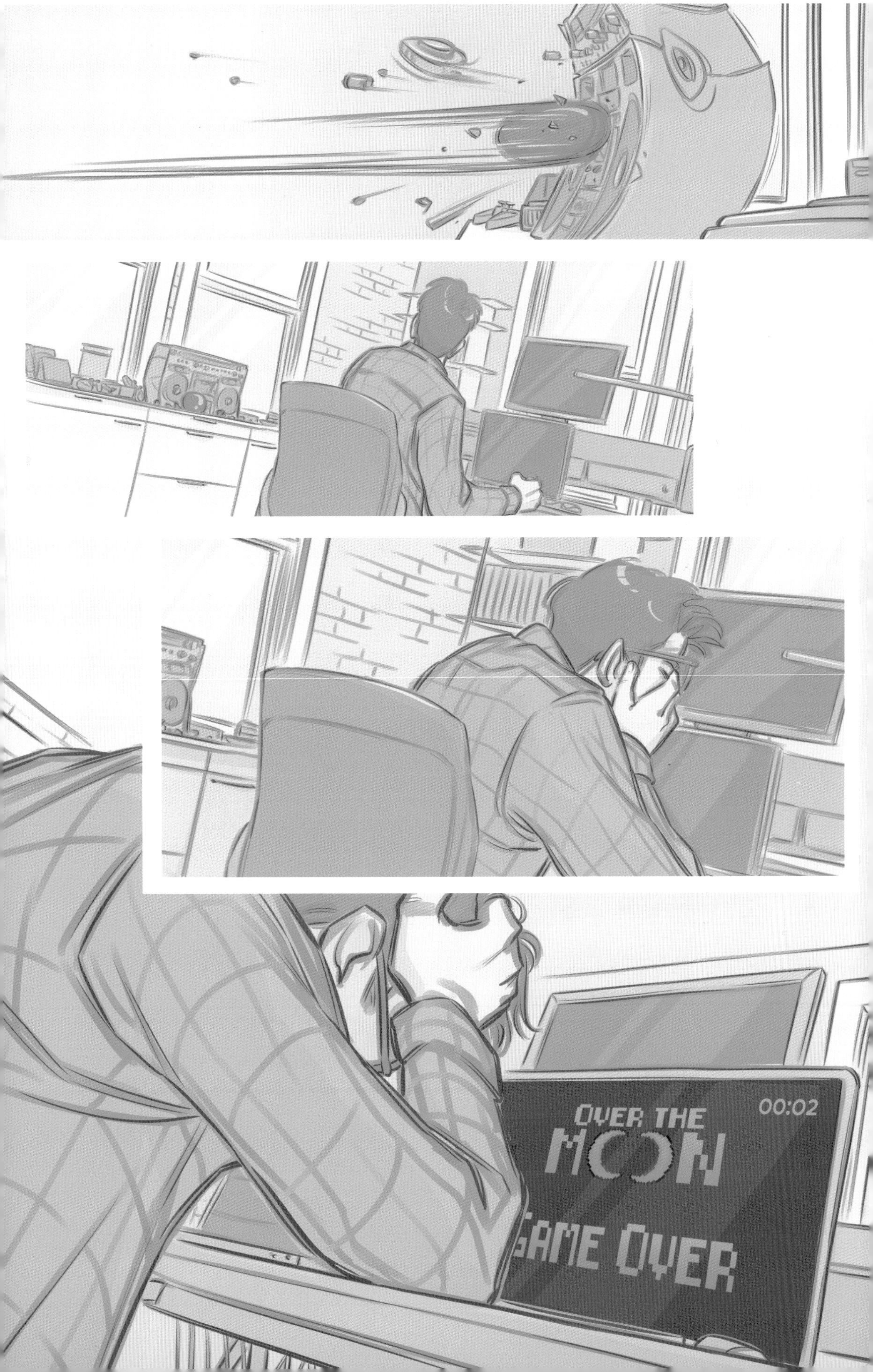
00:02
OVER THE
MOON
GAME OVER

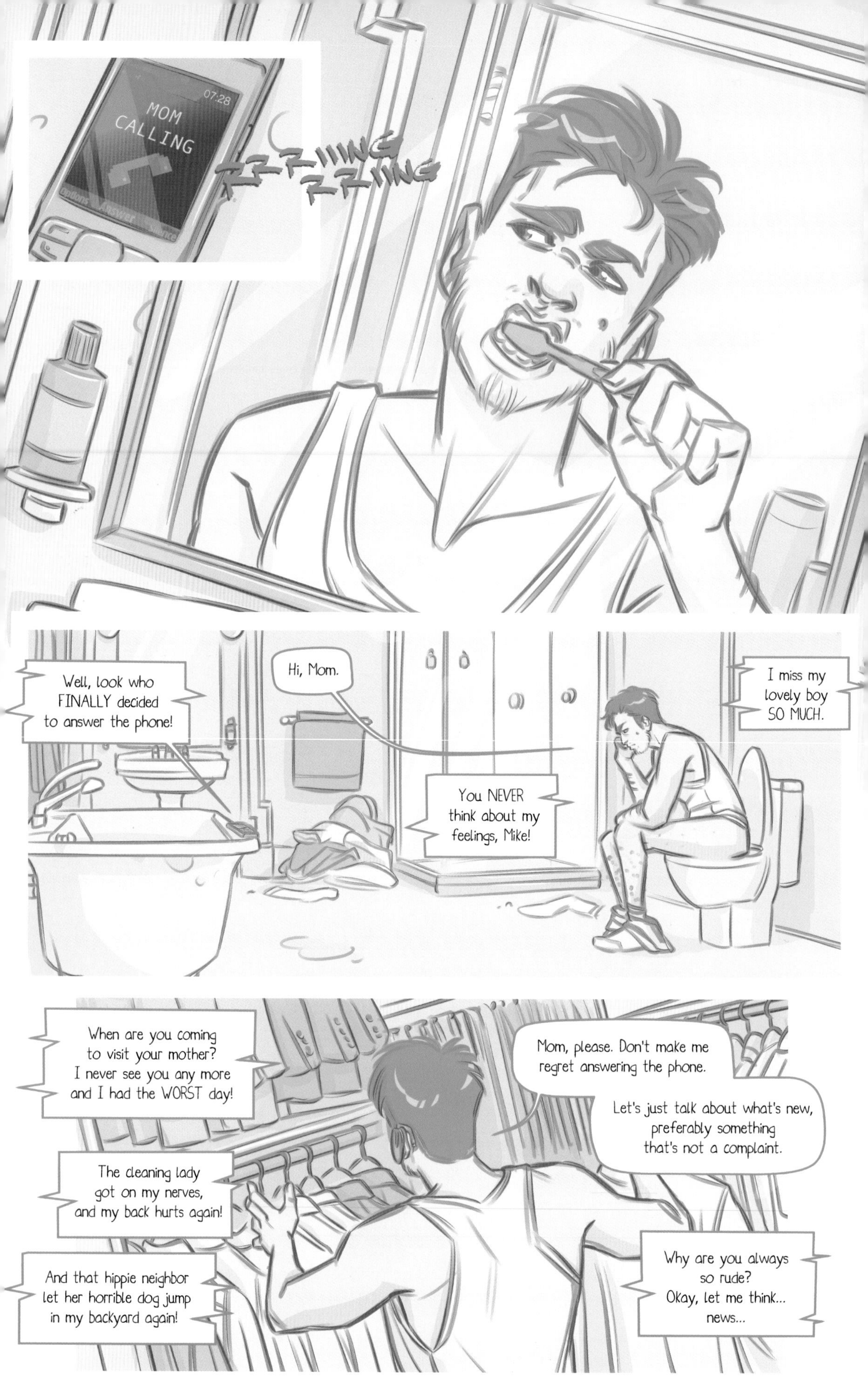
07:28
MOM CALLING
options ANSWER silence
RRRIIIING RRIIING
Well, look who FINALLY decided to answer the phone!
Hi, Mom.
I miss my lovely boy SO MUCH.
You NEVER think about my feelings, Mike!
When are you coming to visit your mother? I never see you any more and I had the WORST day!
Mom, please. Don't make me regret answering the phone.
Let's just talk about what's new, preferably something that's not a complaint.
The cleaning lady got on my nerves, and my back hurts again!
And that hippie neighbor let her horrible dog jump in my backyard again!
Why are you always so rude? Okay, let me think... news...

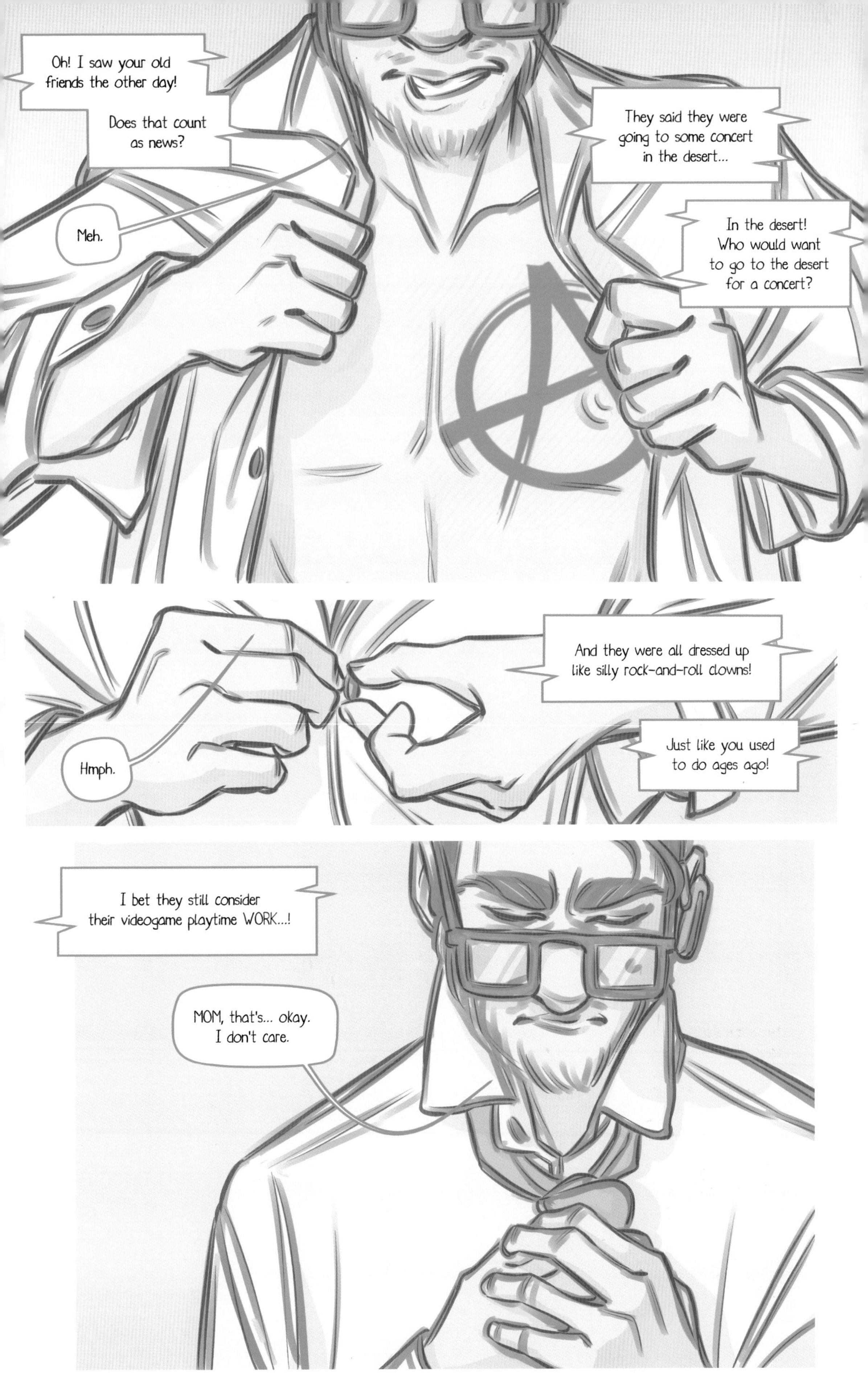
Oh! I saw your old friends the other day!
Does that count as news?
Meh.
They said they were going to some concert in the desert...
In the desert! Who would want to go to the desert for a concert?
And they were all dressed up like silly rock-and-roll clowns!
Hmph.
Just like you used to do ages ago!
I bet they still consider their videogame playtime WORK...!
MOM, that's... okay. I don't care.

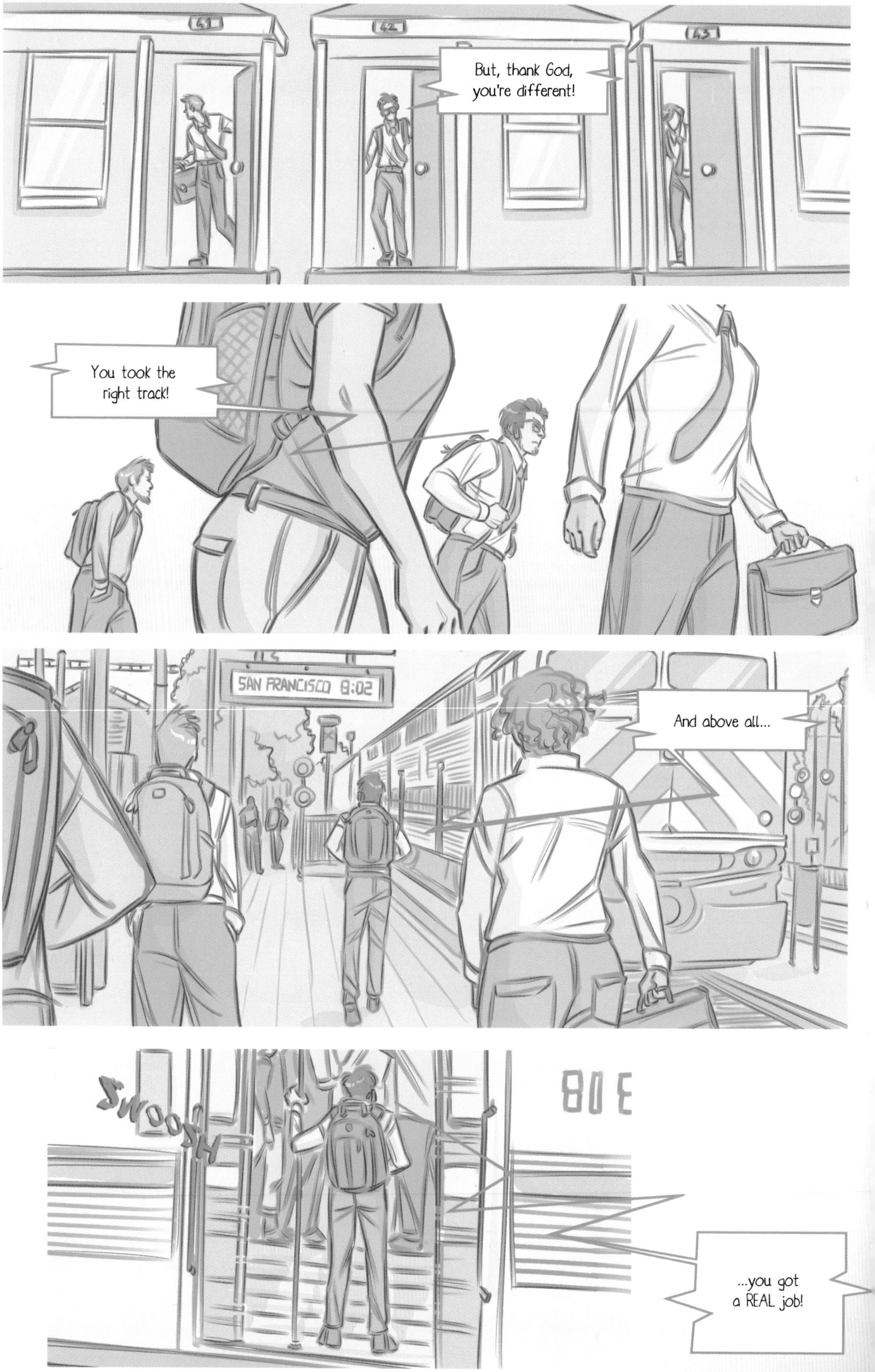

But, thank God, you're different!
You took the right track!
SAN FRANCISCO 8:02
And above all...
SWOOSH
...you got a REAL job!

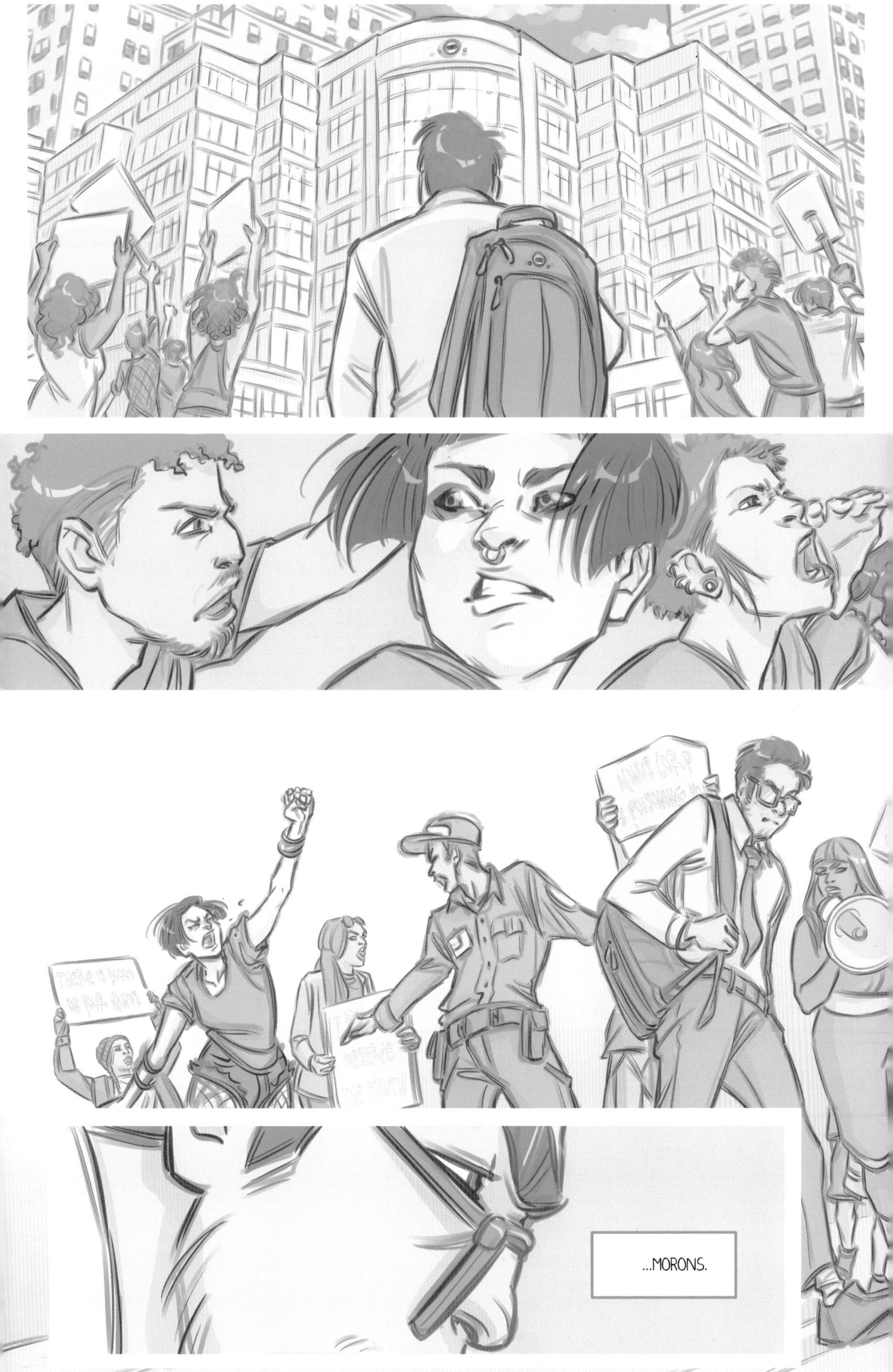
...MORONS.

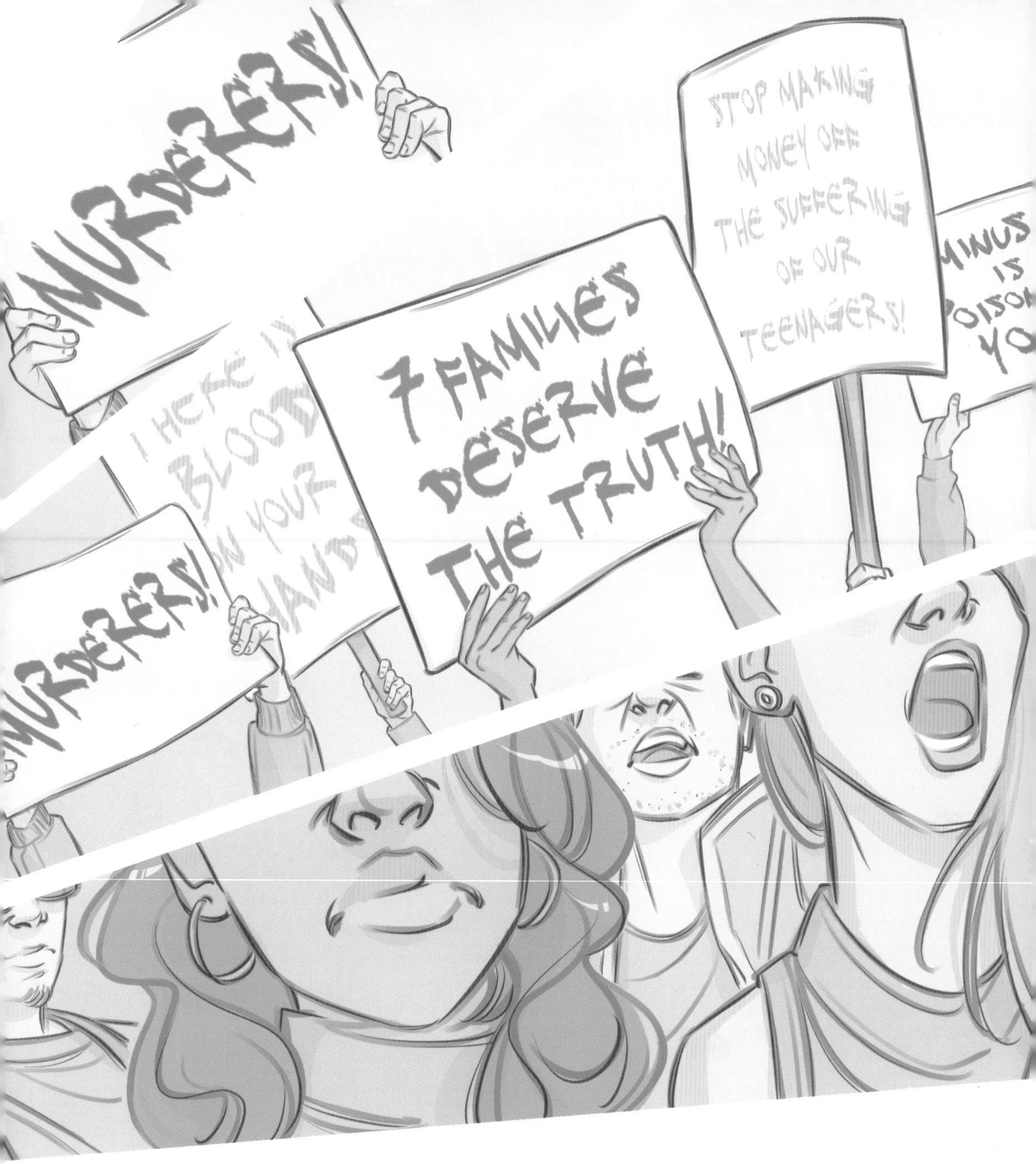
MURDERERS!
7 FAMILIES DESERVE THE TRUTH!
STOP MAKING MONEY OFF THE SUFFERING OF OUR TEENAGERS!
MURDERERS!

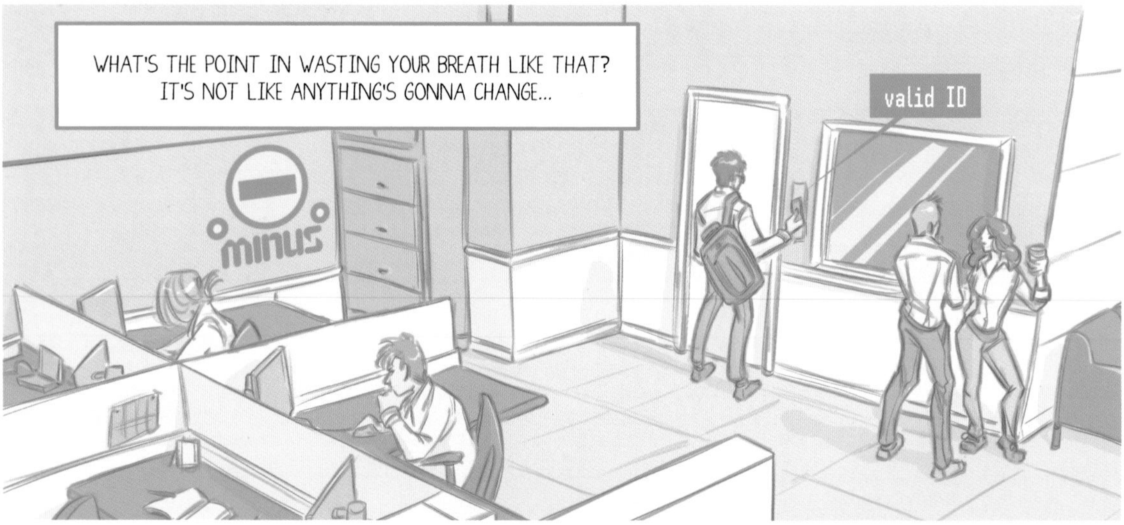
WHAT'S THE POINT IN WASTING YOUR BREATH LIKE THAT? IT'S NOT LIKE ANYTHING'S GONNA CHANGE...
minus
valid ID

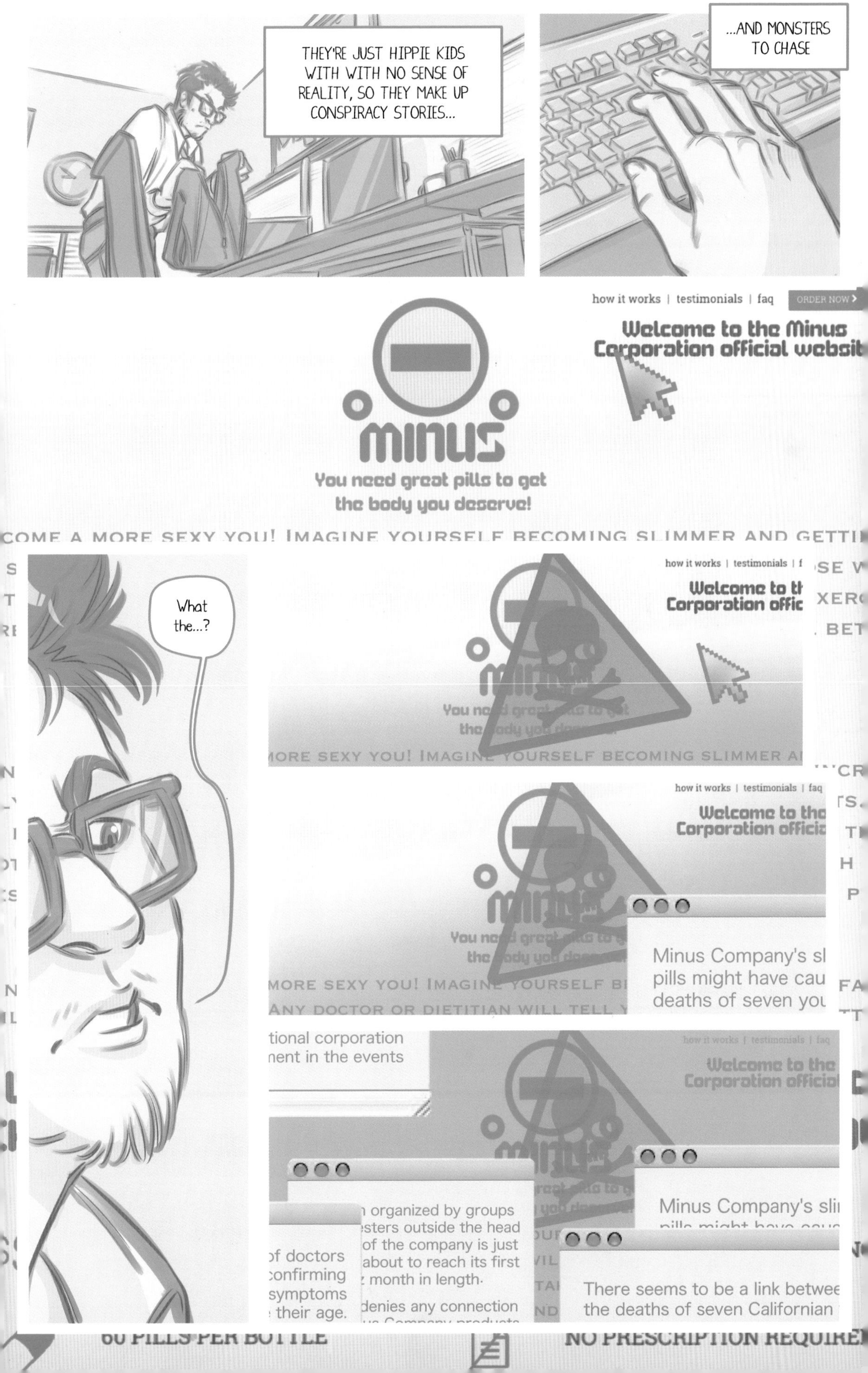
THEY'RE JUST HIPPIE KIDS WITH WITH NO SENSE OF REALITY, SO THEY MAKE UP CONSPIRACY STORIES...
...AND MONSTERS TO CHASE
how it works | testimonials | faq
ORDER NOW
Welcome to the Minus Corporation official websit
MINUS
You need great pills to get the body you deserve!
COME A MORE SEXY YOU! IMAGINE YOURSELF BECOMING SLIMMER AND GETTI
What the...?
MORE SEXY YOU! IMAGINE YOURSELF BECOMING SLIMMER A
Minus Company's sl
pills might have cau
deaths of seven you
ANY DOCTOR OR DIETITIAN WILL TELL Y
tional corporation
nent in the events
n organized by groups
sters outside the head
of the company is just
about to reach its first
month in length.
denies any connection
of doctors
confirming
symptoms
their age.
Minus Company's sli
There seems to be a link betwee
the deaths of seven Californian
60 PILLS PER BOTTLE
NO PRESCRIPTION REQUIRE

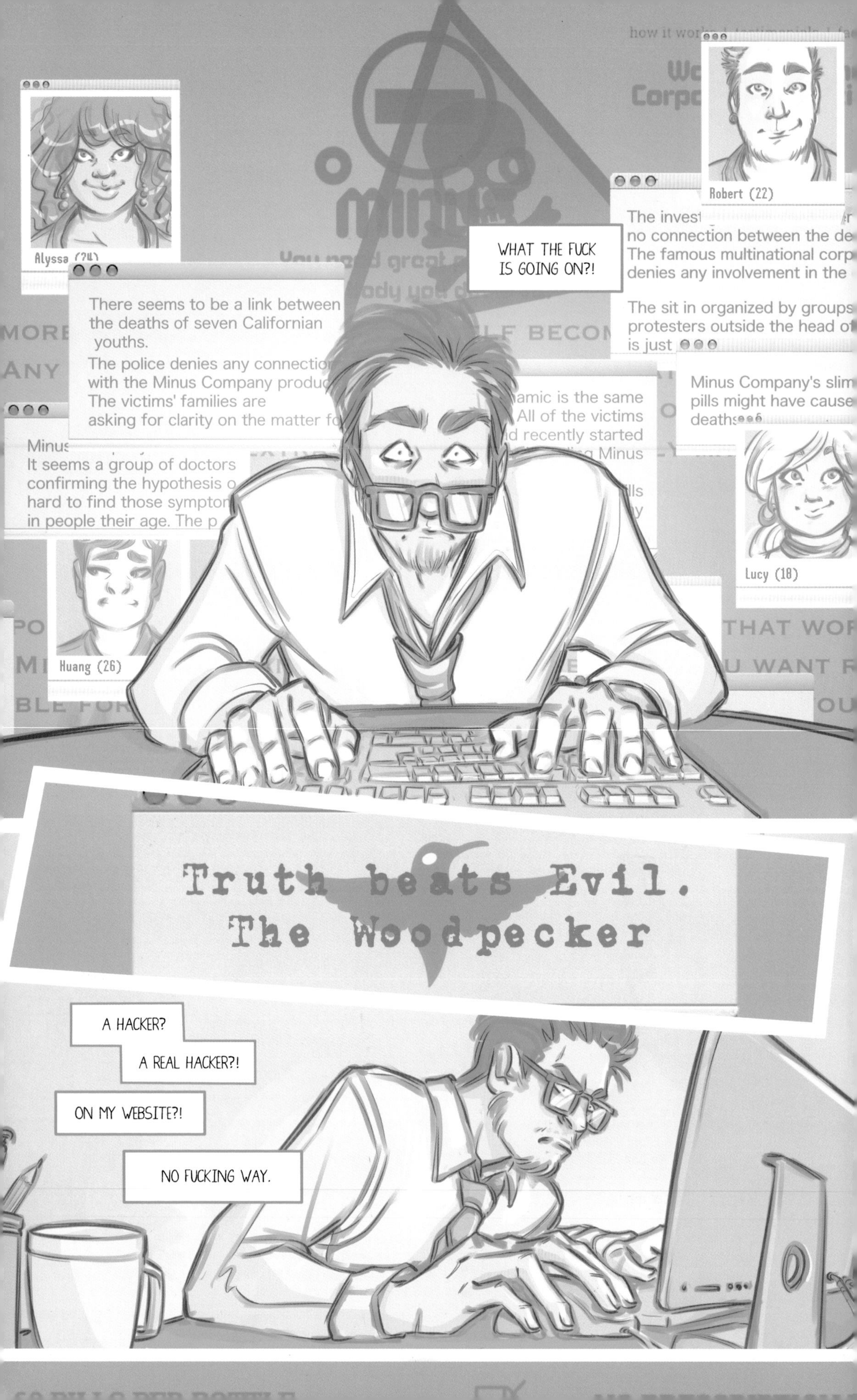

Alyssa (24)
There seems to be a link between the deaths of seven Californian youths.
The police denies any connectio
with the Minus Company produc
The victims' families are asking for clarity on the matter fo
Minus
It seems a group of doctors confirming the hypothesis o hard to find those sympton in people their age. The p
Huang (26)
WHAT THE FUCK IS GOING ON?!
Robert (22)
The invest
no connection between the de
The famous multinational corp denies any involvement in the
The sit in organized by groups protesters outside the head of is just
amic is the same All of the victims d recently started
Minus Company's slim pills might have cause deaths
Lucy (18)
Truth beats Evil.
The Woodpecker
A HACKER?
A REAL HACKER?!
ON MY WEBSITE?!
NO FUCKING WAY.

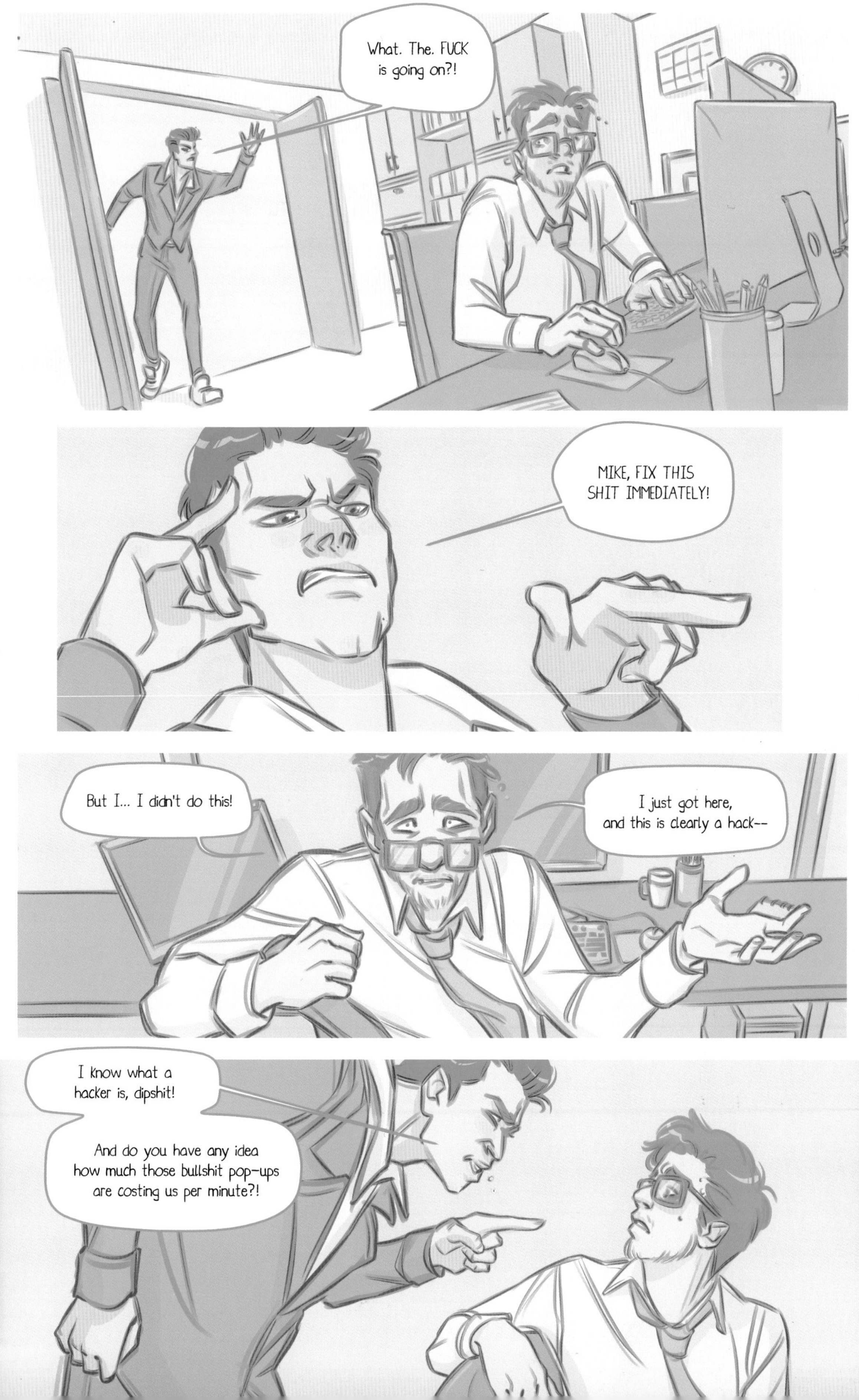
What. The. FUCK is going on?!
MIKE, FIX THIS SHIT IMMEDIATELY!
But I... I didn't do this!
I just got here, and this is clearly a hack--
I know what a hacker is, dipshit!
And do you have any idea how much those bullshit pop-ups are costing us per minute?!

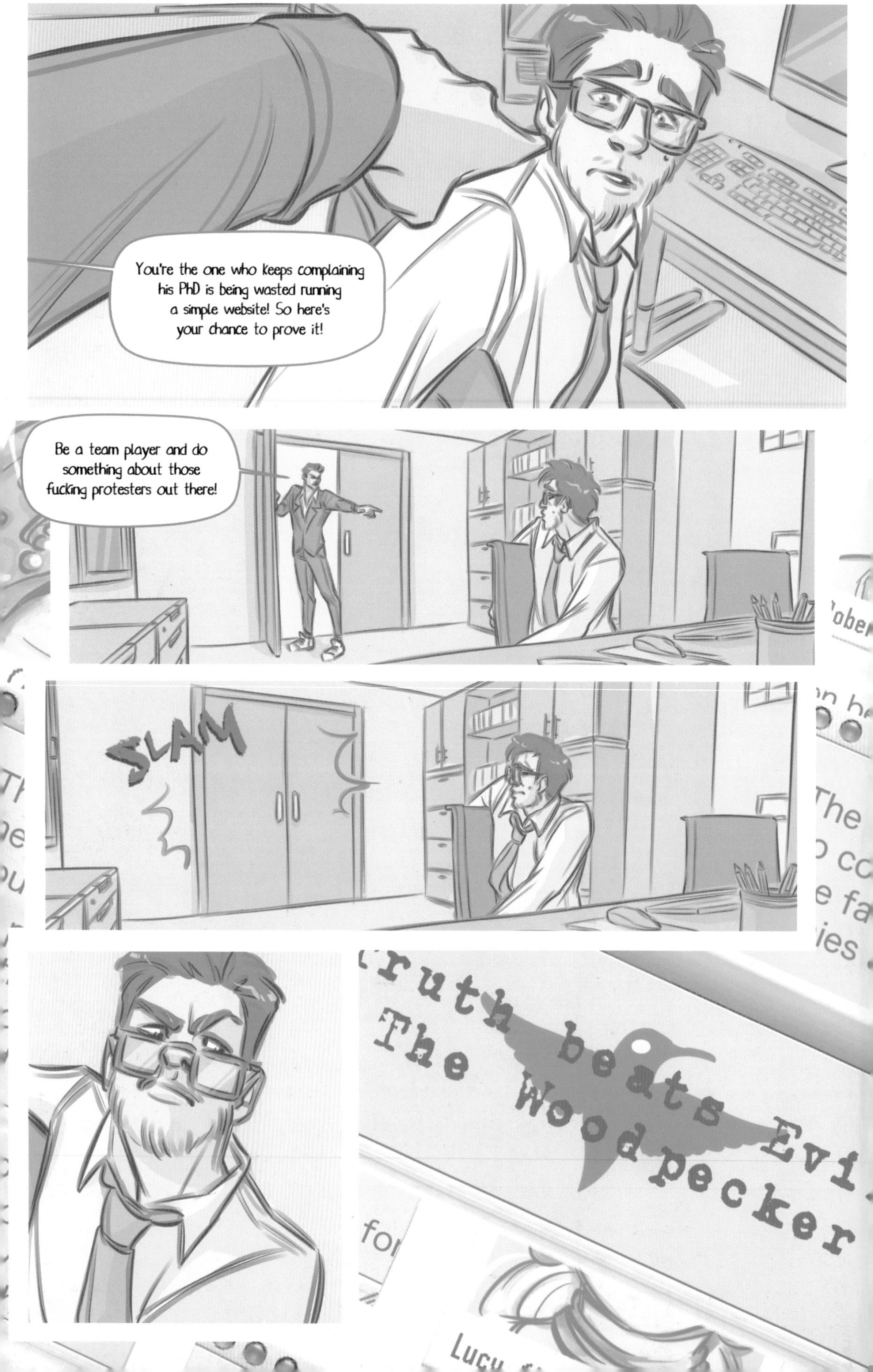
You're the one who keeps complaining his PhD is being wasted running a simple website! So here's your chance to prove it!
Be a team player and do something about those fucking protesters out there!
SLAM
The Woodpecker

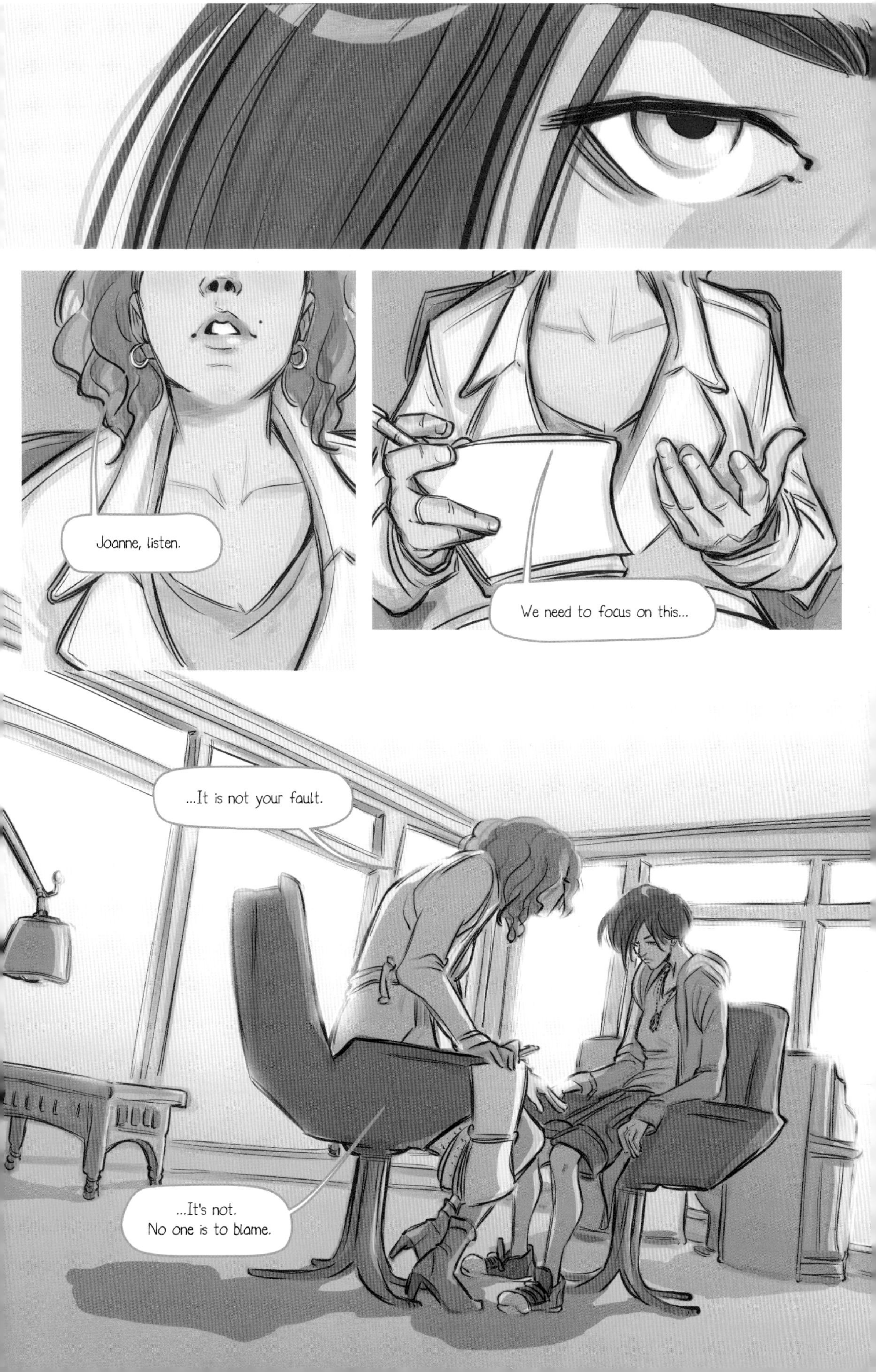
Joanne, listen.
We need to focus on this...
...It is not your fault.
...It's not.
No one is to blame.

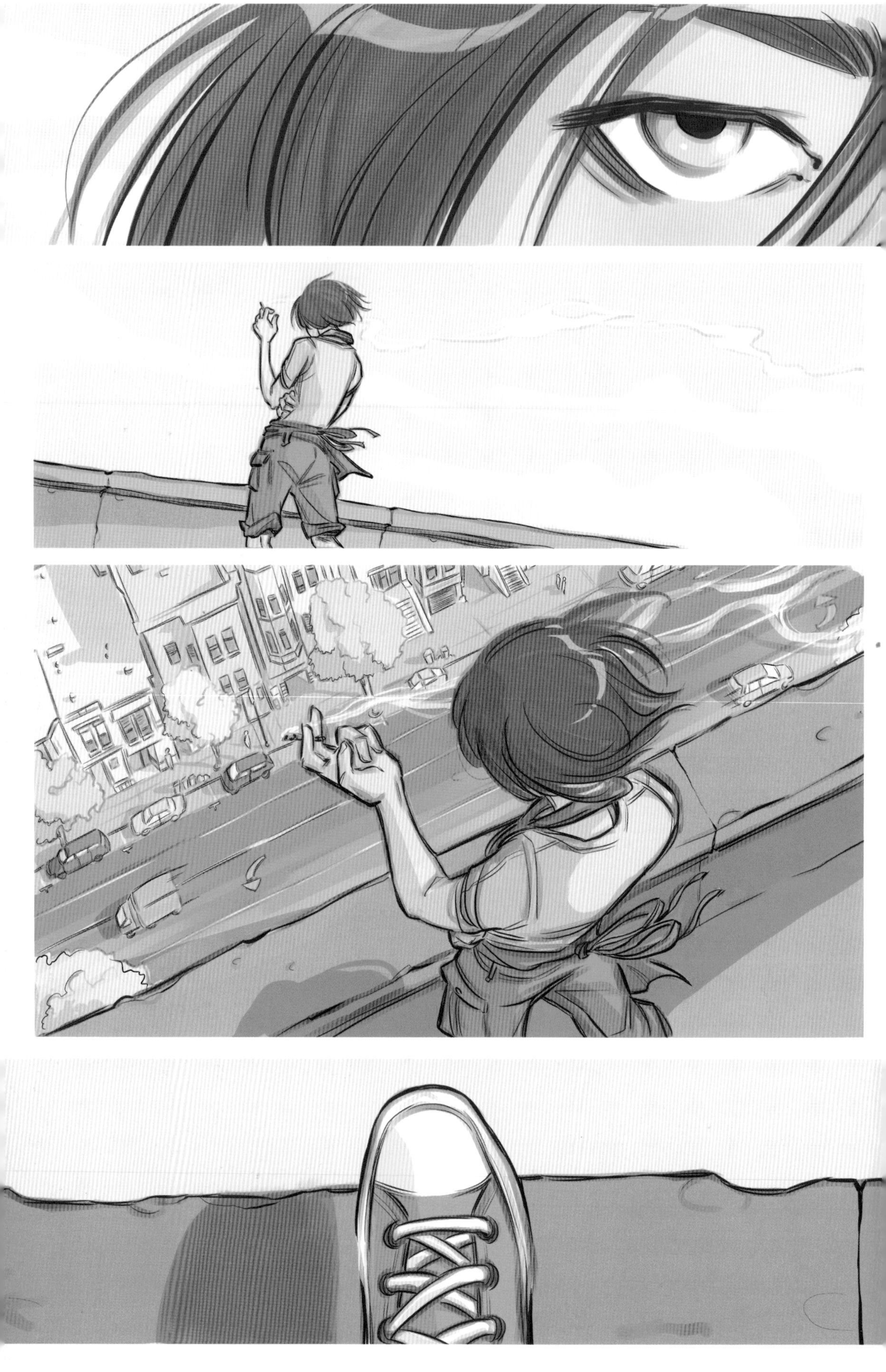

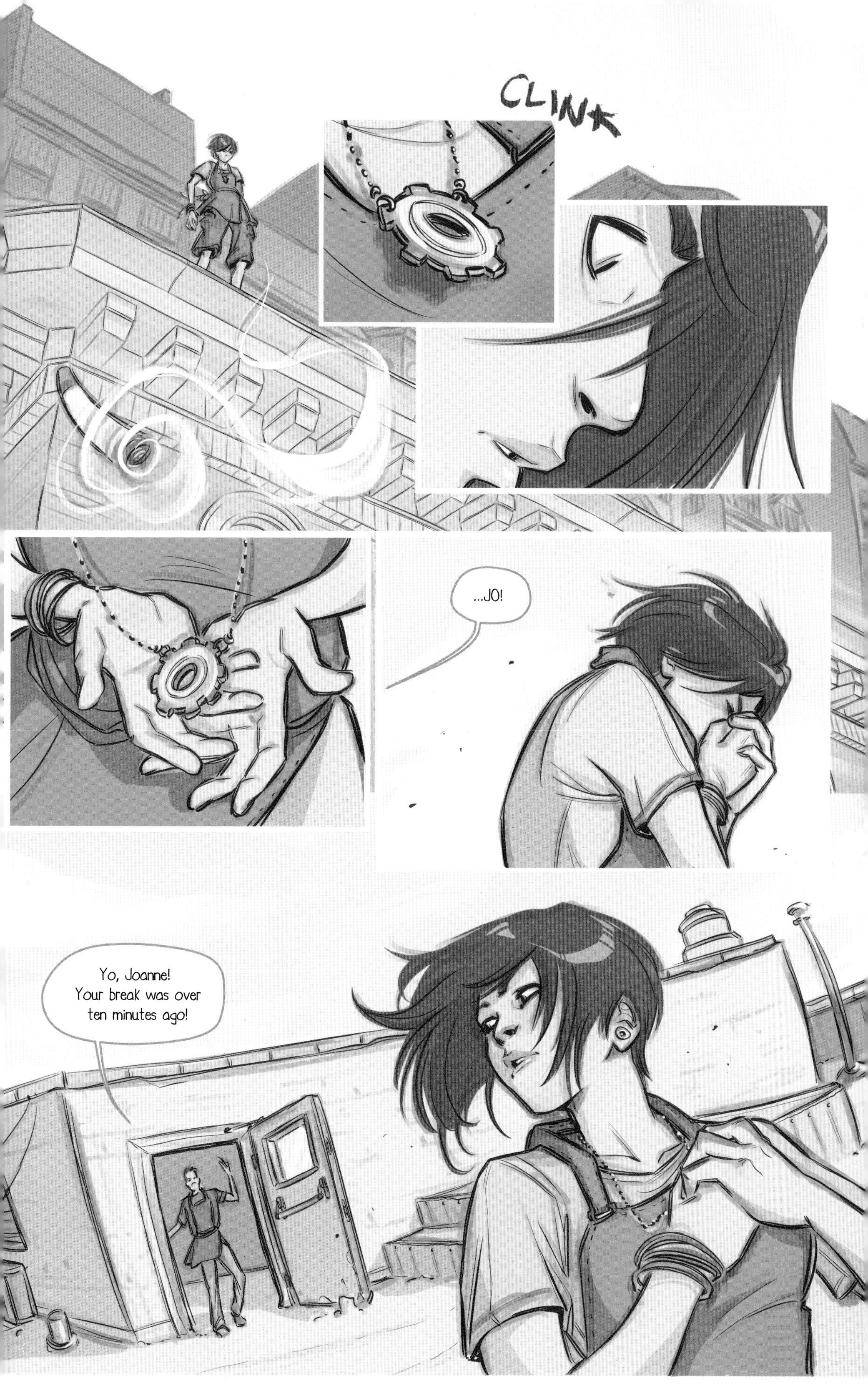
CLINK
...JO!
Yo, Joanne!
Your break was over
ten minutes ago!

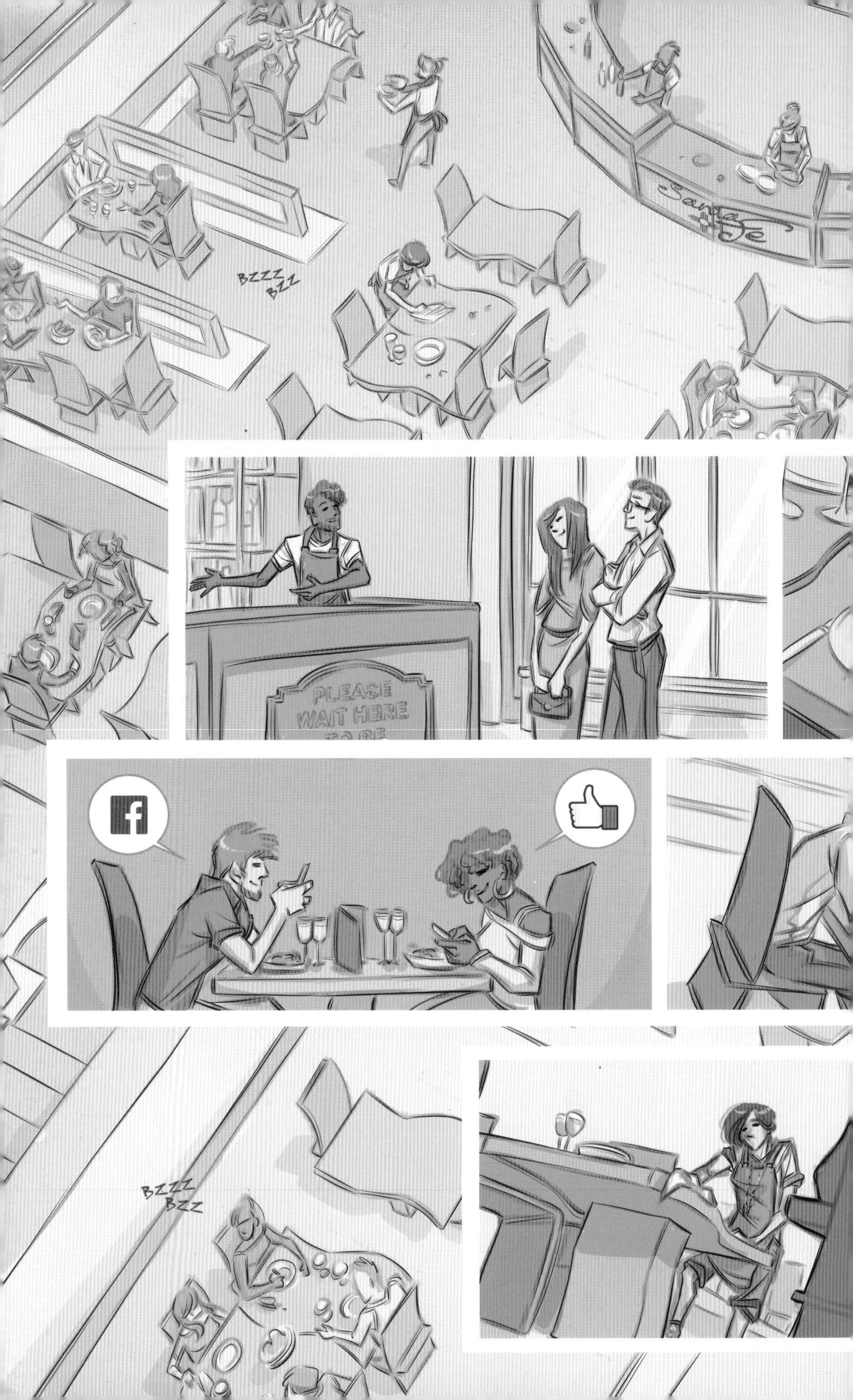
Santa Fe
BZZZ BZZ
PLEASE WAIT HERE
BZZZ BZZ

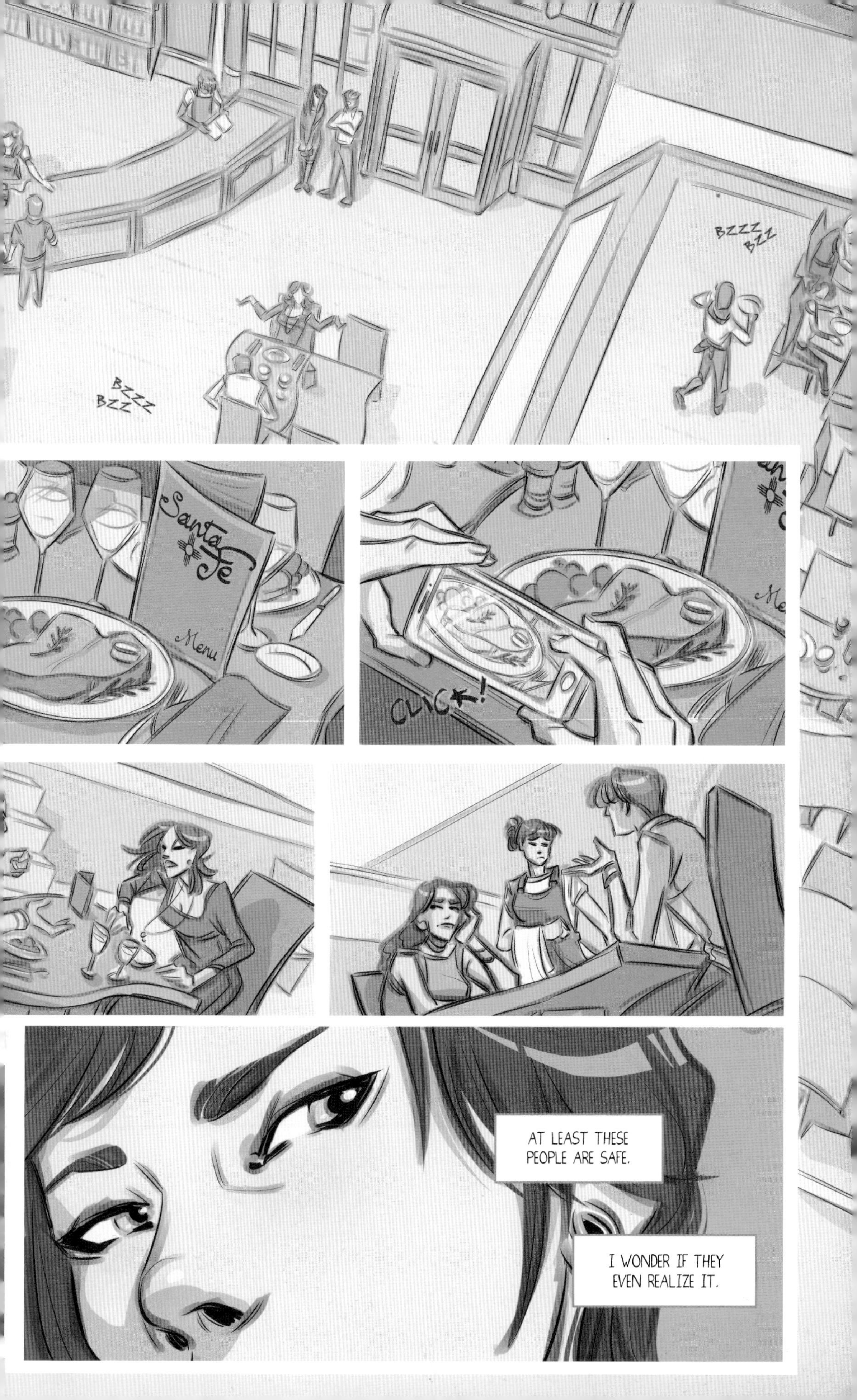
BZZZ
BZZ
BZZZ
BZZ
Santa Fe
Menu
CLICK!
AT LEAST THESE PEOPLE ARE SAFE.
I WONDER IF THEY EVEN REALIZE IT.

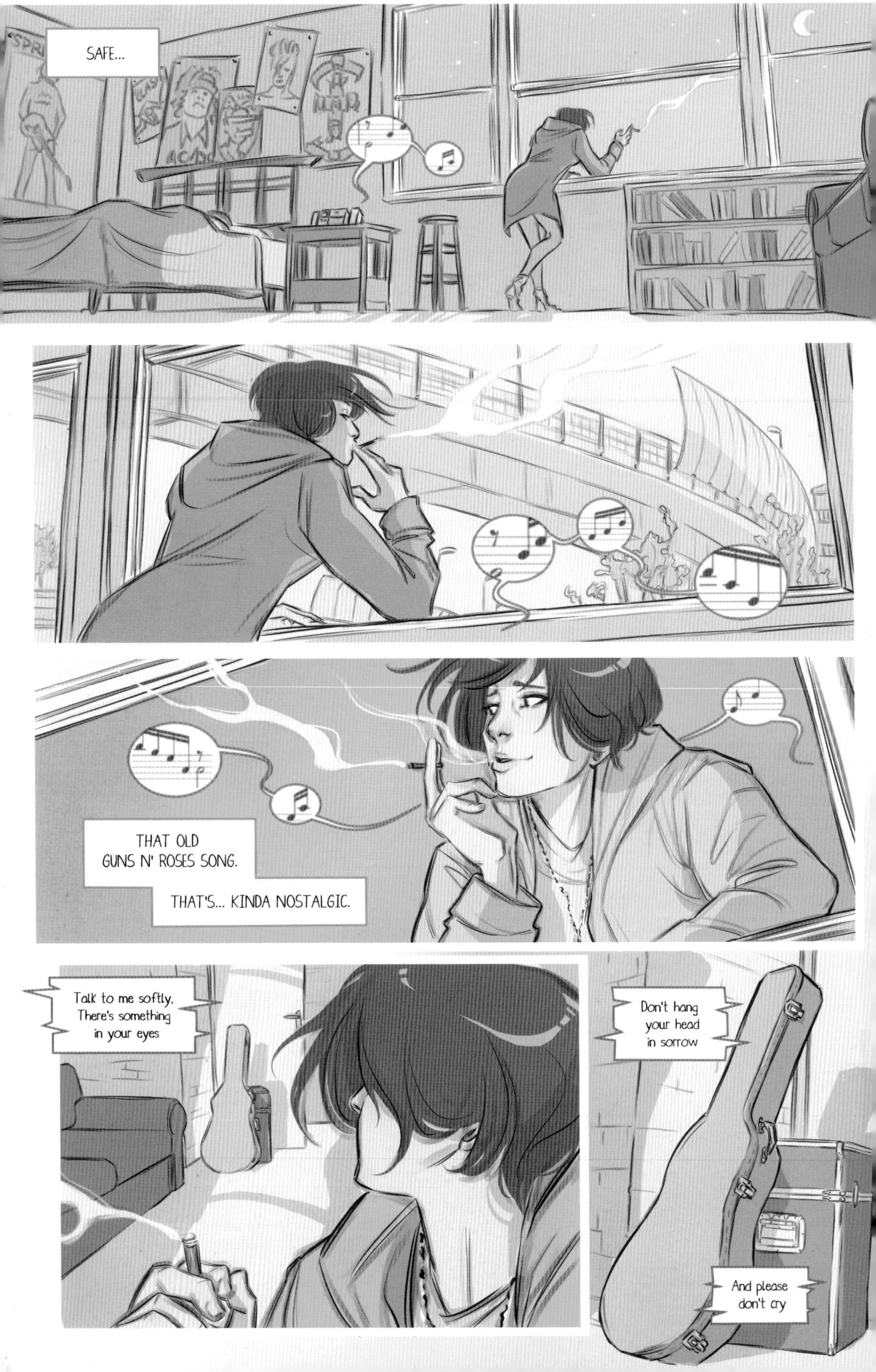
SAFE...
THAT OLD
GUNS N' ROSES SONG.
THAT'S... KINDA NOSTALGIC.
Talk to me softly.
There's something
in your eyes
Don't hang
your head
in sorrow
And please
don't cry

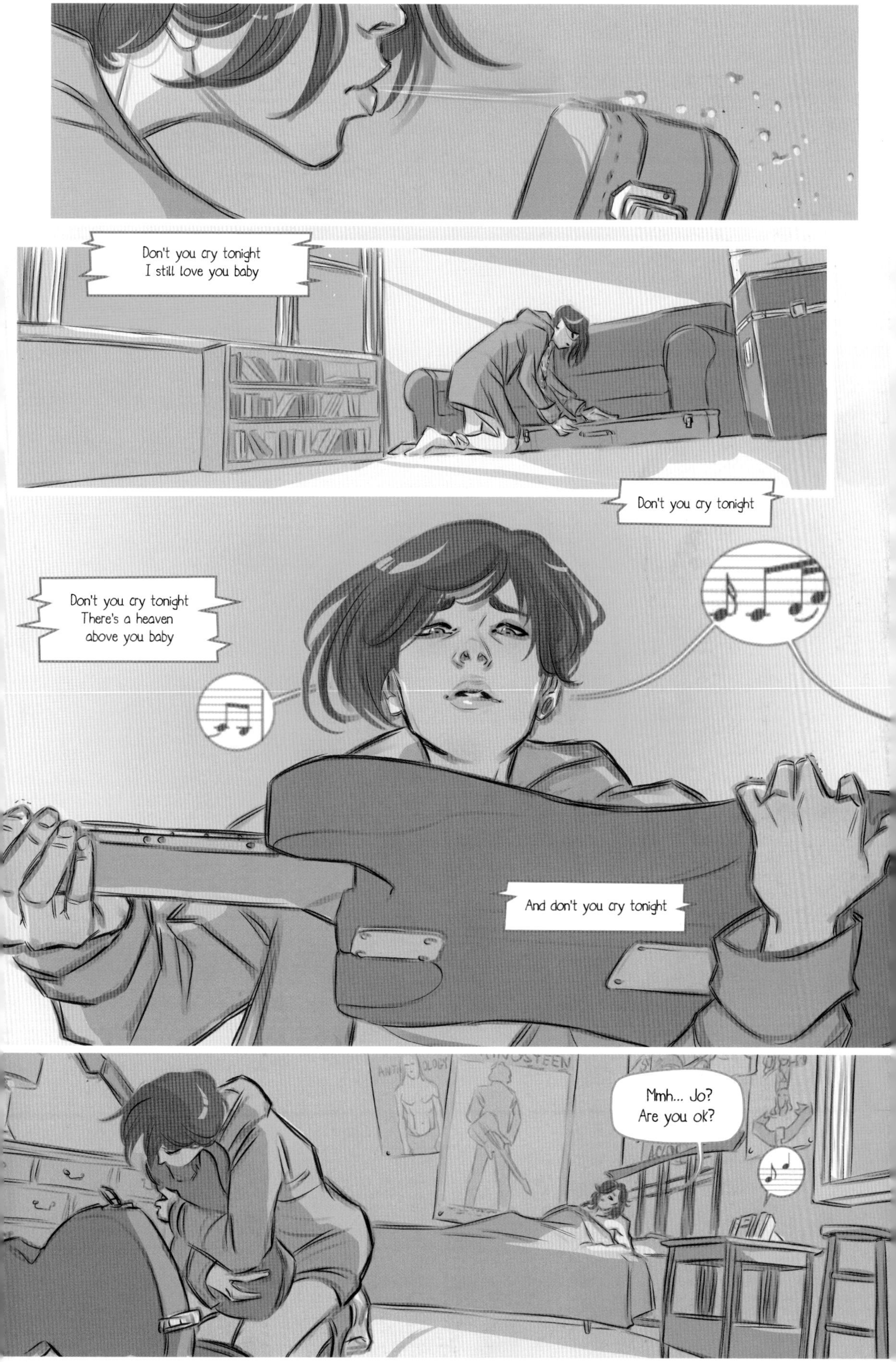
Don't you cry tonight
I still love you baby
Don't you cry tonight
Don't you cry tonight
There's a heaven
above you baby
And don't you cry tonight
Mmh... Jo?
Are you ok?

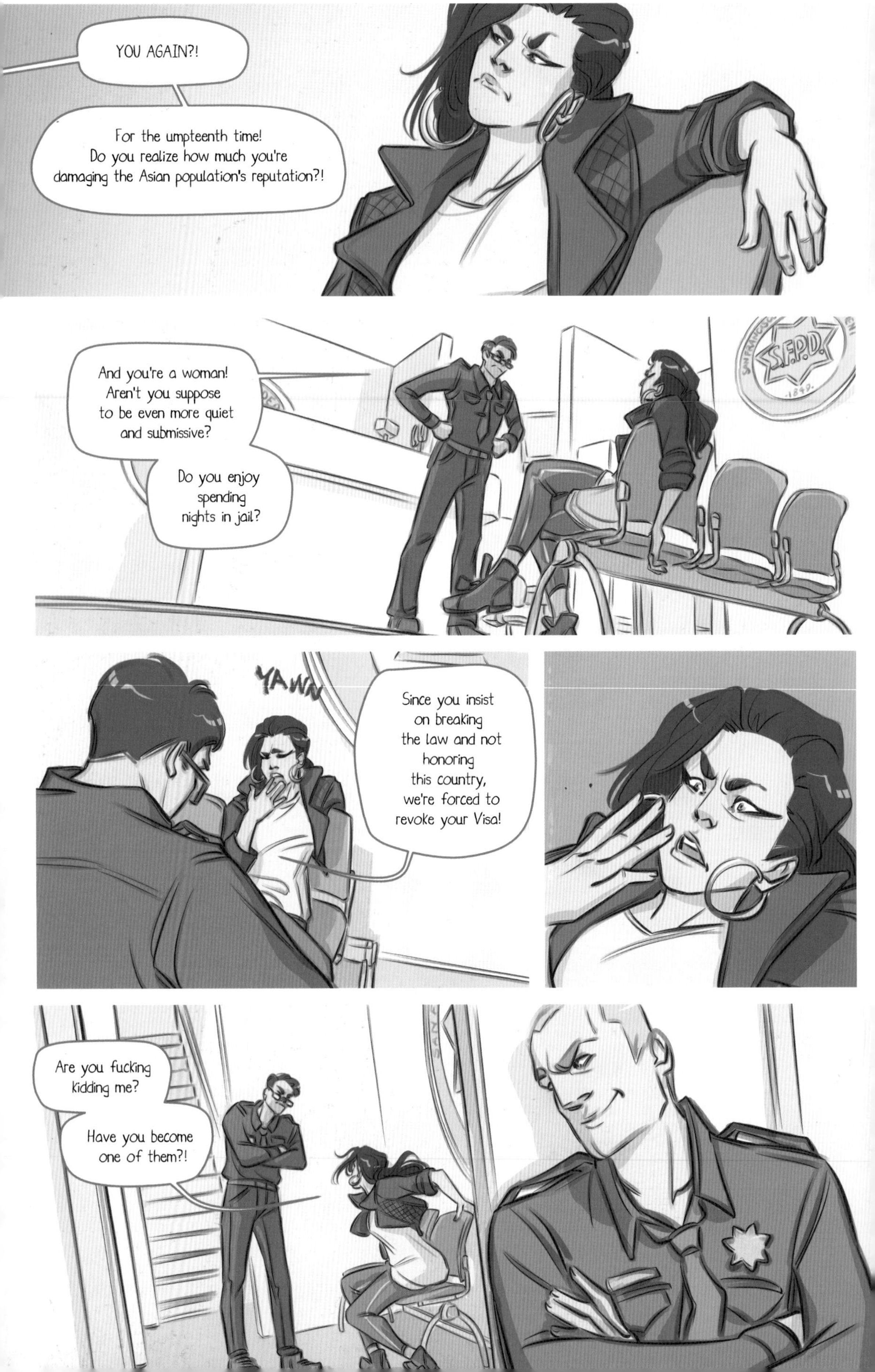
YOU AGAIN?!
For the umpteenth time! Do you realize how much you're damaging the Asian population's reputation?!
And you're a woman! Aren't you suppose to be even more quiet and submissive?
Do you enjoy spending nights in jail?
YAWN
Since you insist on breaking the law and not honoring this country, we're forced to revoke your Visa!
Are you fucking kidding me?
Have you become one of them?!

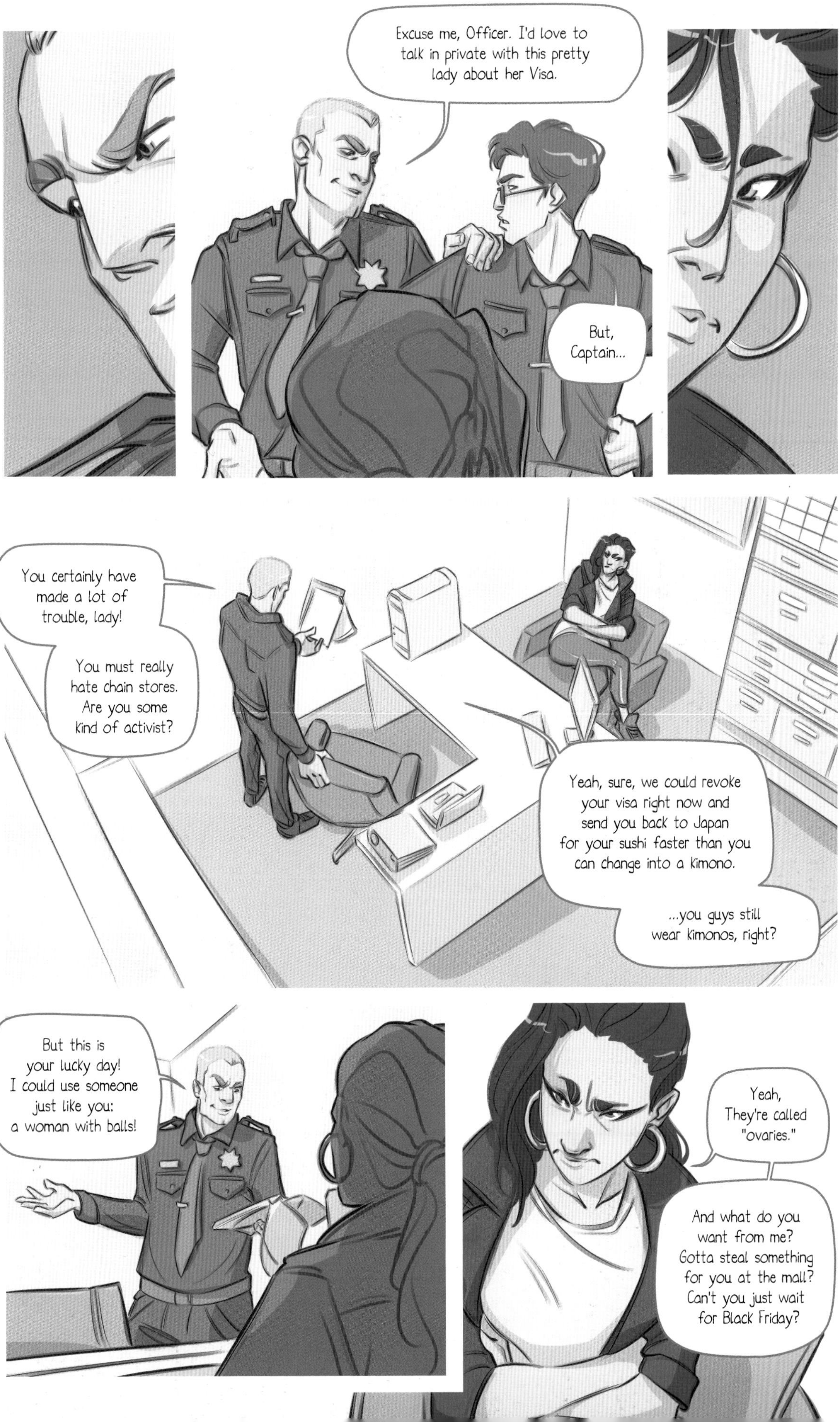
Excuse me, Officer. I'd love to talk in private with this pretty lady about her Visa.
But, Captain...
You certainly have made a lot of trouble, lady!
You must really hate chain stores. Are you some kind of activist?
Yeah, sure, we could revoke your visa right now and send you back to Japan for your sushi faster than you can change into a kimono.
...you guys still wear kimonos, right?
But this is your lucky day! I could use someone just like you: a woman with balls!
Yeah, They're called "ovaries."
And what do you want from me? Gotta steal something for you at the mall? Can't you just wait for Black Friday?

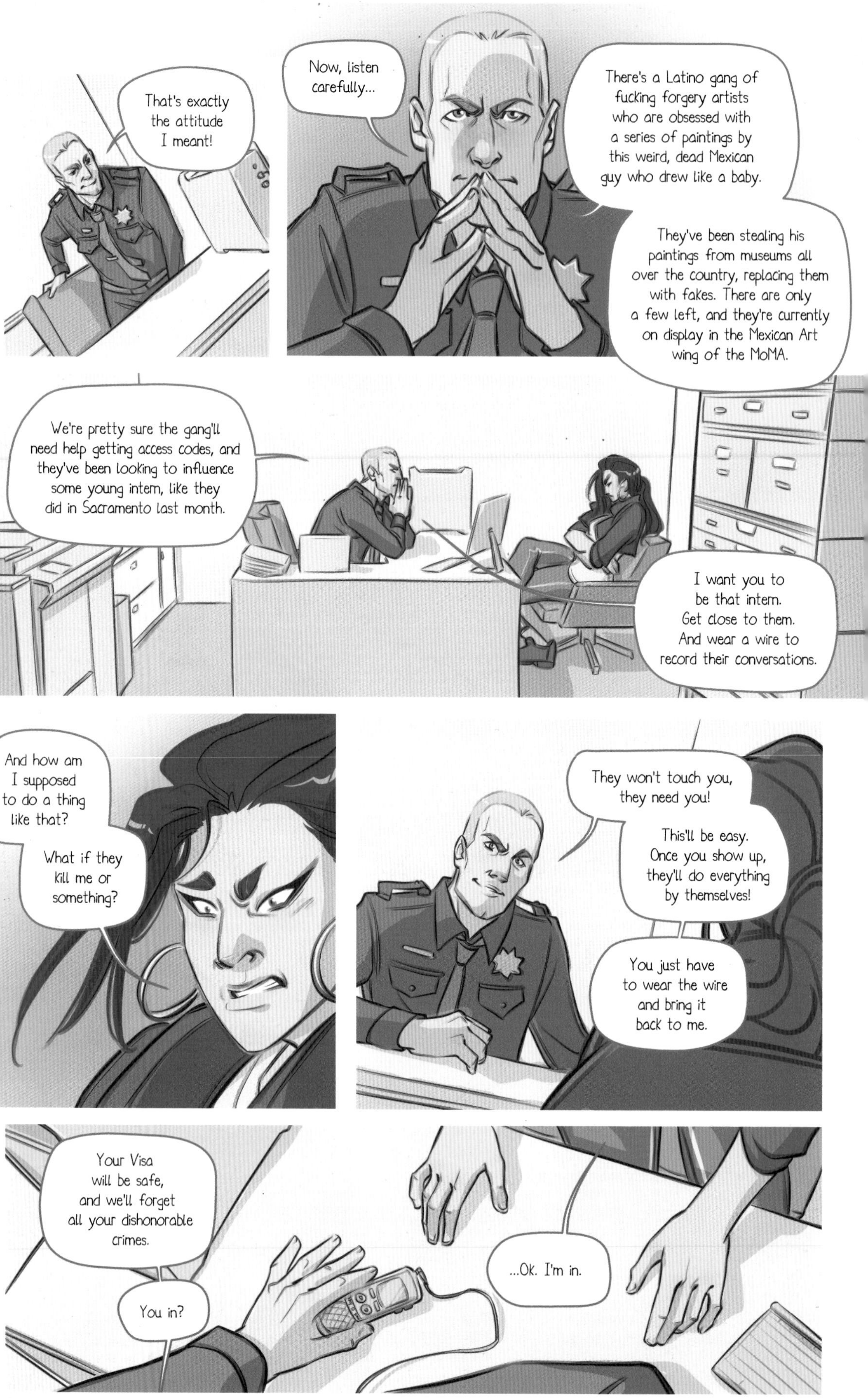
That's exactly the attitude I meant!
Now, listen carefully...
There's a Latino gang of fucking forgery artists who are obsessed with a series of paintings by this weird, dead Mexican guy who drew like a baby.
They've been stealing his paintings from museums all over the country, replacing them with fakes. There are only a few left, and they're currently on display in the Mexican Art wing of the MoMA.
We're pretty sure the gang'll need help getting access codes, and they've been looking to influence some young intern, like they did in Sacramento last month.
I want you to be that intern. Get close to them. And wear a wire to record their conversations.
And how am I supposed to do a thing like that?
What if they kill me or something?
They won't touch you, they need you!
This'll be easy. Once you show up, they'll do everything by themselves!
You just have to wear the wire and bring it back to me.
Your Visa will be safe, and we'll forget all your dishonorable crimes.
You in?
...Ok. I'm in.

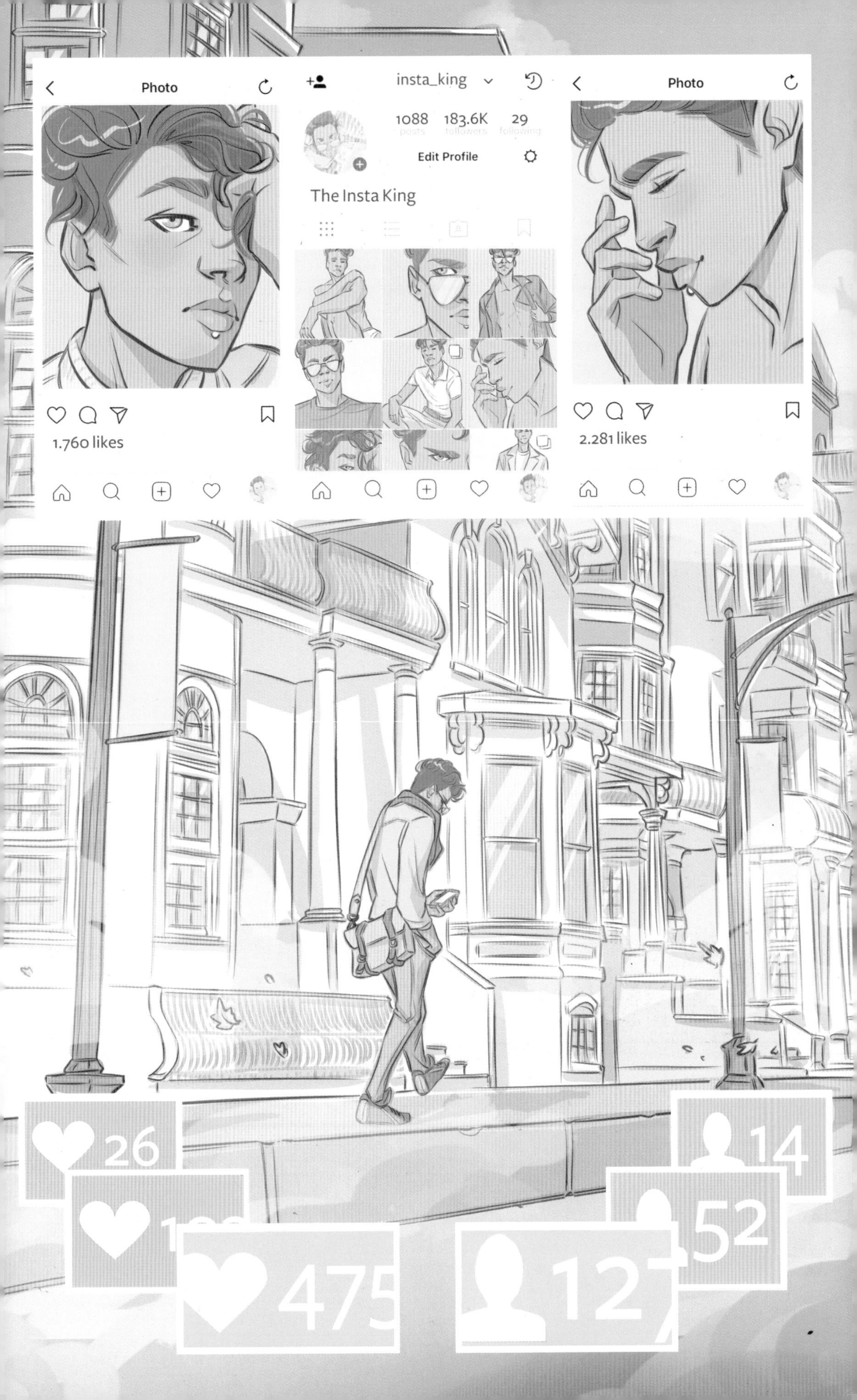

Photo
1.760 likes
insta_king
1088
posts
183.6K
followers
29
following
Edit Profile
The Insta King
Photo
2.281 likes
26
14
52
475
12

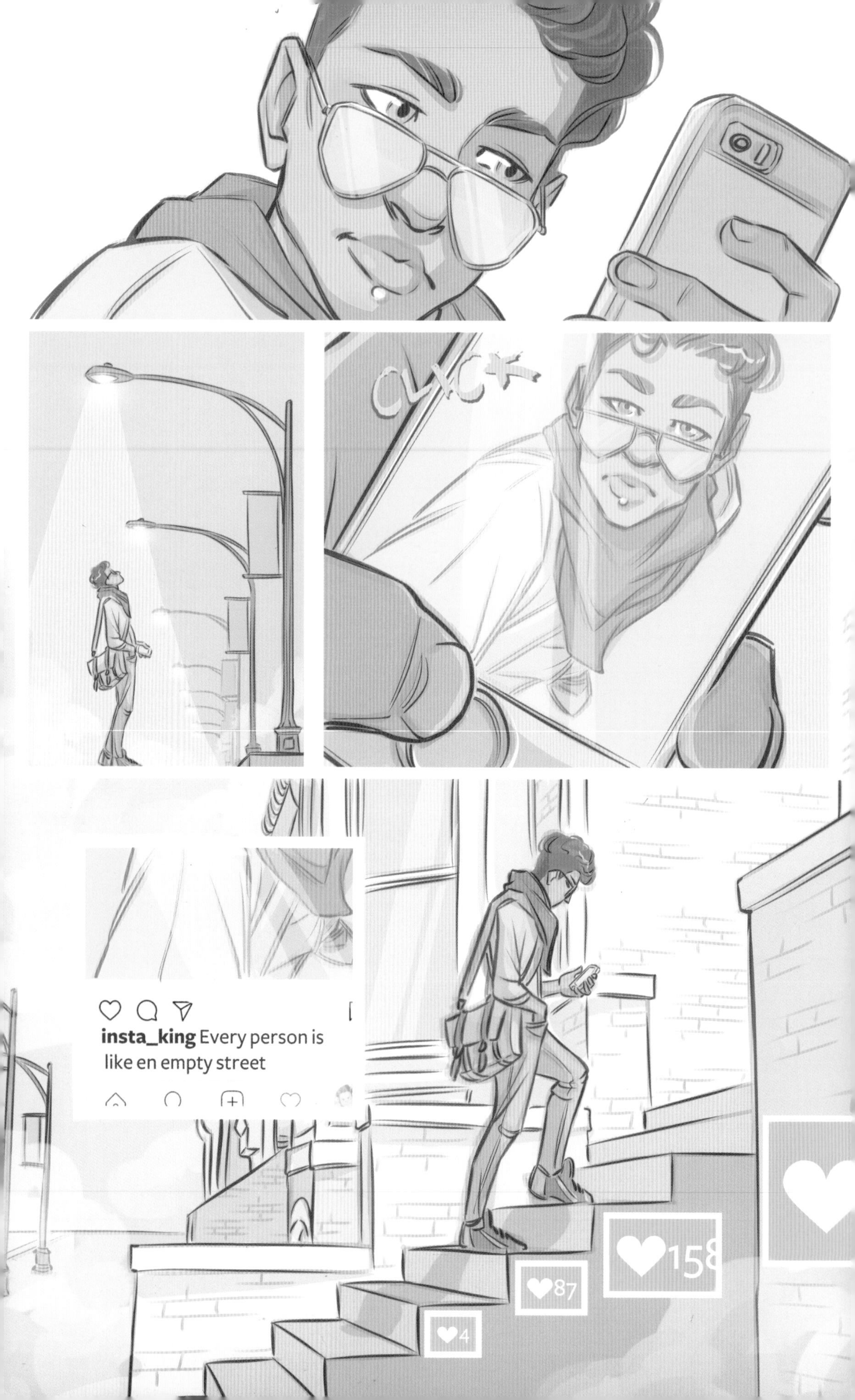
CLICK
insta_king Every person is like en empty street
87
158
4

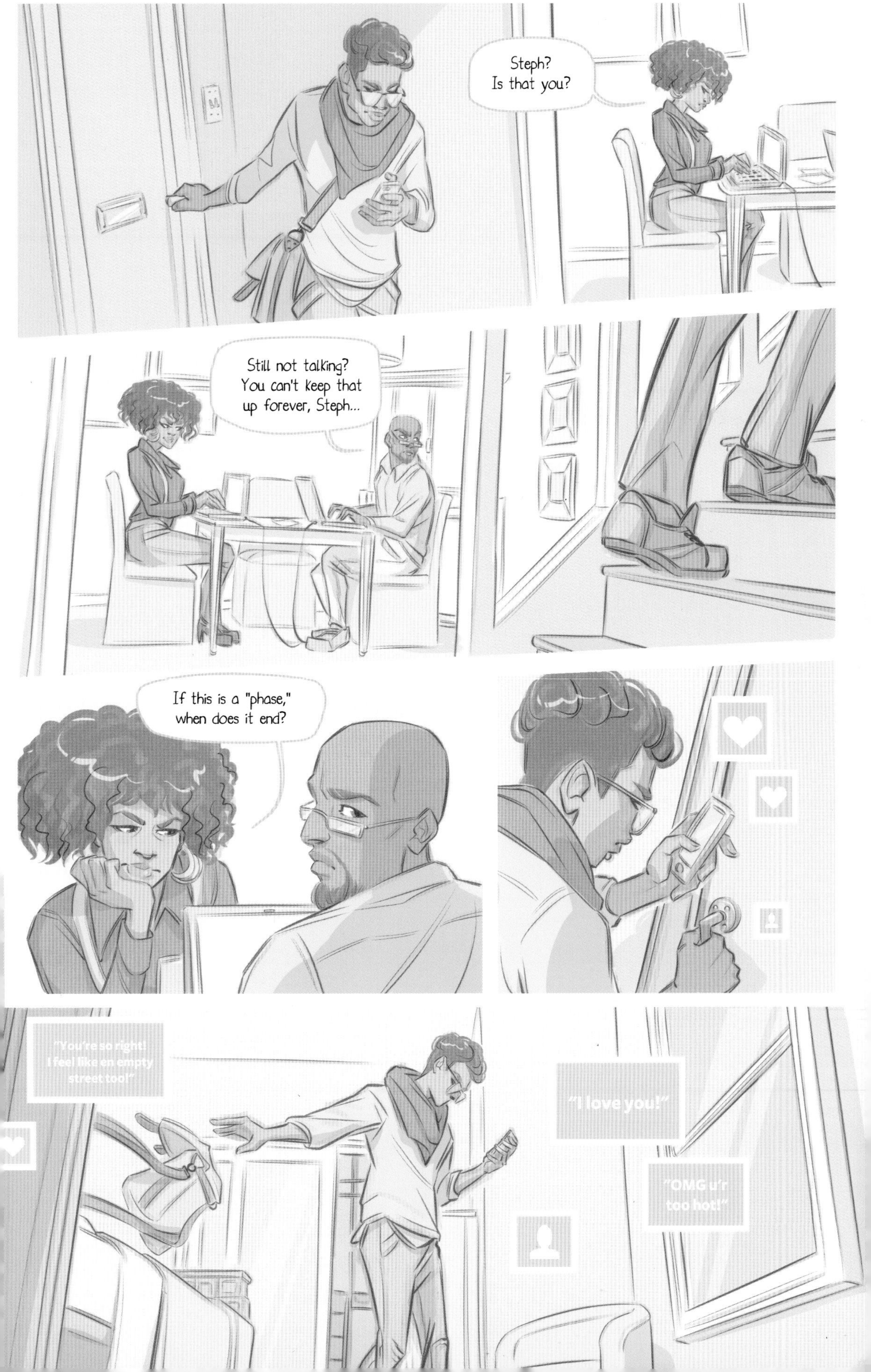
Steph?
Is that you?
Still not talking?
You can't keep that
up forever, Steph...
If this is a "phase,"
when does it end?
"You're so right!
I feel like en empty
street too!"
"I love you!"
"OMG u'r
too hot!"

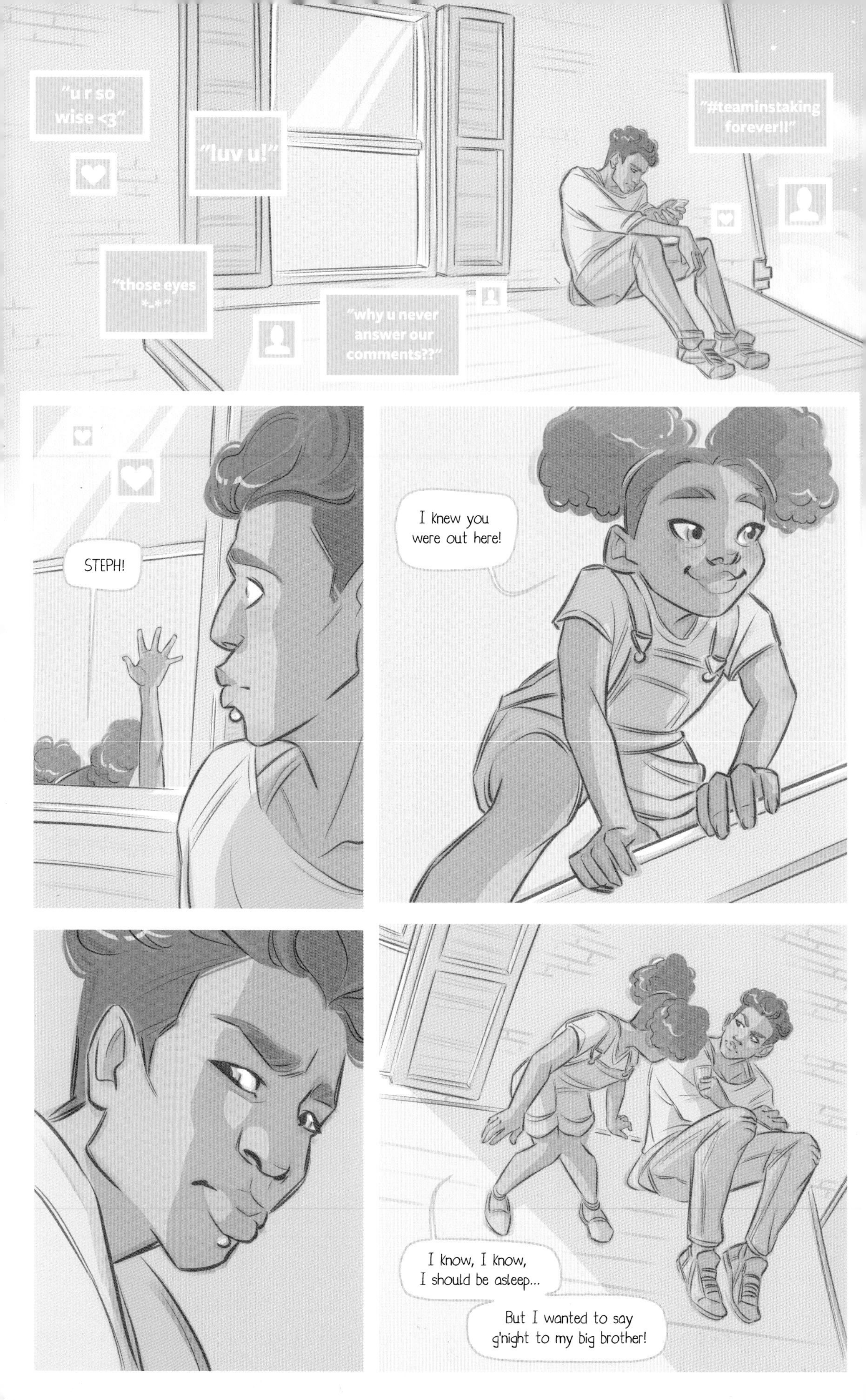

"u r so wise <3"
"luv u!"
"#teaminstaking forever!!"
"those eyes *_*"
"why u never answer our comments??"
STEPH!
I knew you were out here!
I know, I know, I should be asleep...
But I wanted to say g'night to my big brother!

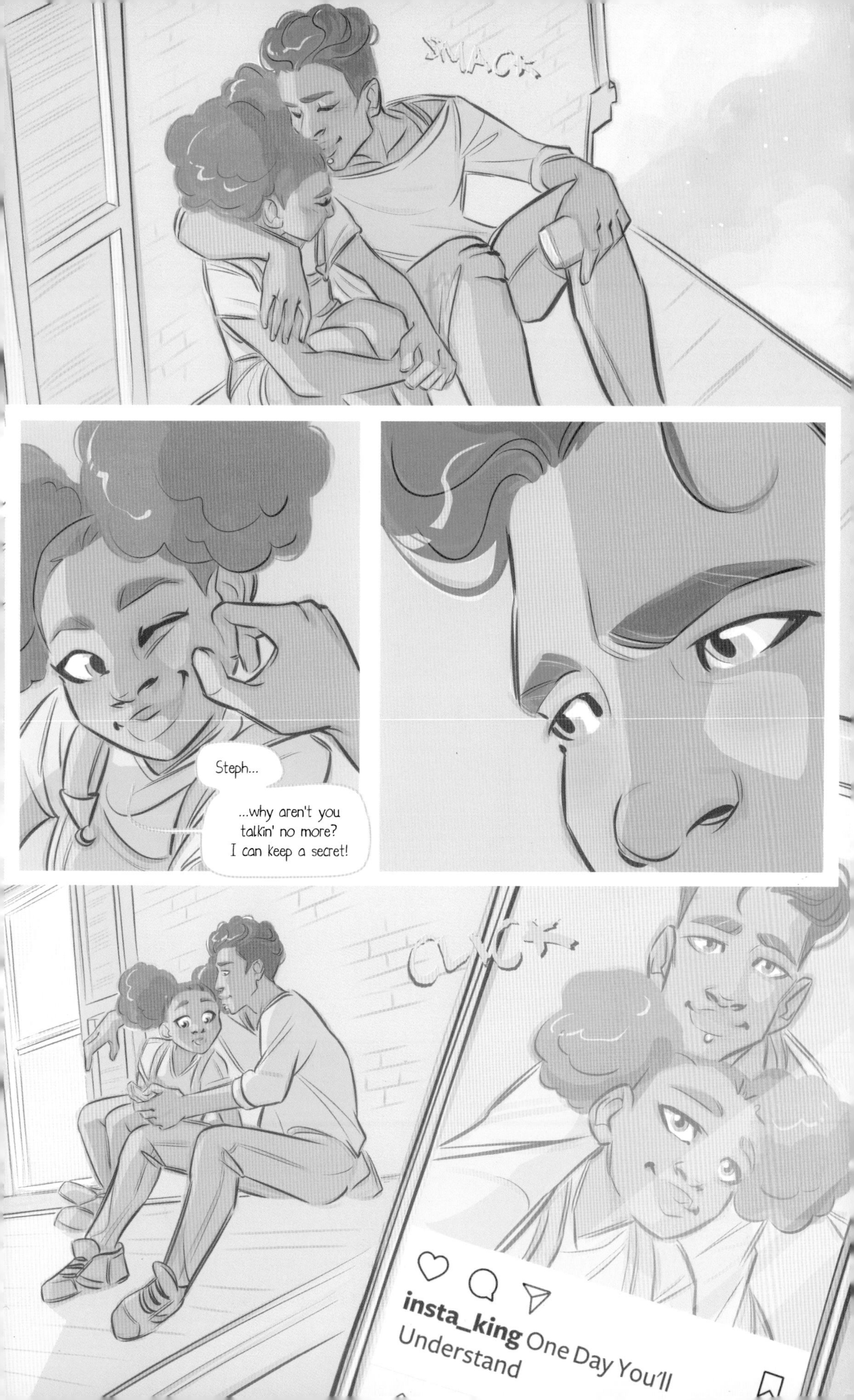
SMACK
Steph...
...why aren't you talkin' no more? I can keep a secret!
CLICK
insta_king One Day You'll Understand

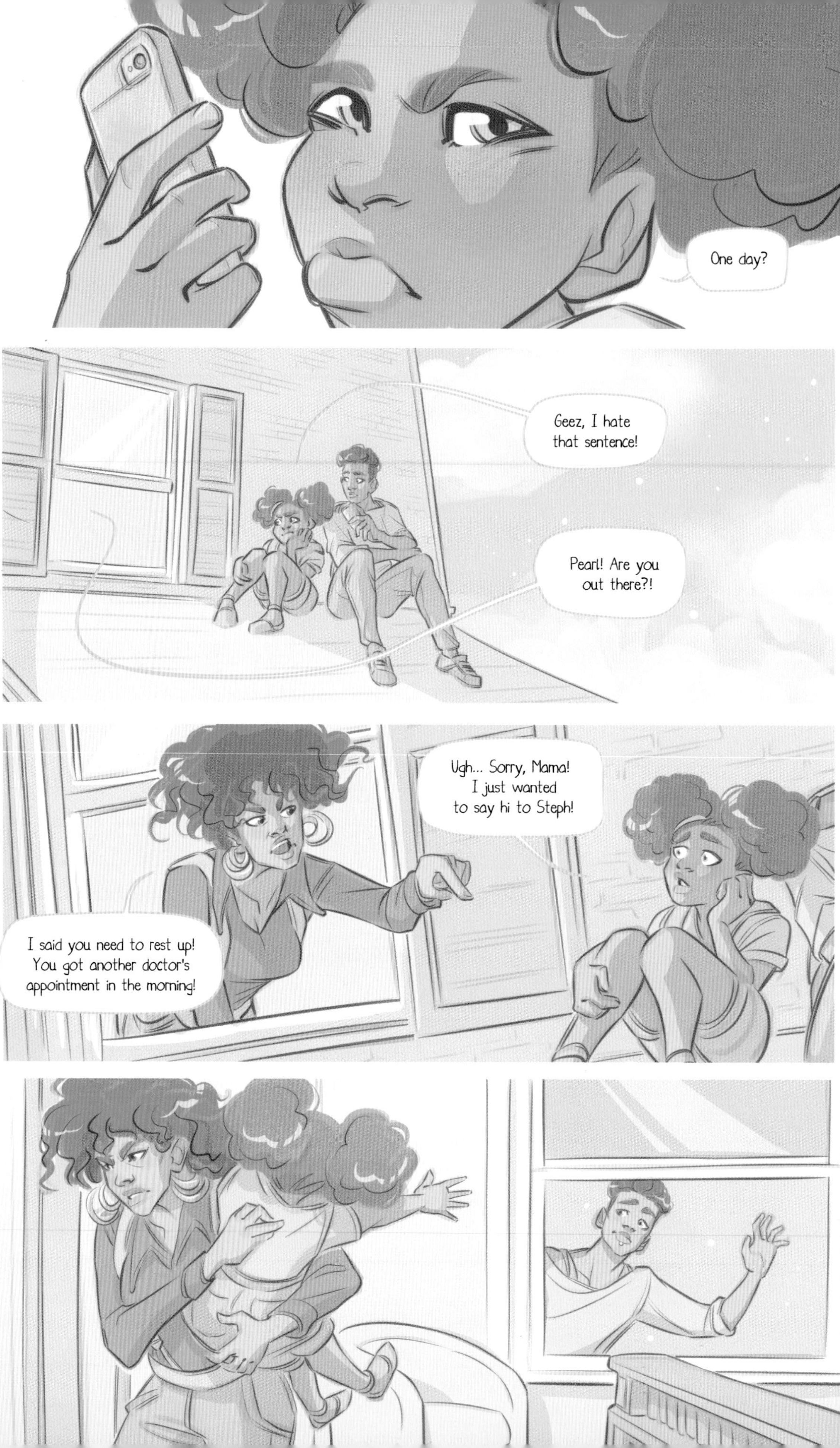
One day?
Geez, I hate that sentence!
Pearl! Are you out there?!
Ugh... Sorry, Mama! I just wanted to say hi to Steph!
I said you need to rest up! You got another doctor's appointment in the morning!

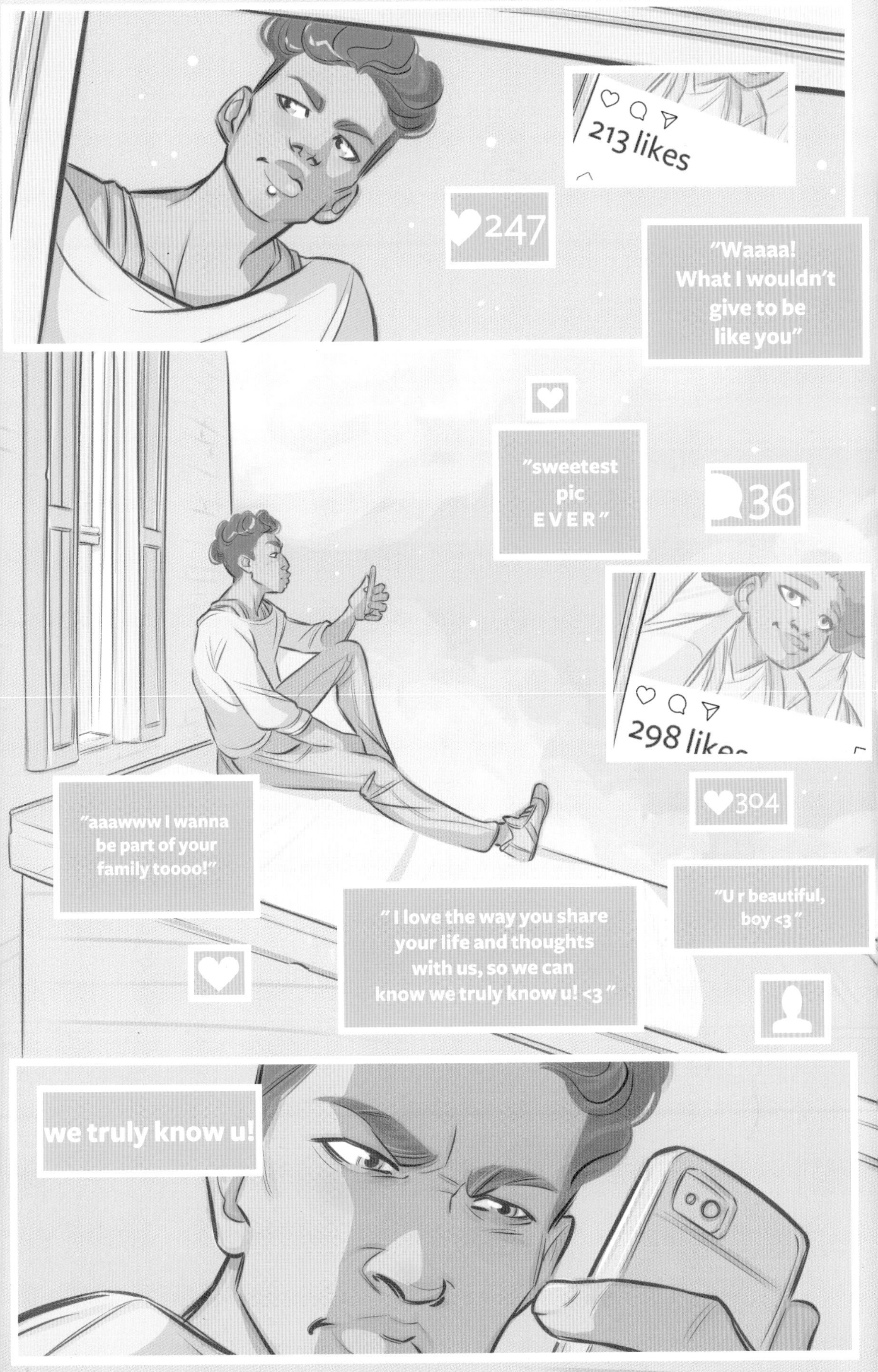
213 likes
247
"Waaaa! What I wouldn't give to be like you"
"sweetest pic EVER"
36
298 likes
304
"aaawww I wanna be part of your family toooo!"
"Ur beautiful, boy <3"
" I love the way you share your life and thoughts with us, so we can know we truly know u! <3 "
we truly know u!

Beep
$$$ HUGE MULTI-BUY SAVINGS
60 PILLS PER BOTTLE
Not now, Mom...
Message 1 of 4
Hey dude! Did you get a chance to look at our game demo? You know your opinion is important to us! :D
We ran into your mom last week. LOL she never changes!

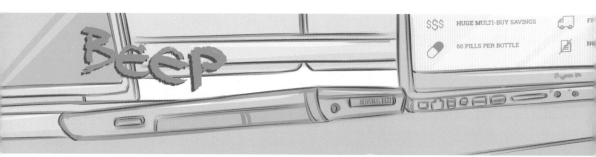

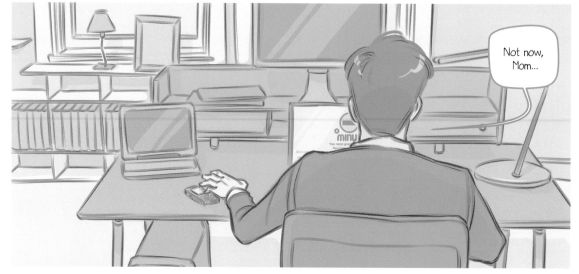

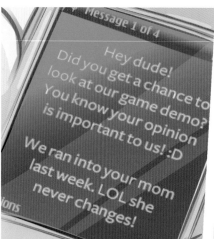

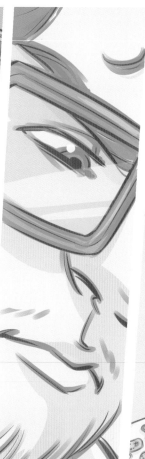

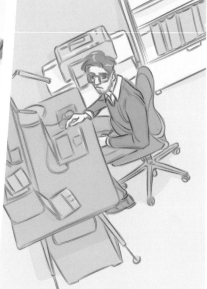

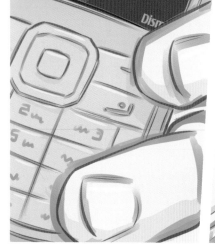

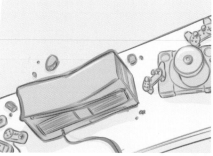

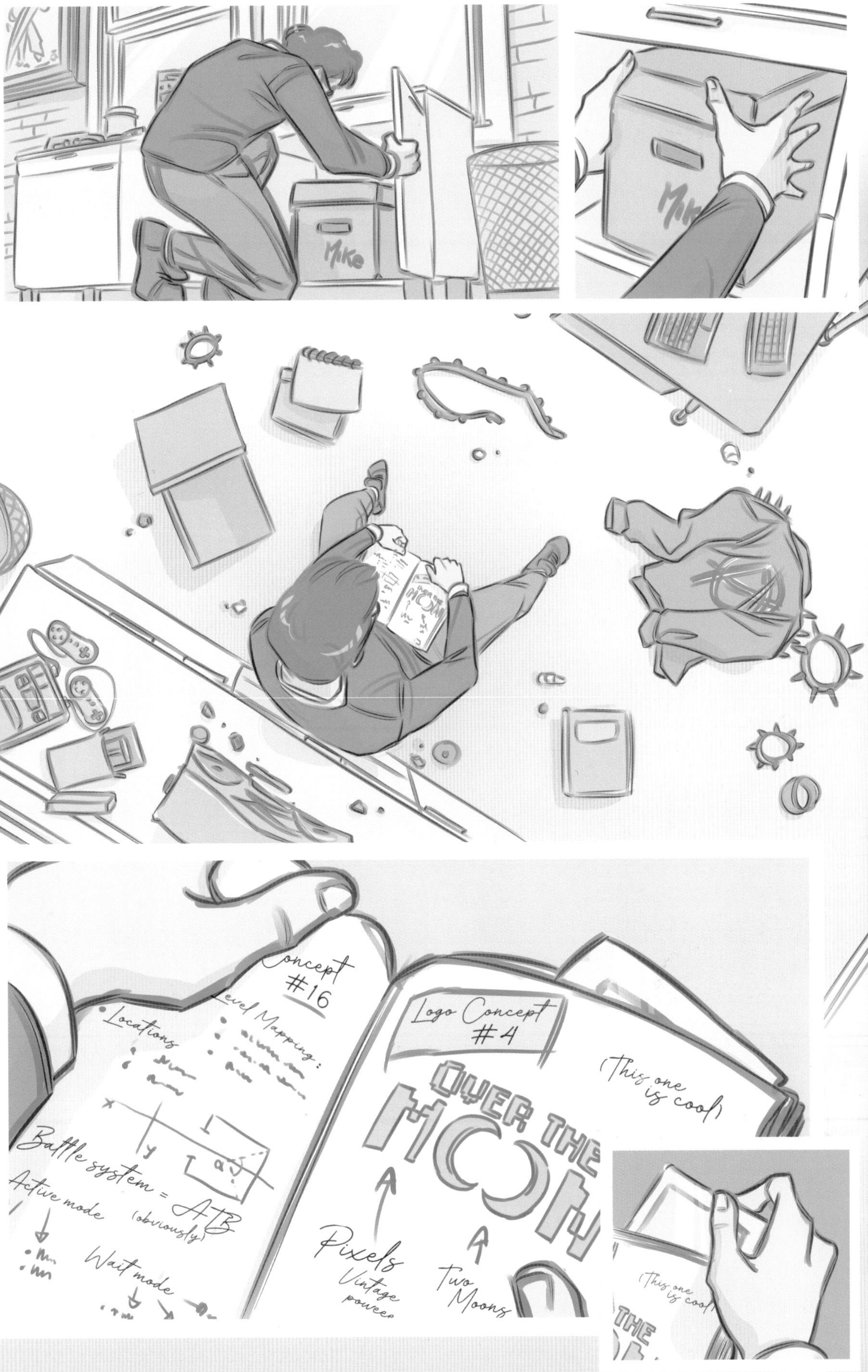

Mike
Mike
oncept #16
Locations
evel Mapping:
Battle system = ATB (obviously)
Active mode
Wait mode
Logo Concept #4
(This one is cool)
OVER THE
MOO
Pixels
Vintage power
Two Moons
(This one is cool)
THE

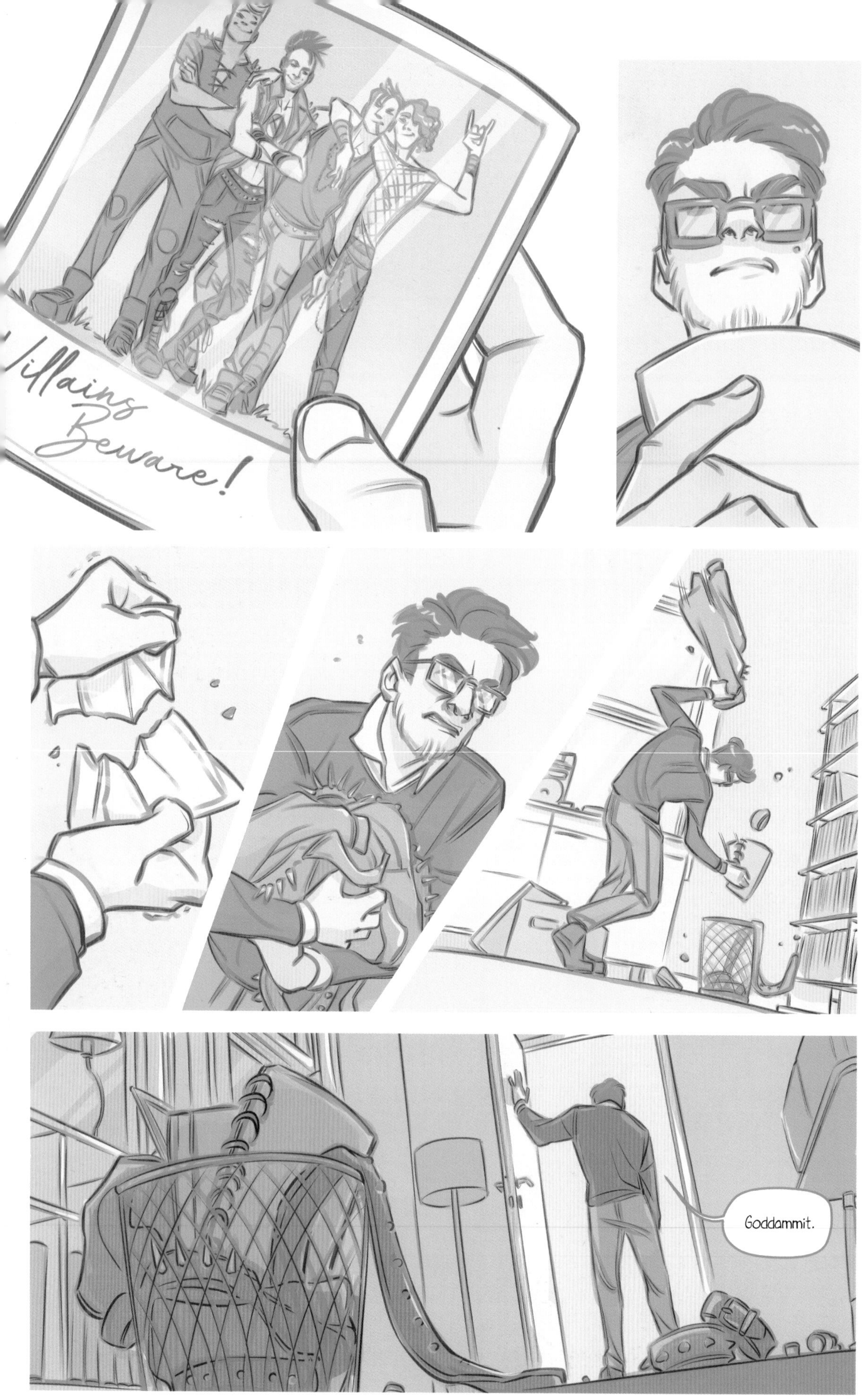
Villains Beware!
Goddammit.

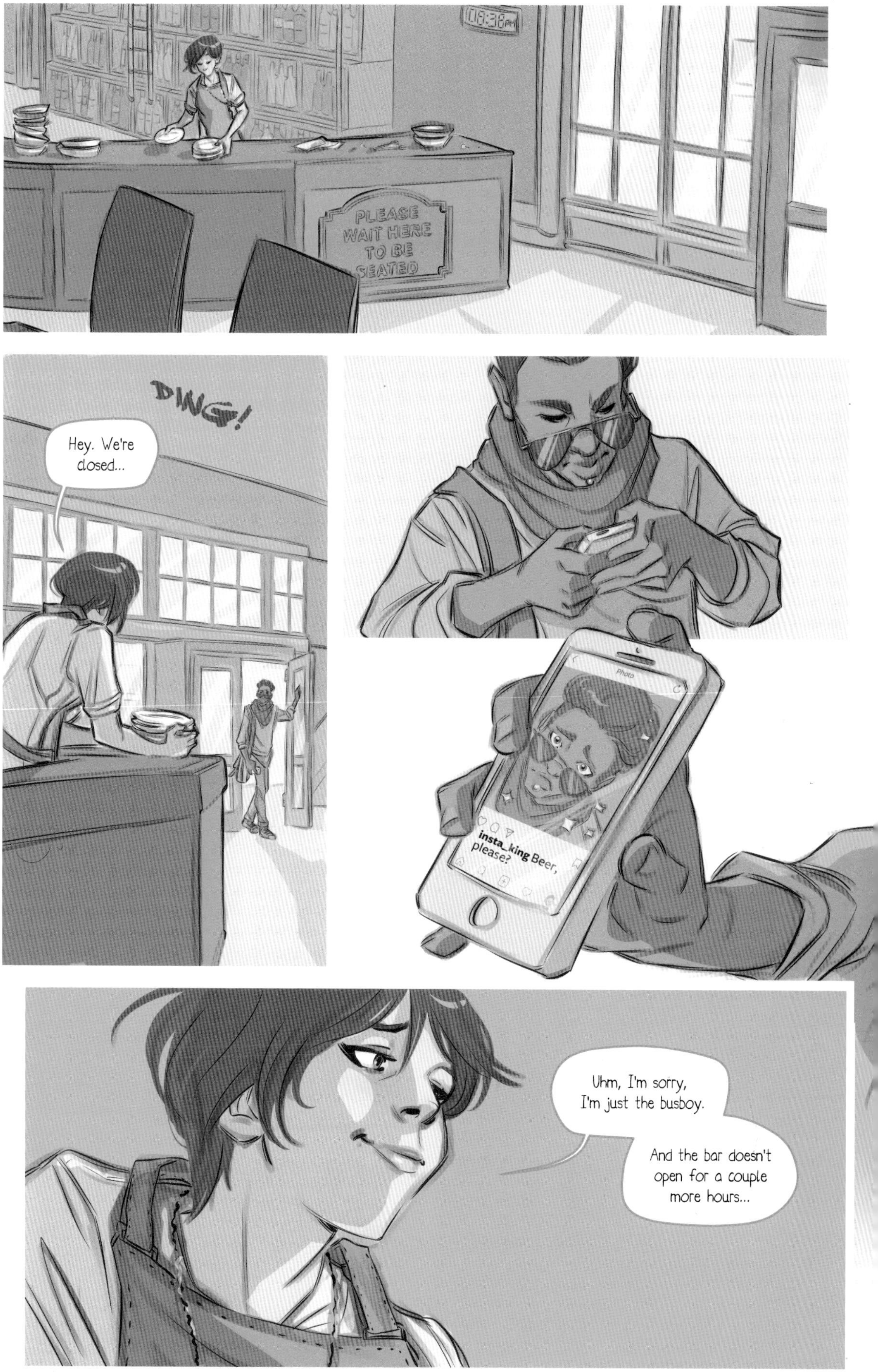
08:38PM
PLEASE WAIT HERE TO BE SEATED
DING!
Hey. We're closed...
Photo
insta_king Beer, please?
Uhm, I'm sorry, I'm just the busboy.
And the bar doesn't open for a couple more hours...

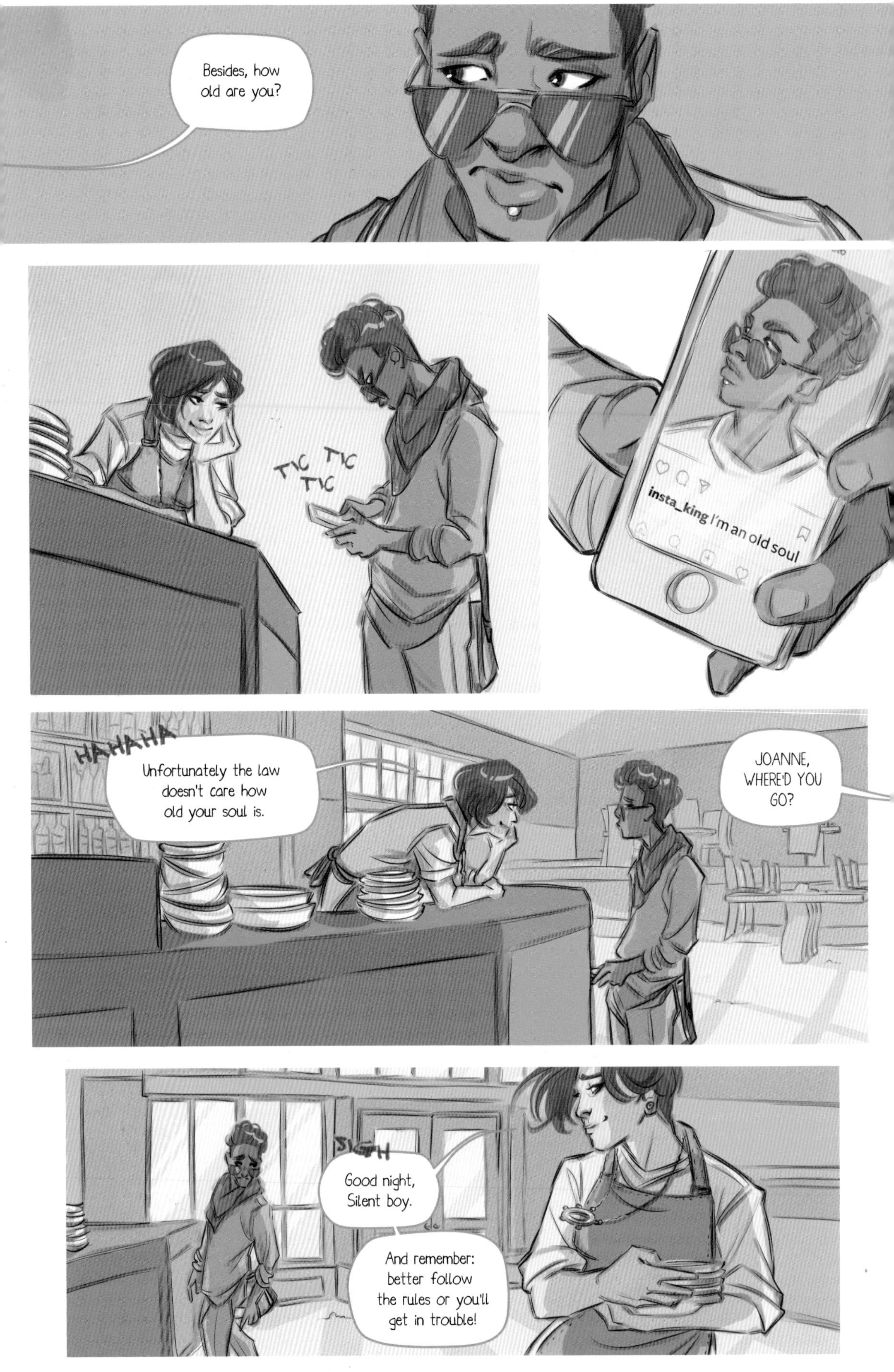
Besides, how old are you?
TIC TIC TIC
insta_king I'm an old soul
HAHAHA
Unfortunately the law doesn't care how old your soul is.
JOANNE, WHERE'D YOU GO?
SIGH
Good night, Silent boy.
And remember: better follow the rules or you'll get in trouble!

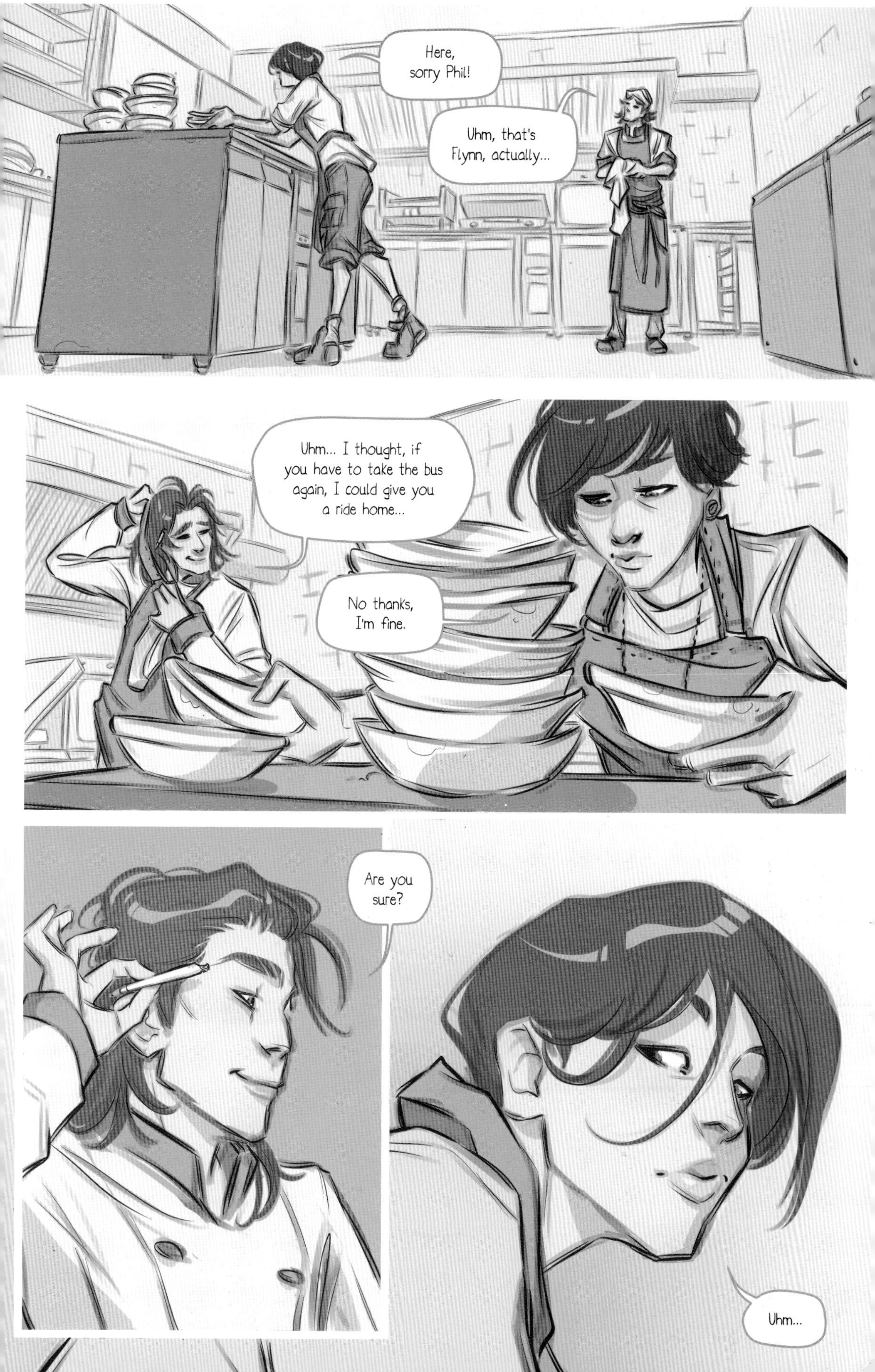
Here, sorry Phil!
Uhm, that's Flynn, actually...
Uhm... I thought, if you have to take the bus again, I could give you a ride home...
No thanks, I'm fine.
Are you sure?
Uhm...

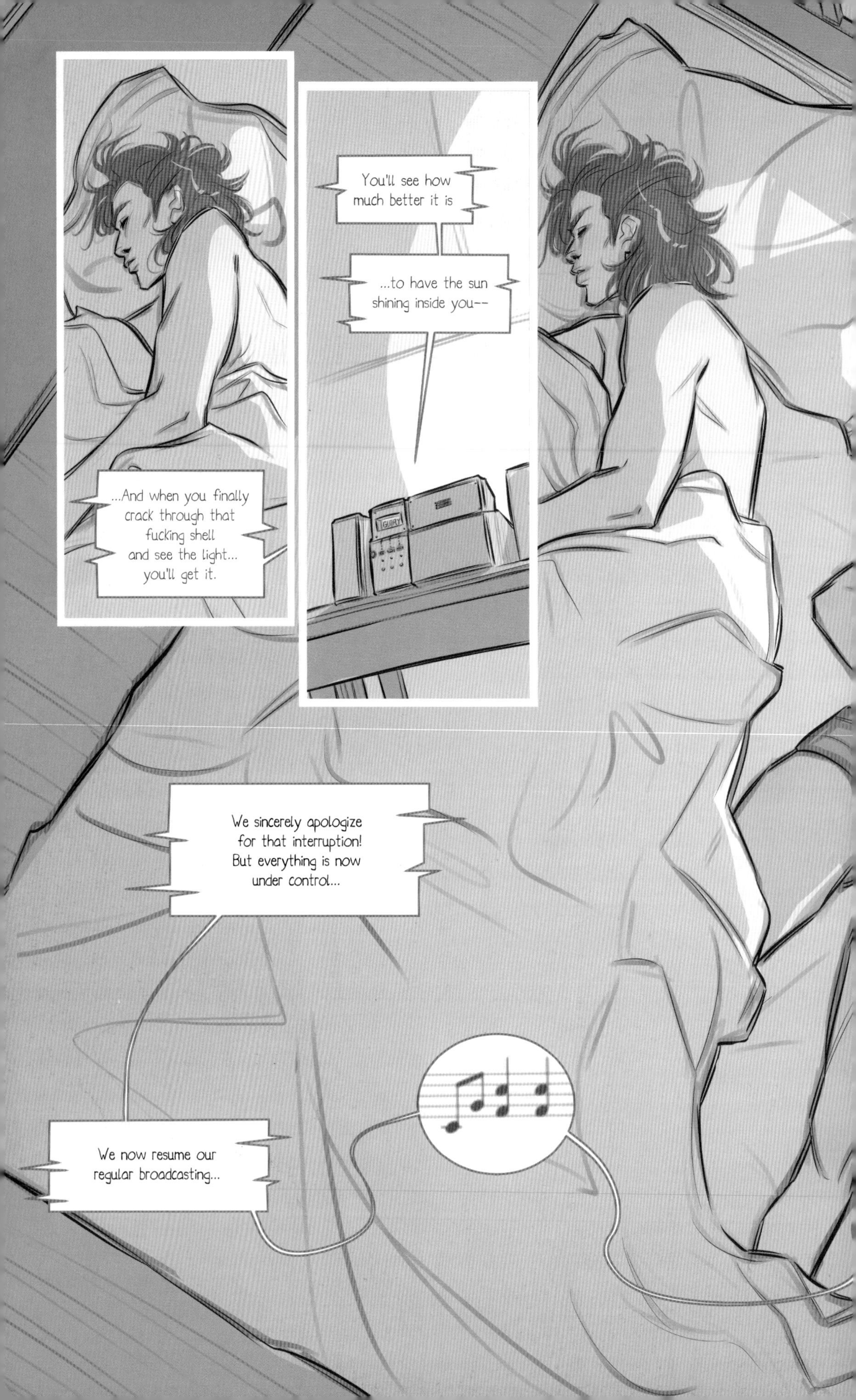
...And when you finally crack through that fucking shell and see the light... you'll get it.
You'll see how much better it is
...to have the sun shining inside you--
We sincerely apologize for that interruption! But everything is now under control...
We now resume our regular broadcasting...

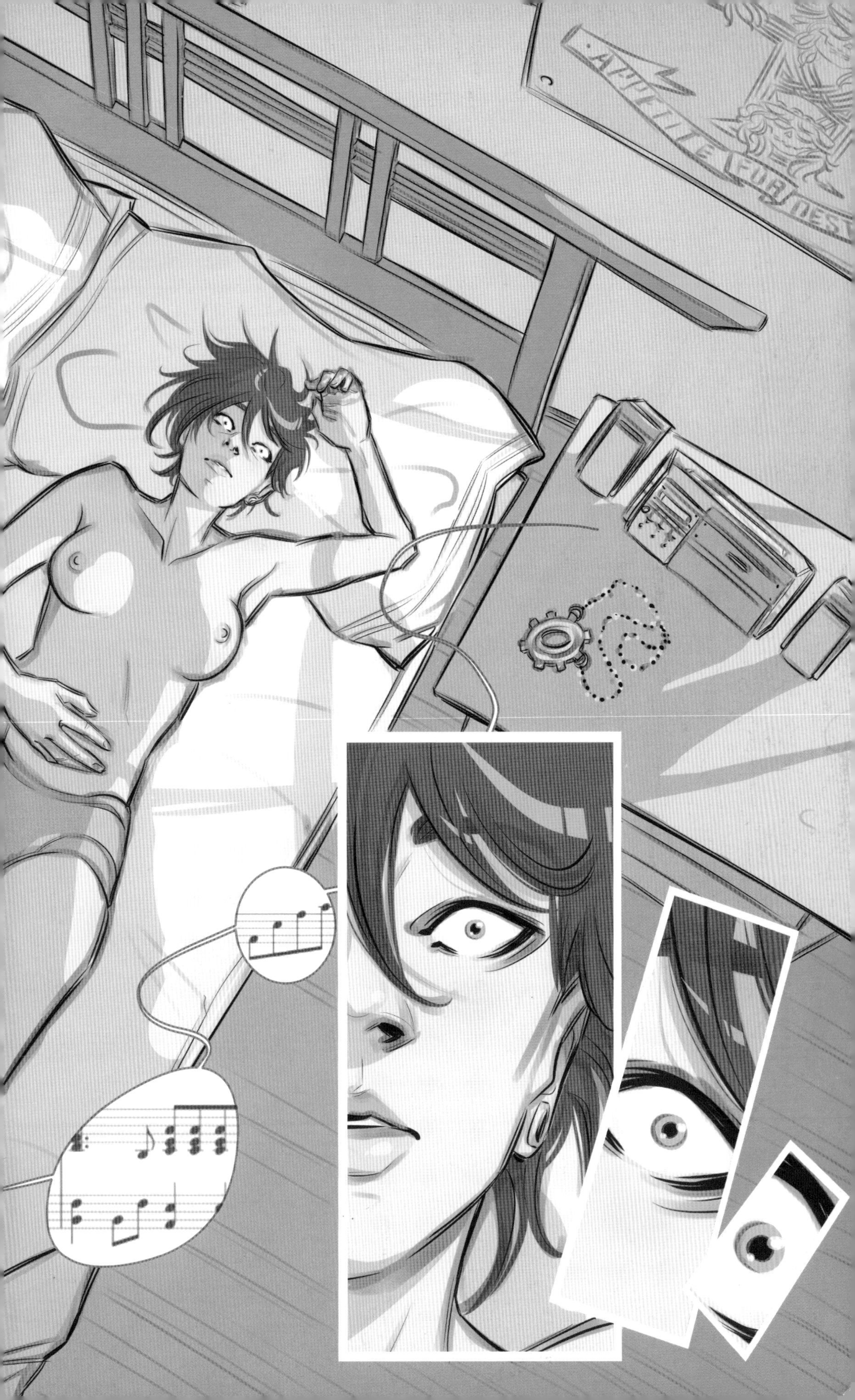
APPETITE FOR DEST

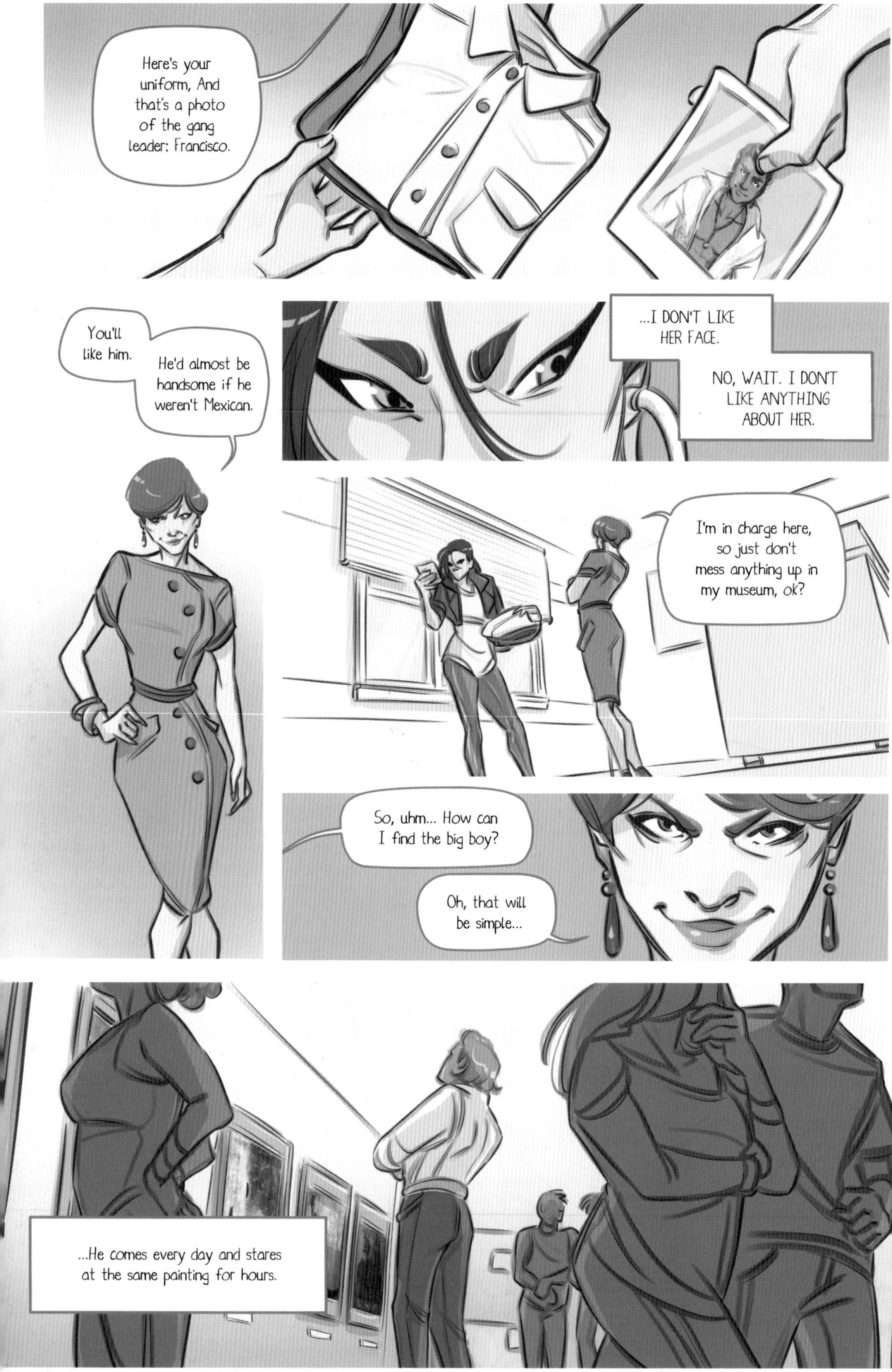
Here's your uniform, And that's a photo of the gang leader: Francisco.
You'll like him.
He'd almost be handsome if he weren't Mexican.
...I DON'T LIKE HER FACE.
NO, WAIT. I DON'T LIKE ANYTHING ABOUT HER.
I'm in charge here, so just don't mess anything up in my museum, ok?
So, uhm... How can I find the big boy?
Oh, that will be simple...
...He comes every day and stares at the same painting for hours.

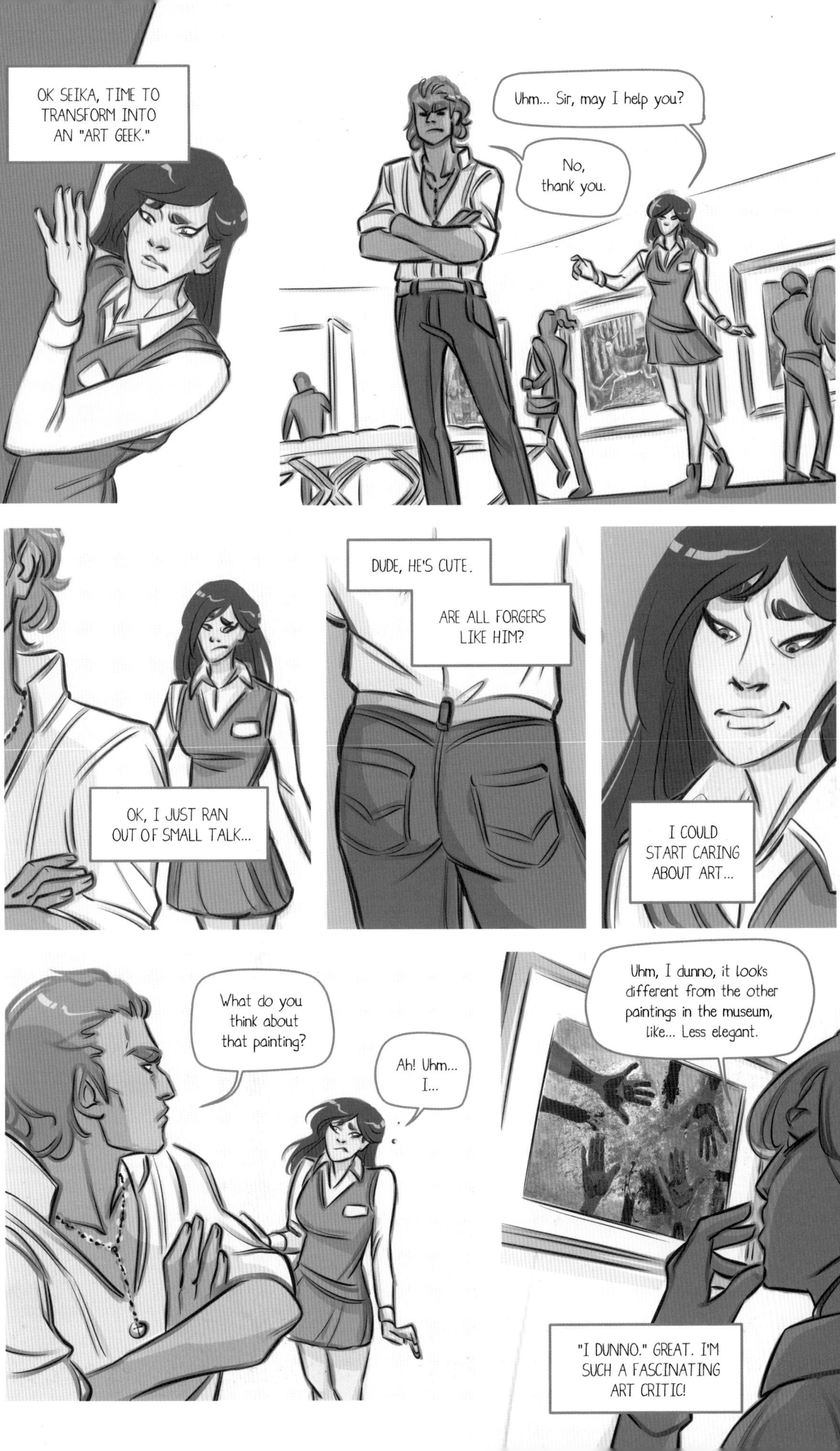
OK SEIKA, TIME TO TRANSFORM INTO AN "ART GEEK."
Uhm... Sir, may I help you?
No, thank you.
OK, I JUST RAN OUT OF SMALL TALK...
DUDE, HE'S CUTE.
ARE ALL FORGERS LIKE HIM?
I COULD START CARING ABOUT ART...
What do you think about that painting?
Ah! Uhm... I...
Uhm, I dunno, it looks different from the other paintings in the museum, like... Less elegant.
"I DUNNO." GREAT. I'M SUCH A FASCINATING ART CRITIC!

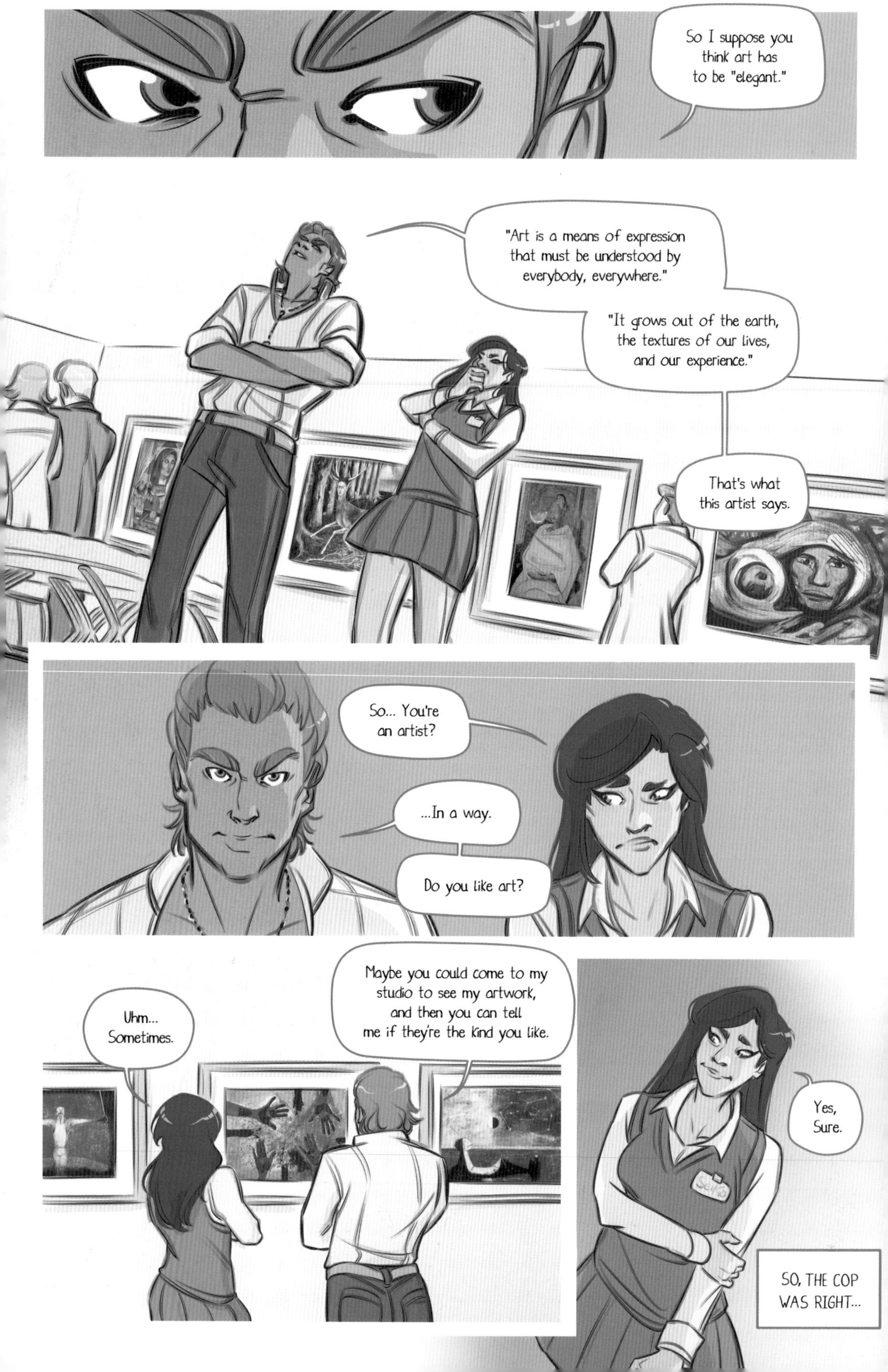

So I suppose you think art has to be "elegant."
"Art is a means of expression that must be understood by everybody, everywhere."
"It grows out of the earth, the textures of our lives, and our experience."
That's what this artist says.
So... You're an artist?
...In a way.
Do you like art?
Uhm... Sometimes.
Maybe you could come to my studio to see my artwork, and then you can tell me if they're the kind you like.
Yes, Sure.
SO, THE COP WAS RIGHT...

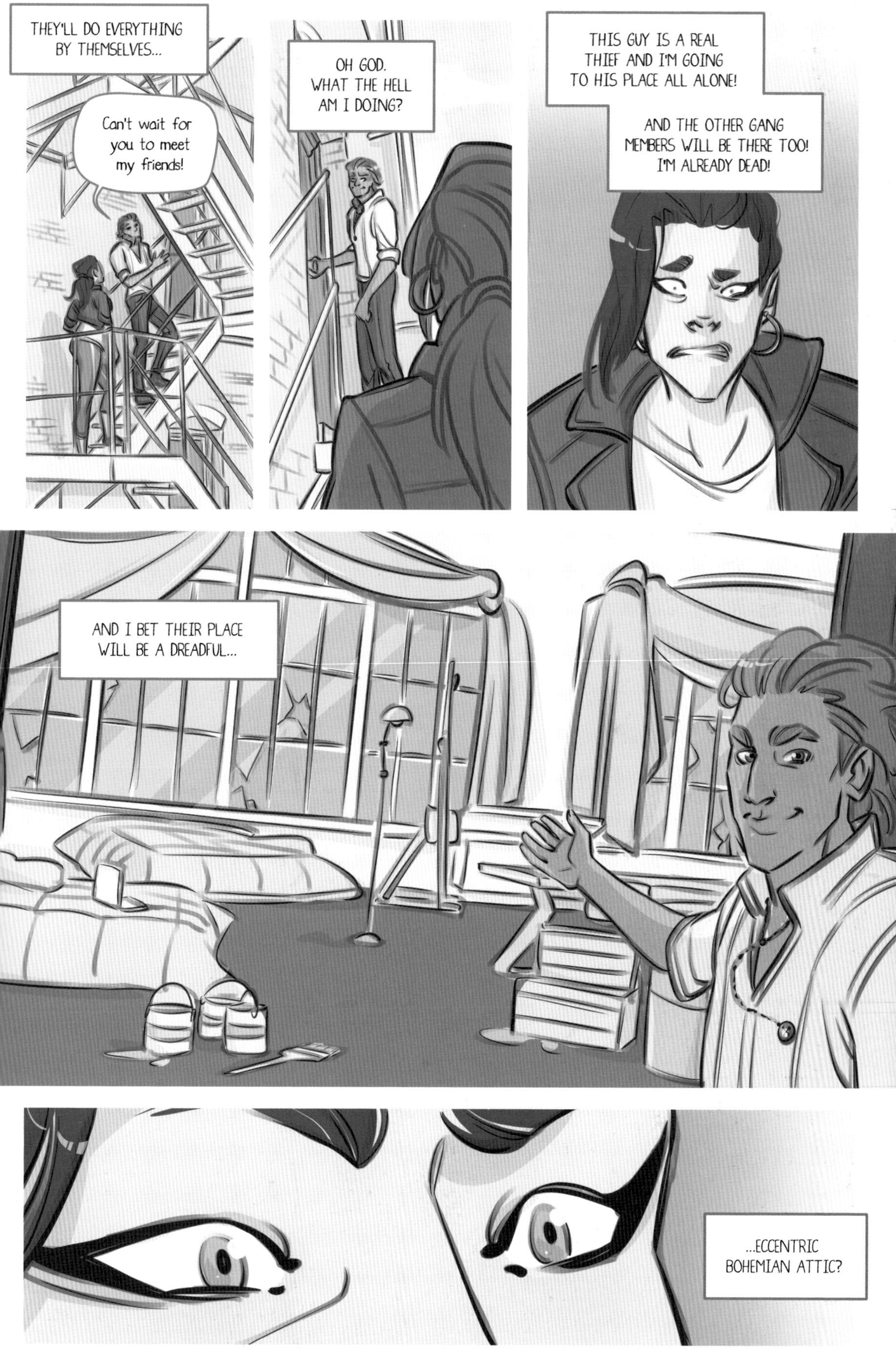
THEY'LL DO EVERYTHING BY THEMSELVES...
Can't wait for you to meet my friends!
OH GOD. WHAT THE HELL AM I DOING?
THIS GUY IS A REAL THIEF AND I'M GOING TO HIS PLACE ALL ALONE!
AND THE OTHER GANG MEMBERS WILL BE THERE TOO! I'M ALREADY DEAD!
AND I BET THEIR PLACE WILL BE A DREADFUL...
...ECCENTRIC BOHEMIAN ATTIC?

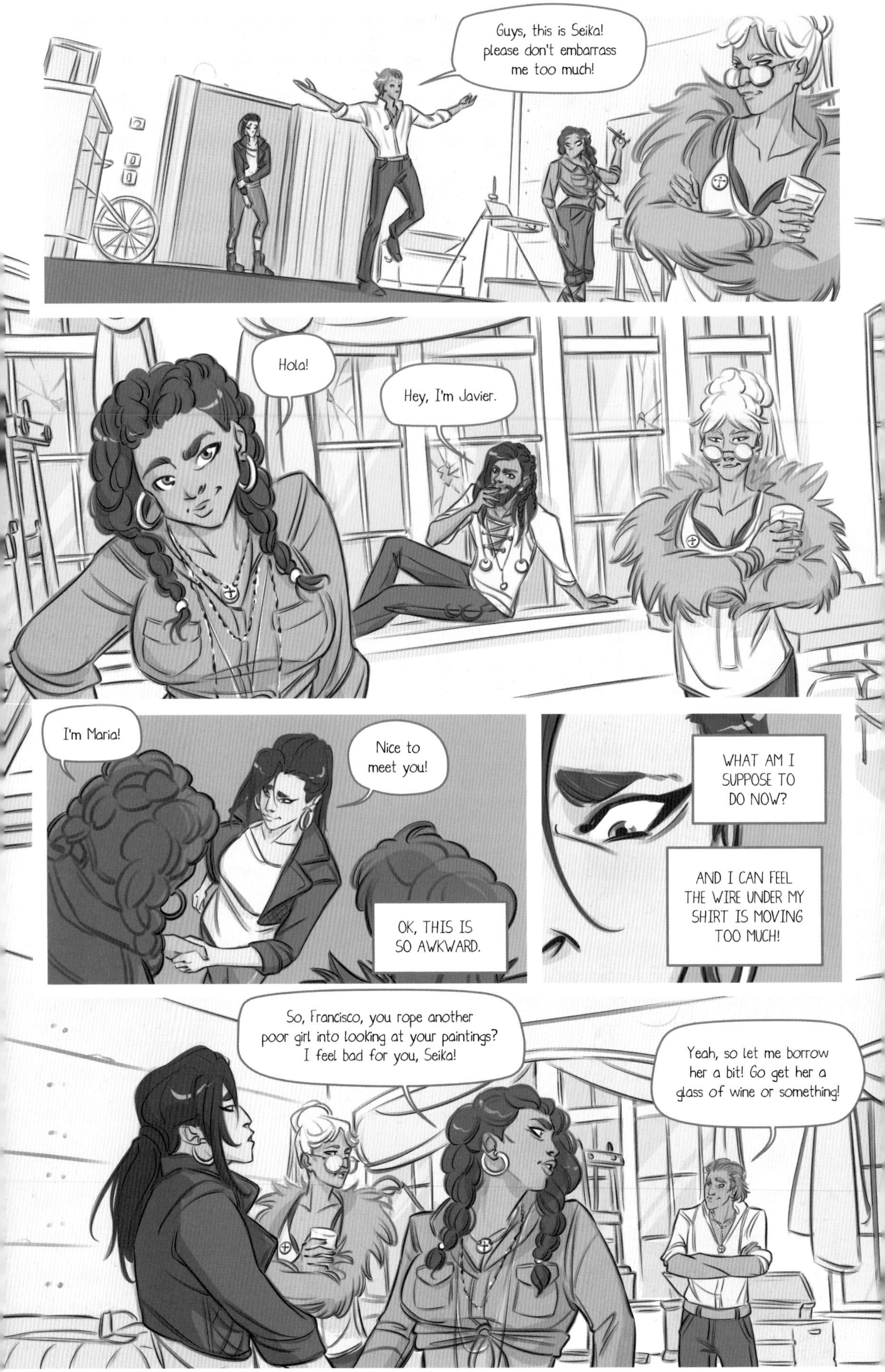

Guys, this is Seika! please don't embarrass me too much!
Hola!
Hey, I'm Javier.
I'm Maria!
Nice to meet you!
OK, THIS IS SO AWKWARD.
WHAT AM I SUPPOSE TO DO NOW?
AND I CAN FEEL THE WIRE UNDER MY SHIRT IS MOVING TOO MUCH!
So, Francisco, you rope another poor girl into looking at your paintings? I feel bad for you, Seika!
Yeah, so let me borrow her a bit! Go get her a glass of wine or something!

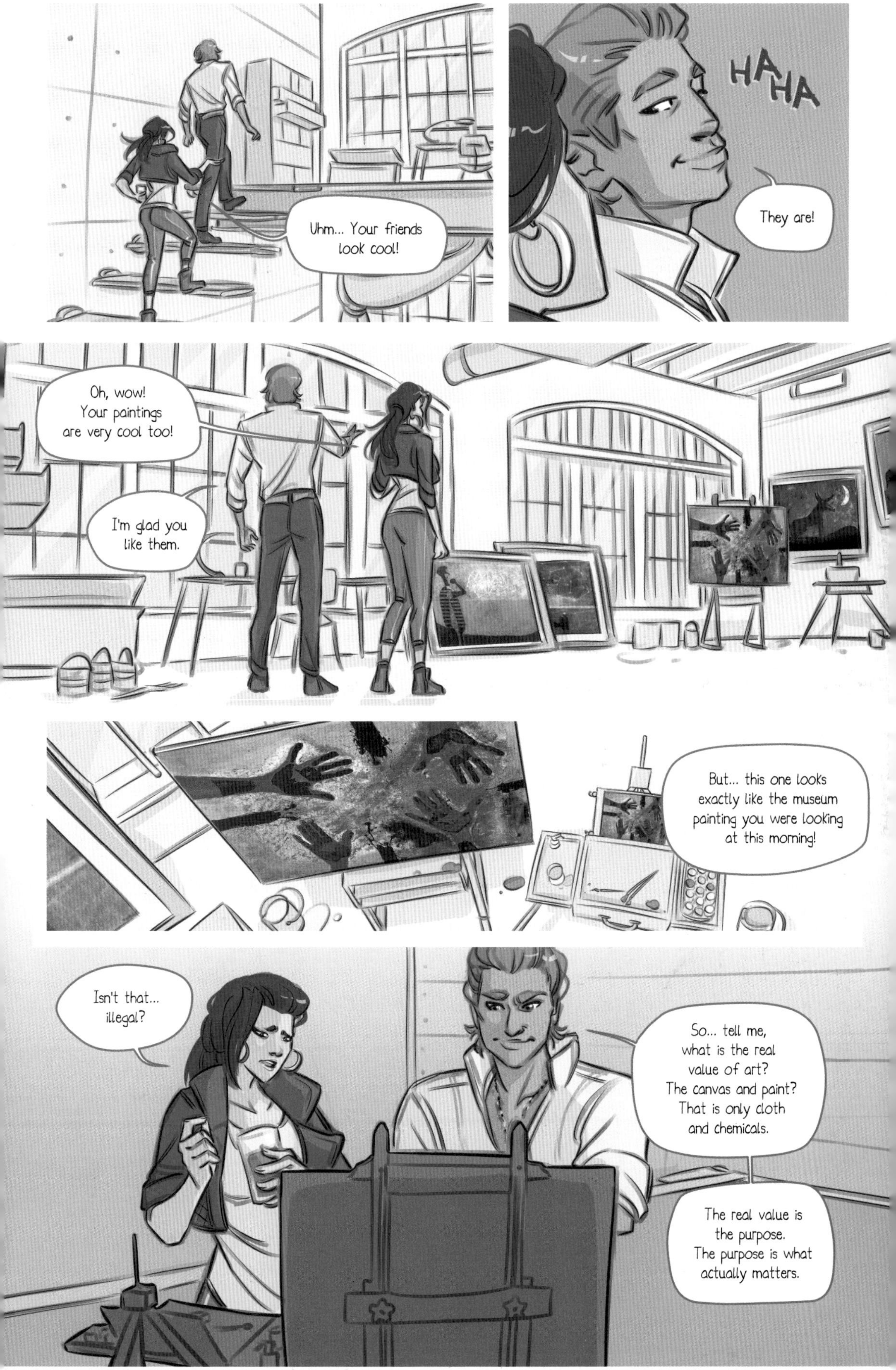
Uhm... Your friends look cool!
HAHA
They are!
Oh, wow! Your paintings are very cool too!
I'm glad you like them.
But... this one looks exactly like the museum painting you were looking at this morning!
Isn't that... illegal?
So... tell me, what is the real value of art? The canvas and paint? That is only cloth and chemicals.
The real value is the purpose. The purpose is what actually matters.

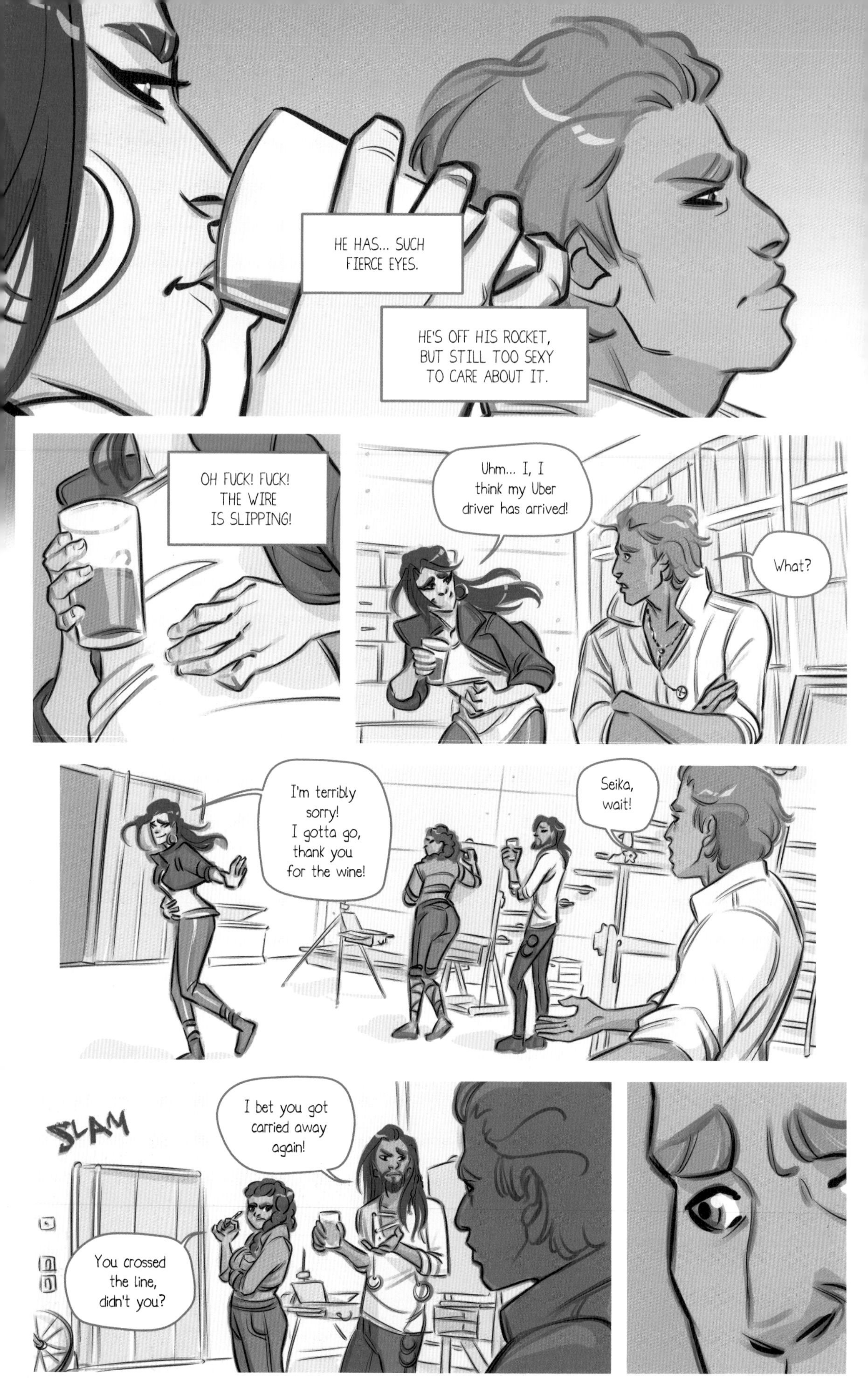
HE HAS... SUCH FIERCE EYES.
HE'S OFF HIS ROCKET, BUT STILL TOO SEXY TO CARE ABOUT IT.
OH FUCK! FUCK! THE WIRE IS SLIPPING!
Uhm... I, I think my Uber driver has arrived!
What?
I'm terribly sorry! I gotta go, thank you for the wine!
Seika, wait!
SLAM
I bet you got carried away again!
You crossed the line, didn't you?

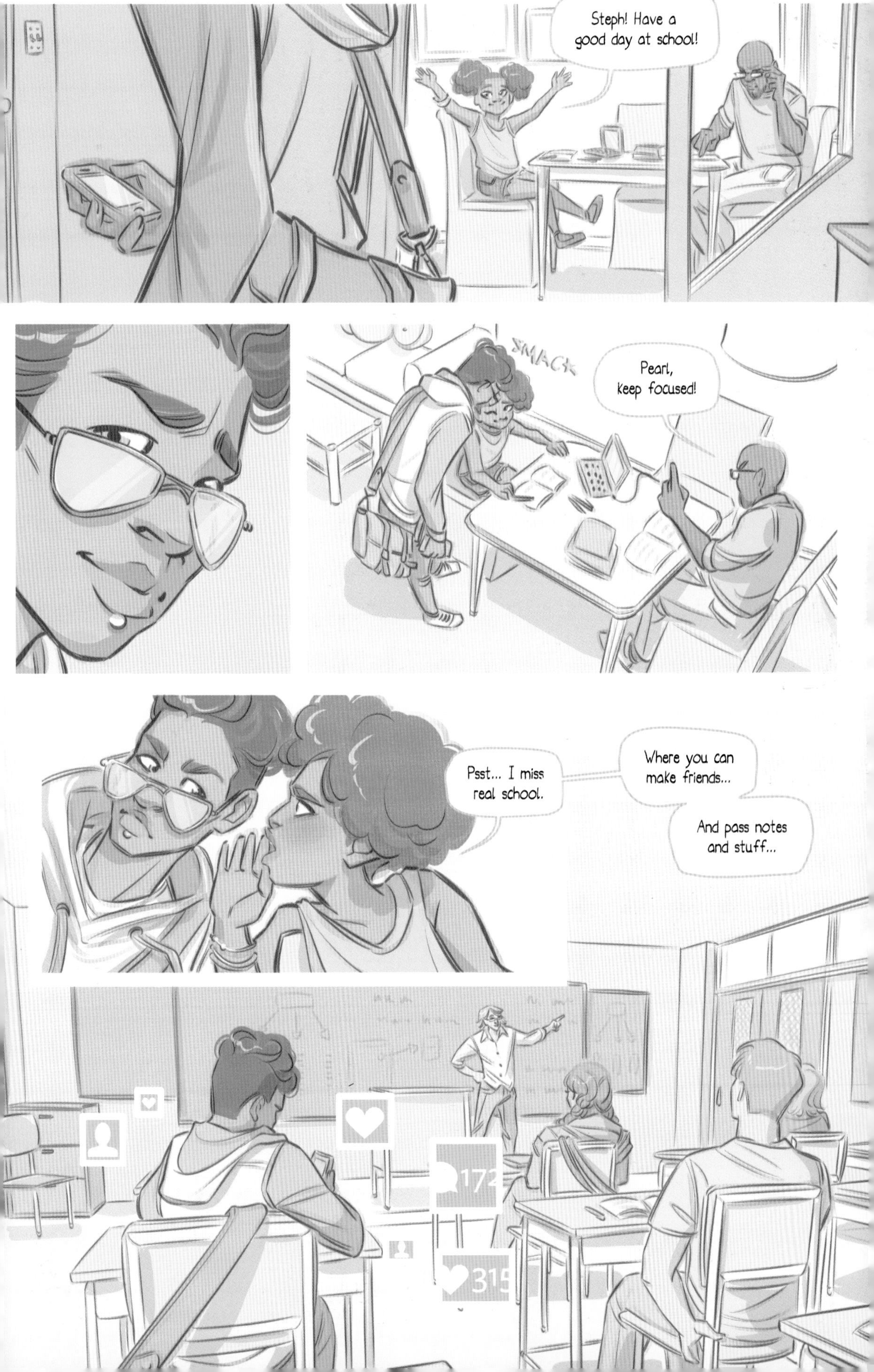
Steph! Have a good day at school!
SMACK
Pearl, keep focused!
Psst... I miss real school.
Where you can make friends...
And pass notes and stuff...
172
315

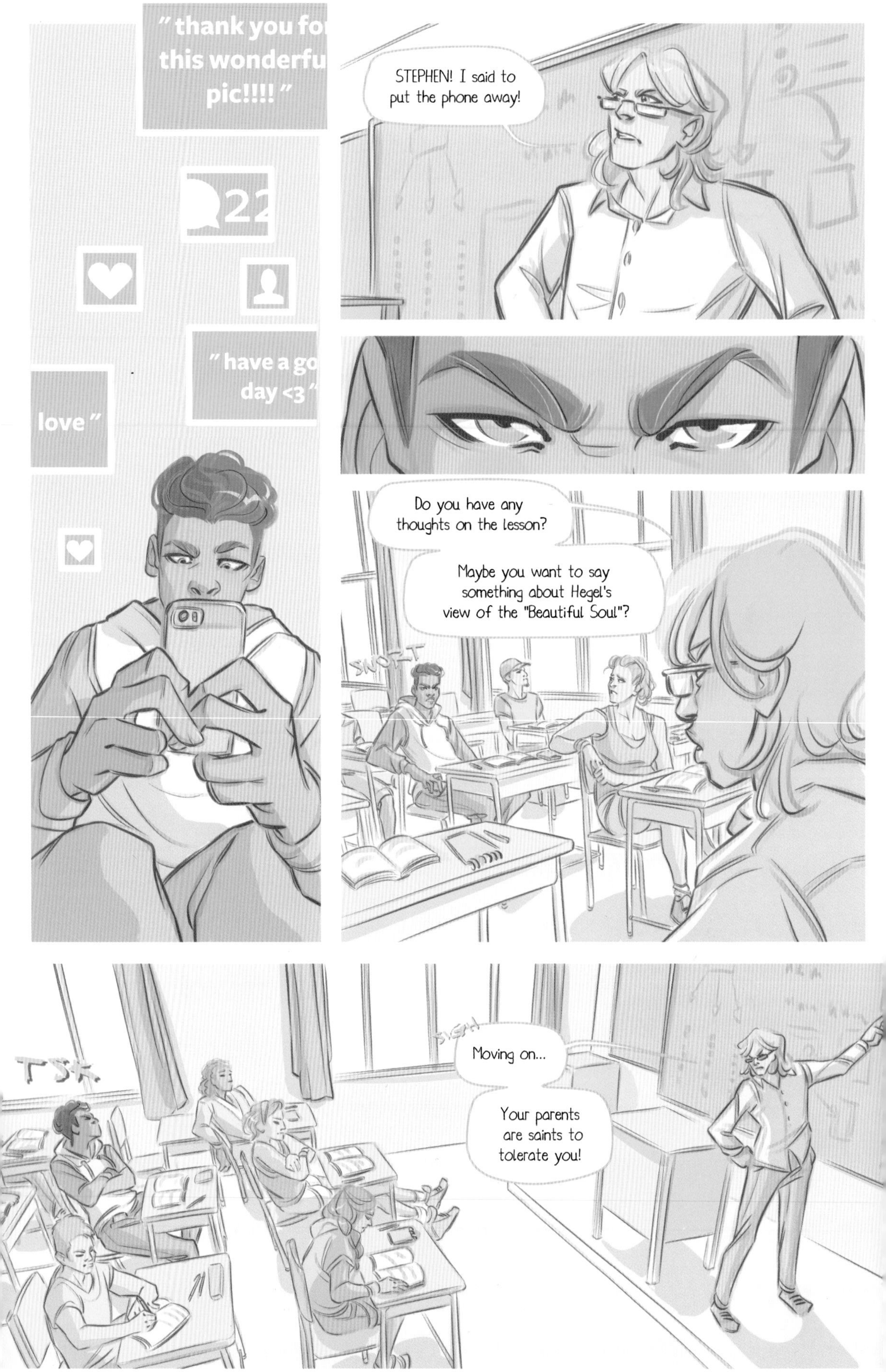

" thank you fo
this wonderfu
pic!!!! "
22
" have a go
day <3 "
love "
STEPHEN! I said to put the phone away!
Do you have any thoughts on the lesson?
Maybe you want to say something about Hegel's view of the "Beautiful Soul"?
SNORT
TSK.
SIGH
Moving on...
Your parents are saints to tolerate you!

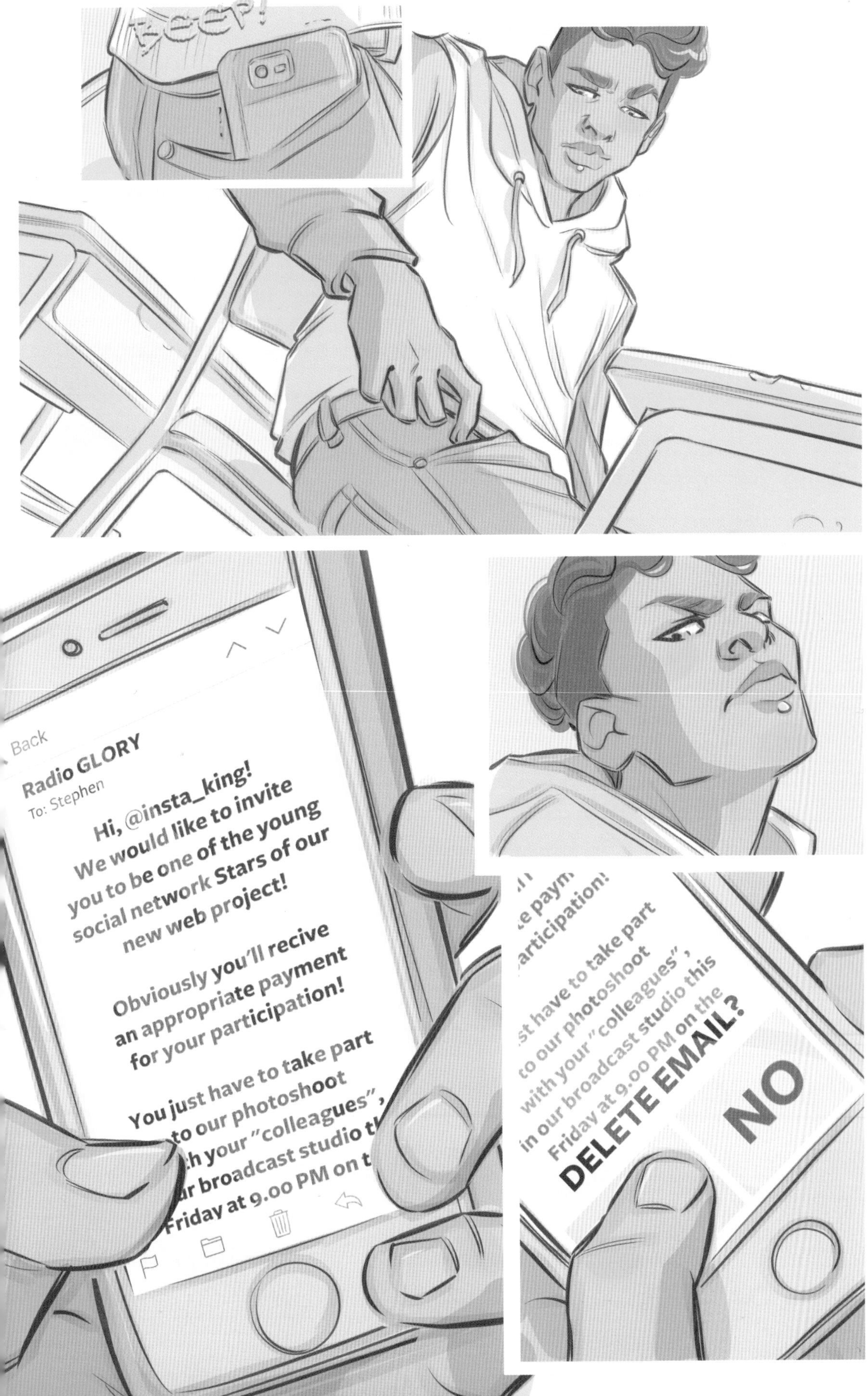

BEEP!
Back
Radio GLORY
To: Stephen
Hi, @insta_king!
We would like to invite you to be one of the young social network Stars of our new web project!
Obviously you'll recive an appropriate payment for your participation!
You just have to take part
to our photoshoot
th your "colleagues",
ur broadcast studio th
Friday at 9.00 PM on t
articipation!
st have to take part
to our photoshoot
with your "colleagues",
in our broadcast studio this
Friday at 9.00 PM on the
DELETE EMAIL?
NO

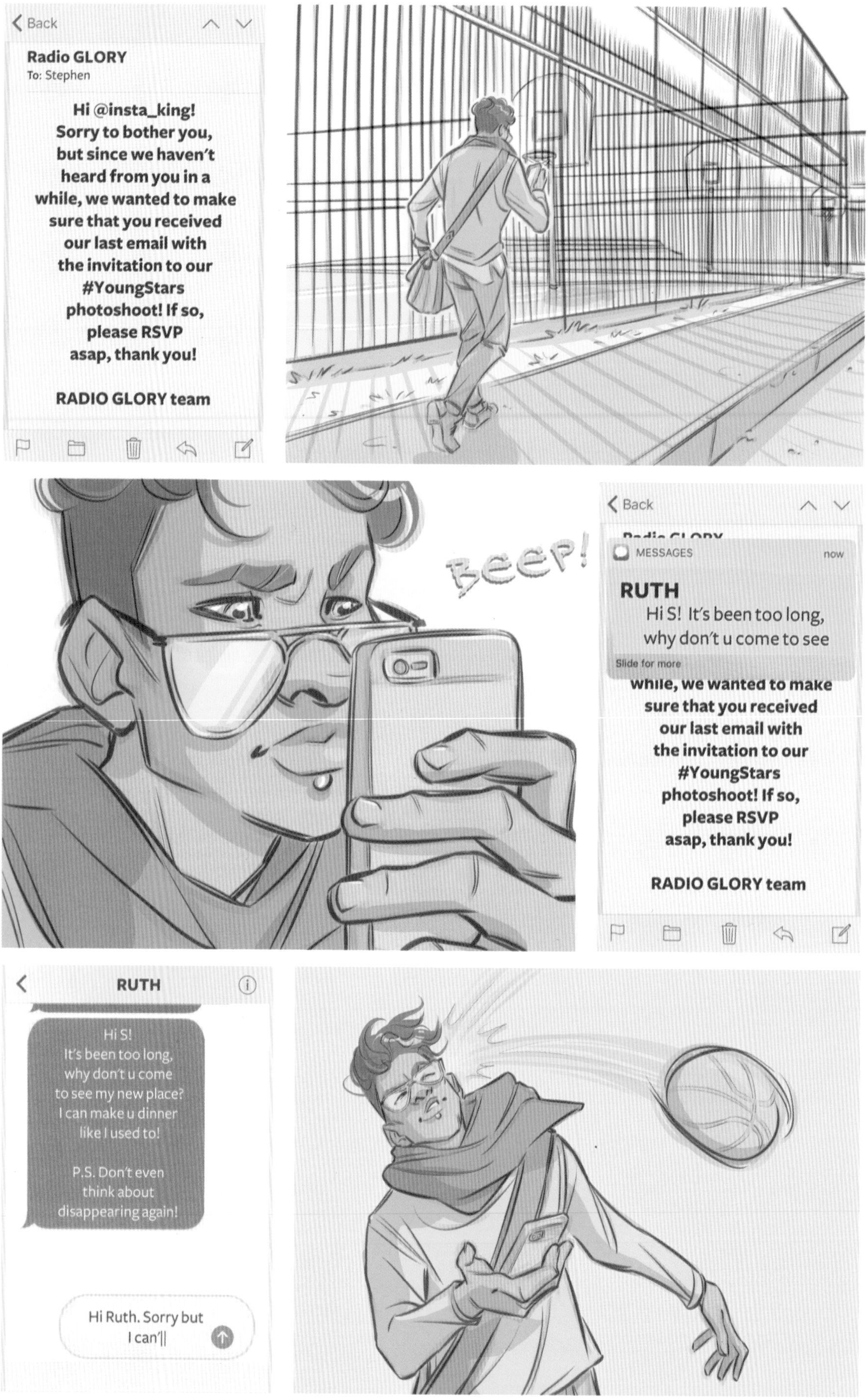

Back
Radio GLORY
To: Stephen
Hi @insta_king! Sorry to bother you, but since we haven't heard from you in a while, we wanted to make sure that you received our last email with the invitation to our #YoungStars photoshoot! If so, please RSVP asap, thank you!
RADIO GLORY team
BEEP!
Back
MESSAGES
now
RUTH
Hi S! It's been too long, why don't u come to see
Slide for more
while, we wanted to make sure that you received our last email with the invitation to our #YoungStars photoshoot! If so, please RSVP asap, thank you!
RADIO GLORY team
RUTH
Hi S! It's been too long, why don't u come to see my new place? I can make u dinner like I used to!
P.S. Don't even think about disappearing again!
Hi Ruth. Sorry but I can'

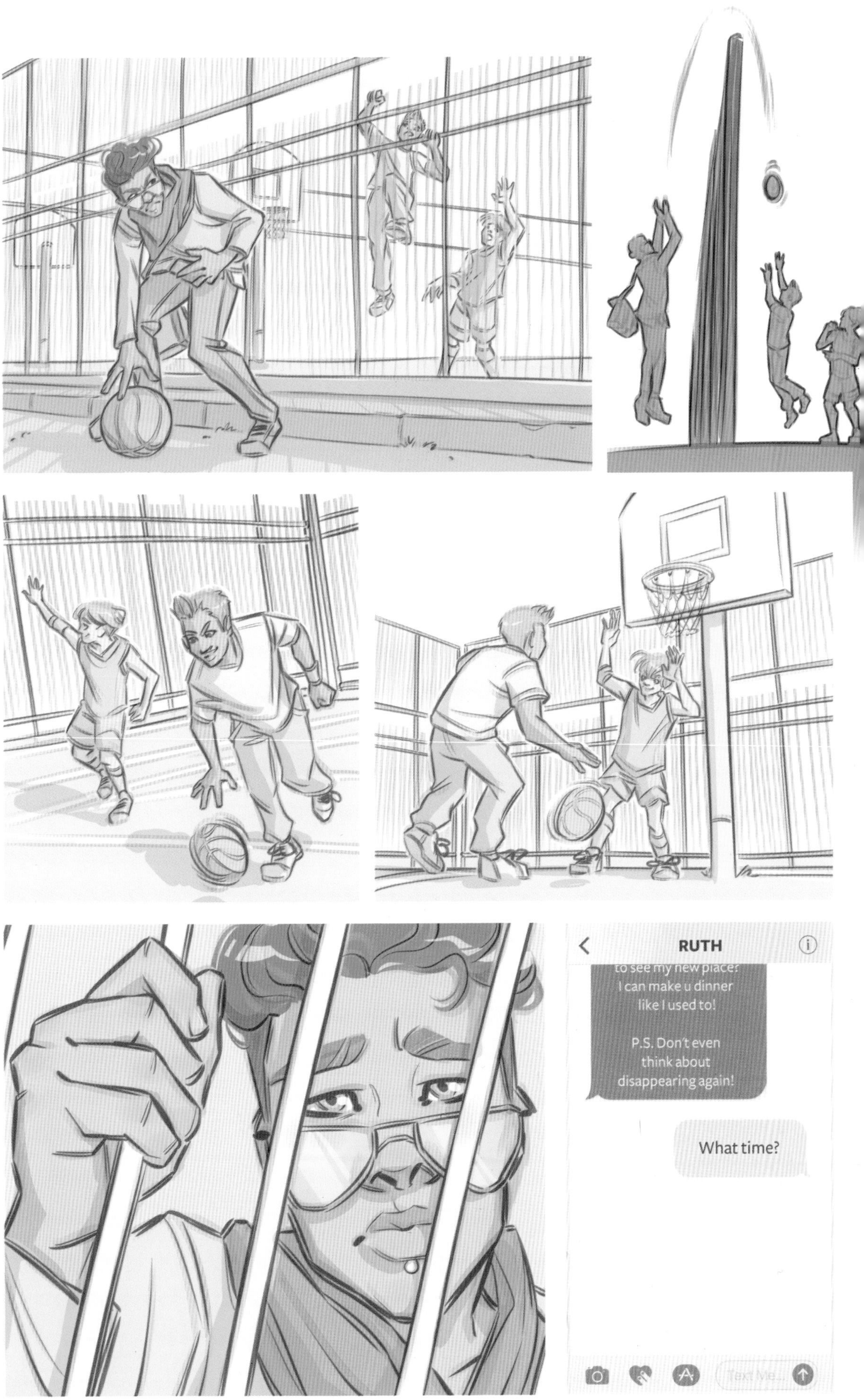
RUTH
to see my new place?
I can make u dinner
like I used to!
P.S. Don't even
think about
disappearing again!
What time?

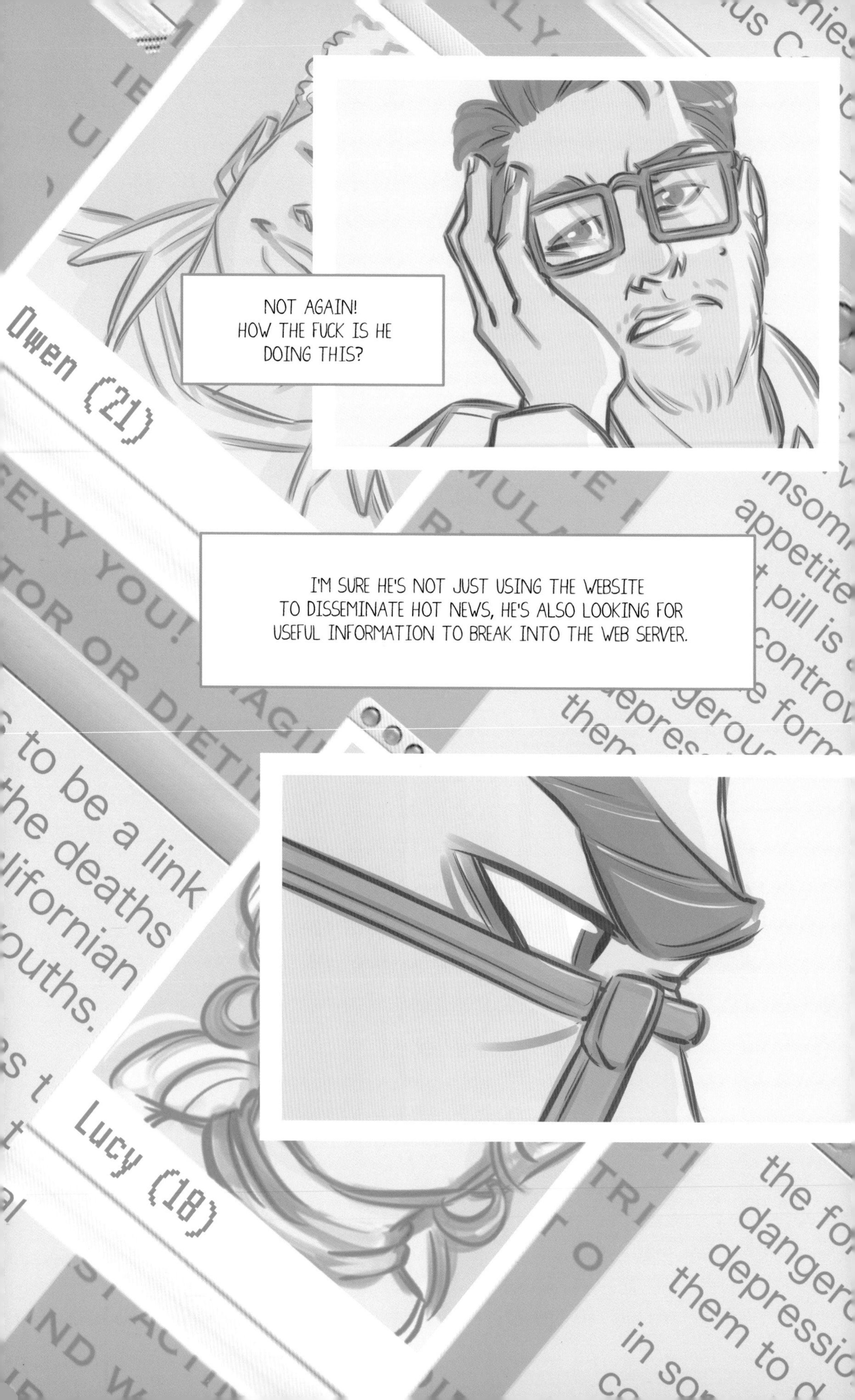
Owen (21)
NOT AGAIN! HOW THE FUCK IS HE DOING THIS?
I'M SURE HE'S NOT JUST USING THE WEBSITE TO DISSEMINATE HOT NEWS, HE'S ALSO LOOKING FOR USEFUL INFORMATION TO BREAK INTO THE WEB SERVER.
Lucy (18)

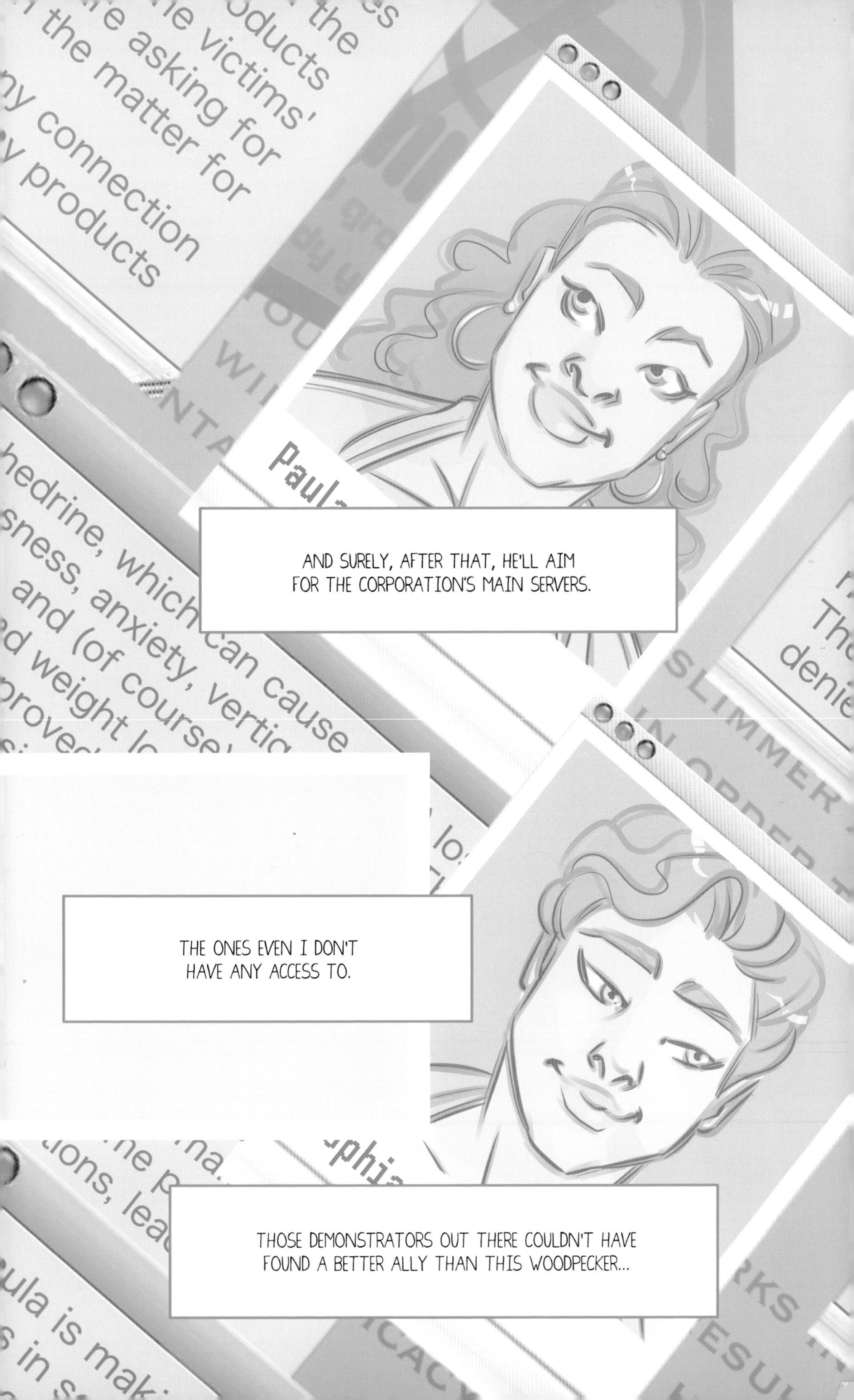

AND SURELY, AFTER THAT, HE'LL AIM FOR THE CORPORATION'S MAIN SERVERS.
THE ONES EVEN I DON'T HAVE ANY ACCESS TO.
THOSE DEMONSTRATORS OUT THERE COULDN'T HAVE FOUND A BETTER ALLY THAN THIS WOODPECKER...

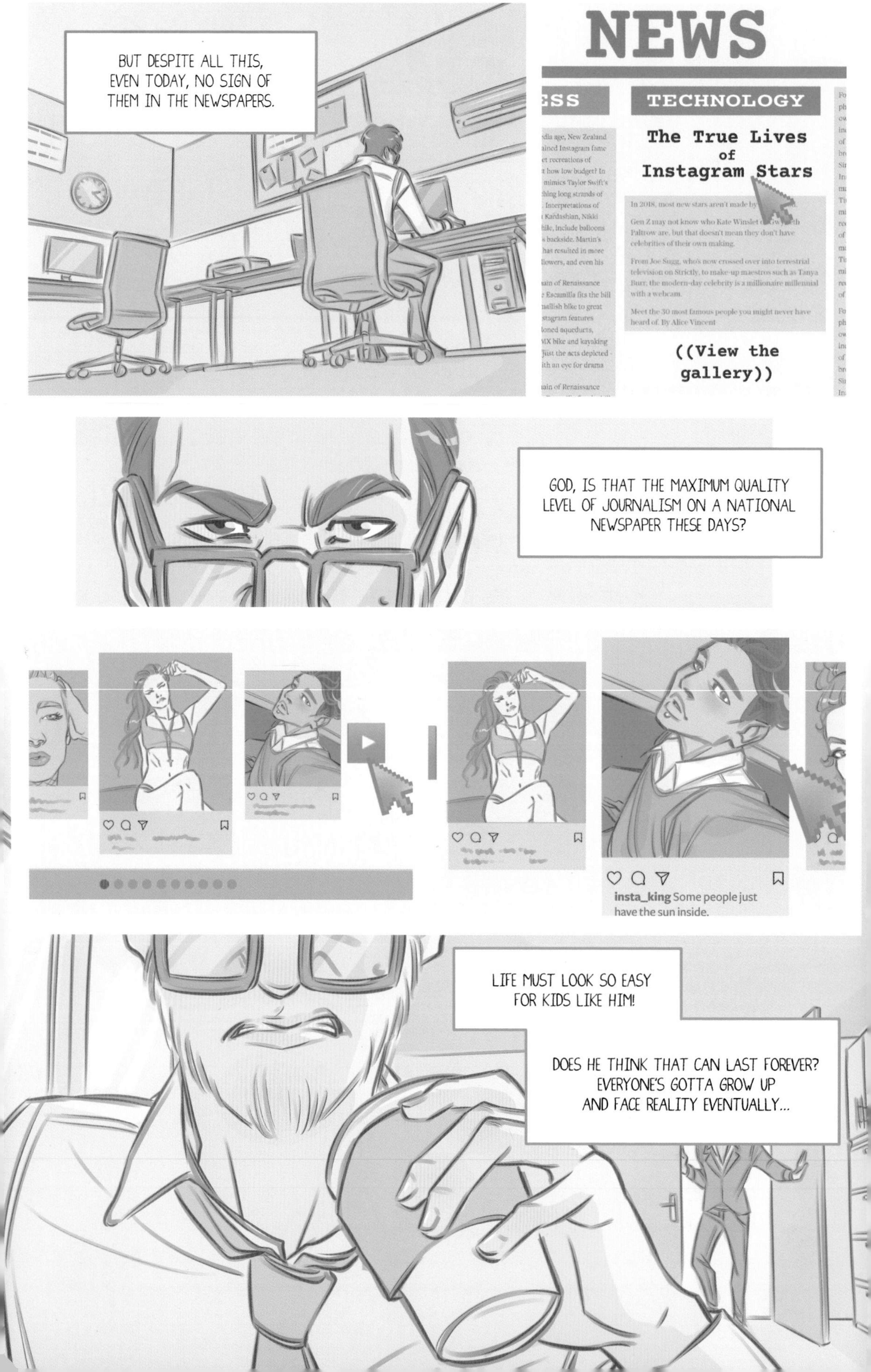
BUT DESPITE ALL THIS, EVEN TODAY, NO SIGN OF THEM IN THE NEWSPAPERS.
NEWS
TECHNOLOGY
The True Lives of Instagram Stars
In 2018, most new stars aren't made by
Paltrow are, but that doesn't mean they don't have celebrities of their own making.
From Joe Sugg, who's now crossed over into terrestrial television on Strictly, to make-up maestros such as Tanya Burr, the modern-day celebrity is a millionaire millennial with a webcam.
Meet the 30 most famous people you might never have heard of. By Alice Vincent
((View the gallery))
GOD, IS THAT THE MAXIMUM QUALITY LEVEL OF JOURNALISM ON A NATIONAL NEWSPAPER THESE DAYS?
insta_king Some people just have the sun inside.
LIFE MUST LOOK SO EASY FOR KIDS LIKE HIM!
DOES HE THINK THAT CAN LAST FOREVER? EVERYONE'S GOTTA GROW UP AND FACE REALITY EVENTUALLY...

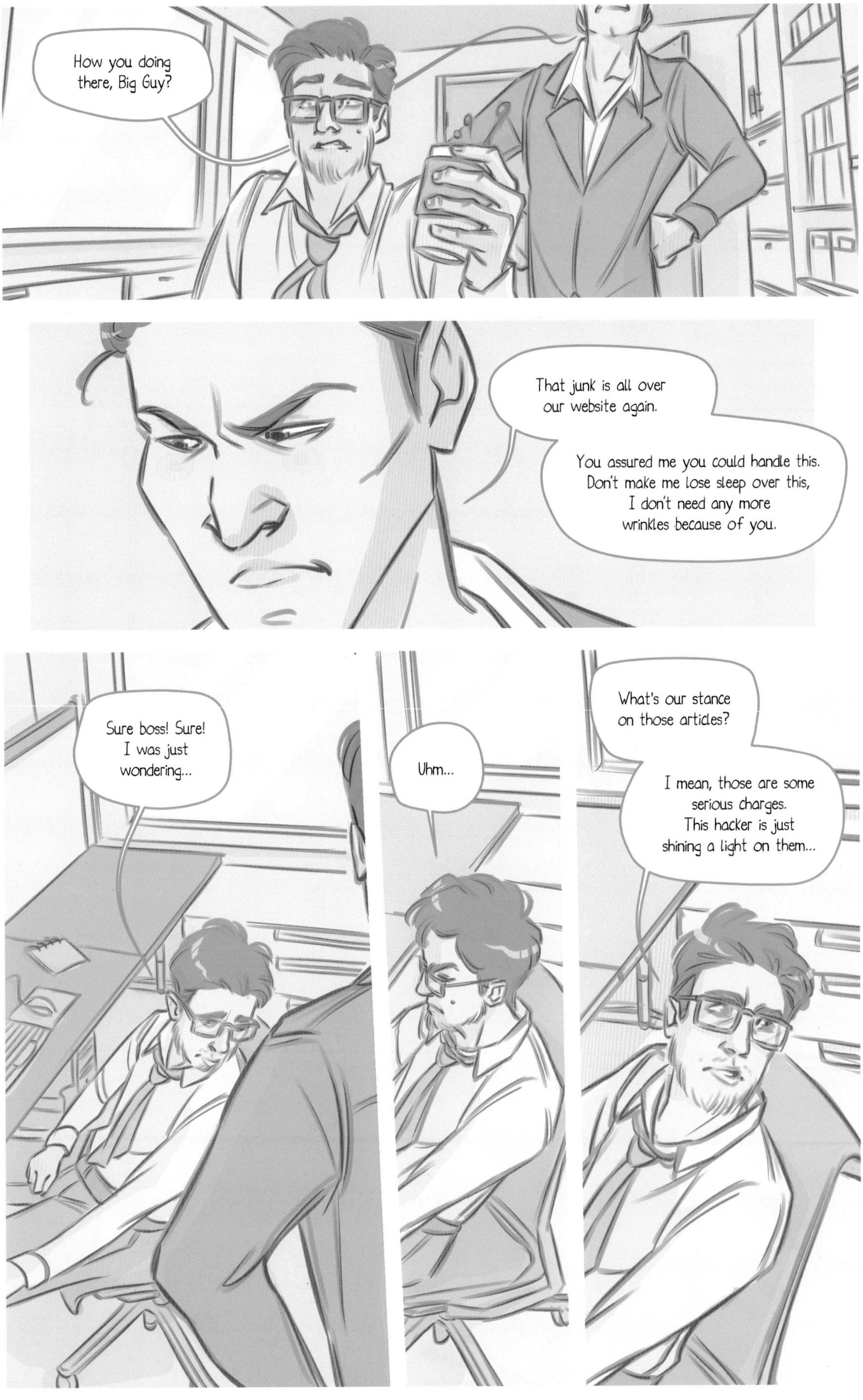
How you doing there, Big Guy?
That junk is all over our website again.
You assured me you could handle this. Don't make me lose sleep over this, I don't need any more wrinkles because of you.
Sure boss! Sure! I was just wondering...
Uhm...
What's our stance on those articles?
I mean, those are some serious charges. This hacker is just shining a light on them...

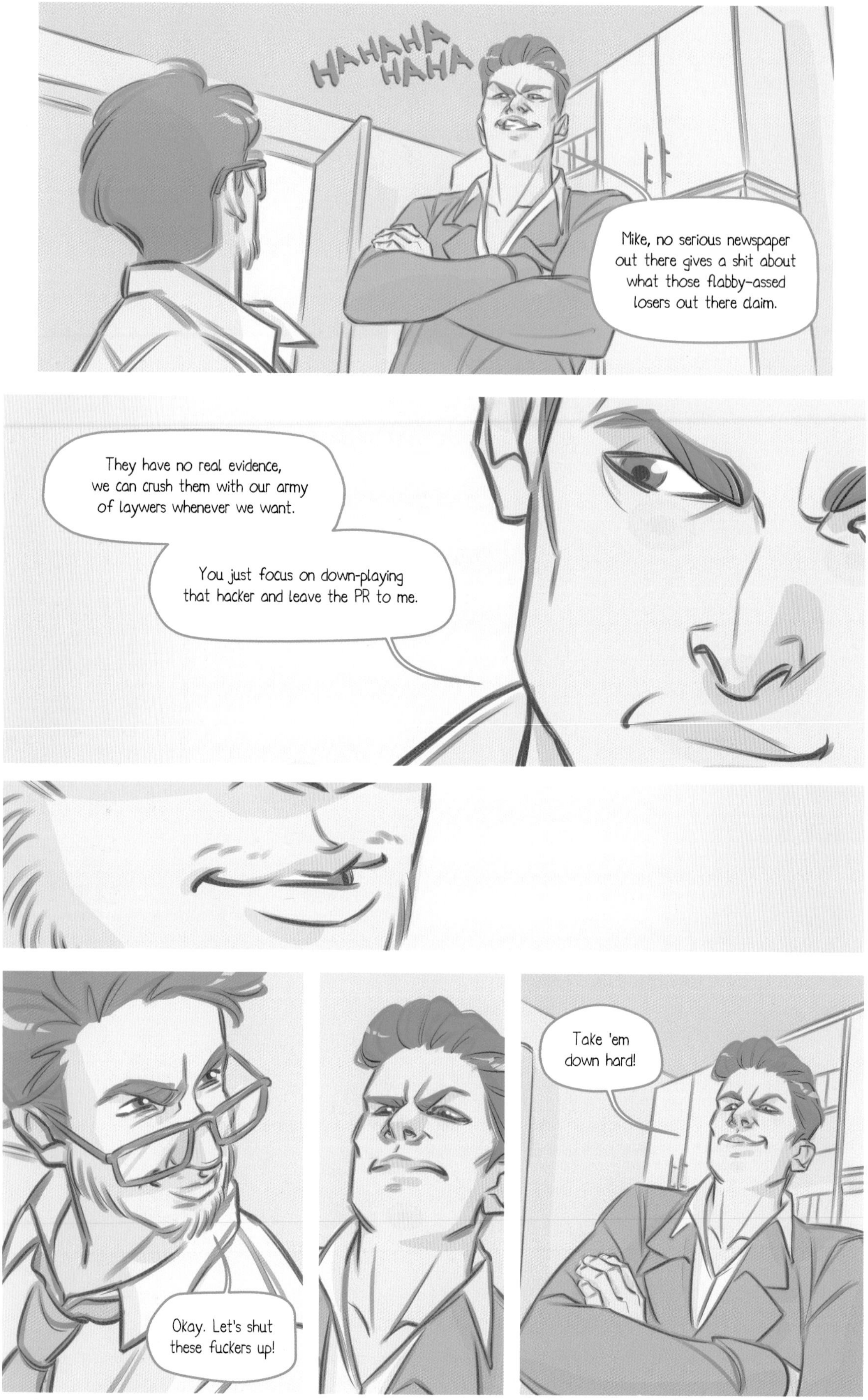
HAHAHA HAHA
Mike, no serious newspaper out there gives a shit about what those flabby-assed losers out there claim.
They have no real evidence, we can crush them with our army of laywers whenever we want.
You just focus on down-playing that hacker and leave the PR to me.
Okay. Let's shut these fuckers up!
Take 'em down hard!

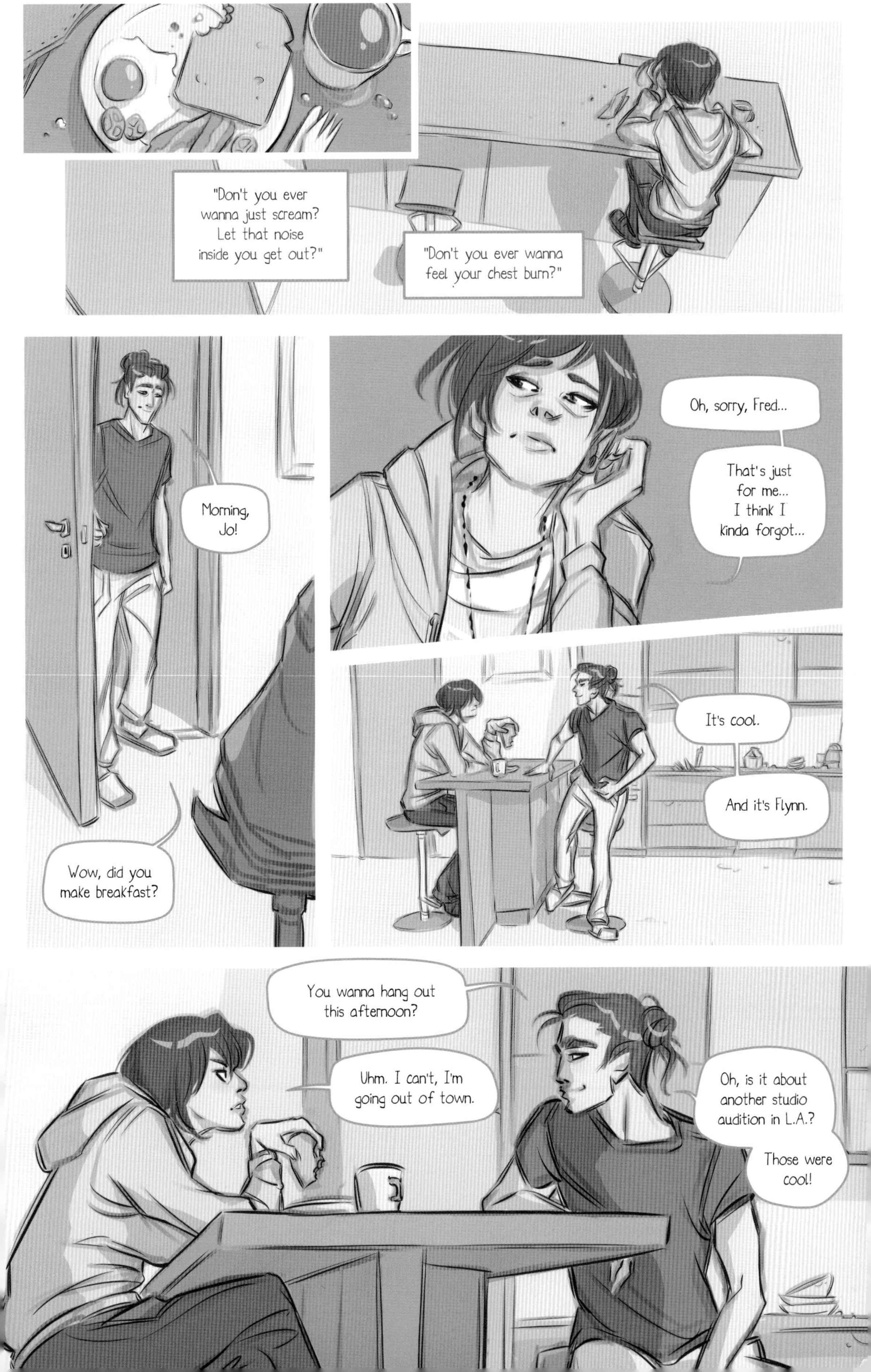
"Don't you ever wanna just scream? Let that noise inside you get out?"
"Don't you ever wanna feel your chest burn?"
Morning, Jo!
Wow, did you make breakfast?
Oh, sorry, Fred...
That's just for me... I think I kinda forgot...
It's cool.
And it's Flynn.
You wanna hang out this afternoon?
Uhm. I can't, I'm going out of town.
Oh, is it about another studio audition in L.A.?
Those were cool!

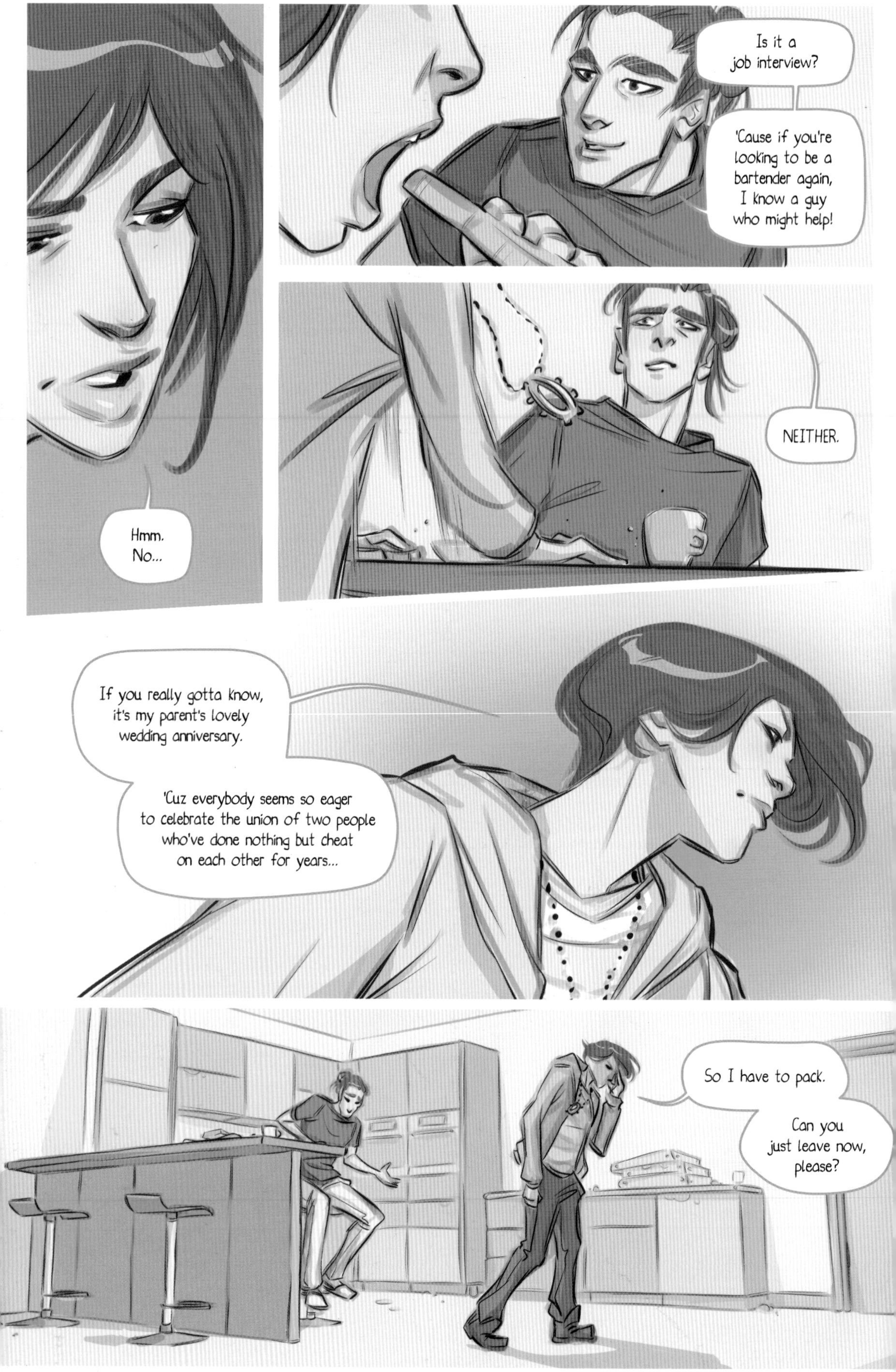
Is it a job interview?
'Cause if you're looking to be a bartender again, I know a guy who might help!
Hmm. No...
NEITHER.
If you really gotta know, it's my parent's lovely wedding anniversary.
'Cuz everybody seems so eager to celebrate the union of two people who've done nothing but cheat on each other for years...
So I have to pack.
Can you just leave now, please?

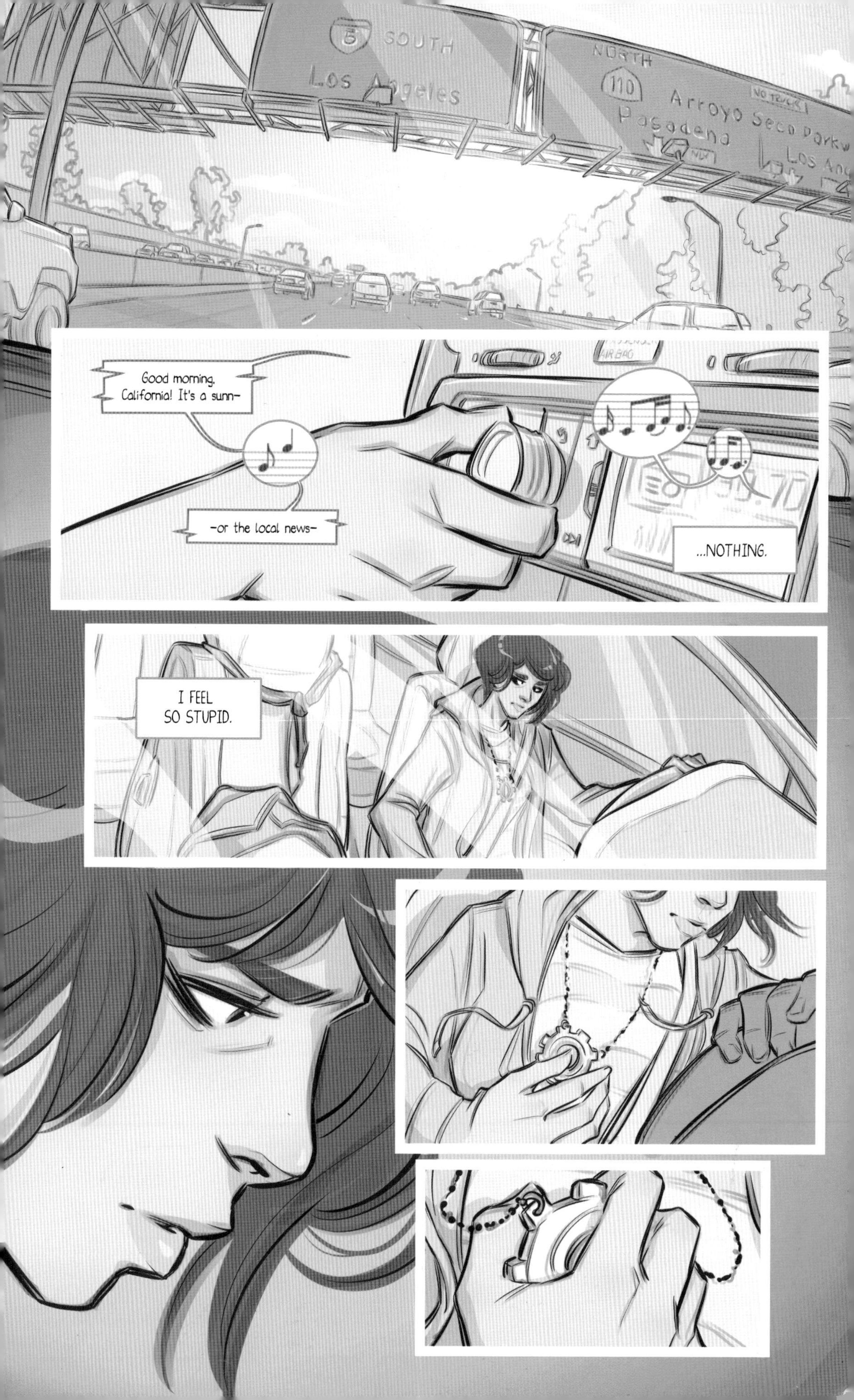

5 SOUTH
Los Angeles
NORTH
110
Arroyo Seco
Pasadena
Good morning, California! It's a sunn–
–or the local news–
...NOTHING.
I FEEL SO STUPID.

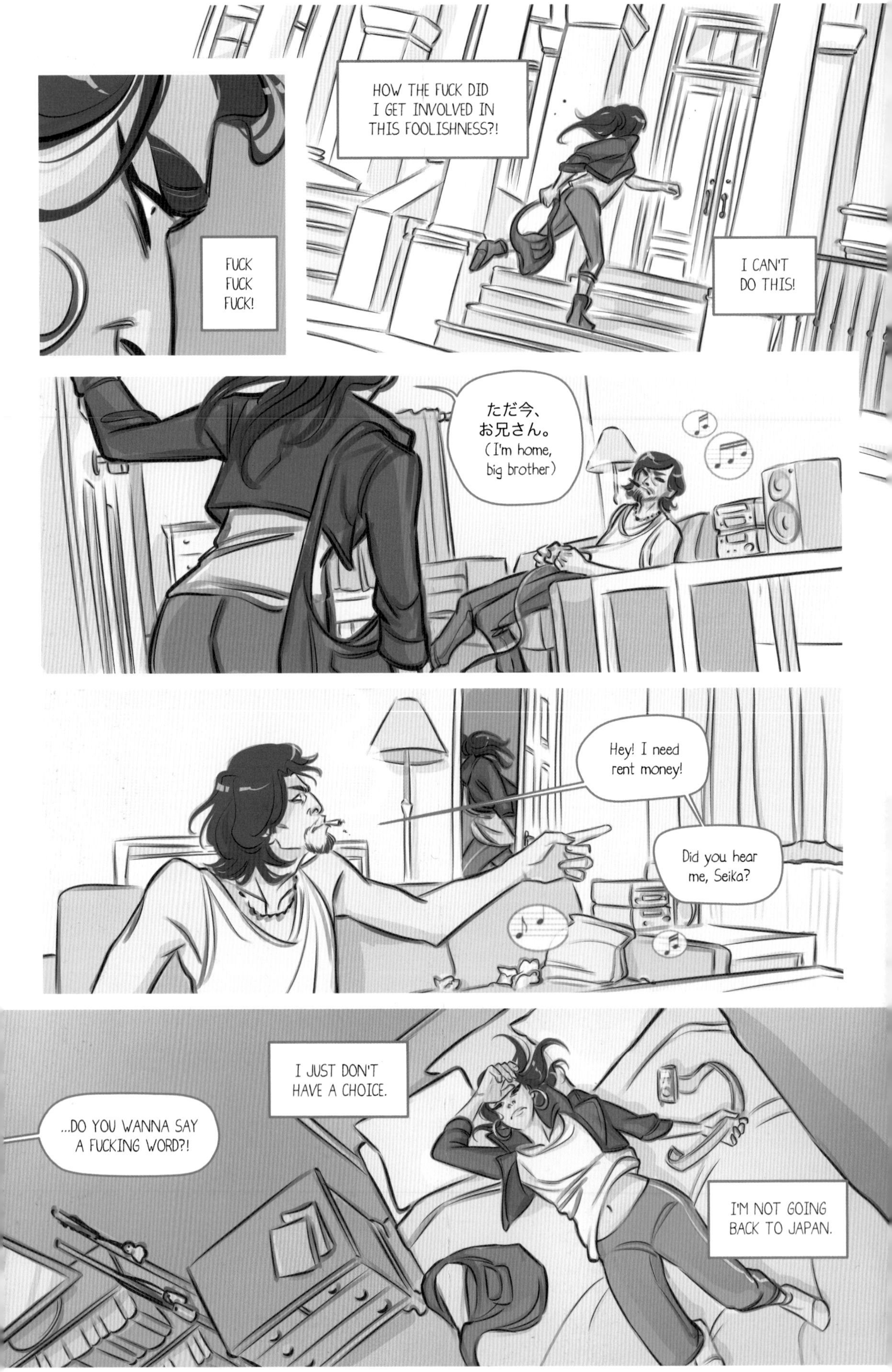
FUCK
FUCK
FUCK!
HOW THE FUCK DID
I GET INVOLVED IN
THIS FOOLISHNESS?!
I CAN'T
DO THIS!
ただ今、
お兄さん。
(I'm home,
big brother)
Hey! I need
rent money!
Did you hear
me, Seika?
I JUST DON'T
HAVE A CHOICE.
...DO YOU WANNA SAY
A FUCKING WORD?!
I'M NOT GOING
BACK TO JAPAN.

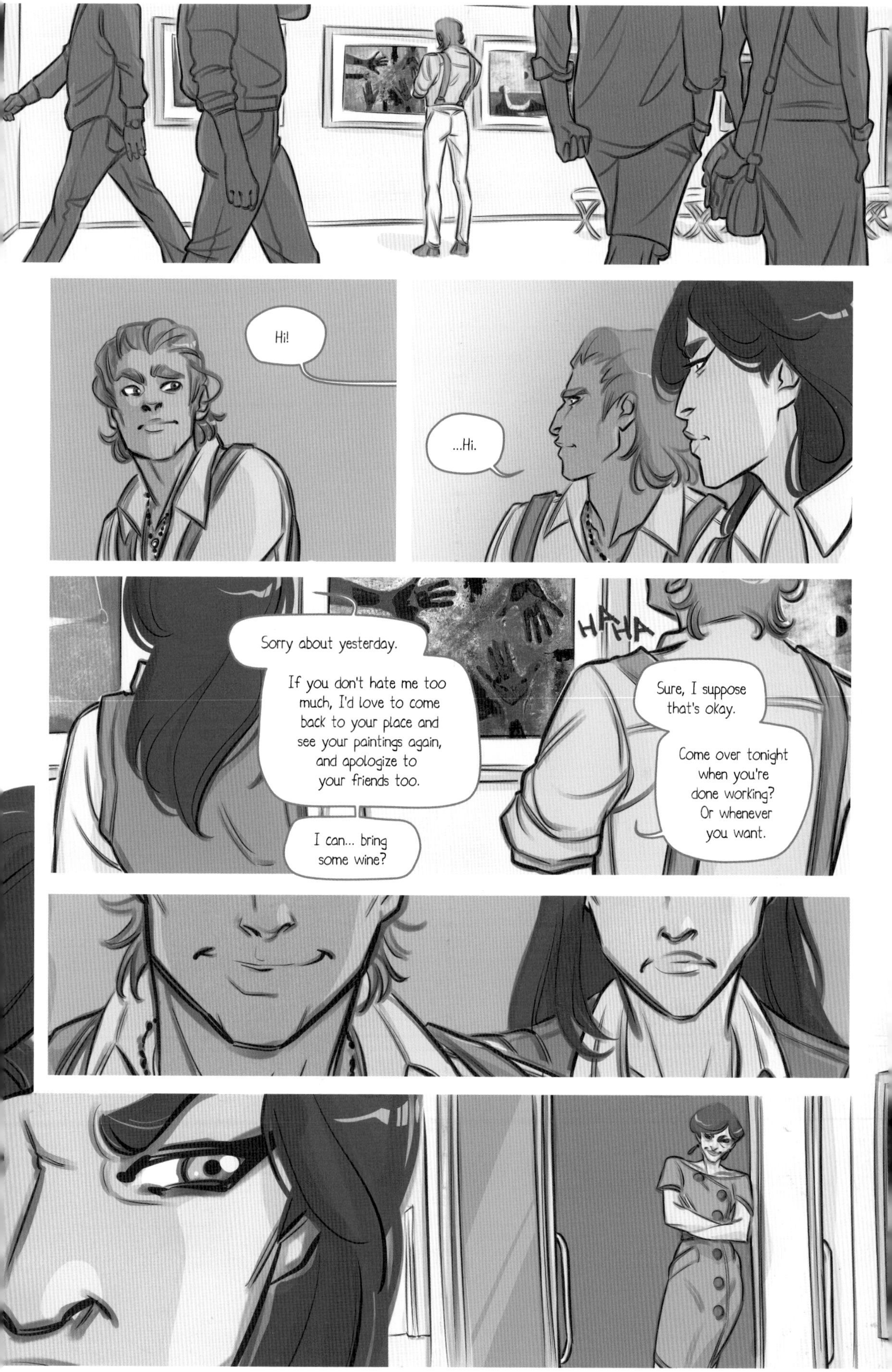
Hi!
...Hi.
Sorry about yesterday.
If you don't hate me too much, I'd love to come back to your place and see your paintings again, and apologize to your friends too.
I can... bring some wine?
HAHA
Sure, I suppose that's okay.
Come over tonight when you're done working? Or whenever you want.

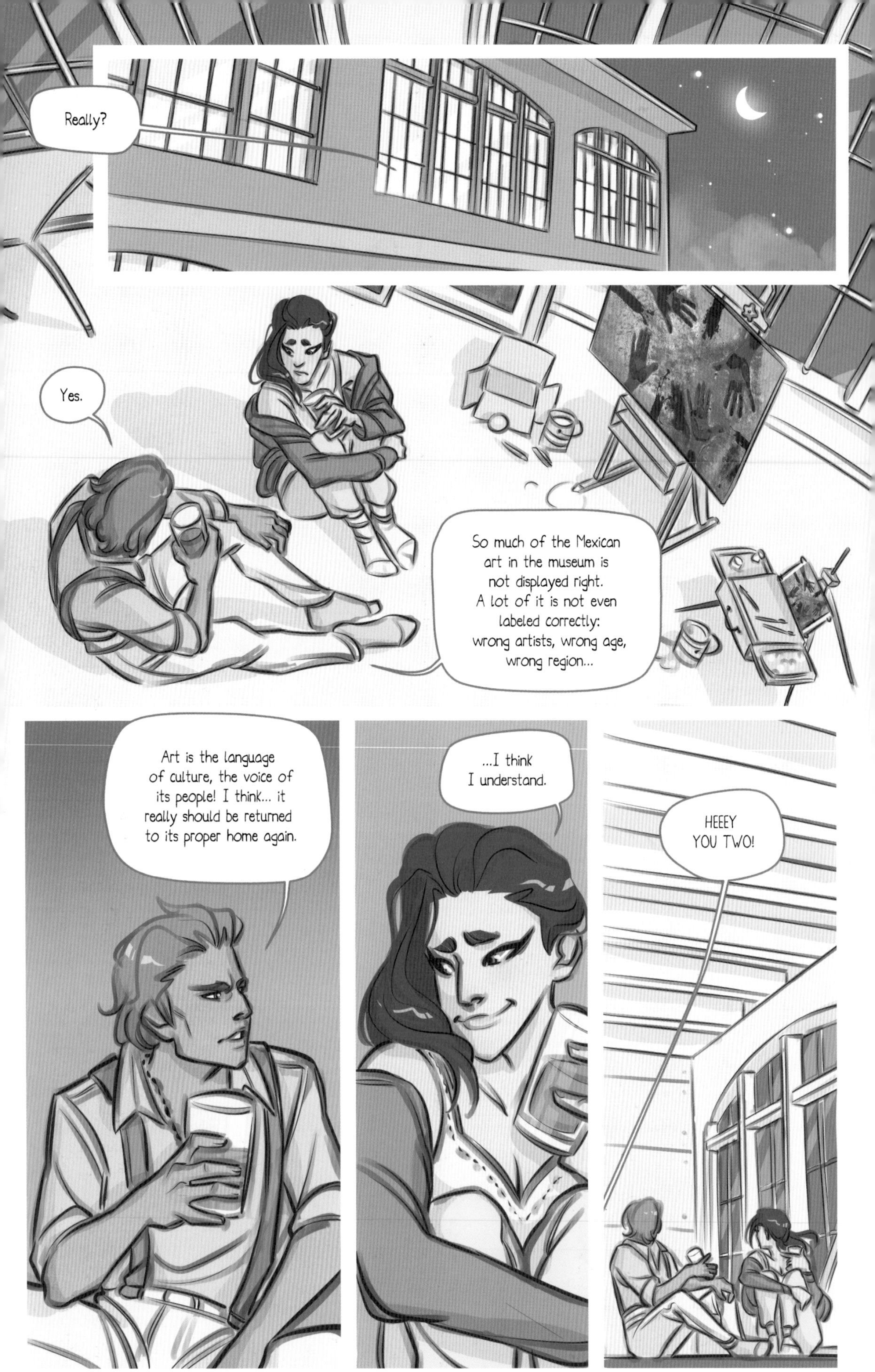
Really?
Yes.
So much of the Mexican art in the museum is not displayed right. A lot of it is not even labeled correctly: wrong artists, wrong age, wrong region...
Art is the language of culture, the voice of its people! I think... it really should be returned to its proper home again.
...I think I understand.
HEEEY YOU TWO!

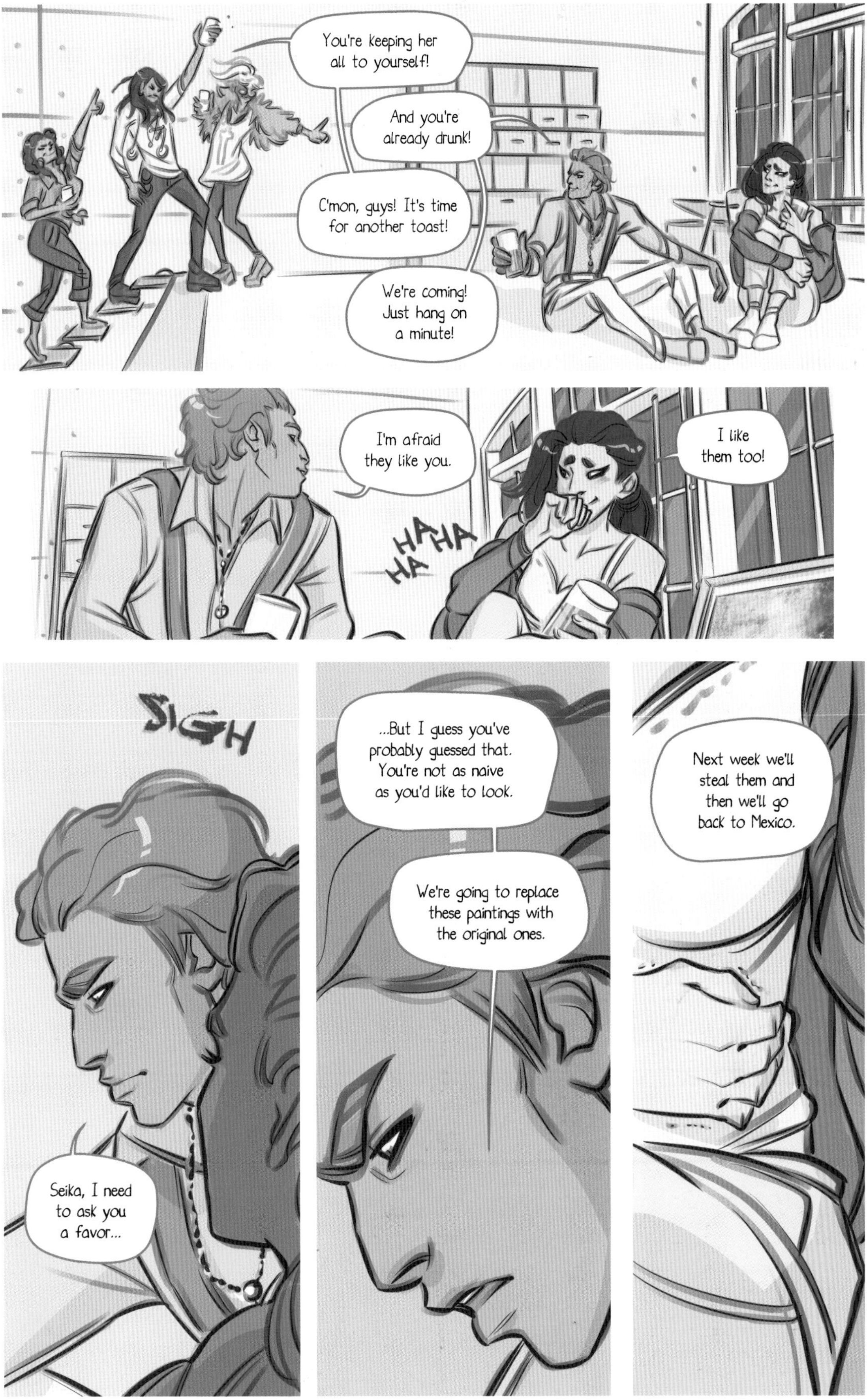

You're keeping her all to yourself!
And you're already drunk!
C'mon, guys! It's time for another toast!
We're coming! Just hang on a minute!
I'm afraid they like you.
HAHAHA
I like them too!
SIGH
Seika, I need to ask you a favor...
...But I guess you've probably guessed that. You're not as naive as you'd like to look.
We're going to replace these paintings with the original ones.
Next week we'll steal them and then we'll go back to Mexico.

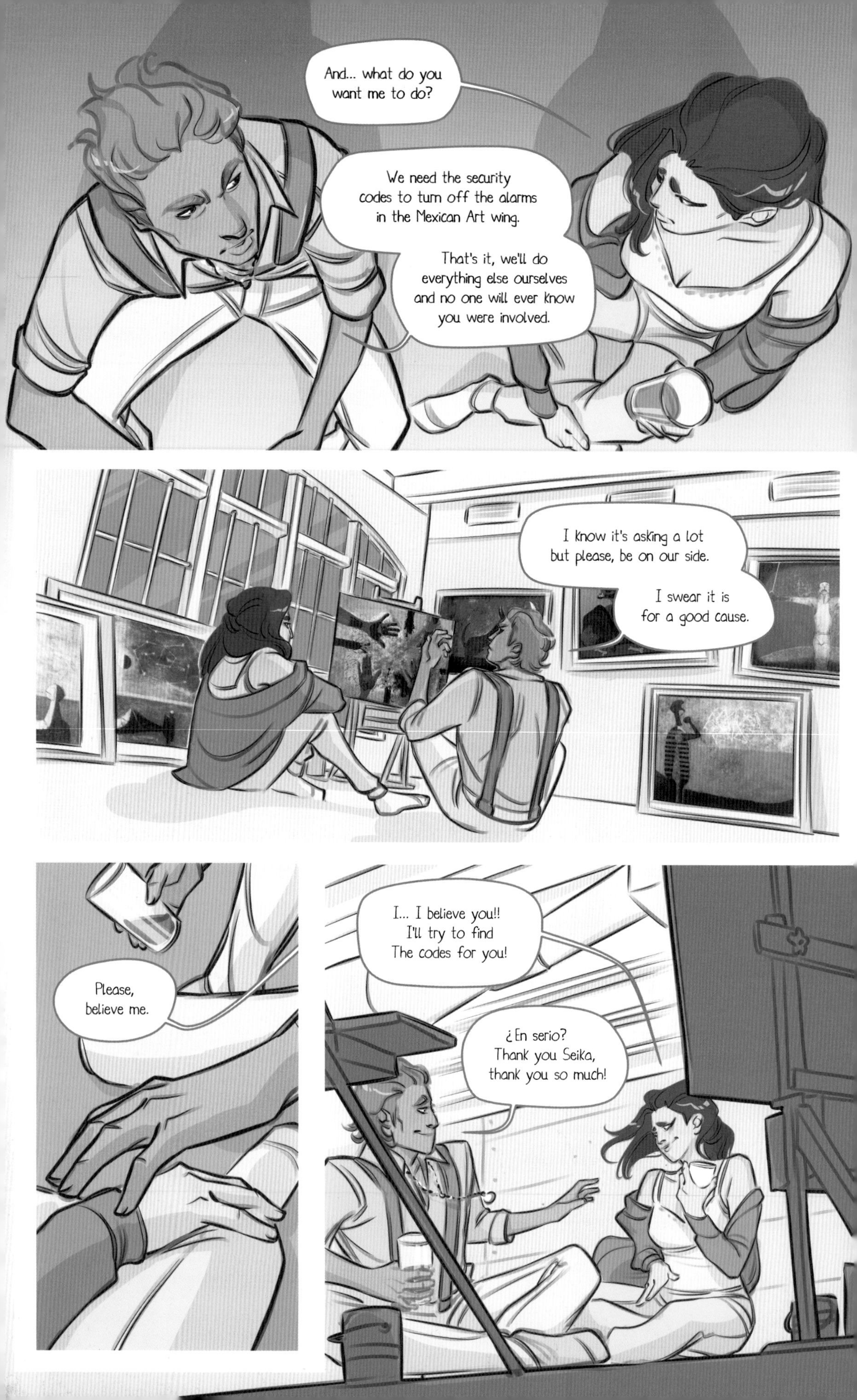
And... what do you want me to do?
We need the security codes to turn off the alarms in the Mexican Art wing.
That's it, we'll do everything else ourselves and no one will ever know you were involved.
I know it's asking a lot but please, be on our side.
I swear it is for a good cause.
Please, believe me.
I... I believe you!! I'll try to find The codes for you!
¿En serio? Thank you Seika, thank you so much!

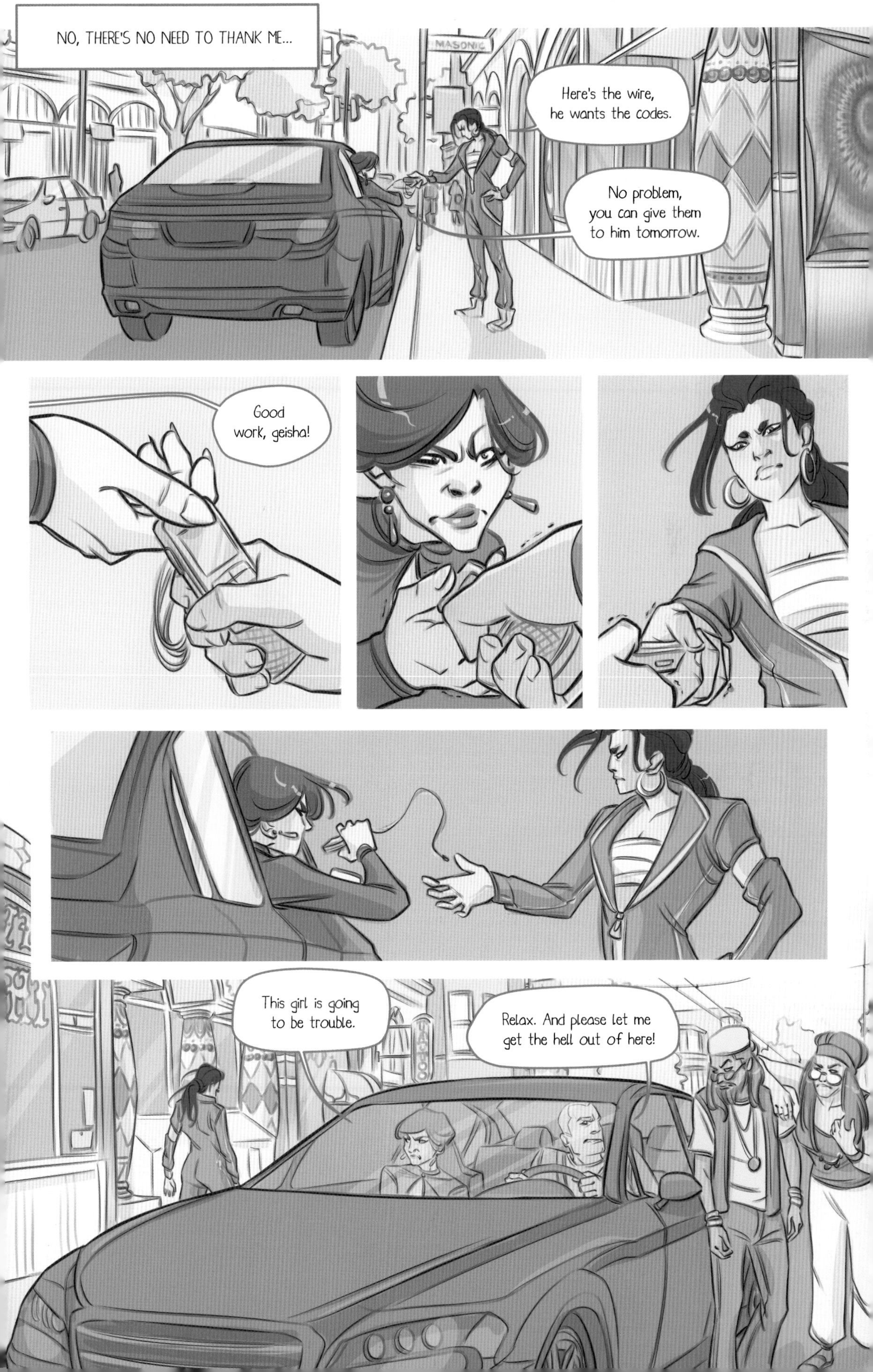
NO, THERE'S NO NEED TO THANK ME...
MASONIC
Here's the wire, he wants the codes.
No problem, you can give them to him tomorrow.
Good work, geisha!
This girl is going to be trouble.
Relax. And please let me get the hell out of here!

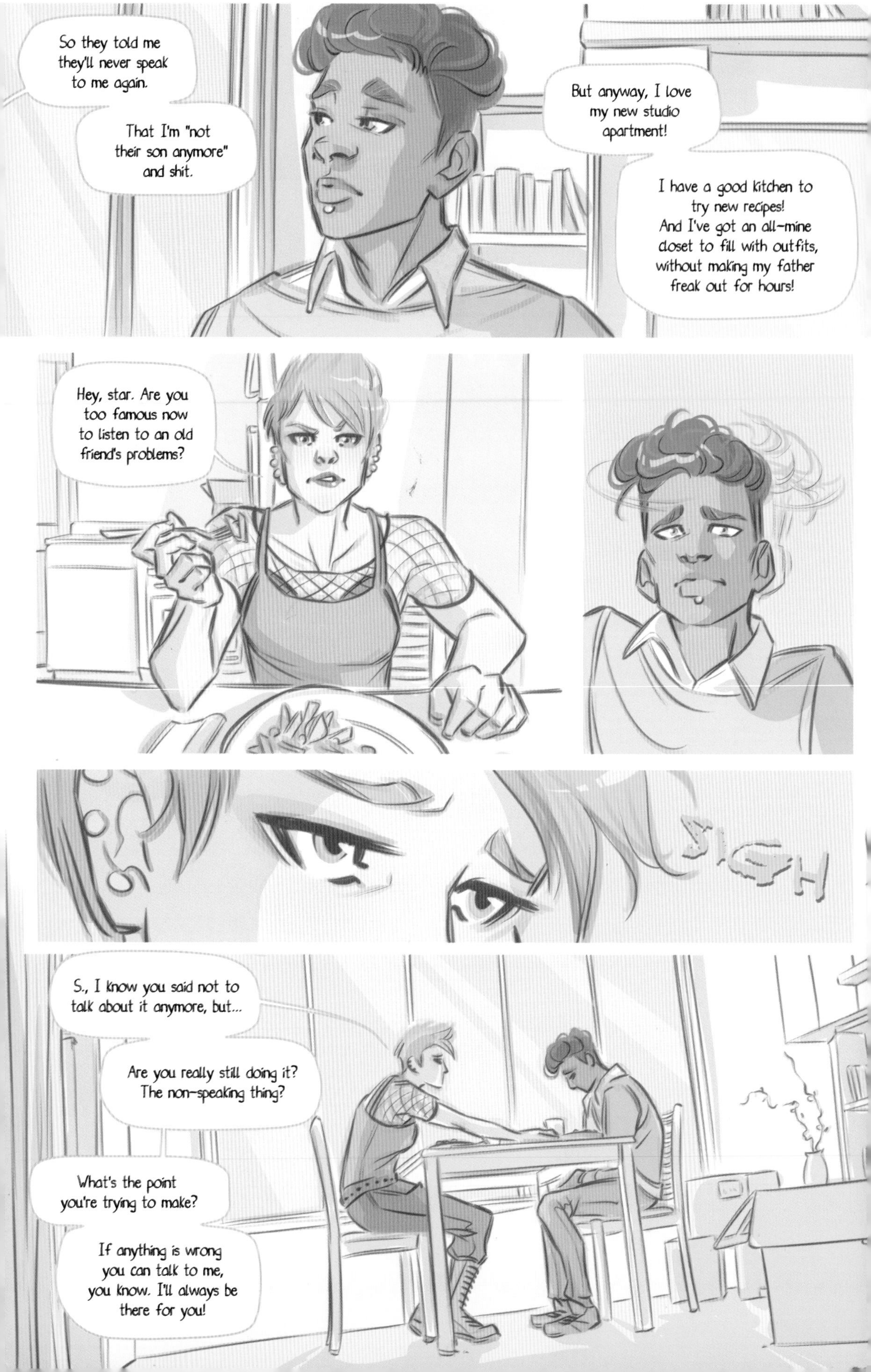
So they told me they'll never speak to me again.
That I'm "not their son anymore" and shit.
But anyway, I love my new studio apartment!
I have a good kitchen to try new recipes! And I've got an all-mine closet to fill with outfits, without making my father freak out for hours!
Hey, star. Are you too famous now to listen to an old friend's problems?
SIGH
S., I know you said not to talk about it anymore, but...
Are you really still doing it? The non-speaking thing?
What's the point you're trying to make?
If anything is wrong you can talk to me, you know. I'll always be there for you!

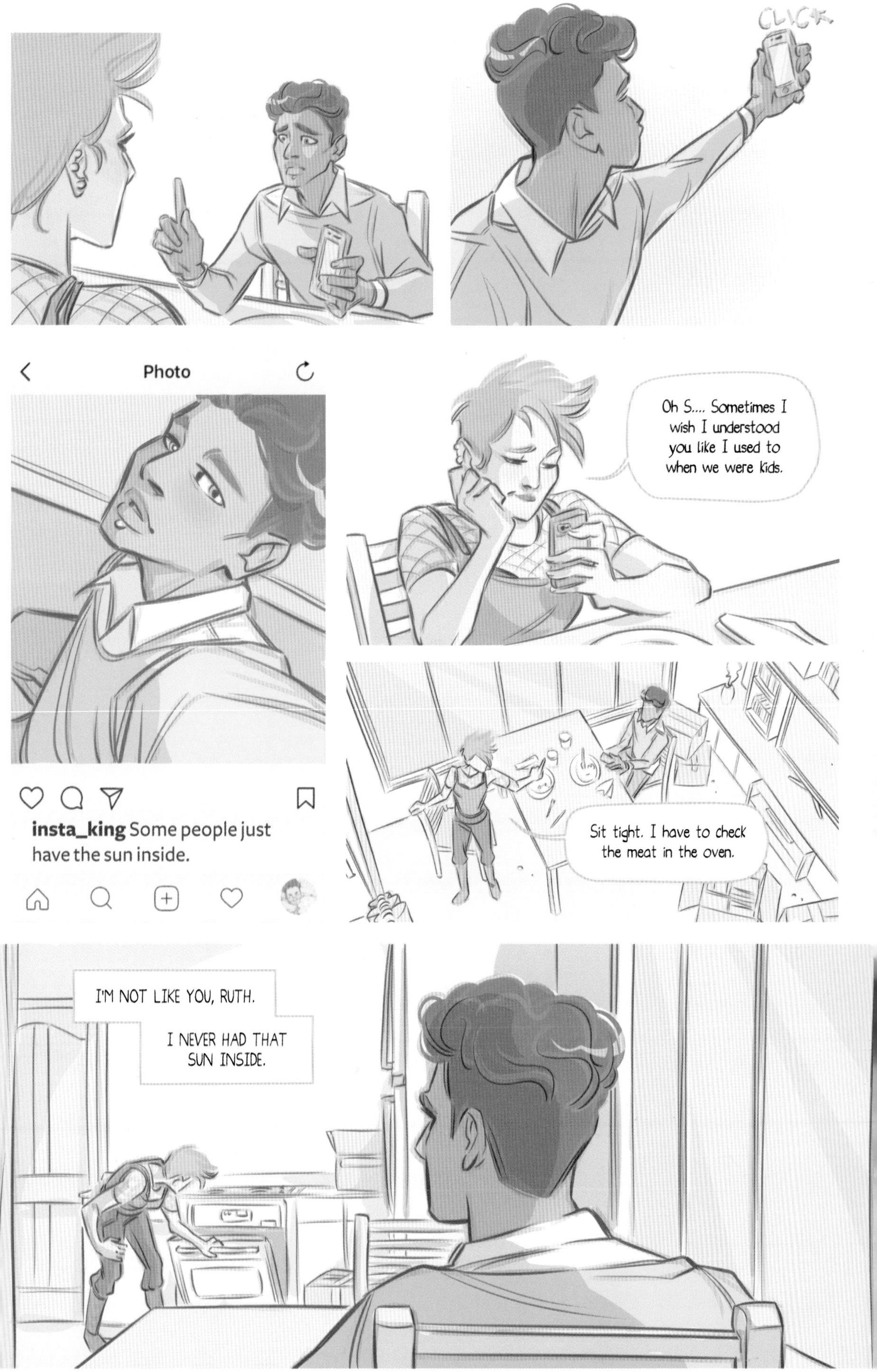
CLICK
Photo
insta_king Some people just have the sun inside.
Oh S.... Sometimes I wish I understood you like I used to when we were kids.
Sit tight. I have to check the meat in the oven.
I'M NOT LIKE YOU, RUTH.
I NEVER HAD THAT SUN INSIDE.

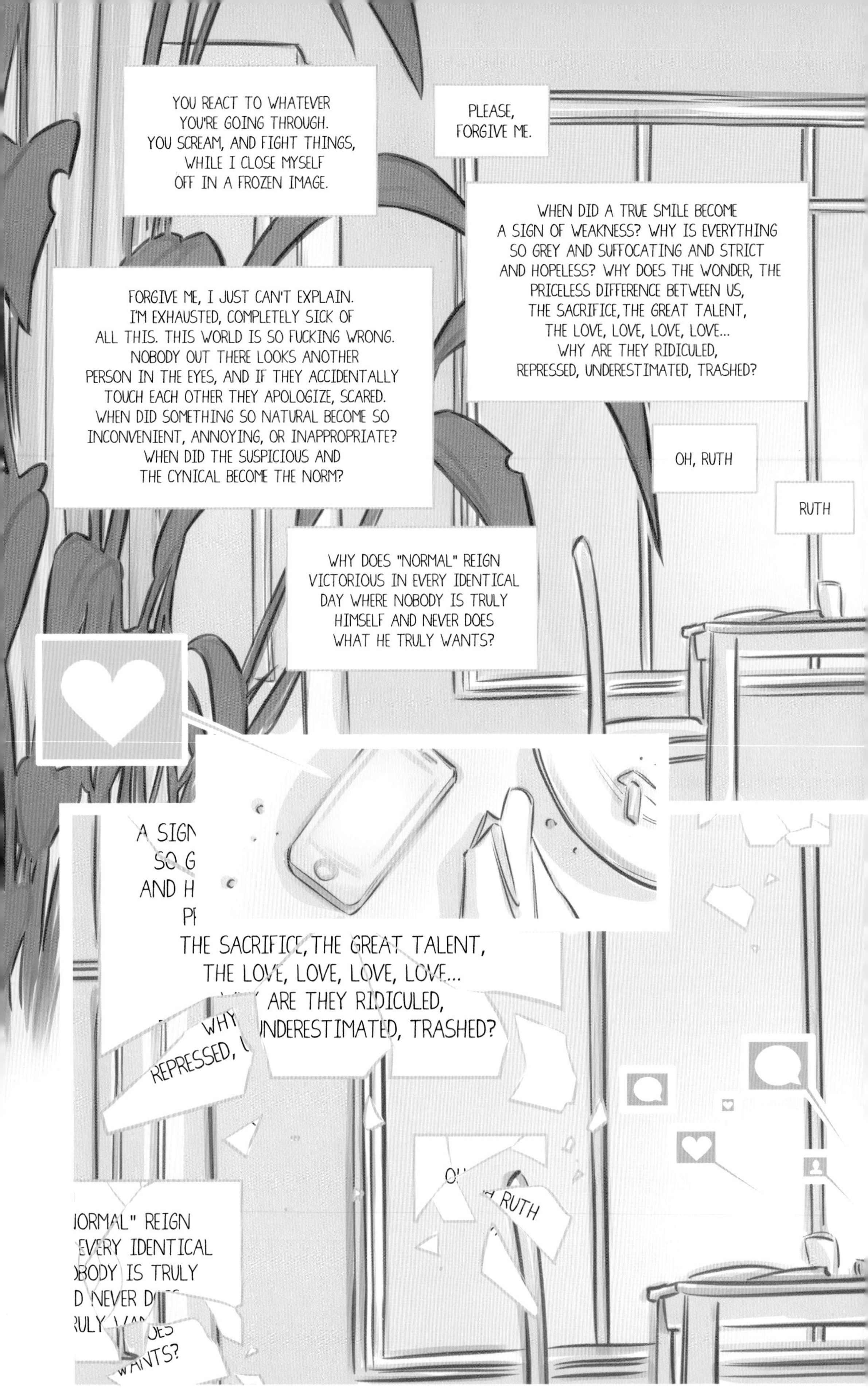
YOU REACT TO WHATEVER YOU'RE GOING THROUGH. YOU SCREAM, AND FIGHT THINGS, WHILE I CLOSE MYSELF OFF IN A FROZEN IMAGE.
PLEASE, FORGIVE ME.
WHEN DID A TRUE SMILE BECOME A SIGN OF WEAKNESS? WHY IS EVERYTHING SO GREY AND SUFFOCATING AND STRICT AND HOPELESS? WHY DOES THE WONDER, THE PRICELESS DIFFERENCE BETWEEN US, THE SACRIFICE, THE GREAT TALENT, THE LOVE, LOVE, LOVE, LOVE... WHY ARE THEY RIDICULED, REPRESSED, UNDERESTIMATED, TRASHED?
FORGIVE ME, I JUST CAN'T EXPLAIN. I'M EXHAUSTED, COMPLETELY SICK OF ALL THIS. THIS WORLD IS SO FUCKING WRONG. NOBODY OUT THERE LOOKS ANOTHER PERSON IN THE EYES, AND IF THEY ACCIDENTALLY TOUCH EACH OTHER THEY APOLOGIZE, SCARED. WHEN DID SOMETHING SO NATURAL BECOME SO INCONVENIENT, ANNOYING, OR INAPPROPRIATE? WHEN DID THE SUSPICIOUS AND THE CYNICAL BECOME THE NORM?
OH, RUTH
RUTH
WHY DOES "NORMAL" REIGN VICTORIOUS IN EVERY IDENTICAL DAY WHERE NOBODY IS TRULY HIMSELF AND NEVER DOES WHAT HE TRULY WANTS?
THE SACRIFICE, THE GREAT TALENT,
THE LOVE, LOVE, LOVE, LOVE...
ARE THEY RIDICULED,
REPRESSED,
UNDERESTIMATED, TRASHED?
RUTH
EVERY IDENTICAL
IS TRULY
WANTS?

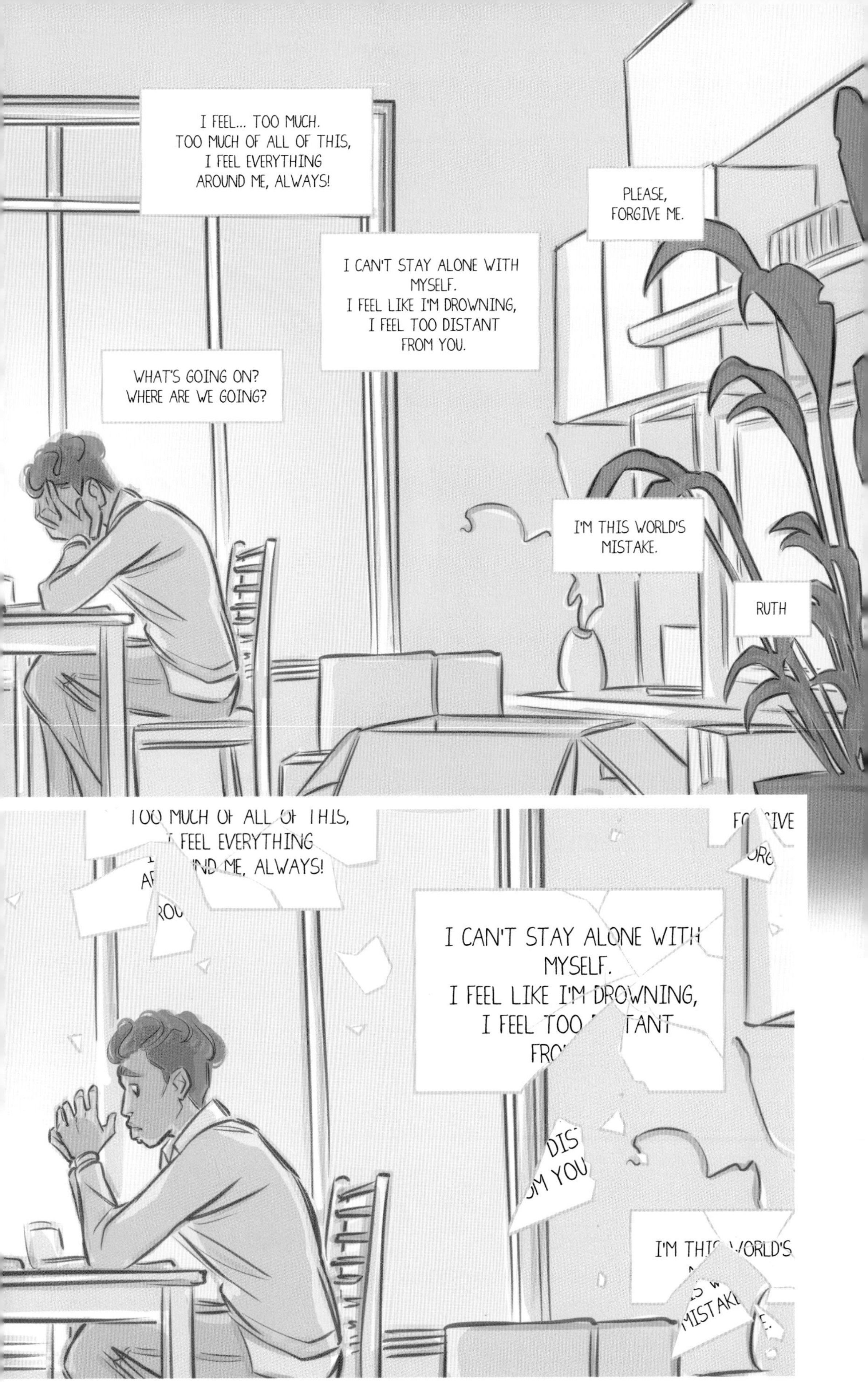

I FEEL... TOO MUCH.
TOO MUCH OF ALL OF THIS,
I FEEL EVERYTHING
AROUND ME, ALWAYS!
I CAN'T STAY ALONE WITH MYSELF.
I FEEL LIKE I'M DROWNING,
I FEEL TOO DISTANT
FROM YOU.
WHAT'S GOING ON?
WHERE ARE WE GOING?
PLEASE,
FORGIVE ME.
I'M THIS WORLD'S
MISTAKE.
RUTH
TOO MUCH OF ALL OF THIS,
I FEEL EVERYTHING
ND ME, ALWAYS!
I CAN'T STAY ALONE WITH
MYSELF.
I FEEL LIKE I'M DROWNING,
I FEEL TOO
TANT
DIS
M YOU
I'M THI
VORLD'S
MISTAK

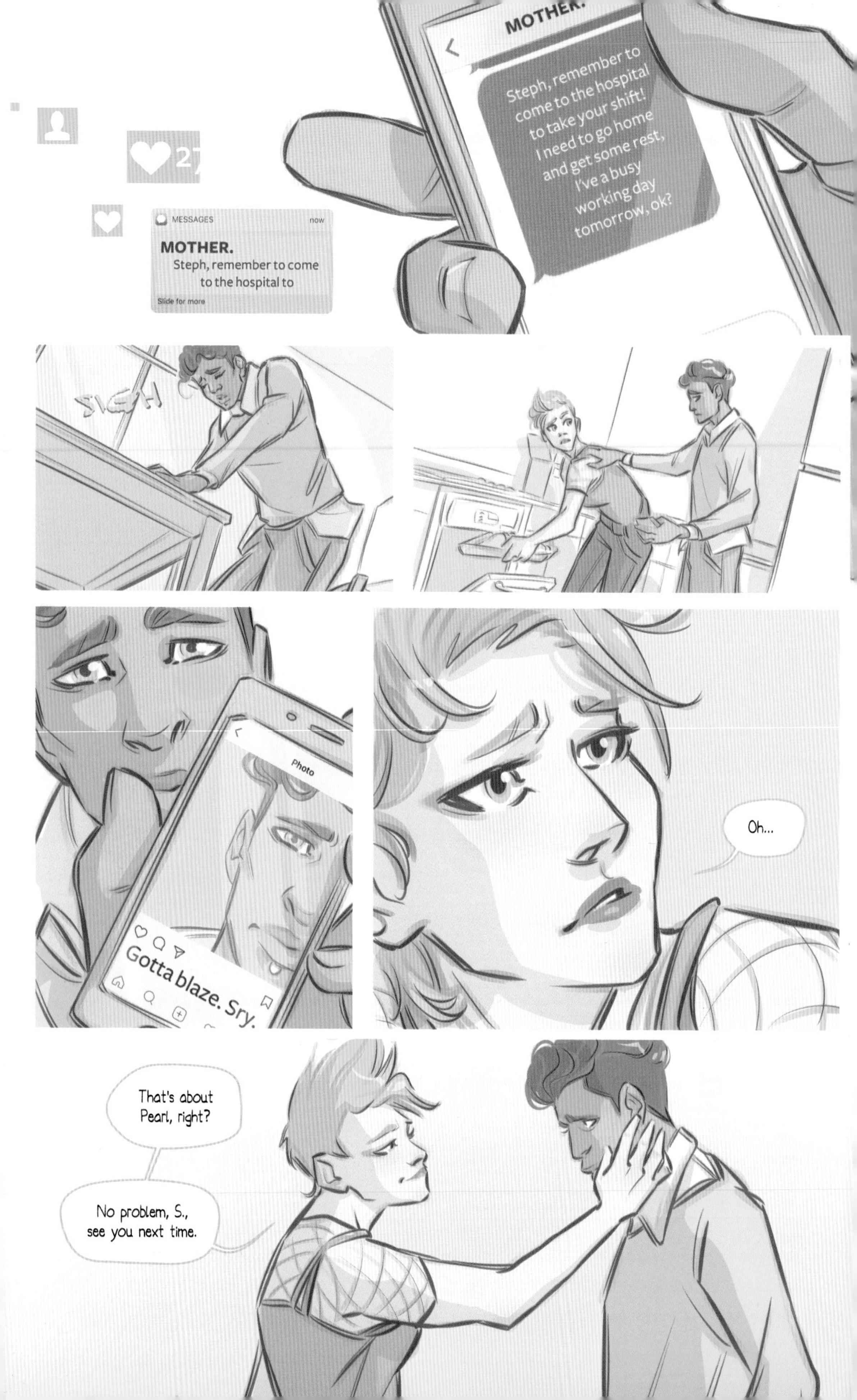
MOTHER.
Steph, remember to come to the hospital to take your shift! I need to go home and get some rest, I've a busy working day tomorrow, ok?
MESSAGES
now
MOTHER.
Steph, remember to come to the hospital to
Slide for more
SIGH
Photo
Gotta blaze. Sry.
Oh...
That's about Pearl, right?
No problem, S., see you next time.

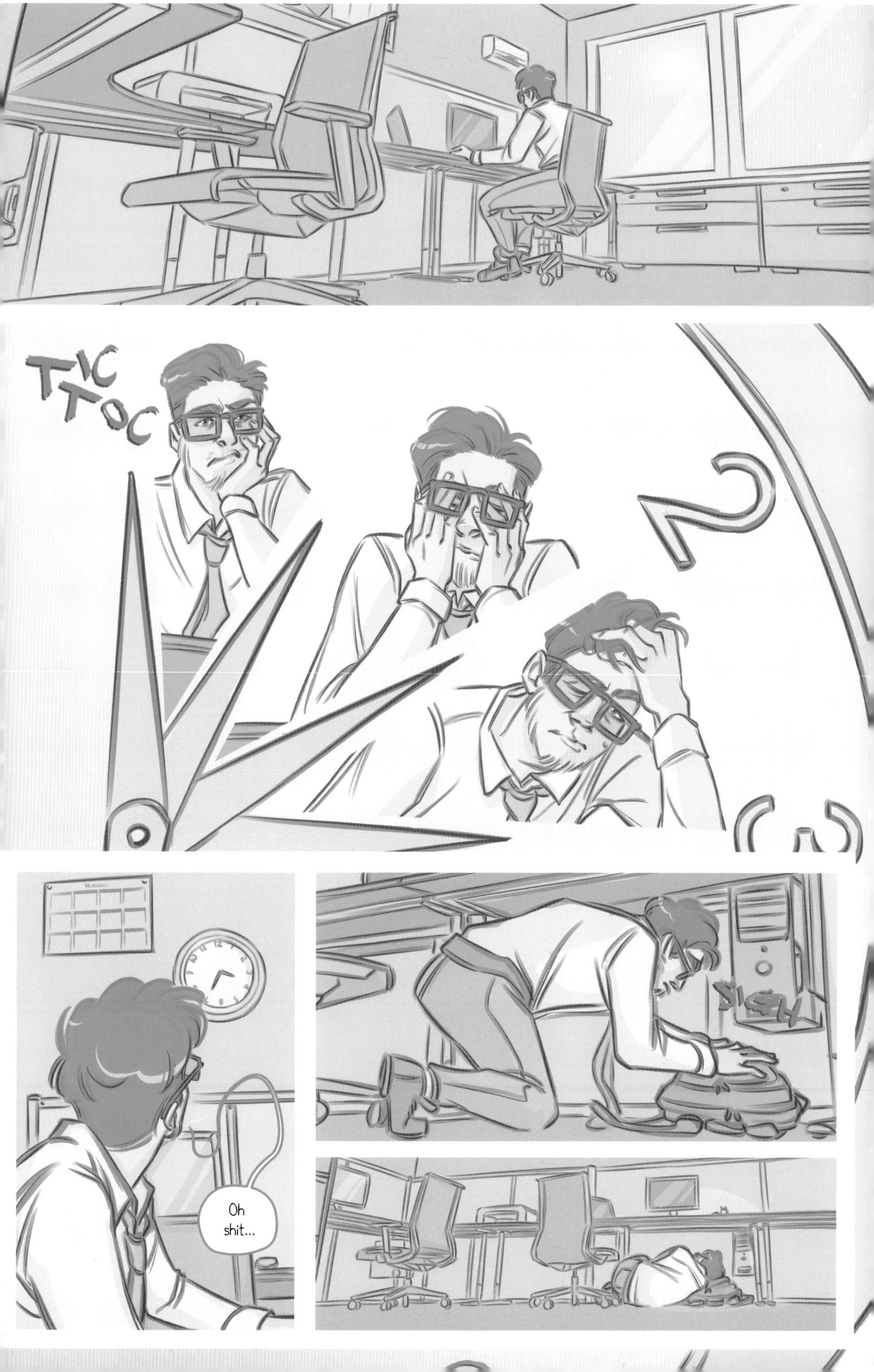
TIC TOC
Oh shit...
SIGH

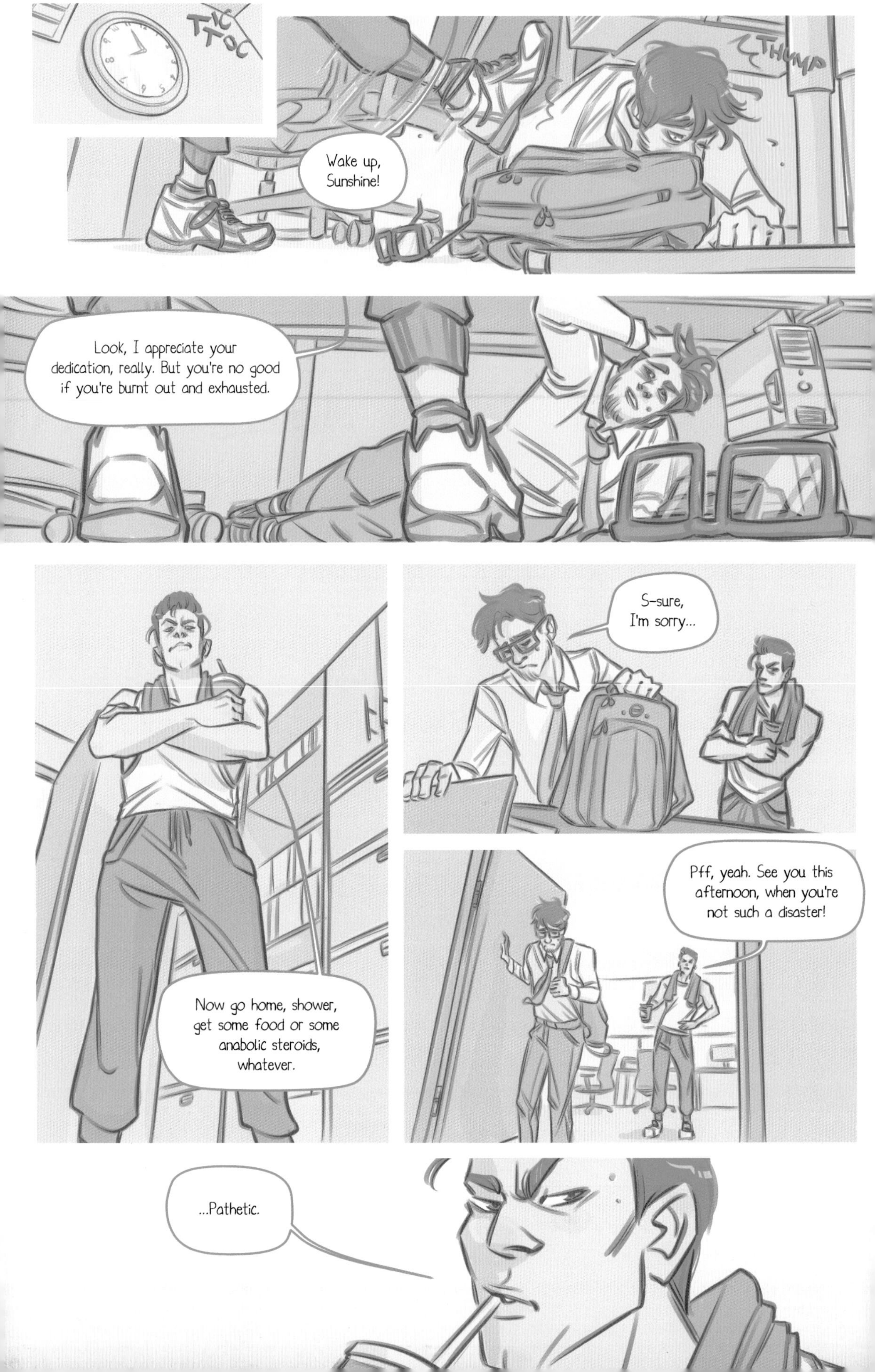
TIC TOC
THUMP
Wake up, Sunshine!
Look, I appreciate your dedication, really. But you're no good if you're burnt out and exhausted.
Now go home, shower, get some food or some anabolic steroids, whatever.
S-sure, I'm sorry...
Pff, yeah. See you this afternoon, when you're not such a disaster!
...Pathetic.

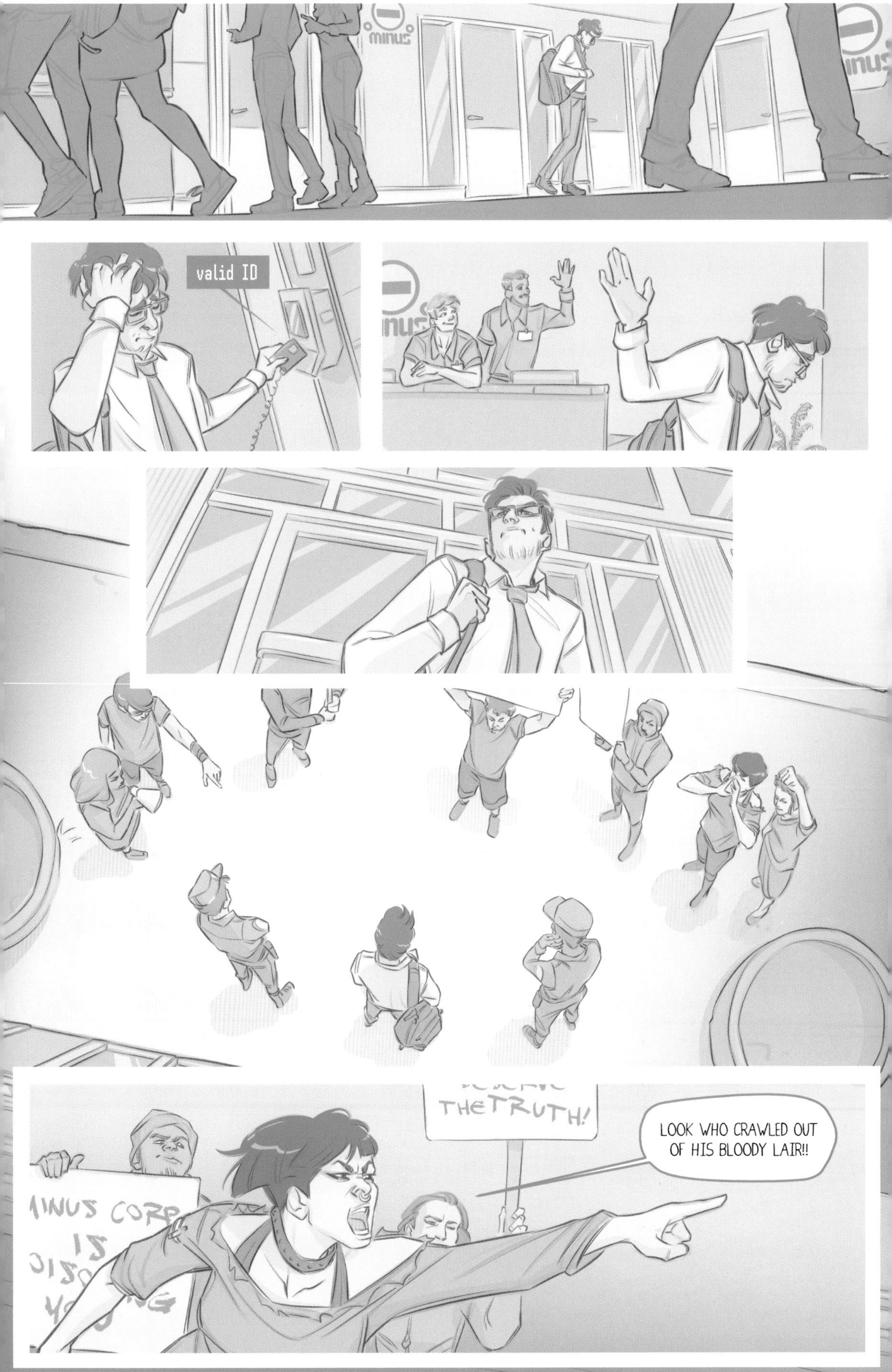
minus
valid ID
THE TRUTH!
LOOK WHO CRAWLED OUT OF HIS BLOODY LAIR!!

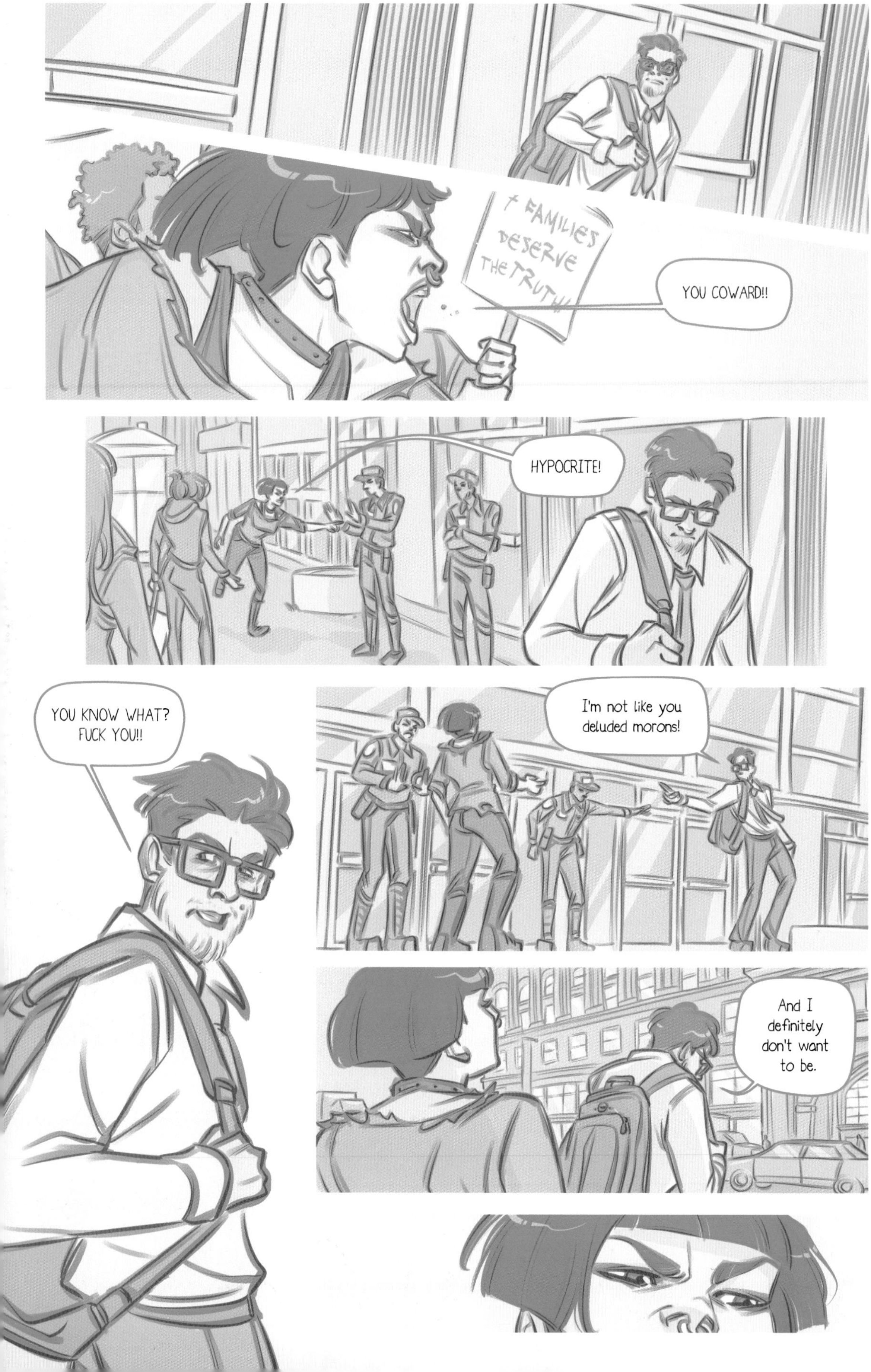

FAMILIES DESERVE THE TRUTH!
YOU COWARD!!
HYPOCRITE!
YOU KNOW WHAT? FUCK YOU!!
I'm not like you deluded morons!
And I definitely don't want to be.

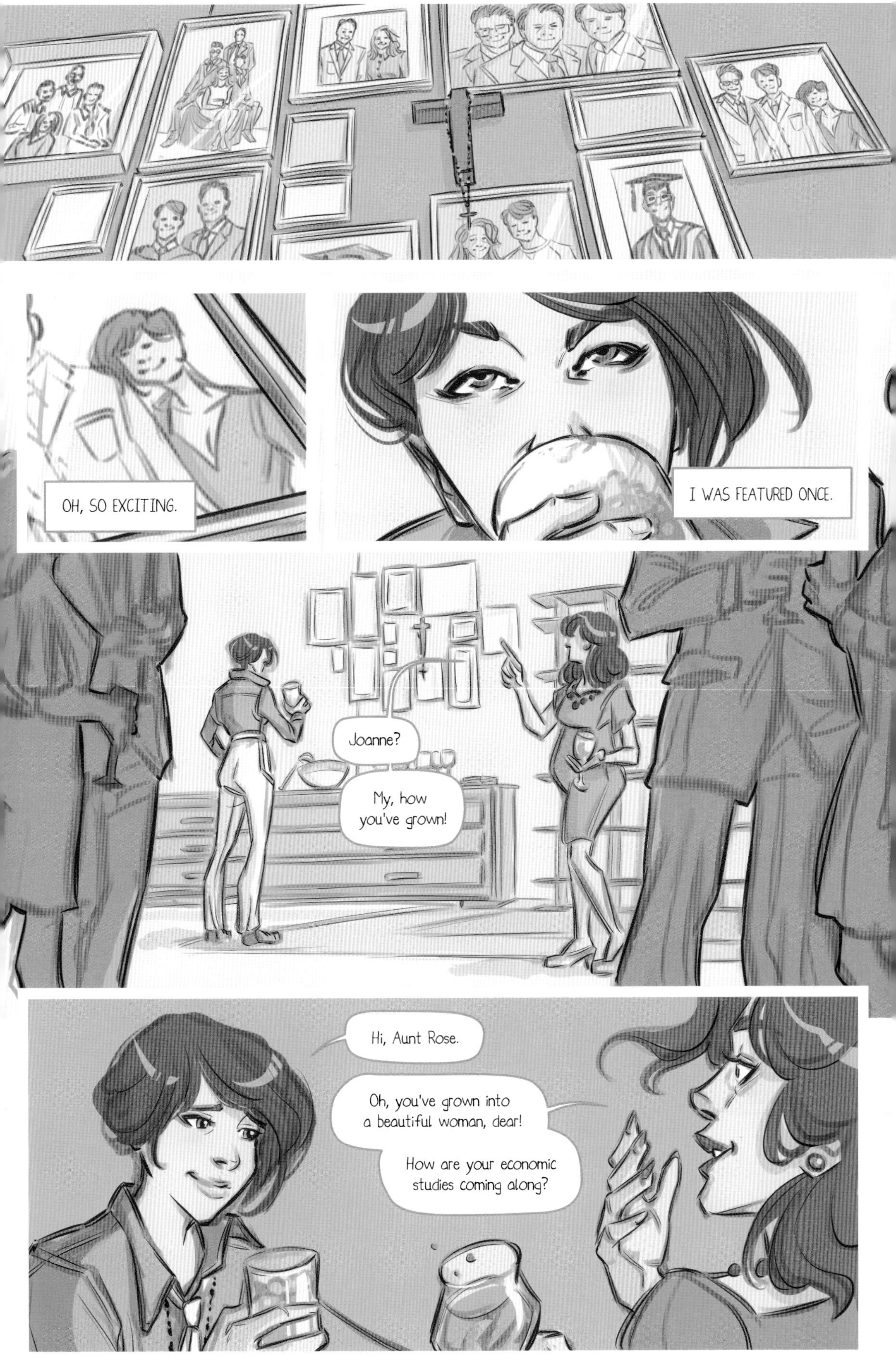
OH, SO EXCITING.
I WAS FEATURED ONCE.
Joanne?
My, how you've grown!
Hi, Aunt Rose.
Oh, you've grown into a beautiful woman, dear!
How are your economic studies coming along?

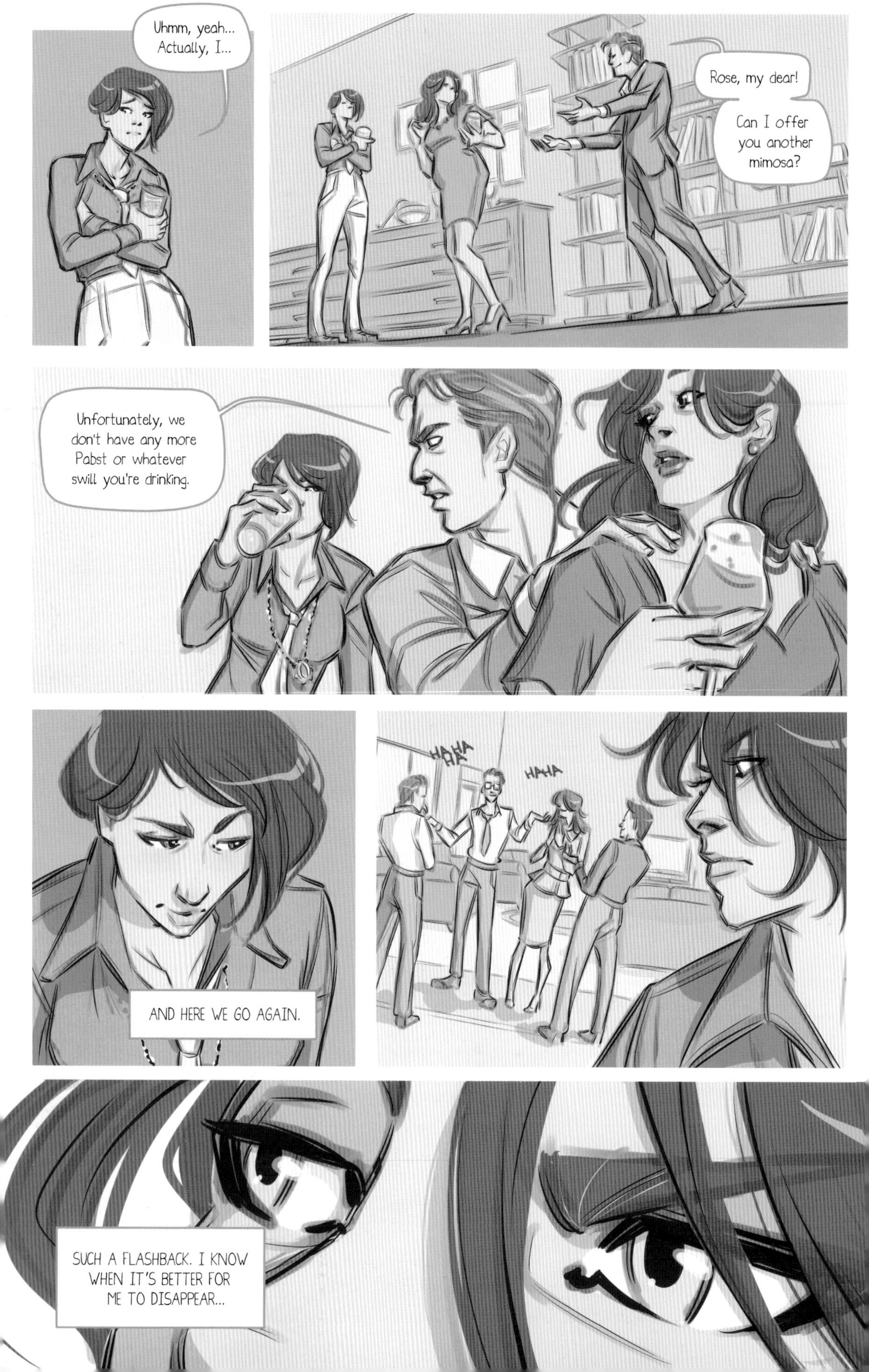
Uhmm, yeah...
Actually, I...
Rose, my dear!
Can I offer you another mimosa?
Unfortunately, we don't have any more Pabst or whatever swill you're drinking.
AND HERE WE GO AGAIN.
HAHA HA
HAHA
SUCH A FLASHBACK. I KNOW WHEN IT'S BETTER FOR ME TO DISAPPEAR...

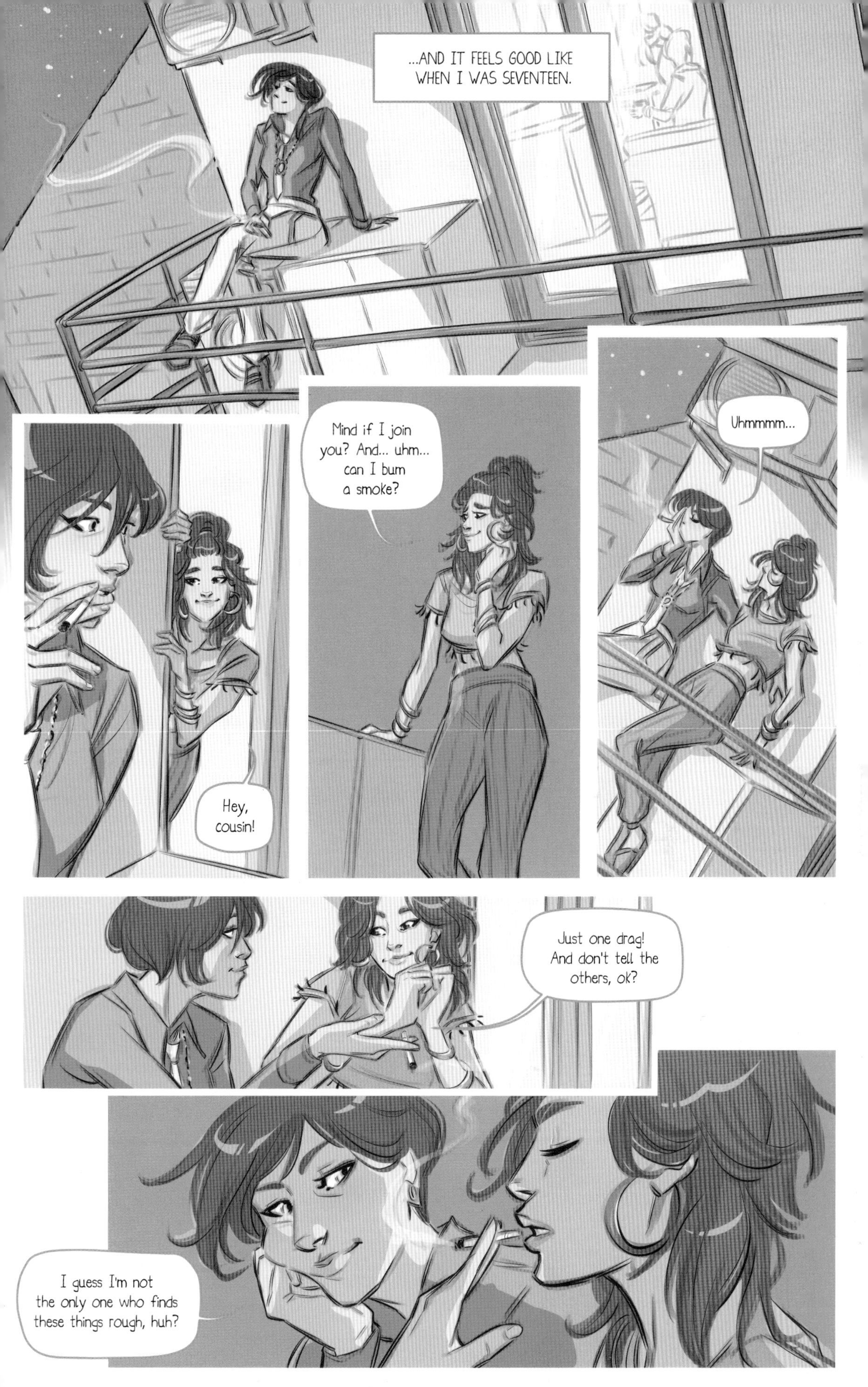
...AND IT FEELS GOOD LIKE WHEN I WAS SEVENTEEN.
Hey, cousin!
Mind if I join you? And... uhm... can I bum a smoke?
Uhmmmm...
Just one drag! And don't tell the others, ok?
I guess I'm not the only one who finds these things rough, huh?

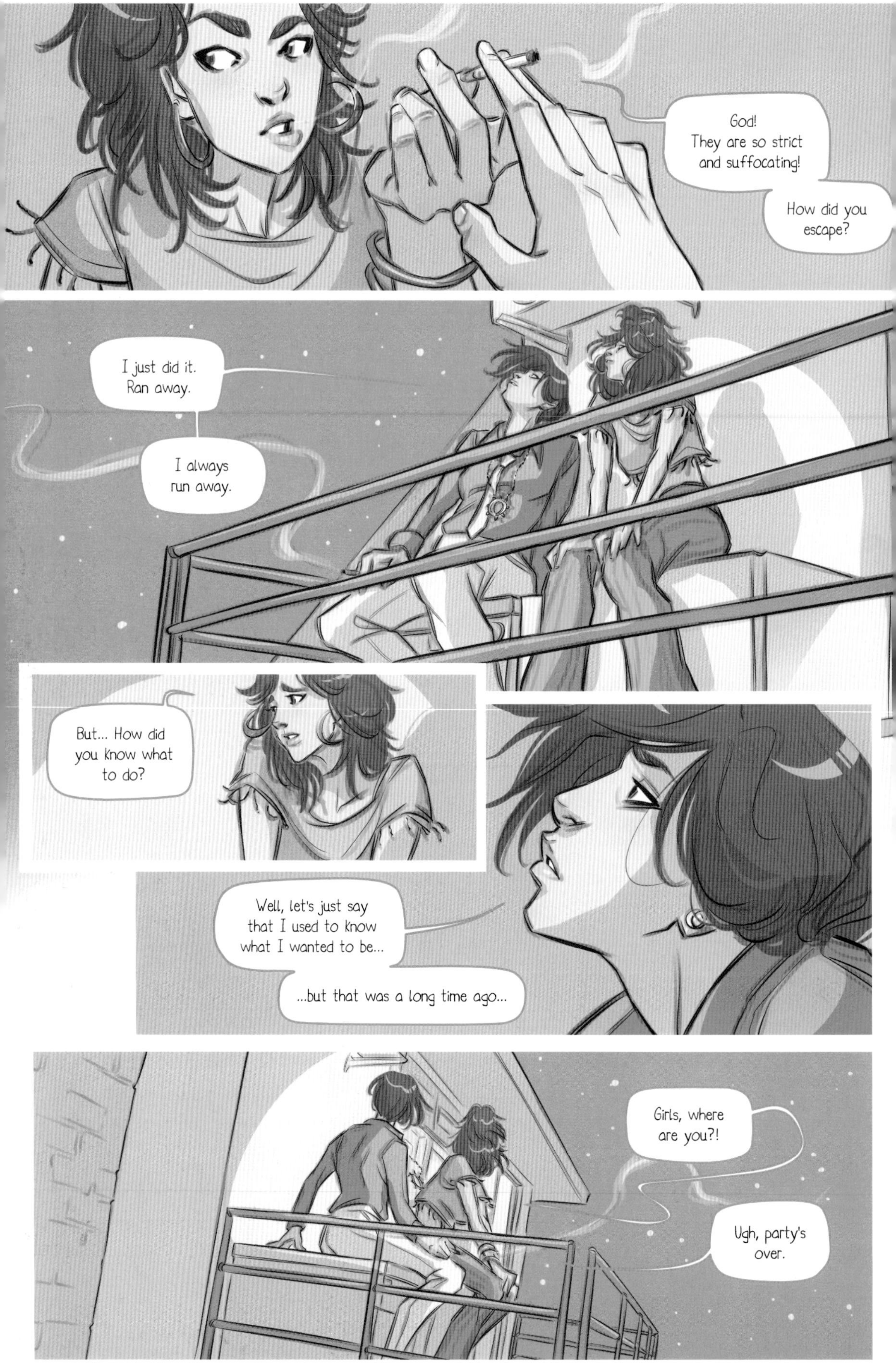
God!
They are so strict
and suffocating!
How did you
escape?
I just did it.
Ran away.
I always
run away.
But... How did
you know what
to do?
Well, let's just say
that I used to know
what I wanted to be...
...but that was a long time ago...
Girls, where
are you?!
Ugh, party's
over.

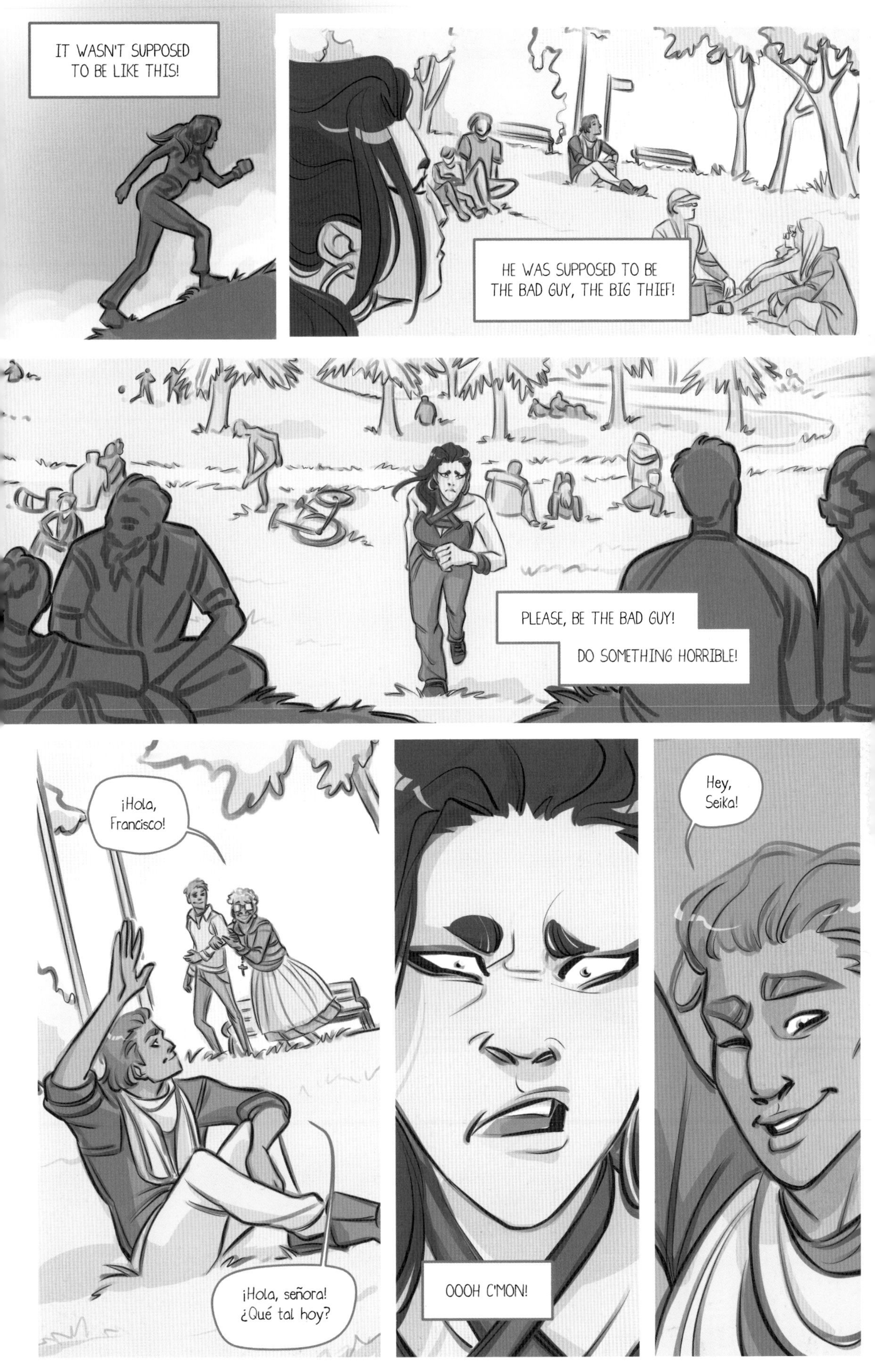
IT WASN'T SUPPOSED TO BE LIKE THIS!
HE WAS SUPPOSED TO BE THE BAD GUY, THE BIG THIEF!
PLEASE, BE THE BAD GUY!
DO SOMETHING HORRIBLE!
¡Hola, Francisco!
¡Hola, señora! ¿Qué tal hoy?
OOOH C'MON!
Hey, Seika!

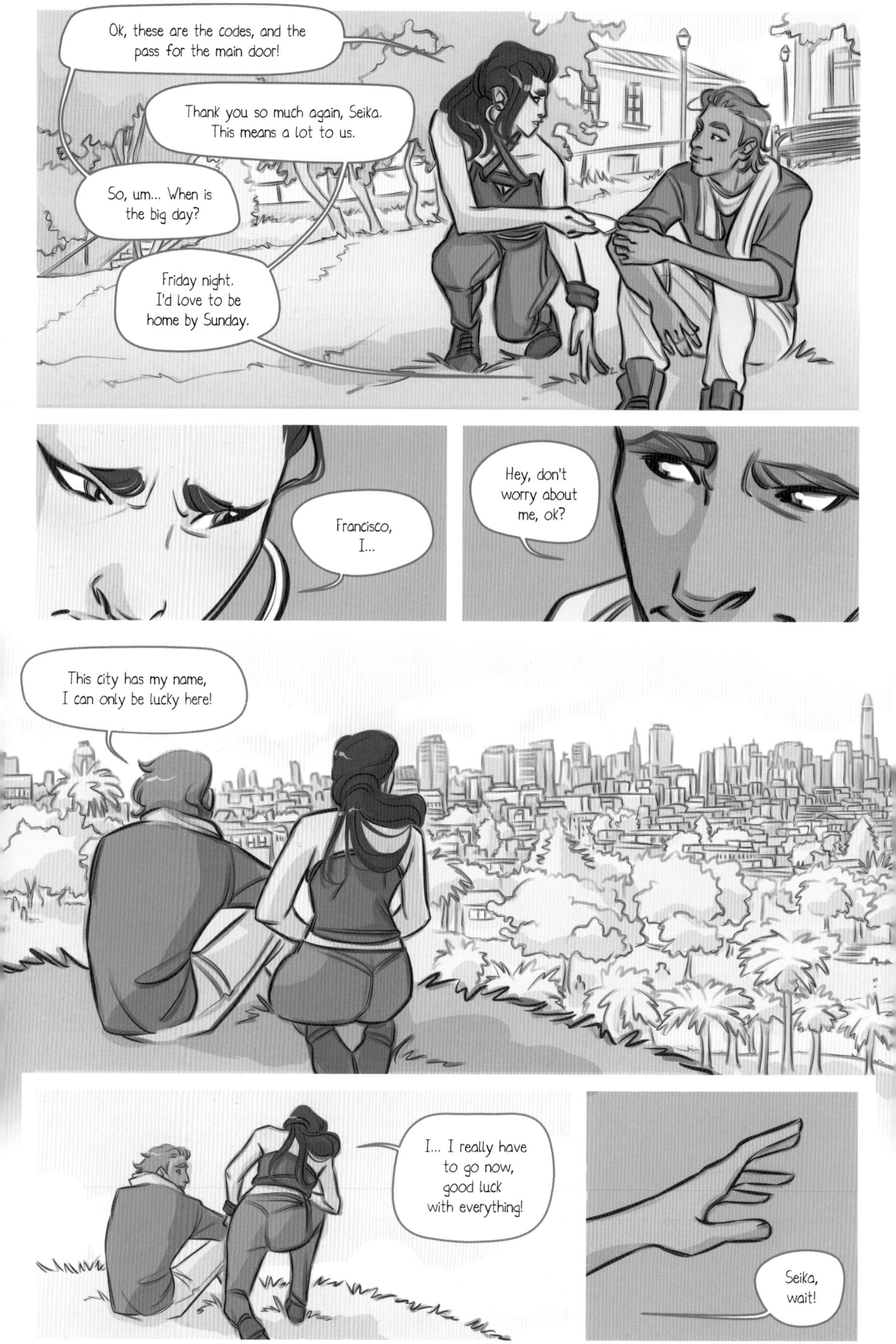
Ok, these are the codes, and the pass for the main door!
Thank you so much again, Seika. This means a lot to us.
So, um... When is the big day?
Friday night. I'd love to be home by Sunday.
Francisco, I...
Hey, don't worry about me, ok?
This city has my name, I can only be lucky here!
I... I really have to go now, good luck with everything!
Seika, wait!

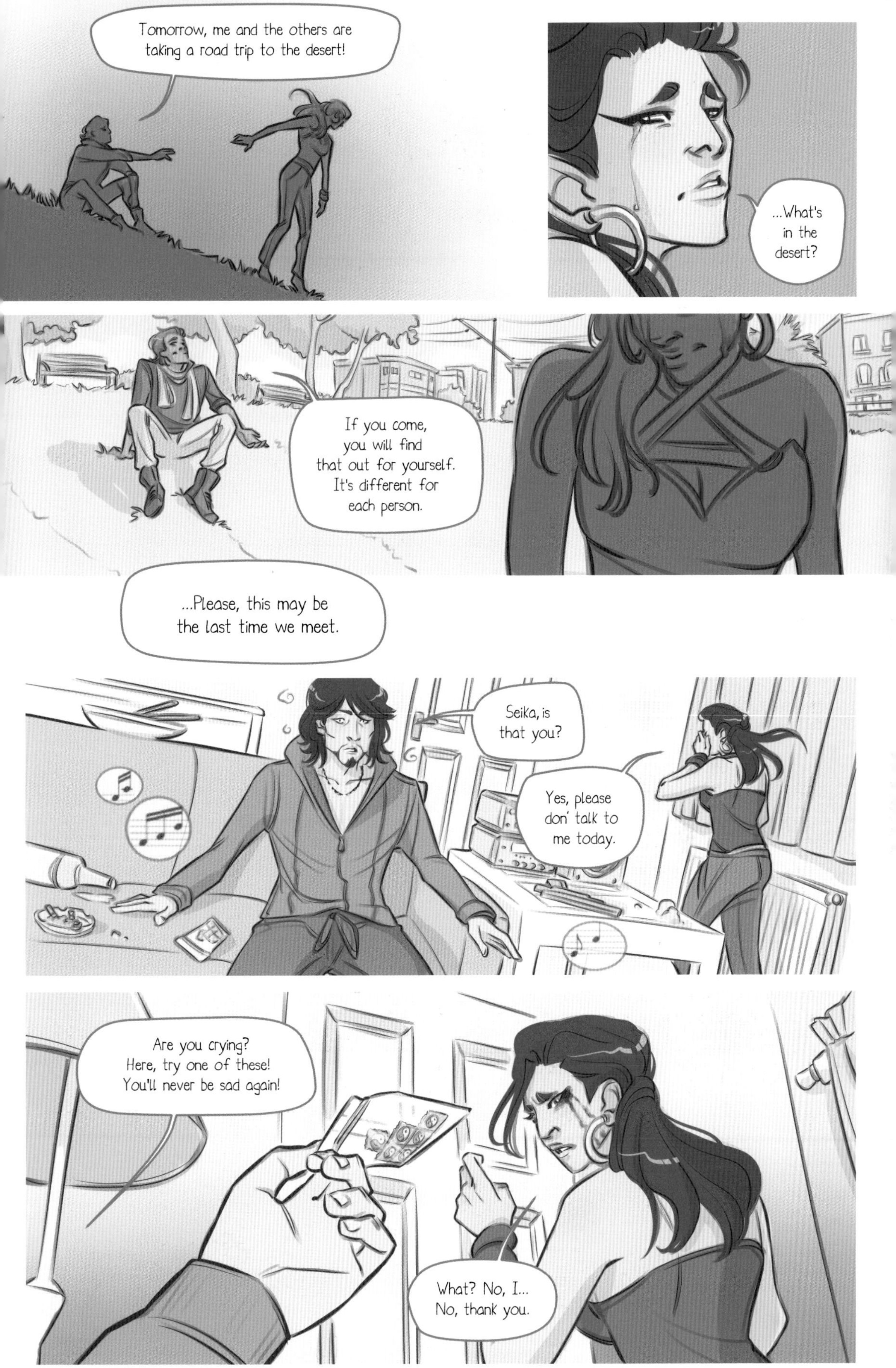
Tomorrow, me and the others are taking a road trip to the desert!
...What's in the desert?
If you come, you will find that out for yourself. It's different for each person.
...Please, this may be the last time we meet.
Seika, is that you?
Yes, please don' talk to me today.
Are you crying? Here, try one of these! You'll never be sad again!
What? No, I... No, thank you.

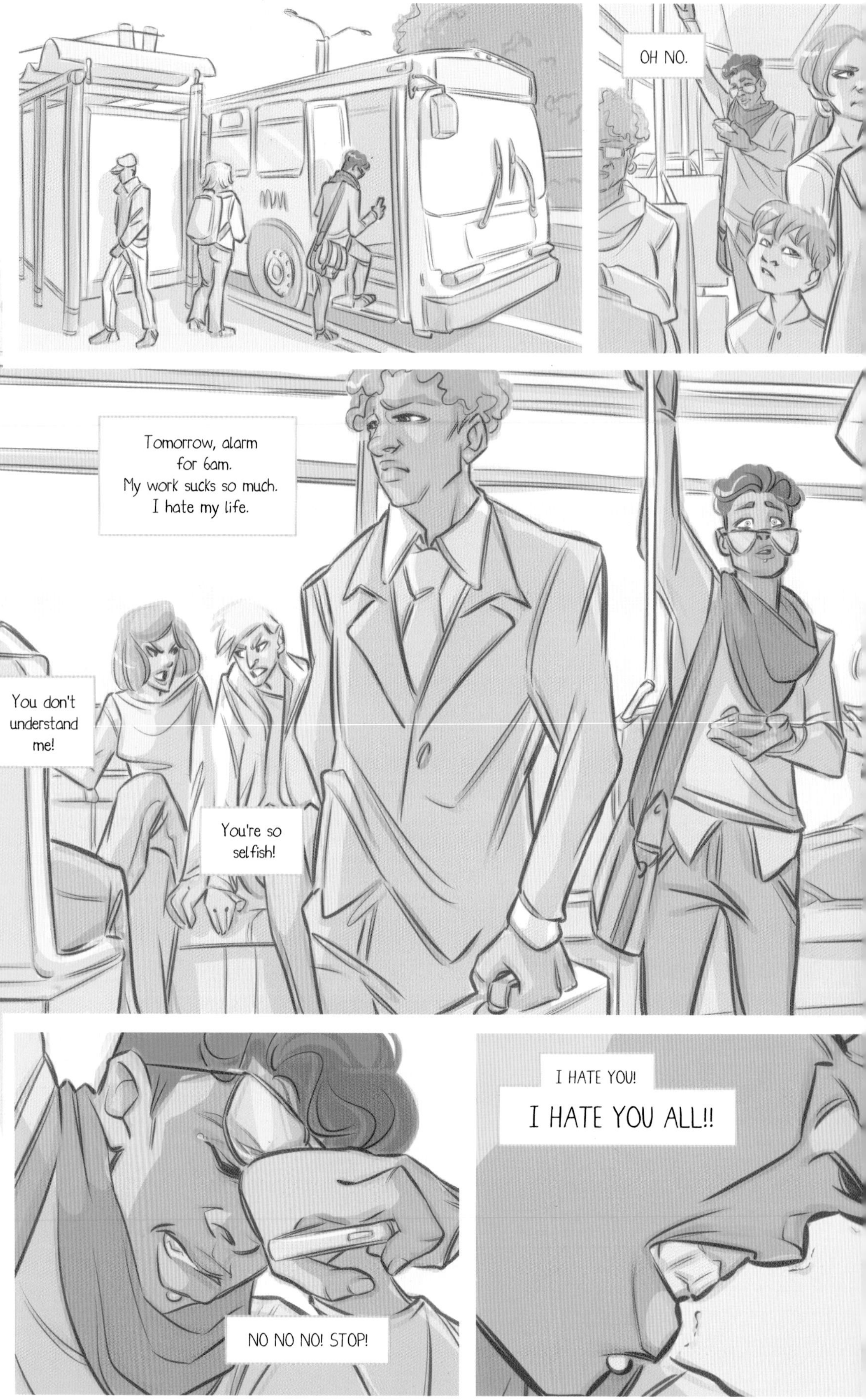
OH NO.
Tomorrow, alarm for 6am. My work sucks so much. I hate my life.
You don't understand me!
You're so selfish!
NO NO NO! STOP!
I HATE YOU!
I HATE YOU ALL!!

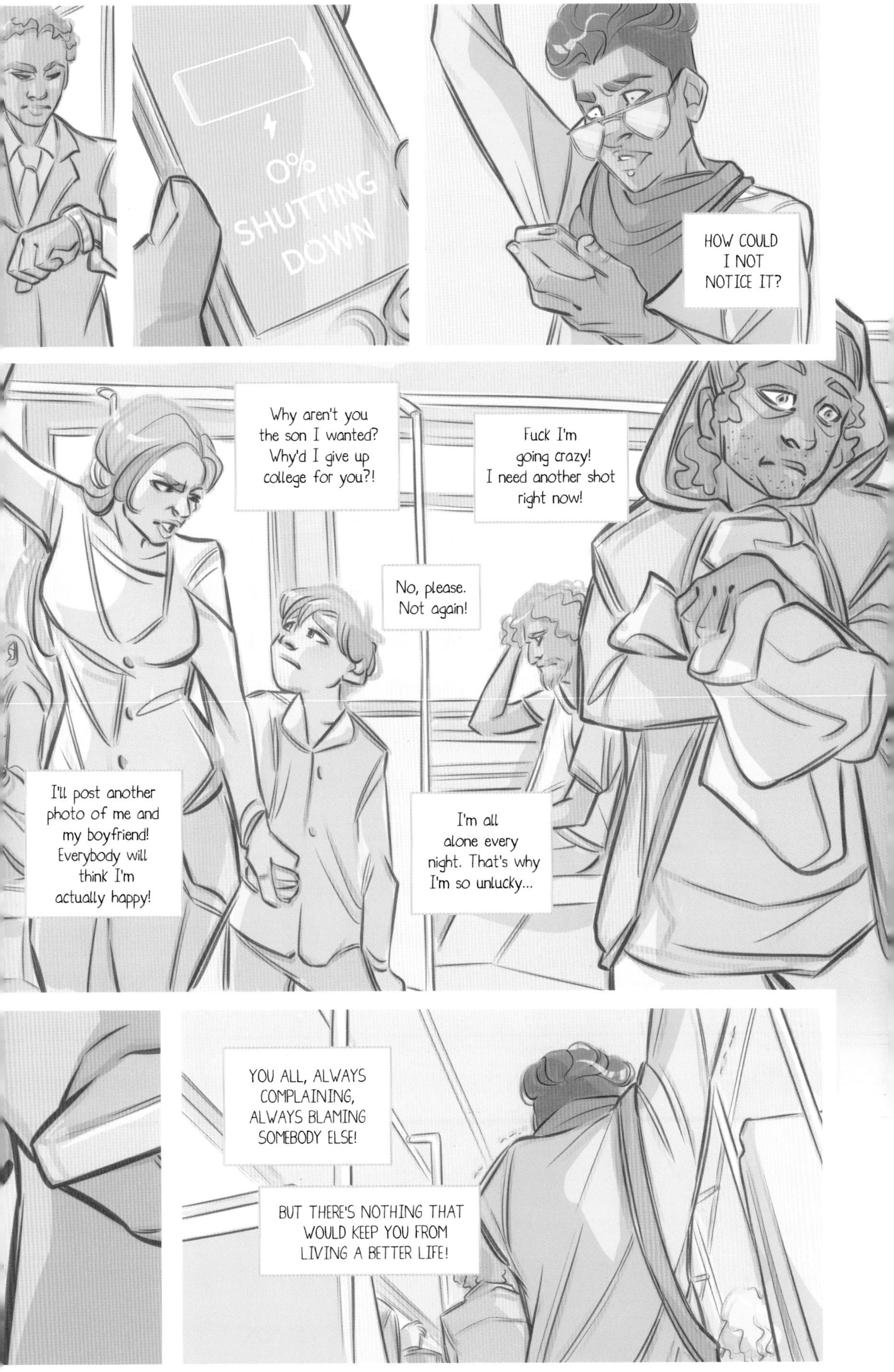
0%
SHUTTING
DOWN
HOW COULD I NOT NOTICE IT?
Why aren't you the son I wanted? Why'd I give up college for you?!
Fuck I'm going crazy! I need another shot right now!
No, please. Not again!
I'll post another photo of me and my boyfriend! Everybody will think I'm actually happy!
I'm all alone every night. That's why I'm so unlucky...
YOU ALL, ALWAYS COMPLAINING, ALWAYS BLAMING SOMEBODY ELSE!
BUT THERE'S NOTHING THAT WOULD KEEP YOU FROM LIVING A BETTER LIFE!

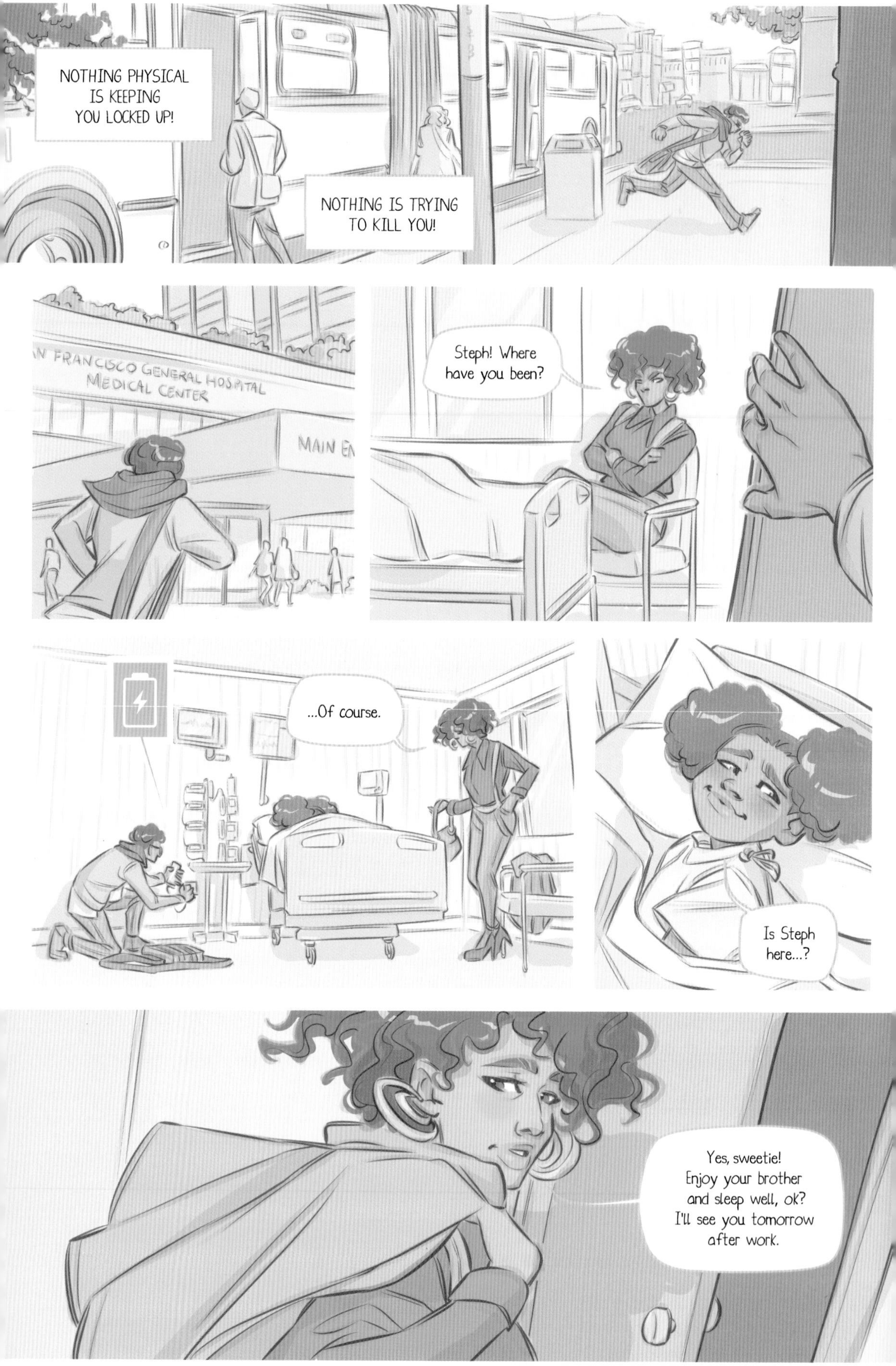
NOTHING PHYSICAL IS KEEPING YOU LOCKED UP!
NOTHING IS TRYING TO KILL YOU!
N FRANCISCO GENERAL HOSPITAL
MEDICAL CENTER
MAIN EN
Steph! Where have you been?
...Of course.
Is Steph here...?
Yes, sweetie! Enjoy your brother and sleep well, ok? I'll see you tomorrow after work.

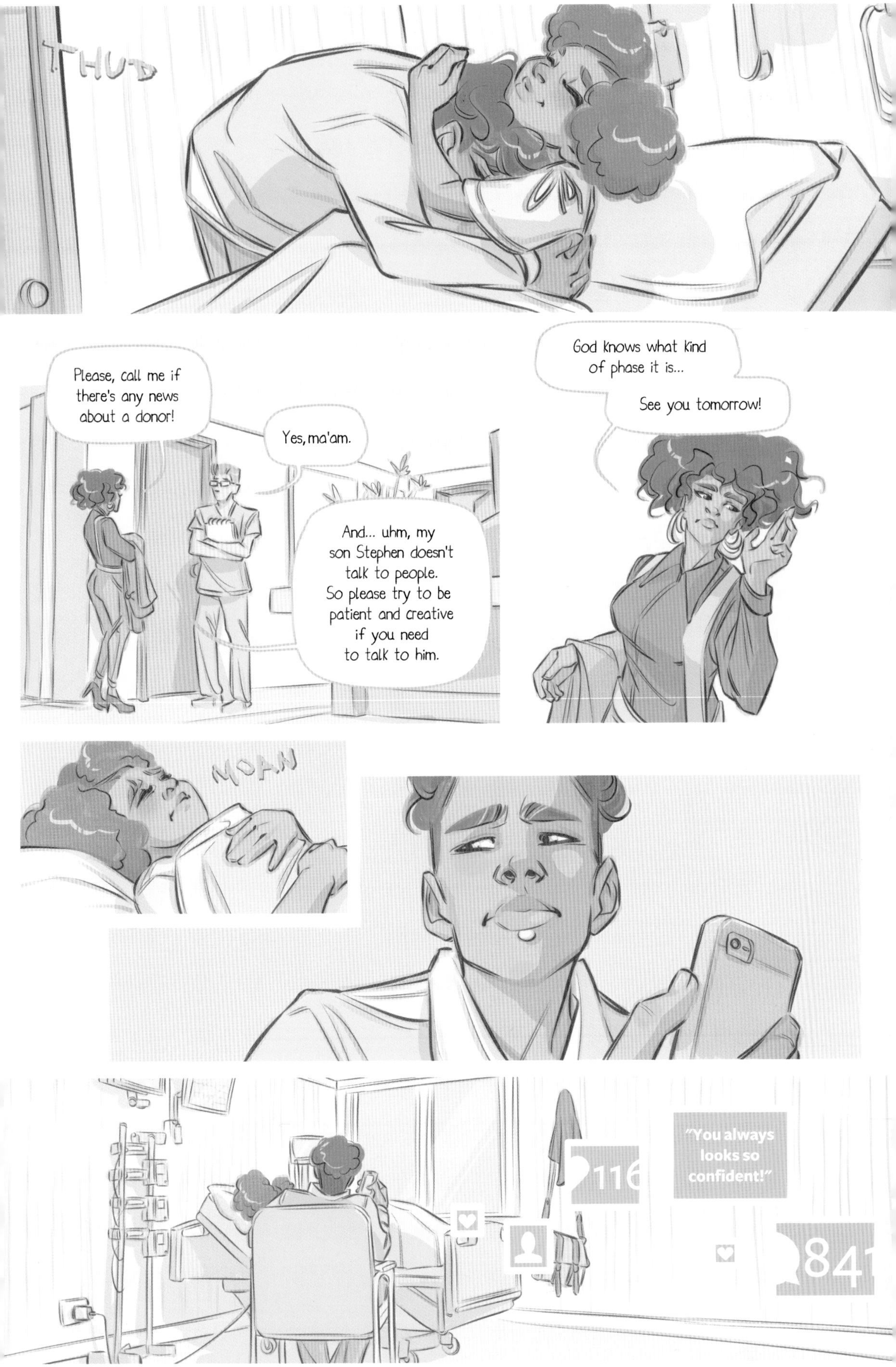
THUD
Please, call me if there's any news about a donor!
Yes, ma'am.
And... uhm, my son Stephen doesn't talk to people. So please try to be patient and creative if you need to talk to him.
God knows what kind of phase it is...
See you tomorrow!
MOAN
116
"You always looks so confident!"
841

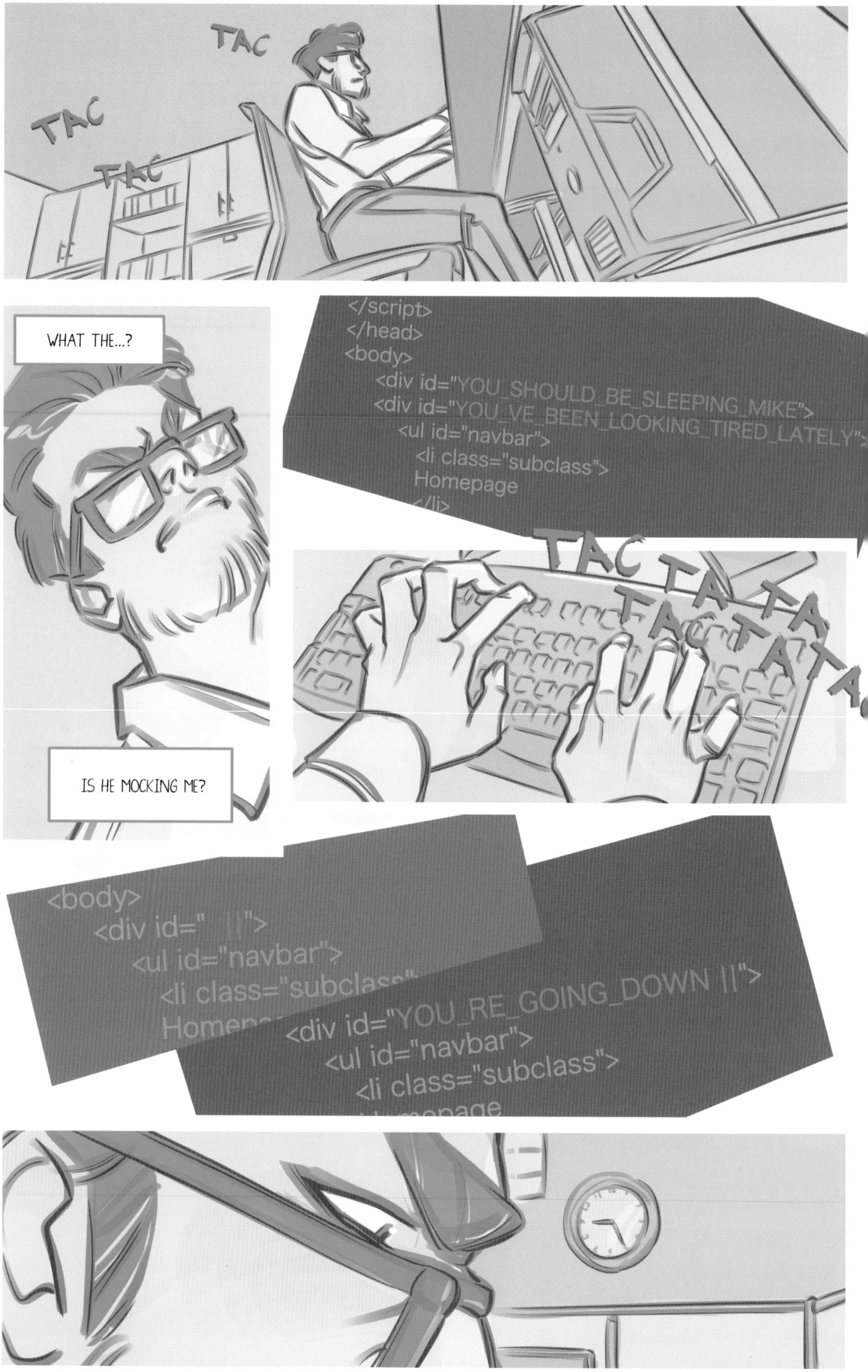
TAC
TAC
TAC
WHAT THE...?
</script>
</head>
<body>
<div id="YOU_SHOULD_BE_SLEEPING_MIKE">
<div id="YOU_VE_BEEN_LOOKING_TIRED_LATELY">
<ul id="navbar">
<li class="subclass">
Homepage
IS HE MOCKING ME?
TAC TA TA
TAC TA TA
<body>
<div id=" ||">
<ul id="navbar">
<div id="YOU_RE_GOING_DOWN ||">
<ul id="navbar">
<li class="subclass">

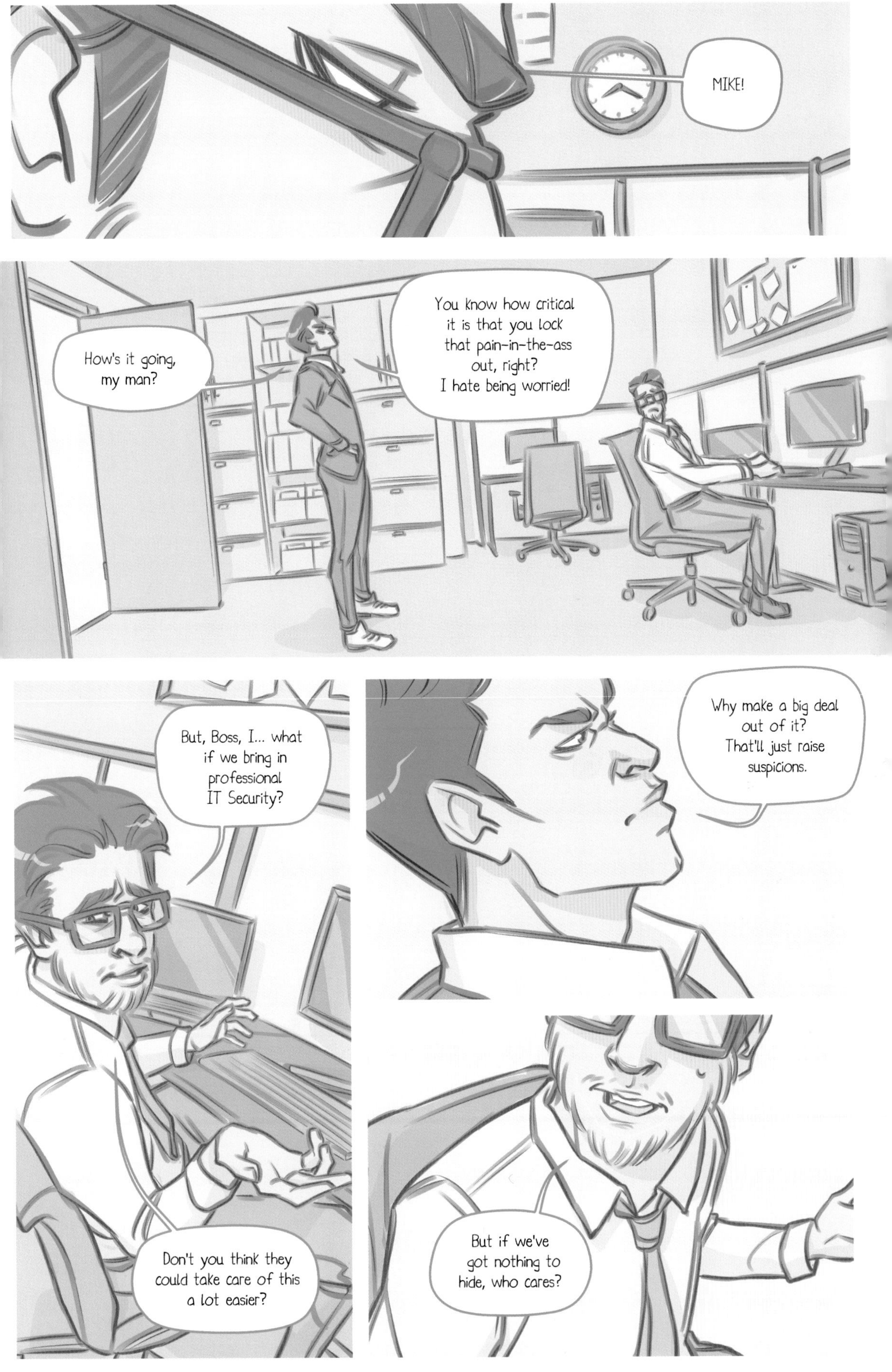
MIKE!
How's it going, my man?
You know how critical it is that you lock that pain-in-the-ass out, right? I hate being worried!
But, Boss, I... what if we bring in professional IT Security?
Don't you think they could take care of this a lot easier?
Why make a big deal out of it? That'll just raise suspicions.
But if we've got nothing to hide, who cares?

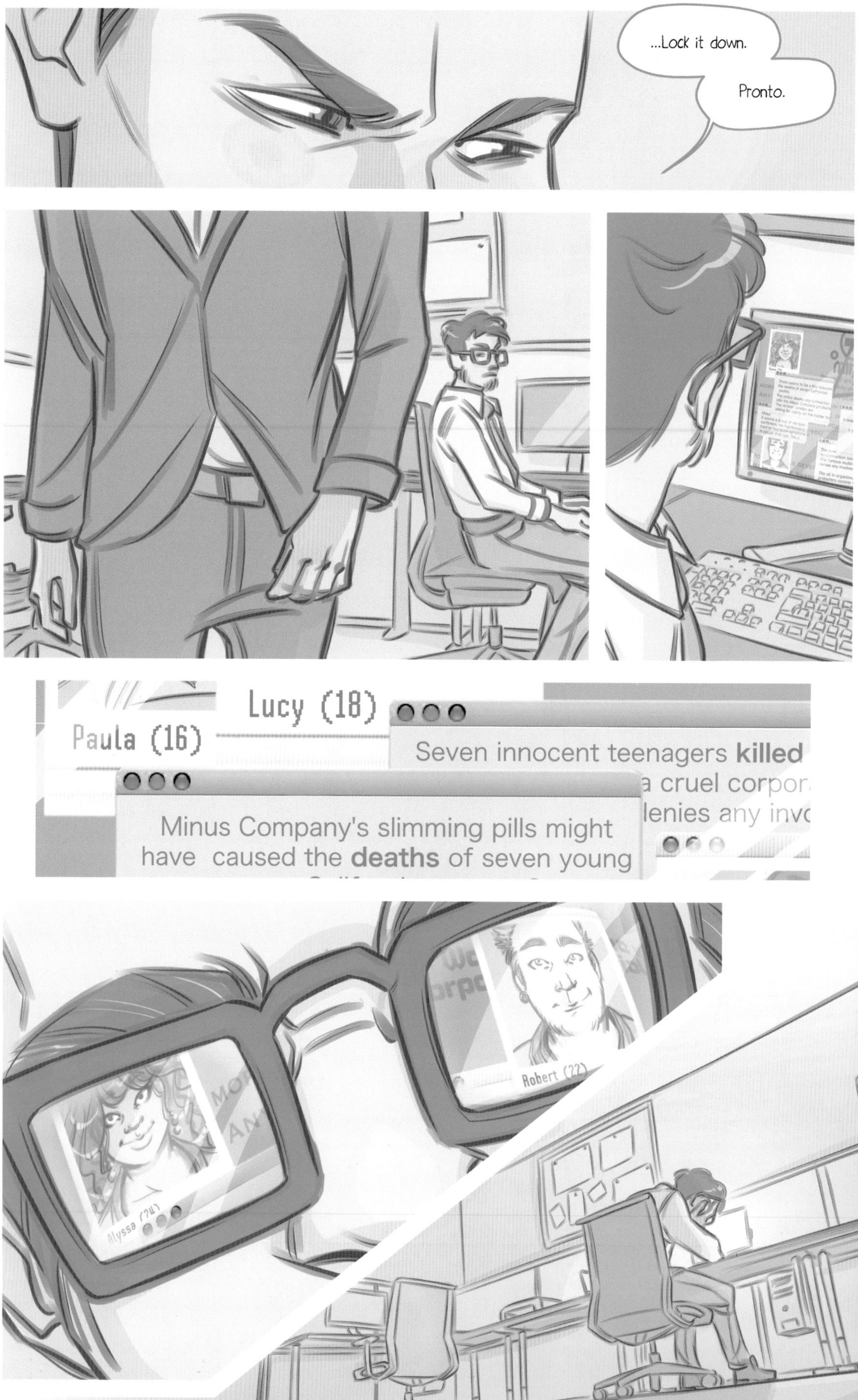
...Lock it down.
Pronto.
Lucy (18)
Paula (16)
Seven innocent teenagers killed
a cruel corpor
lenies any invo
Minus Company's slimming pills might
have caused the deaths of seven young
Robert (22)
Alyssa (24)

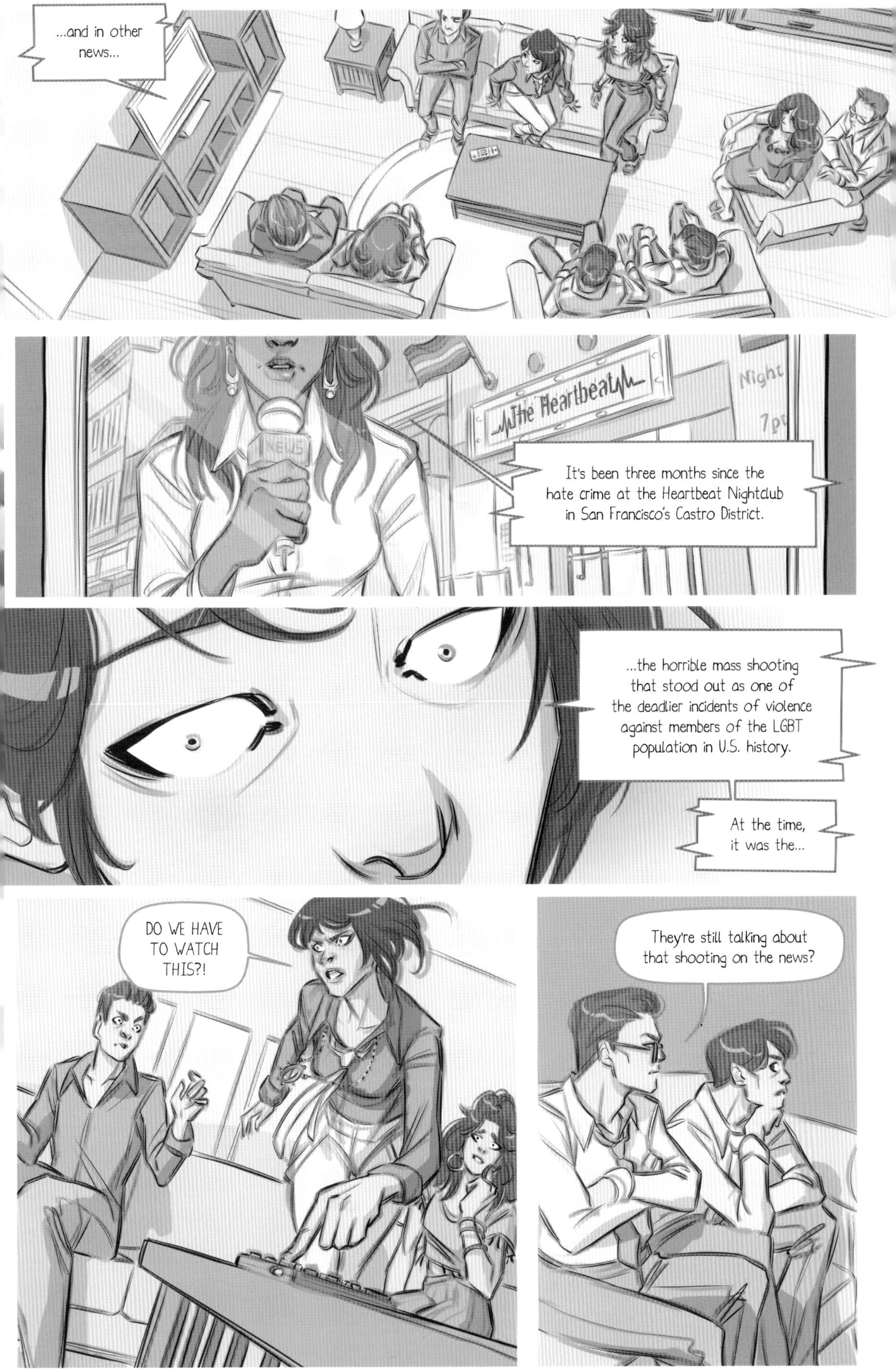
...and in other news...
The Heartbeat
Night
7p
It's been three months since the hate crime at the Heartbeat Nightclub in San Francisco's Castro District.
...the horrible mass shooting that stood out as one of the deadlier incidents of violence against members of the LGBT population in U.S. history.
At the time, it was the...
DO WE HAVE TO WATCH THIS?!
They're still talking about that shooting on the news?

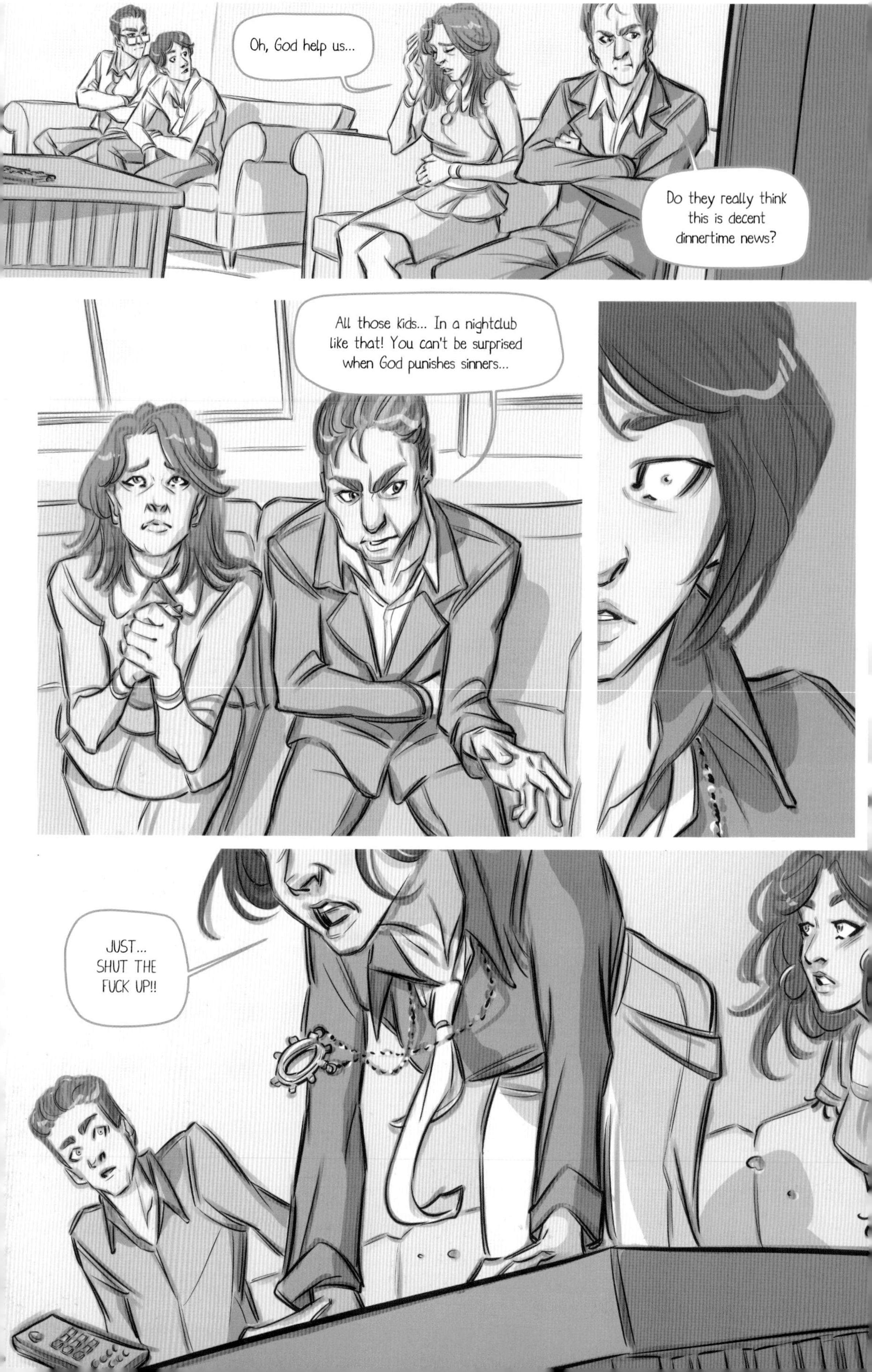
Oh, God help us...
Do they really think this is decent dinnertime news?
All those kids... In a nightclub like that! You can't be surprised when God punishes sinners...
JUST... SHUT THE FUCK UP!!

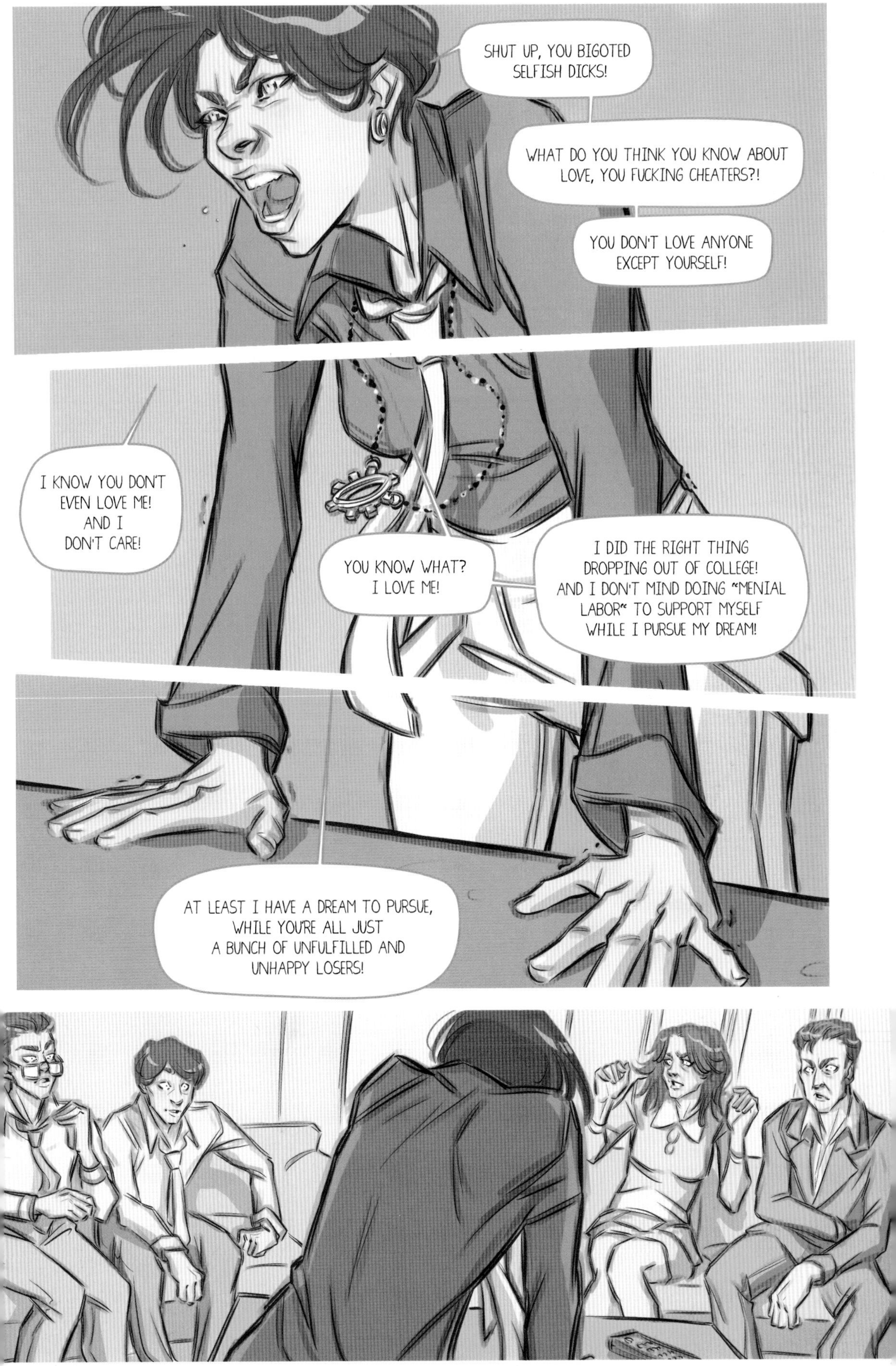
SHUT UP, YOU BIGOTED SELFISH DICKS!
WHAT DO YOU THINK YOU KNOW ABOUT LOVE, YOU FUCKING CHEATERS?!
YOU DON'T LOVE ANYONE EXCEPT YOURSELF!
I KNOW YOU DON'T EVEN LOVE ME! AND I DON'T CARE!
YOU KNOW WHAT? I LOVE ME!
I DID THE RIGHT THING DROPPING OUT OF COLLEGE! AND I DON'T MIND DOING "MENIAL LABOR" TO SUPPORT MYSELF WHILE I PURSUE MY DREAM!
AT LEAST I HAVE A DREAM TO PURSUE, WHILE YOU'RE ALL JUST A BUNCH OF UNFULFILLED AND UNHAPPY LOSERS!

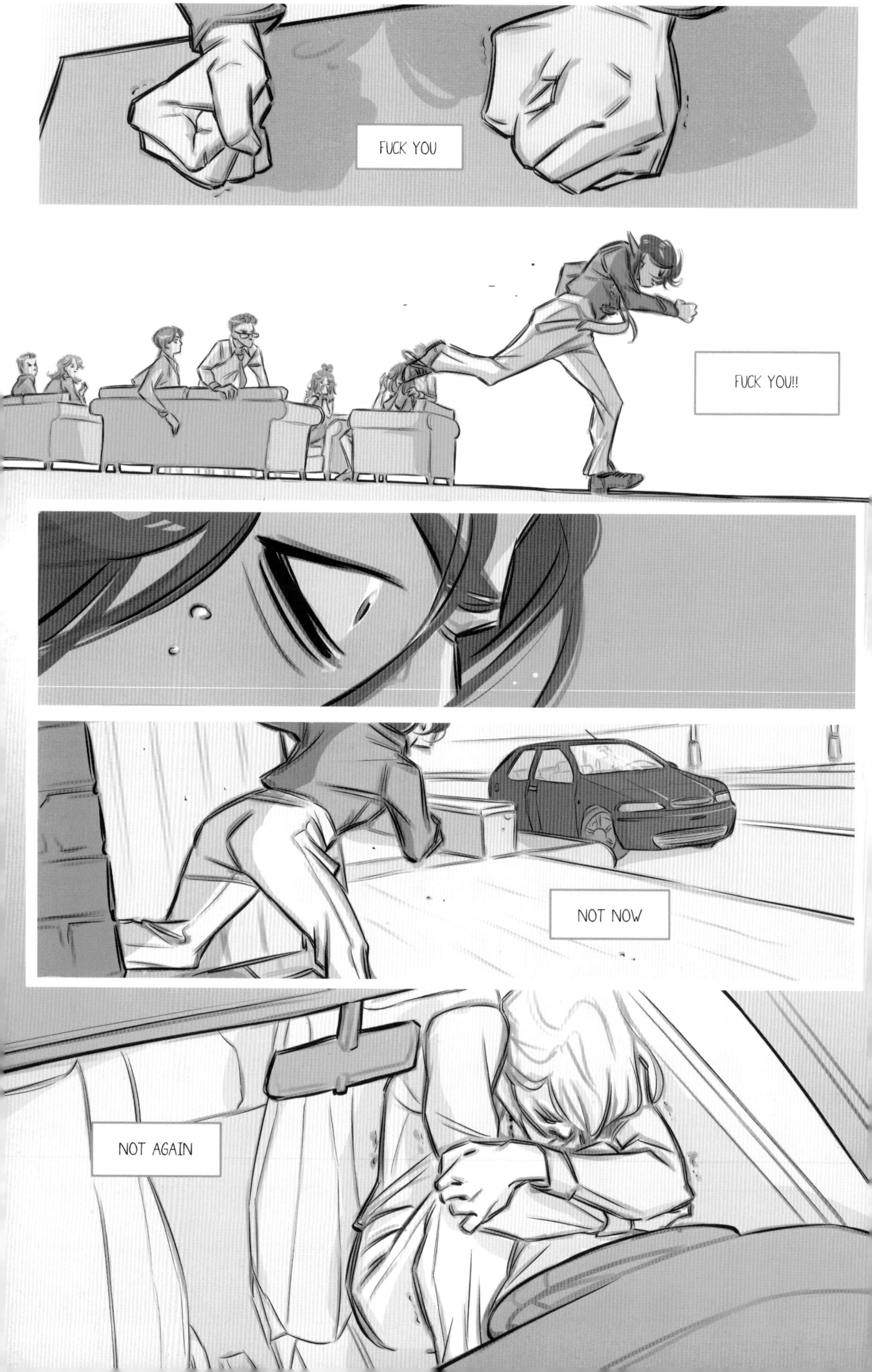
FUCK YOU
FUCK YOU!!
NOT NOW
NOT AGAIN

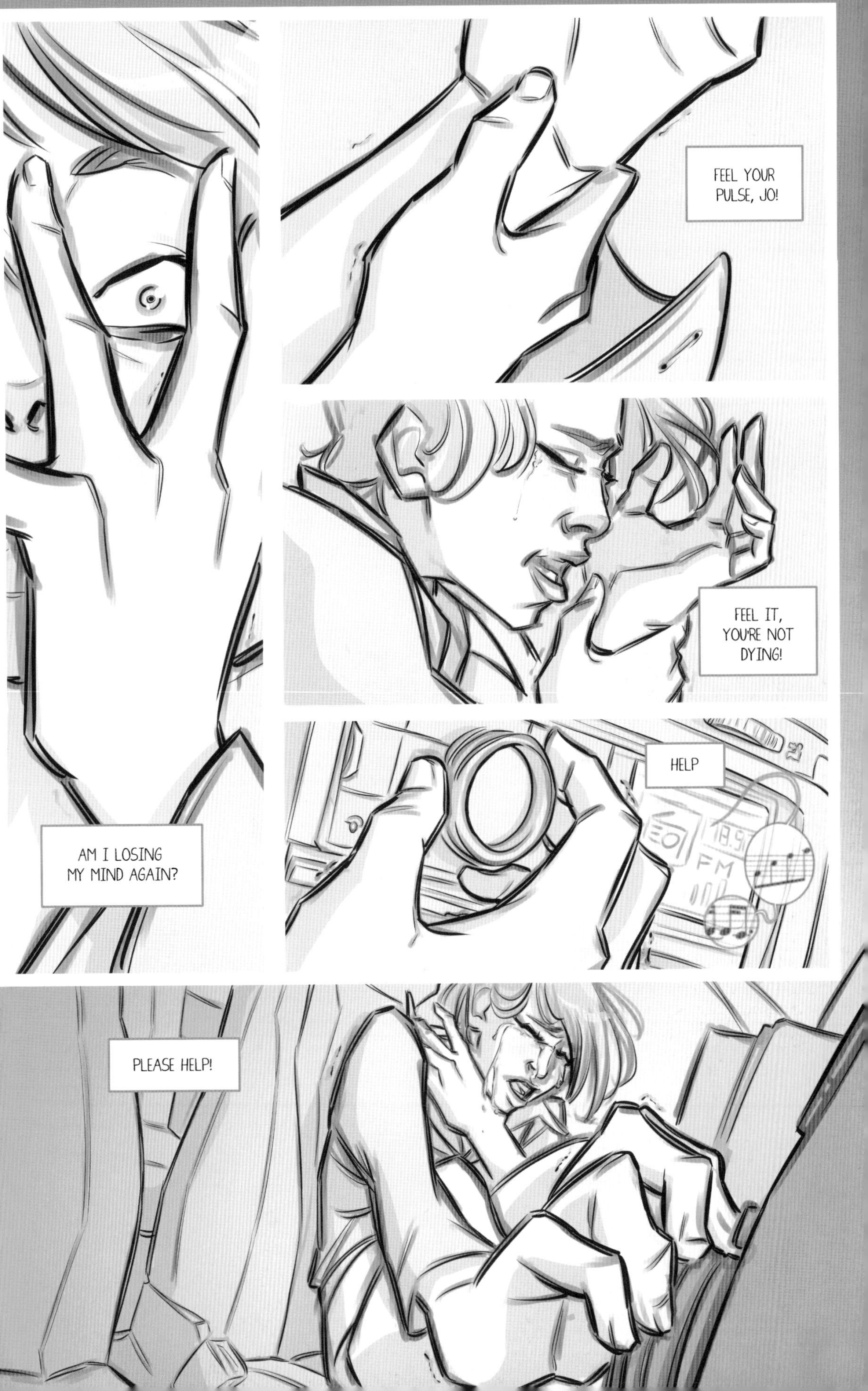
AM I LOSING MY MIND AGAIN?
FEEL YOUR PULSE, JO!
FEEL IT, YOU'RE NOT DYING!
HELP
FM
PLEASE HELP!

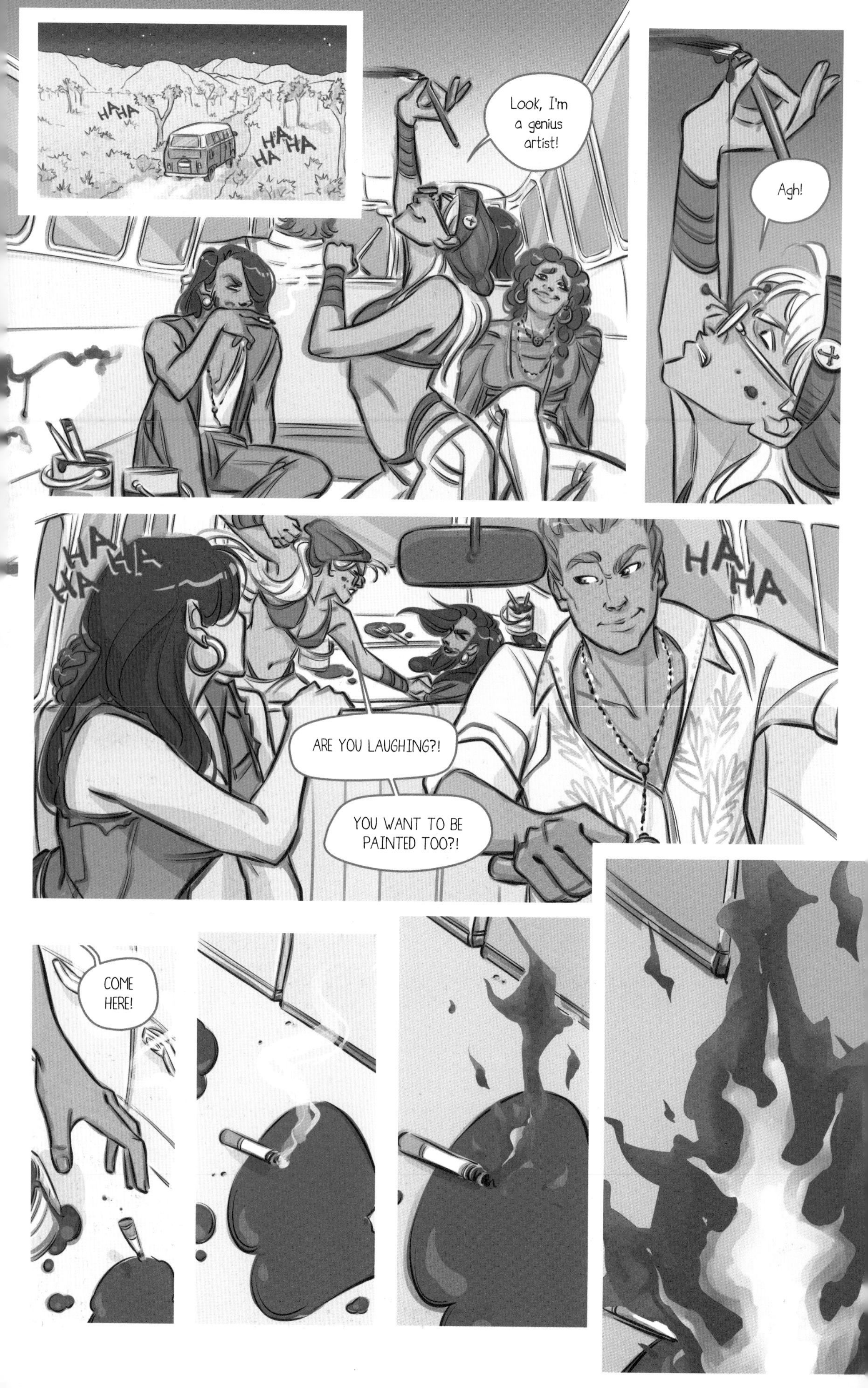
HAHA
HAHA
HA
Look, I'm a genius artist!
Agh!
HAHA
HA
HAHA
ARE YOU LAUGHING?!
YOU WANT TO BE PAINTED TOO?!
COME HERE!

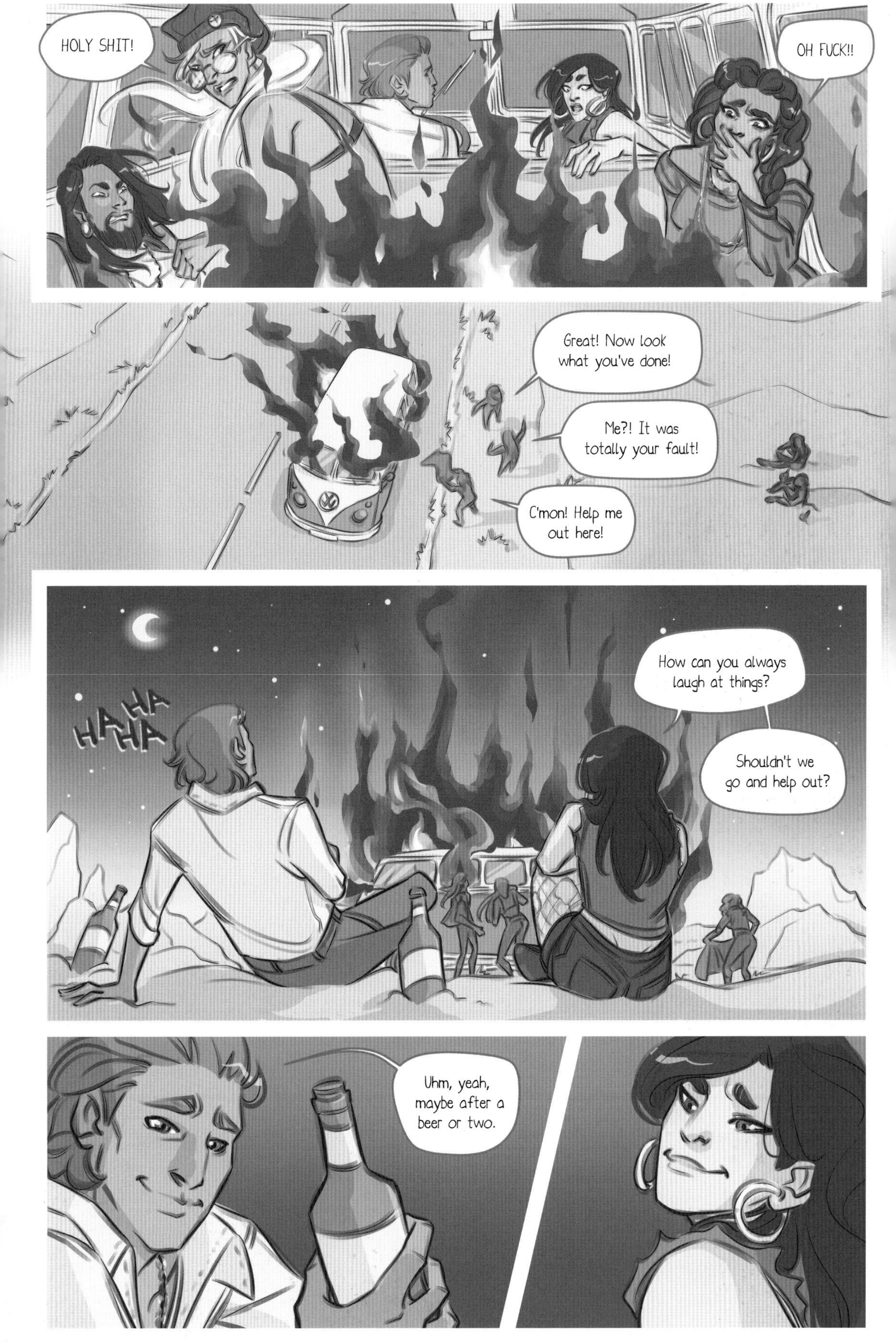
HOLY SHIT!
OH FUCK!!
Great! Now look what you've done!
Me?! It was totally your fault!
C'mon! Help me out here!
HA HA HA HA
How can you always laugh at things?
Shouldn't we go and help out?
Uhm, yeah, maybe after a beer or two.

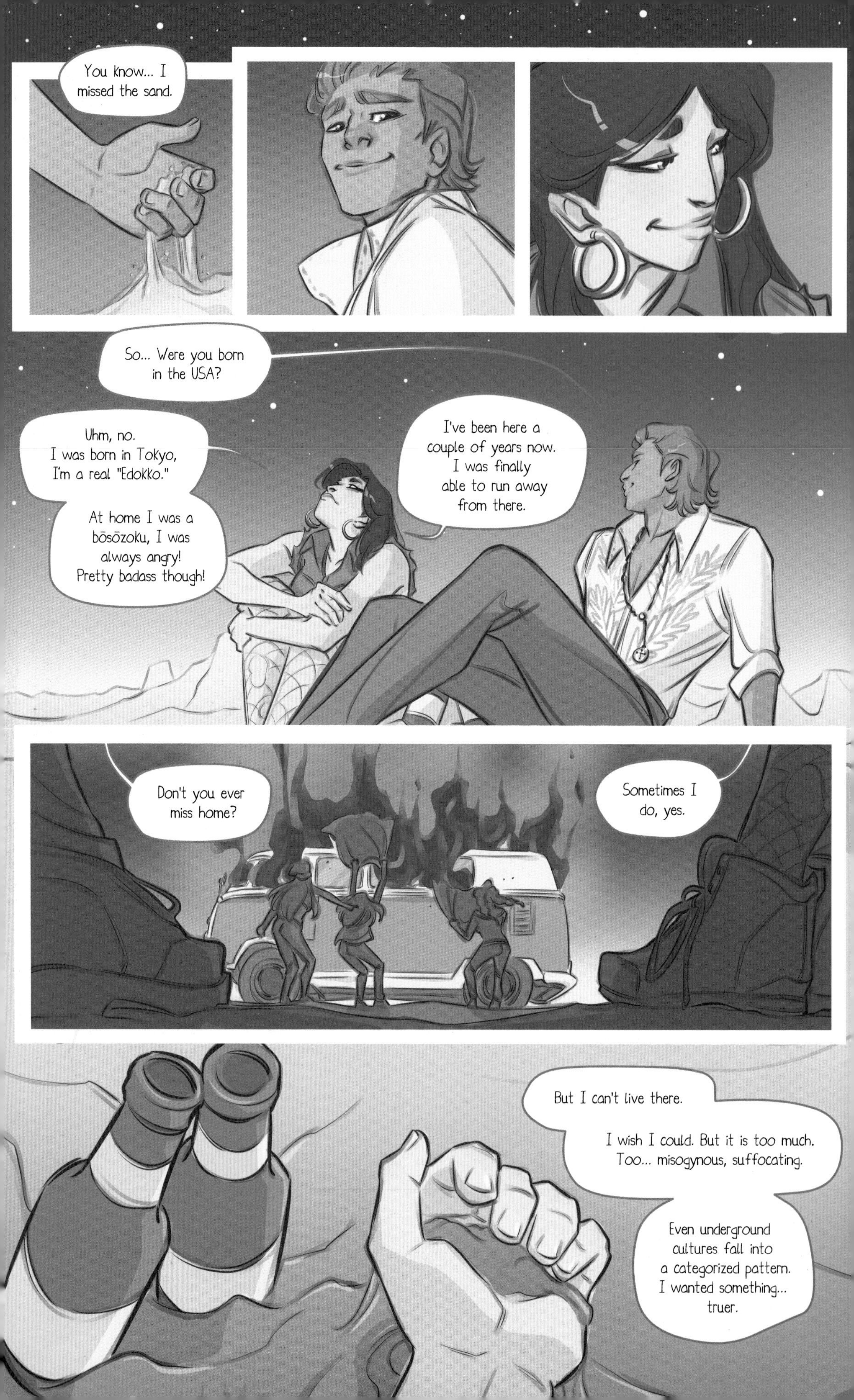

You know... I missed the sand.
So... Were you born in the USA?
Uhm, no. I was born in Tokyo, I'm a real "Edokko."
At home I was a bōsōzoku, I was always angry! Pretty badass though!
I've been here a couple of years now. I was finally able to run away from there.
Don't you ever miss home?
Sometimes I do, yes.
But I can't live there.
I wish I could. But it is too much. Too... misogynous, suffocating.
Even underground cultures fall into a categorized pattern. I wanted something... truer.

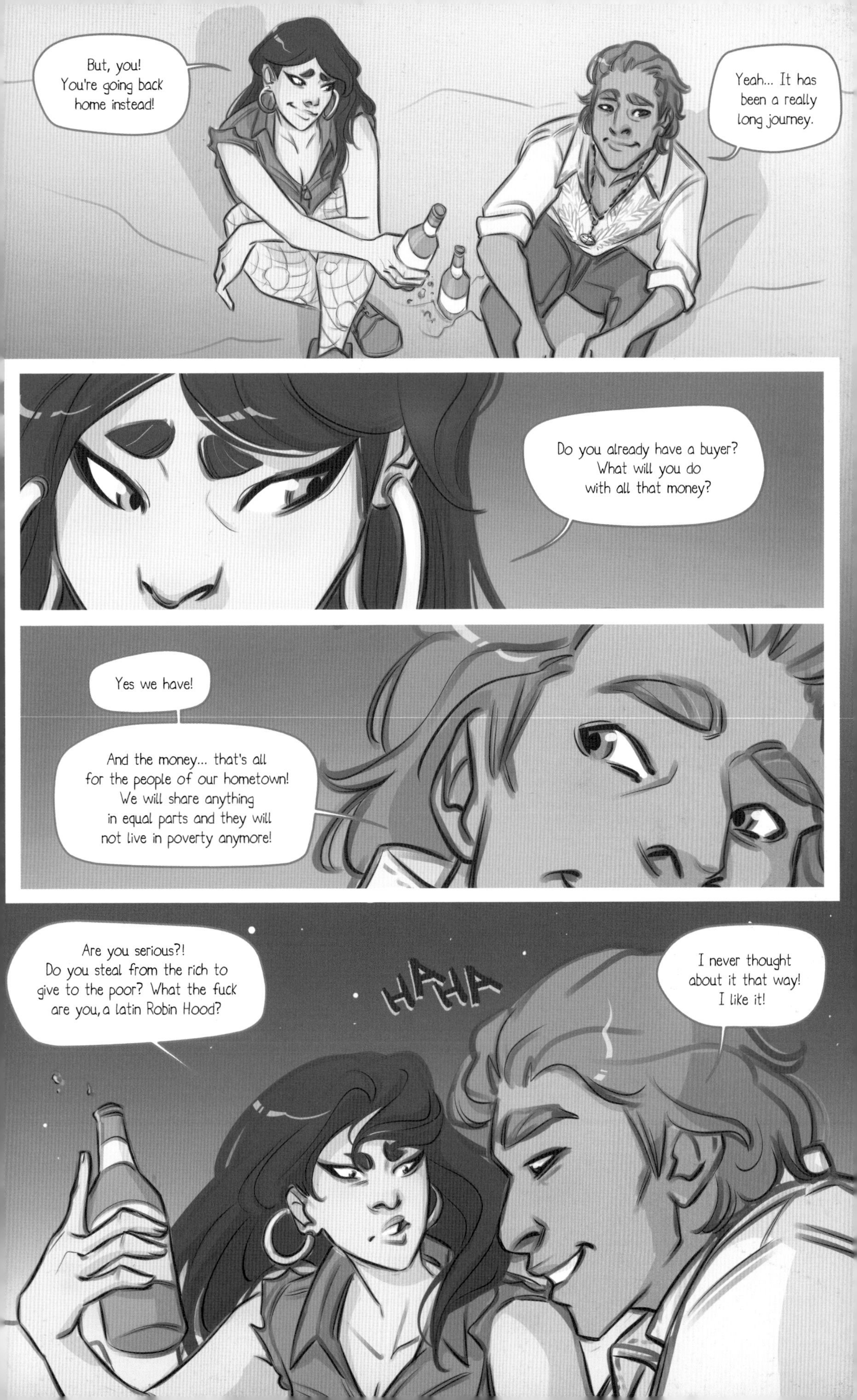
But, you!
You're going back home instead!
Yeah... It has been a really long journey.
Do you already have a buyer? What will you do with all that money?
Yes we have!
And the money... that's all for the people of our hometown! We will share anything in equal parts and they will not live in poverty anymore!
Are you serious?! Do you steal from the rich to give to the poor? What the fuck are you, a latin Robin Hood?
HAHA
I never thought about it that way! I like it!

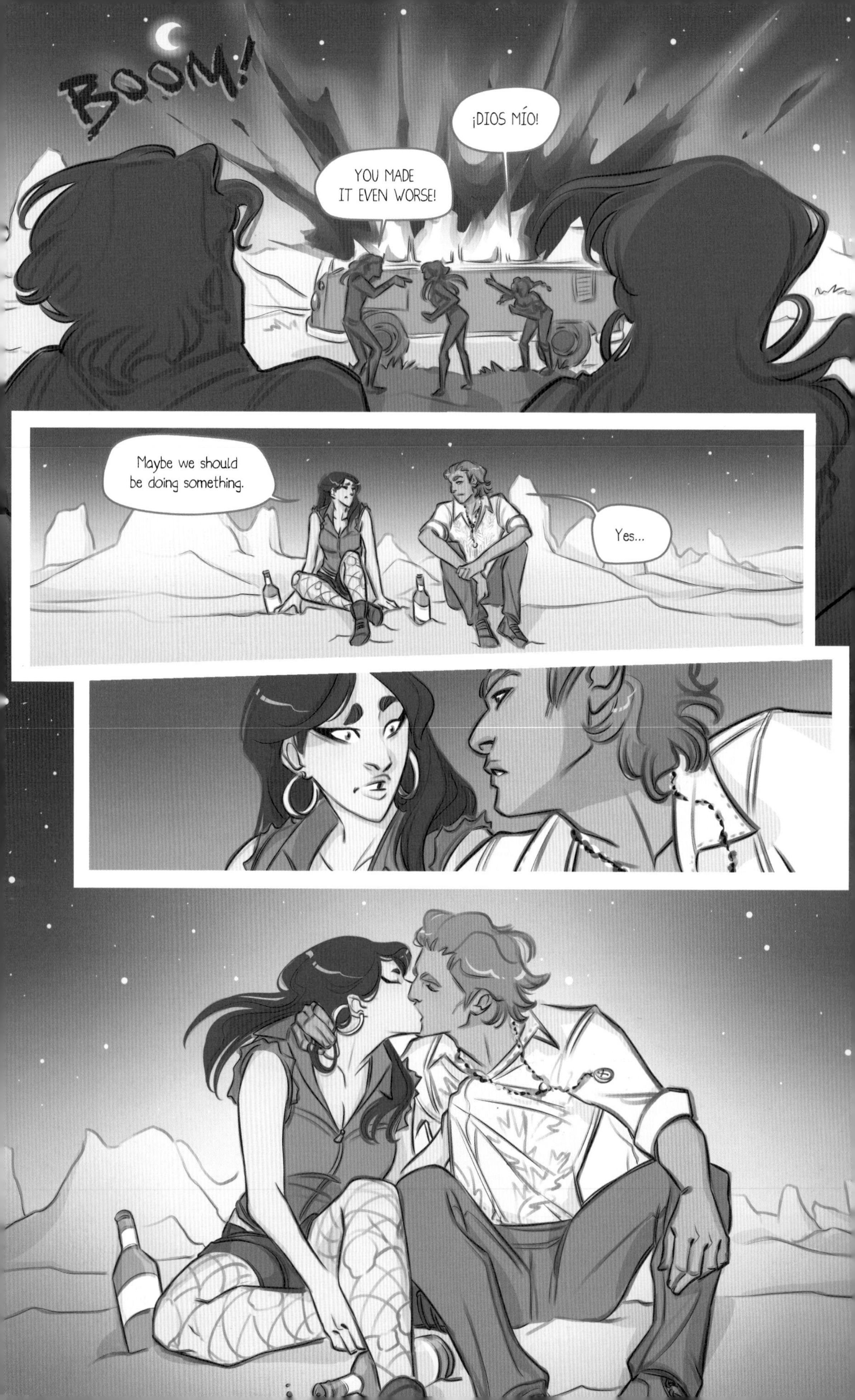
BOOM!
¡DIOS MÍO!
YOU MADE IT EVEN WORSE!
Maybe we should be doing something.
Yes...

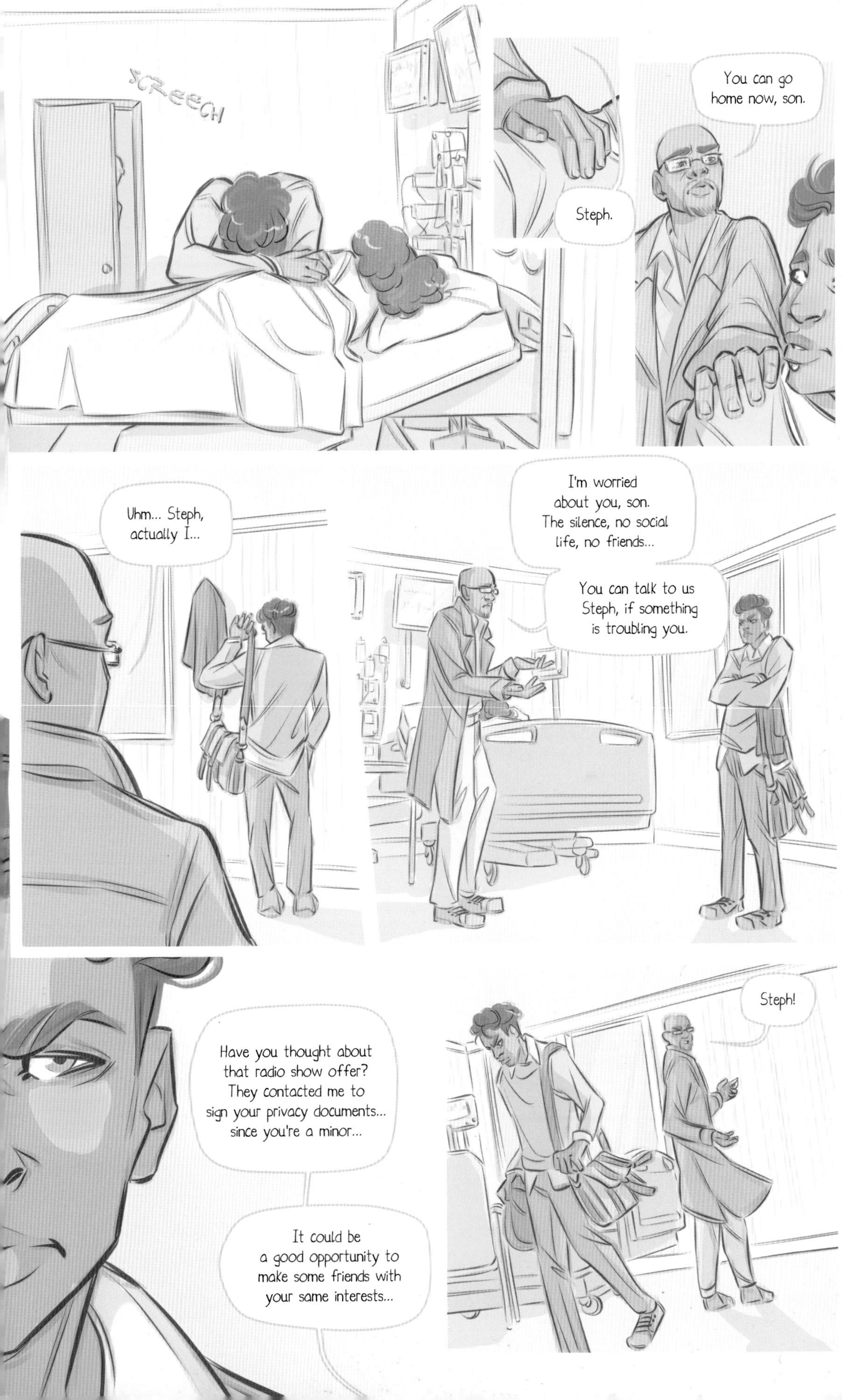
SCREECH
Steph.
You can go home now, son.
Uhm... Steph, actually I...
I'm worried about you, son. The silence, no social life, no friends...
You can talk to us Steph, if something is troubling you.
Have you thought about that radio show offer? They contacted me to sign your privacy documents... since you're a minor...
It could be a good opportunity to make some friends with your same interests...
Steph!

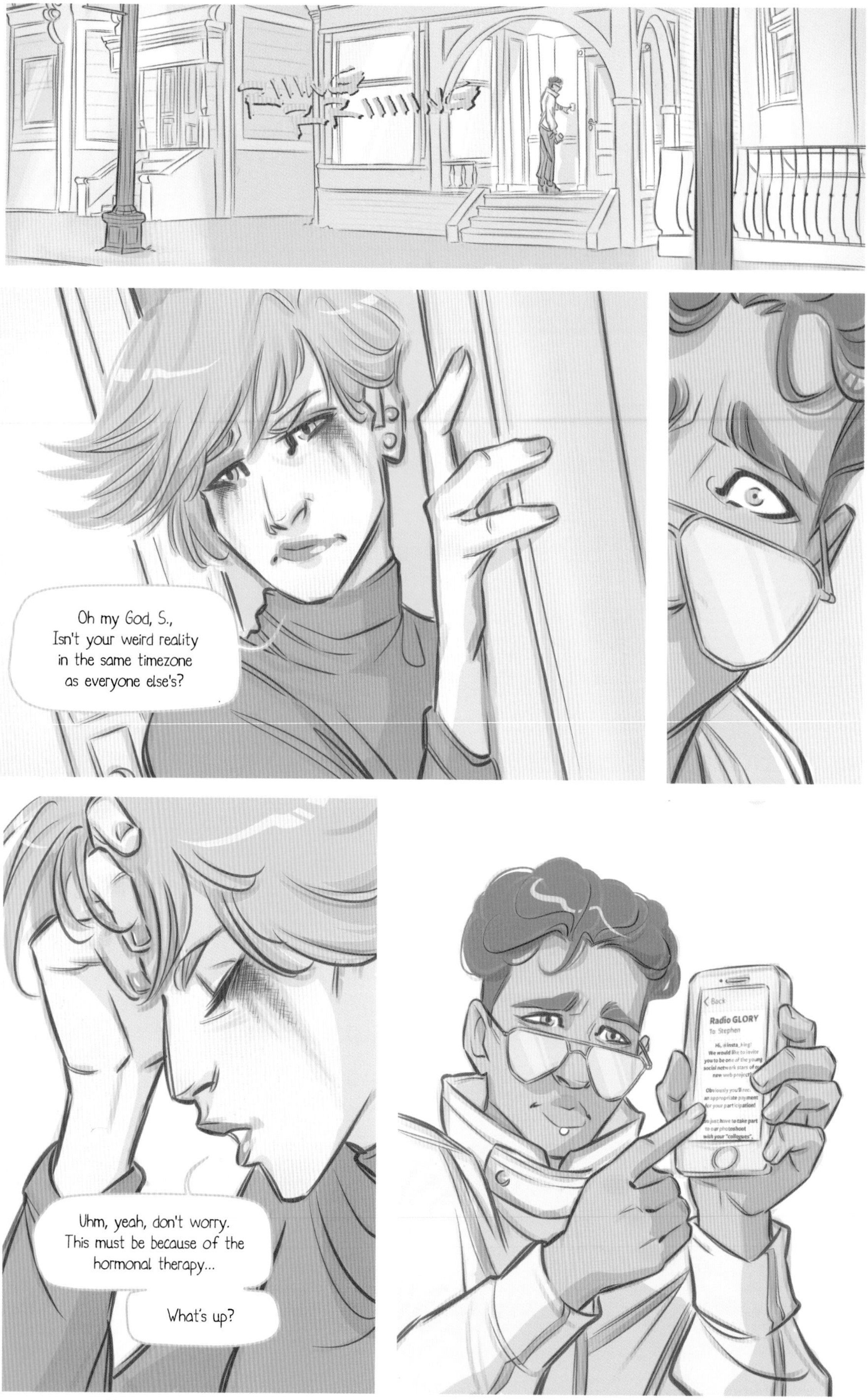
Oh my God, S.,
Isn't your weird reality
in the same timezone
as everyone else's?
Uhm, yeah, don't worry.
This must be because of the
hormonal therapy...
What's up?
Back
Radio GLORY
To: Stephen
Hi, @insta_king!
We would like to invite
you to be one of the young
an appropriate payment
for your participation!
to our photoshoot
with your "collegues".

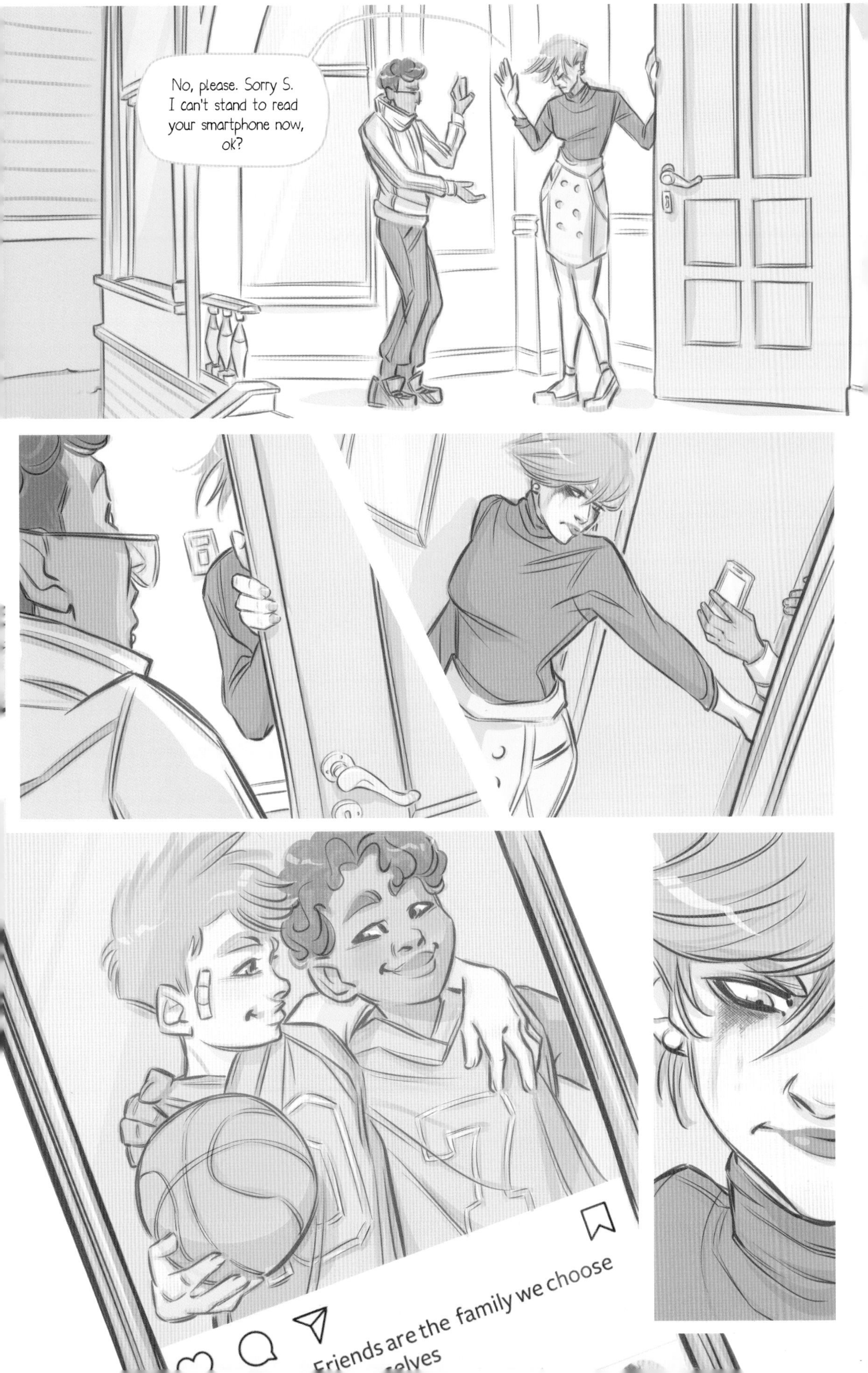
No, please. Sorry S. I can't stand to read your smartphone now, ok?
Friends are the family we choose ...elves

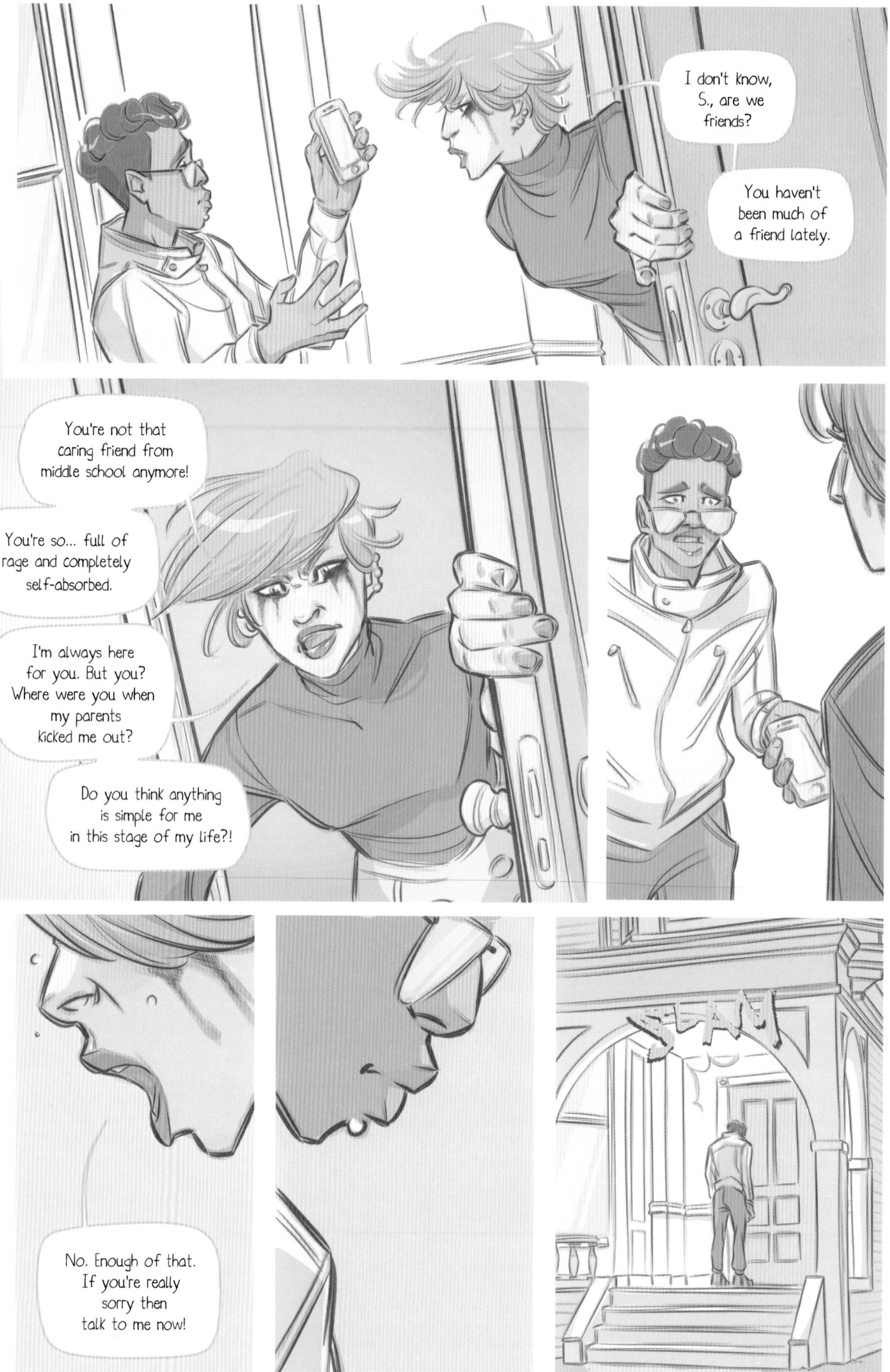
I don't know, S., are we friends?
You haven't been much of a friend lately.
You're not that caring friend from middle school anymore!
You're so... full of rage and completely self-absorbed.
I'm always here for you. But you? Where were you when my parents kicked me out?
Do you think anything is simple for me in this stage of my life?!
No. Enough of that. If you're really sorry then talk to me now!

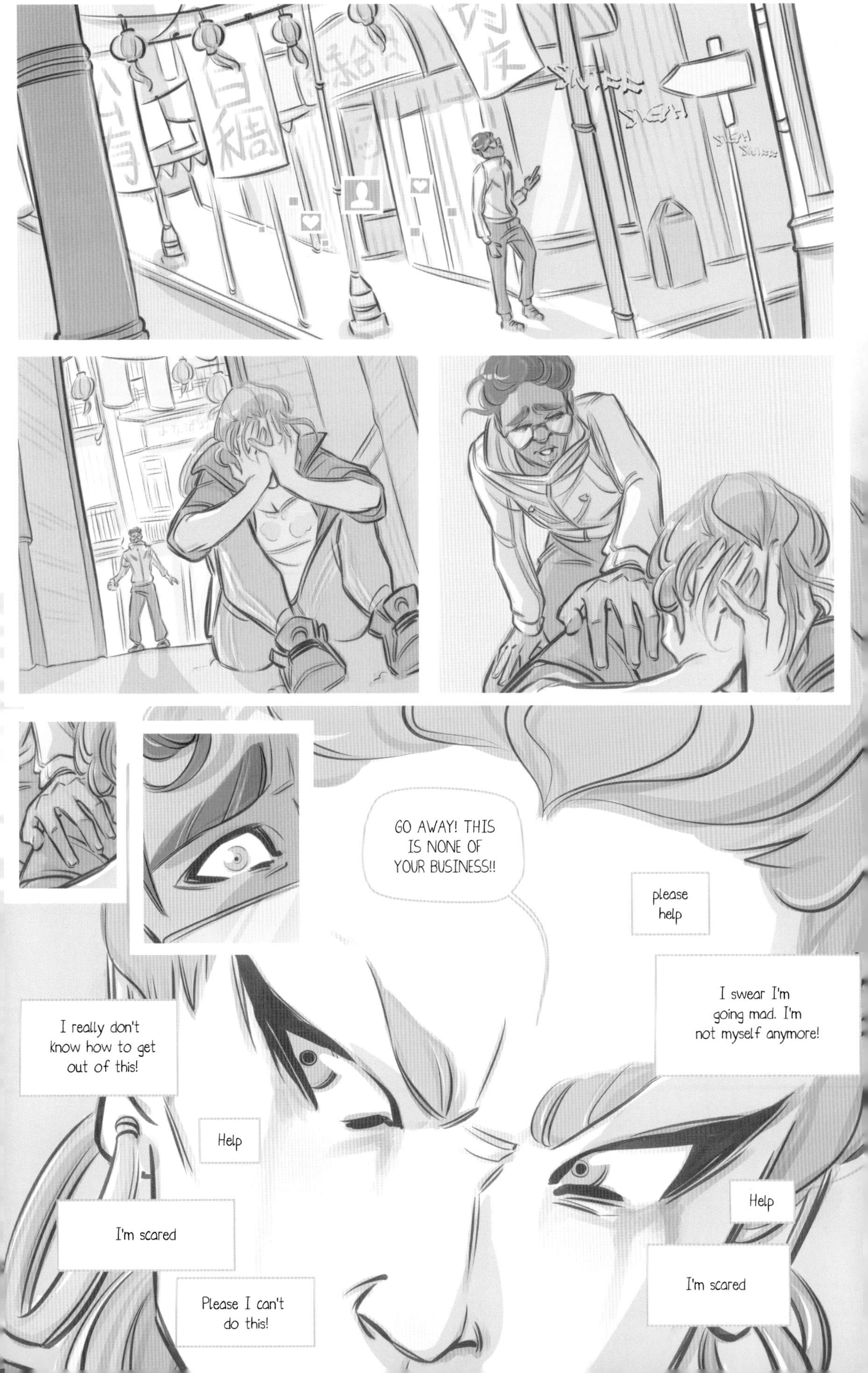
GO AWAY! THIS IS NONE OF YOUR BUSINESS!!
please help
I swear I'm going mad. I'm not myself anymore!
I really don't know how to get out of this!
Help
I'm scared
Please I can't do this!
Help
I'm scared

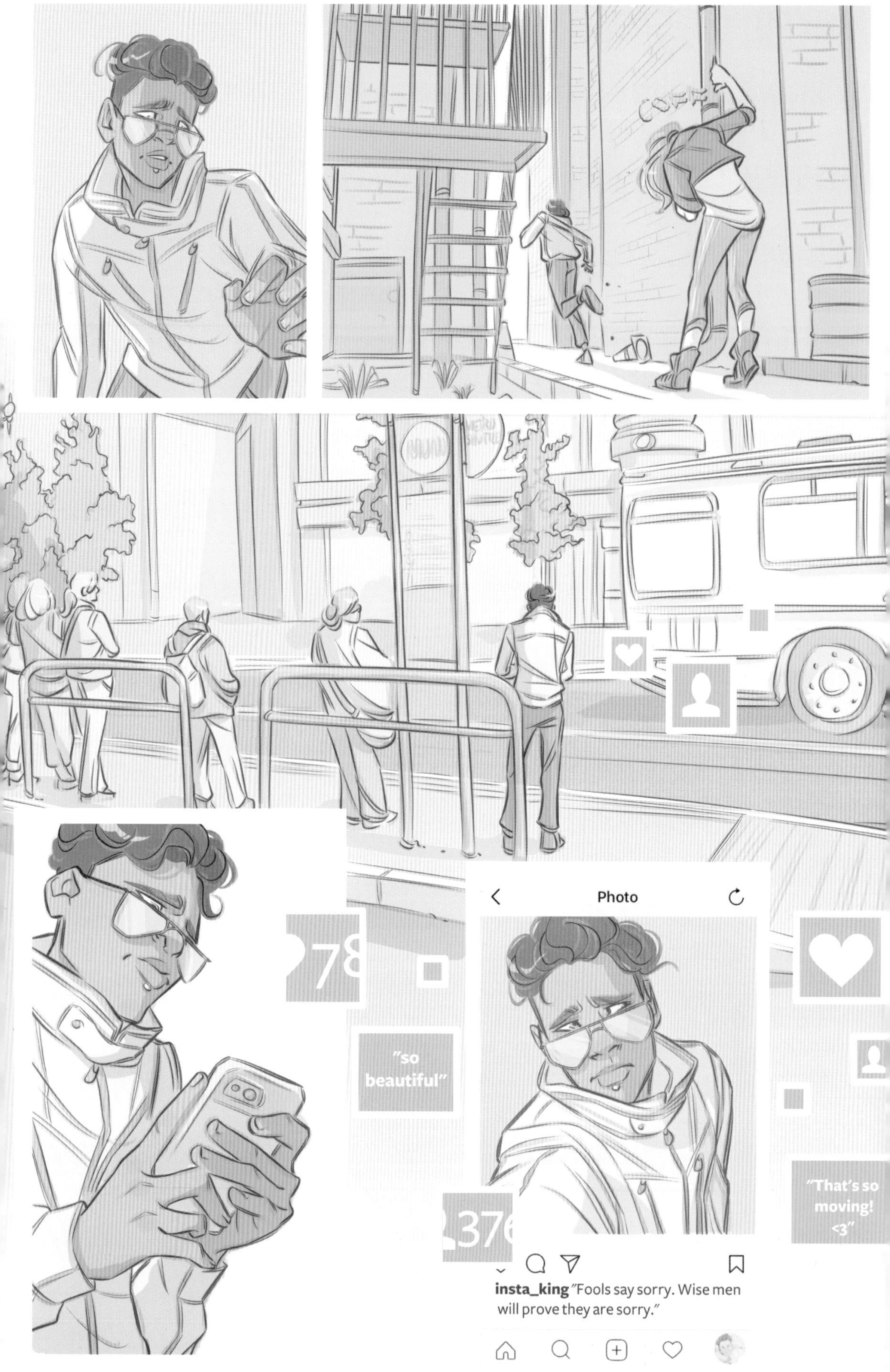
78
"so beautiful"
Photo
376
insta_king "Fools say sorry. Wise men will prove they are sorry."
"That's so moving! <3"

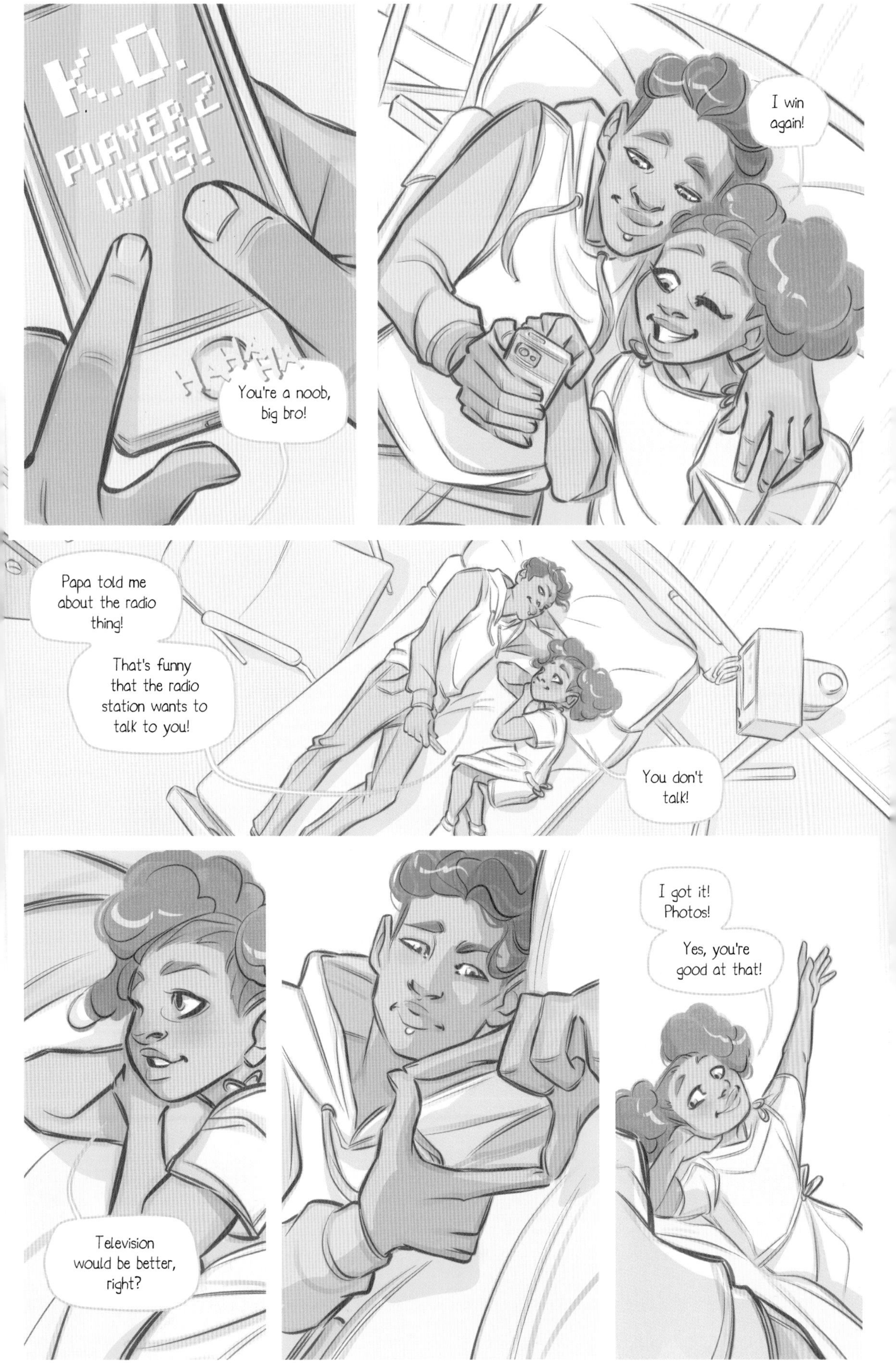
K.O.
PLAYER 2 WINS!
You're a noob, big bro!
I win again!
Papa told me about the radio thing!
That's funny that the radio station wants to talk to you!
You don't talk!
Television would be better, right?
I got it! Photos!
Yes, you're good at that!

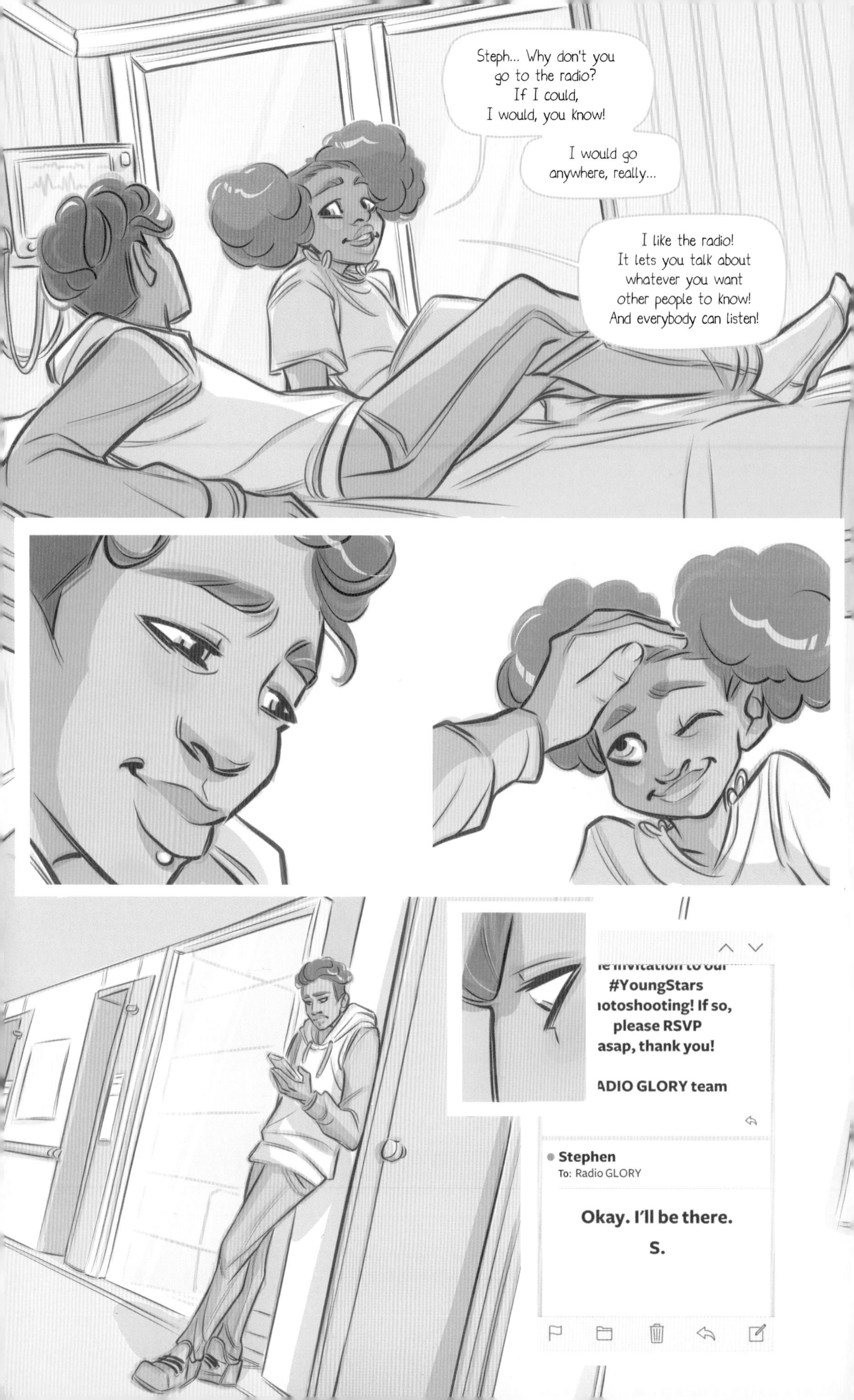
Steph... Why don't you go to the radio? If I could, I would, you know!
I would go anywhere, really...
I like the radio! It lets you talk about whatever you want other people to know! And everybody can listen!
#YoungStars
otoshooting! If so, please RSVP asap, thank you!
ADIO GLORY team
Stephen
To: Radio GLORY
Okay. I'll be there.
S.

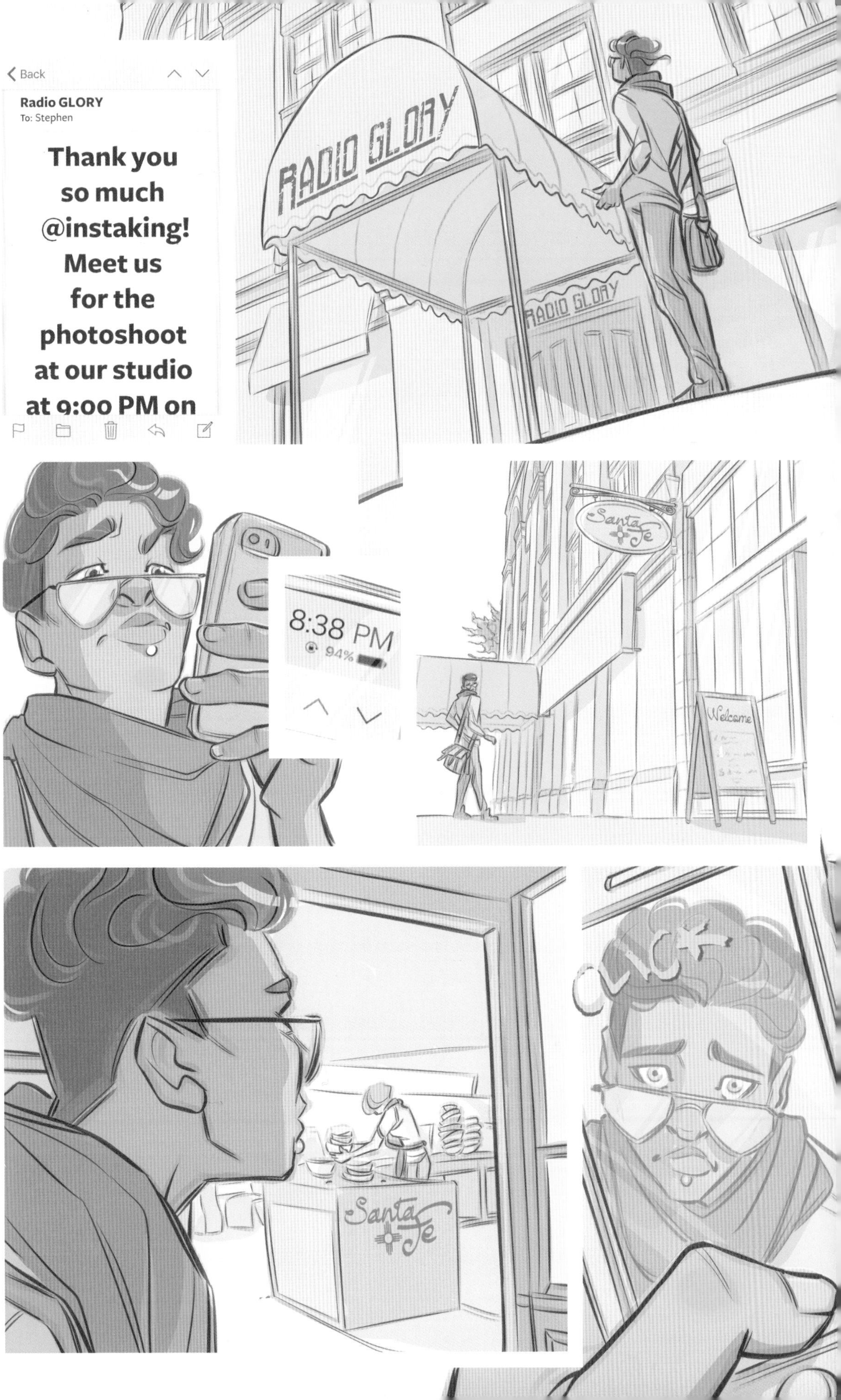

Back
Radio GLORY
To: Stephen
Thank you so much @instaking! Meet us for the photoshoot at our studio at 9:00 PM on
RADIO GLORY
RADIO GLORY
8:38 PM
94%
Santa Fe
Welcome
Santa Fe

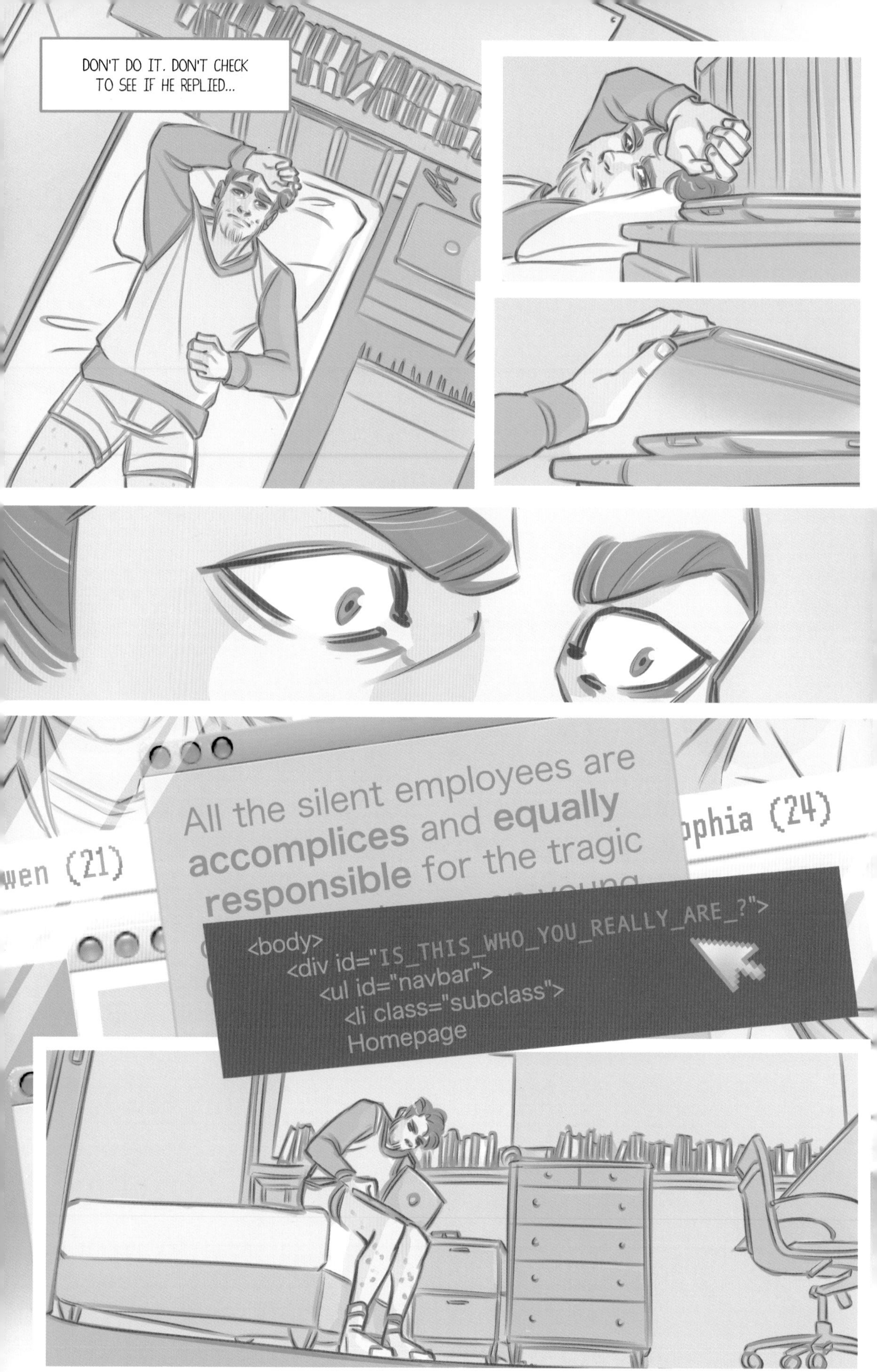
DON'T DO IT. DON'T CHECK TO SEE IF HE REPLIED...
All the silent employees are accomplices and equally responsible for the tragic
wen (21)
phia (24)
<body>
<div id="IS_THIS_WHO_YOU_REALLY_ARE_?">
<div id="navbar">
<ul id="navbar">
<li class="subclass">
Homepage

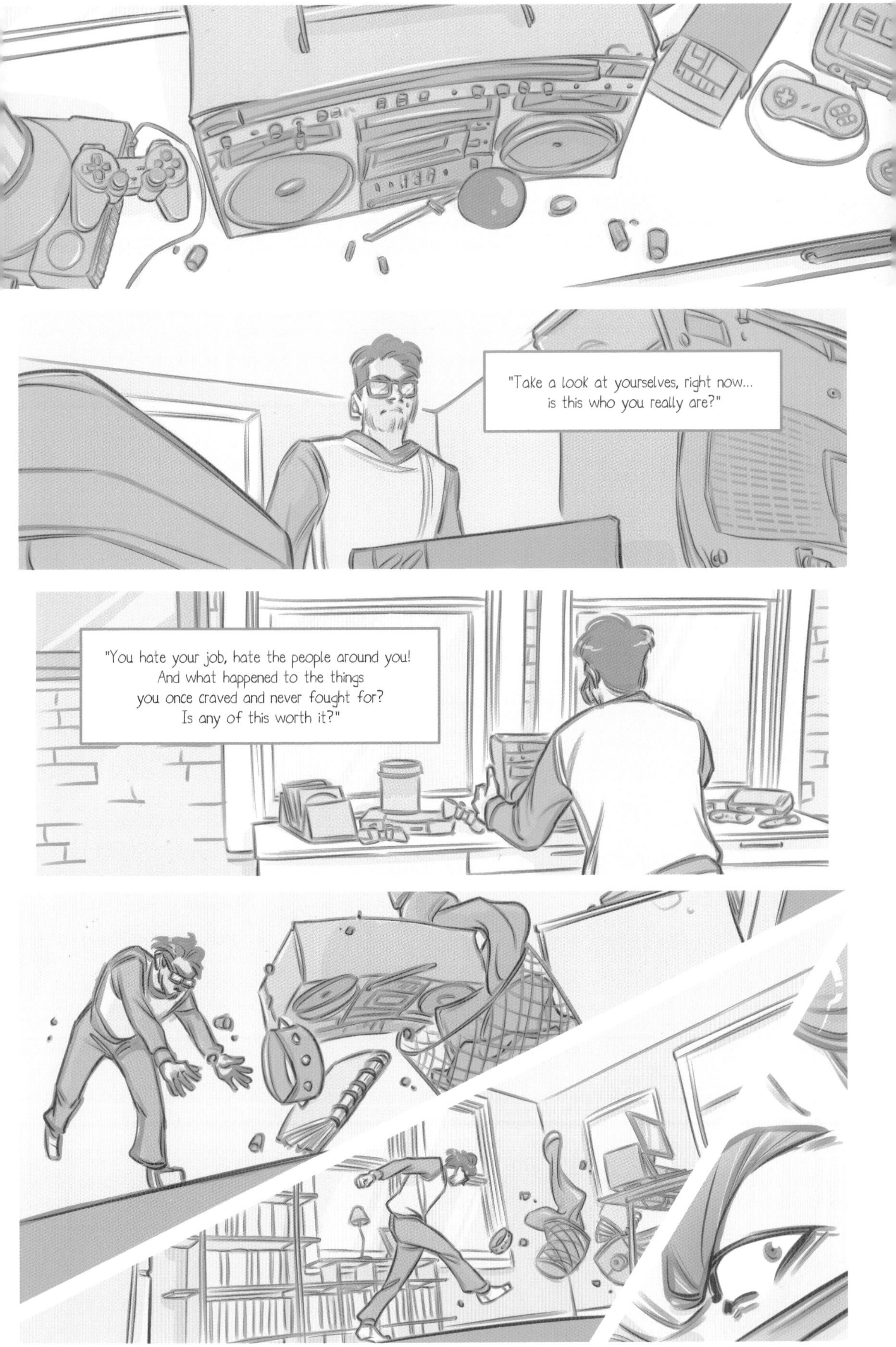
"Take a look at yourselves, right now...
is this who you really are?"
"You hate your job, hate the people around you!
And what happened to the things
you once craved and never fought for?
Is any of this worth it?"

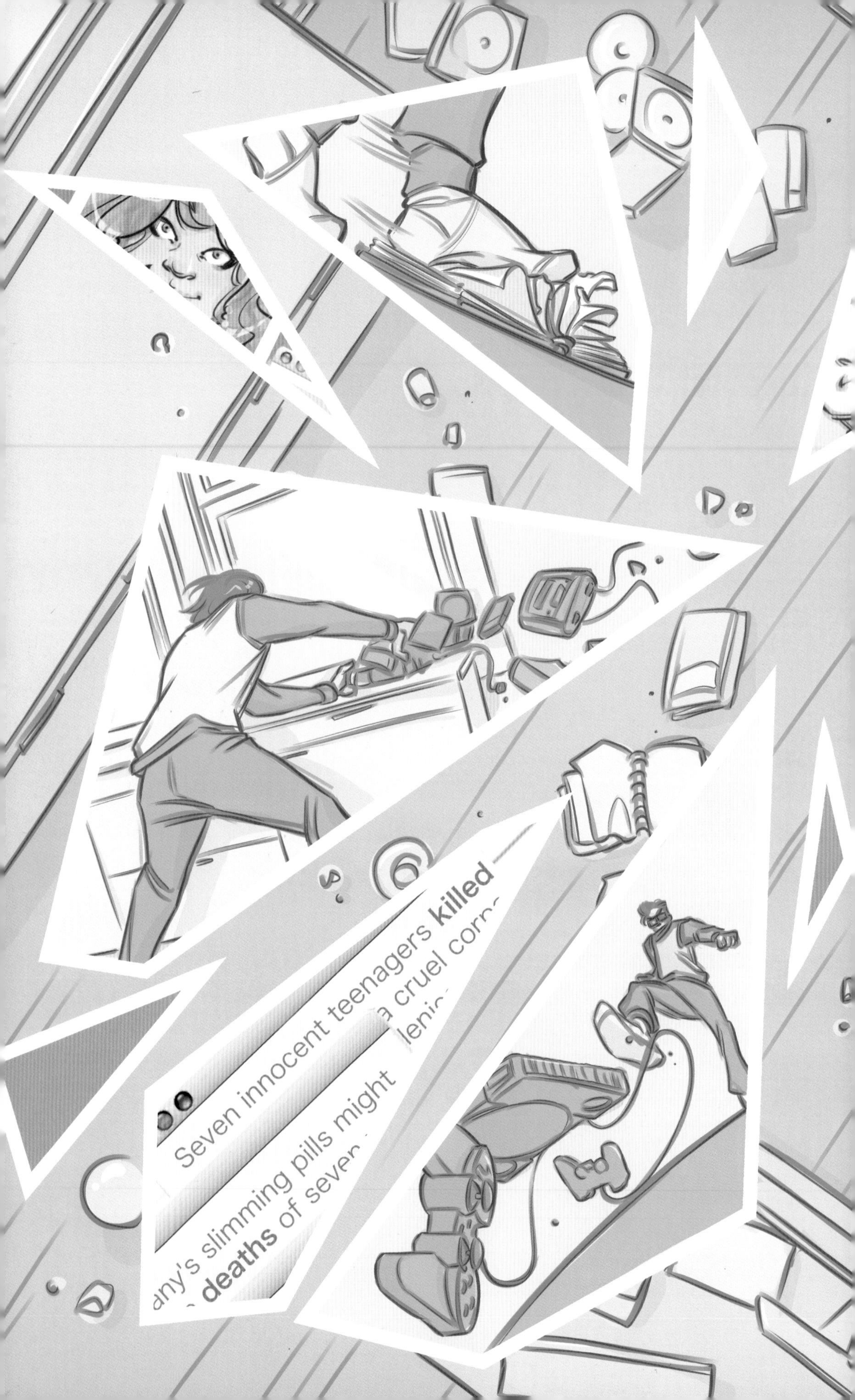
Seven innocent teenagers killed
a cruel corp
any's slimming pills might
deaths of seven

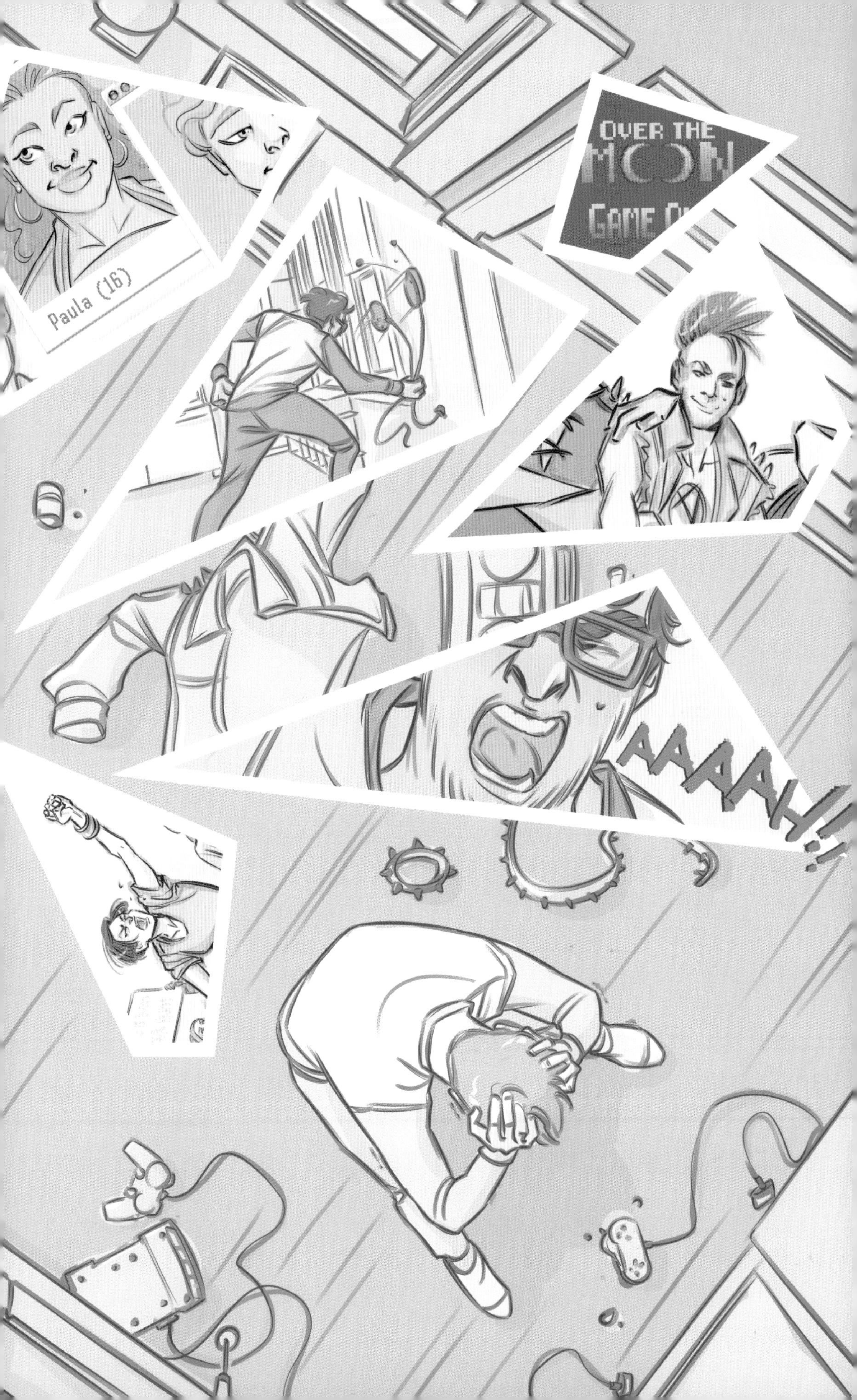
Paula (16)
OVER THE MOON
AAAAH!!

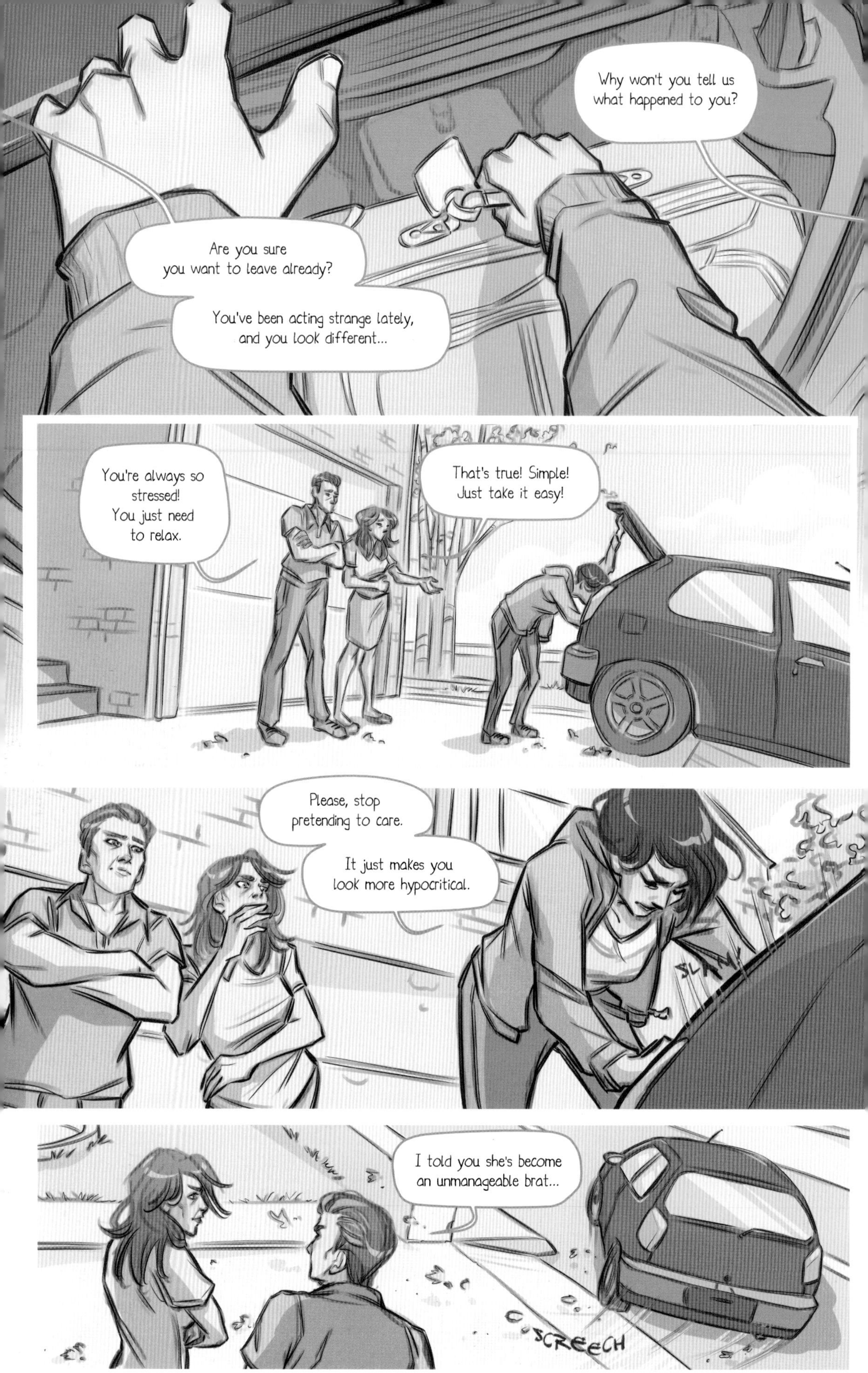
Why won't you tell us what happened to you?
Are you sure you want to leave already?
You've been acting strange lately, and you look different...
You're always so stressed! You just need to relax.
That's true! Simple! Just take it easy!
Please, stop pretending to care.
It just makes you look more hypocritical.
SLAM!
I told you she's become an unmanageable brat...
SCREECH

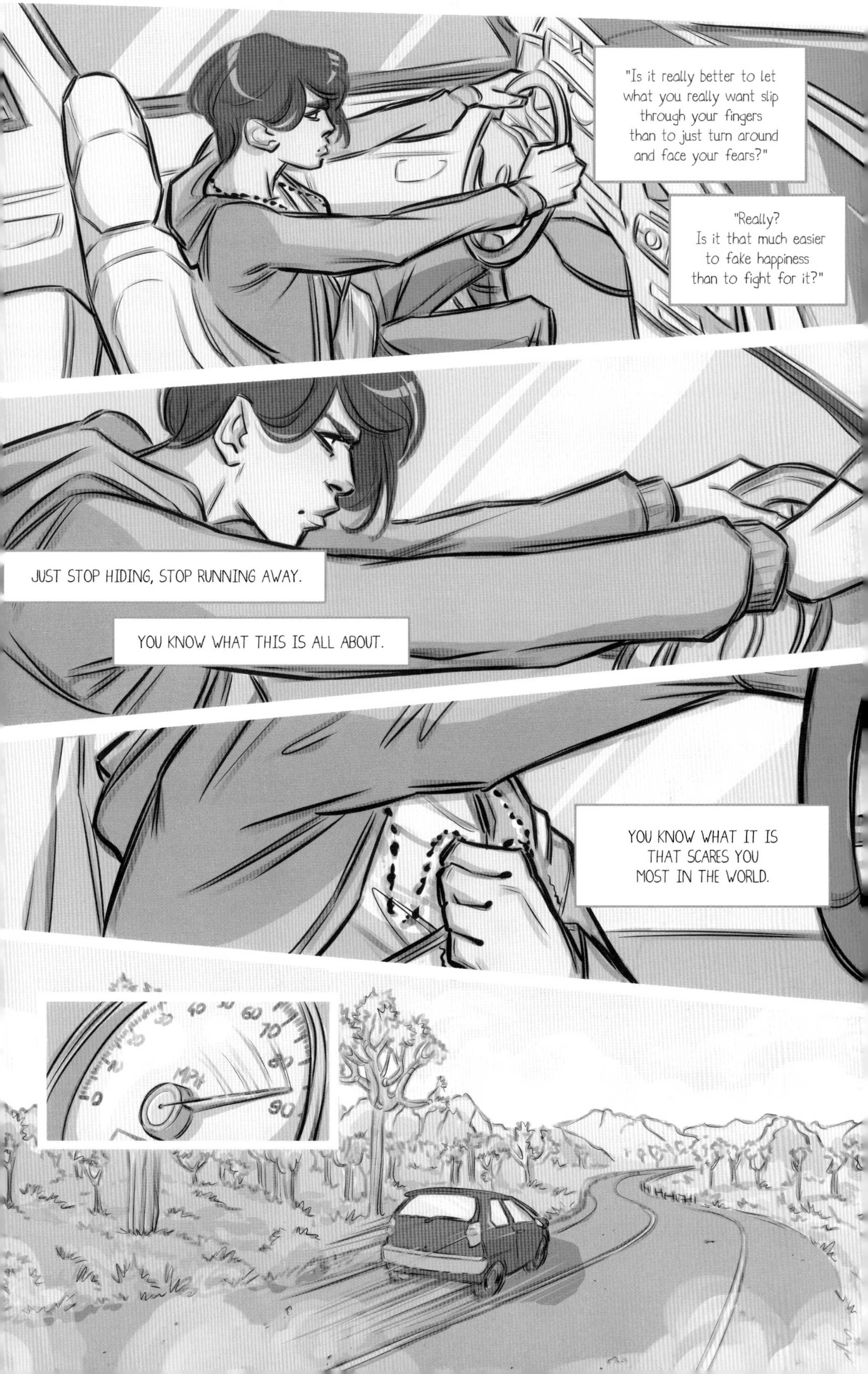
"Is it really better to let what you really want slip through your fingers than to just turn around and face your fears?"
"Really? Is it that much easier to fake happiness than to fight for it?"
JUST STOP HIDING, STOP RUNNING AWAY.
YOU KNOW WHAT THIS IS ALL ABOUT.
YOU KNOW WHAT IT IS THAT SCARES YOU MOST IN THE WORLD.
MPH

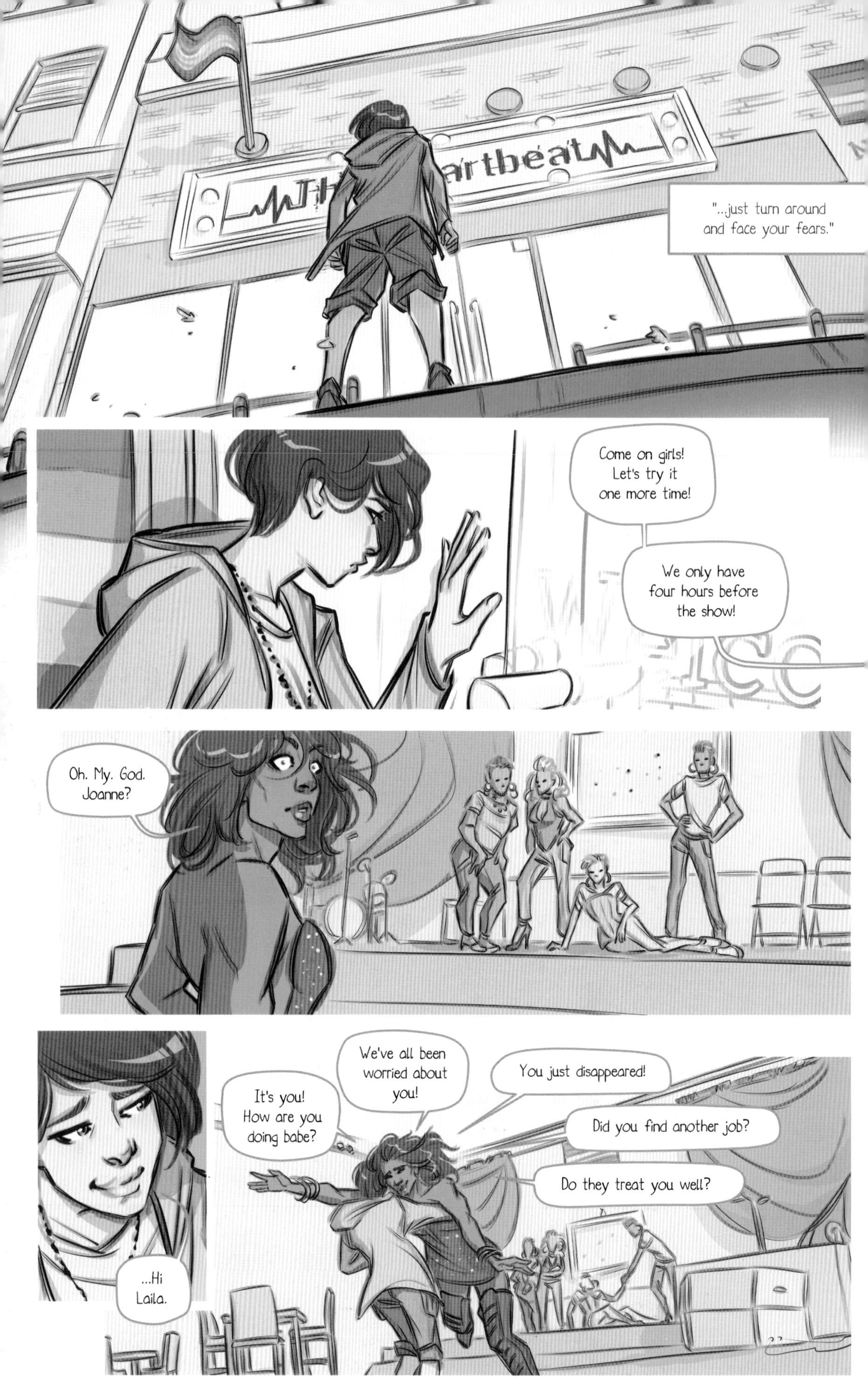

"...just turn around and face your fears."
Come on girls! Let's try it one more time!
We only have four hours before the show!
Oh. My. God. Joanne?
...Hi Laila.
It's you! How are you doing babe?
We've all been worried about you!
You just disappeared!
Did you find another job?
Do they treat you well?

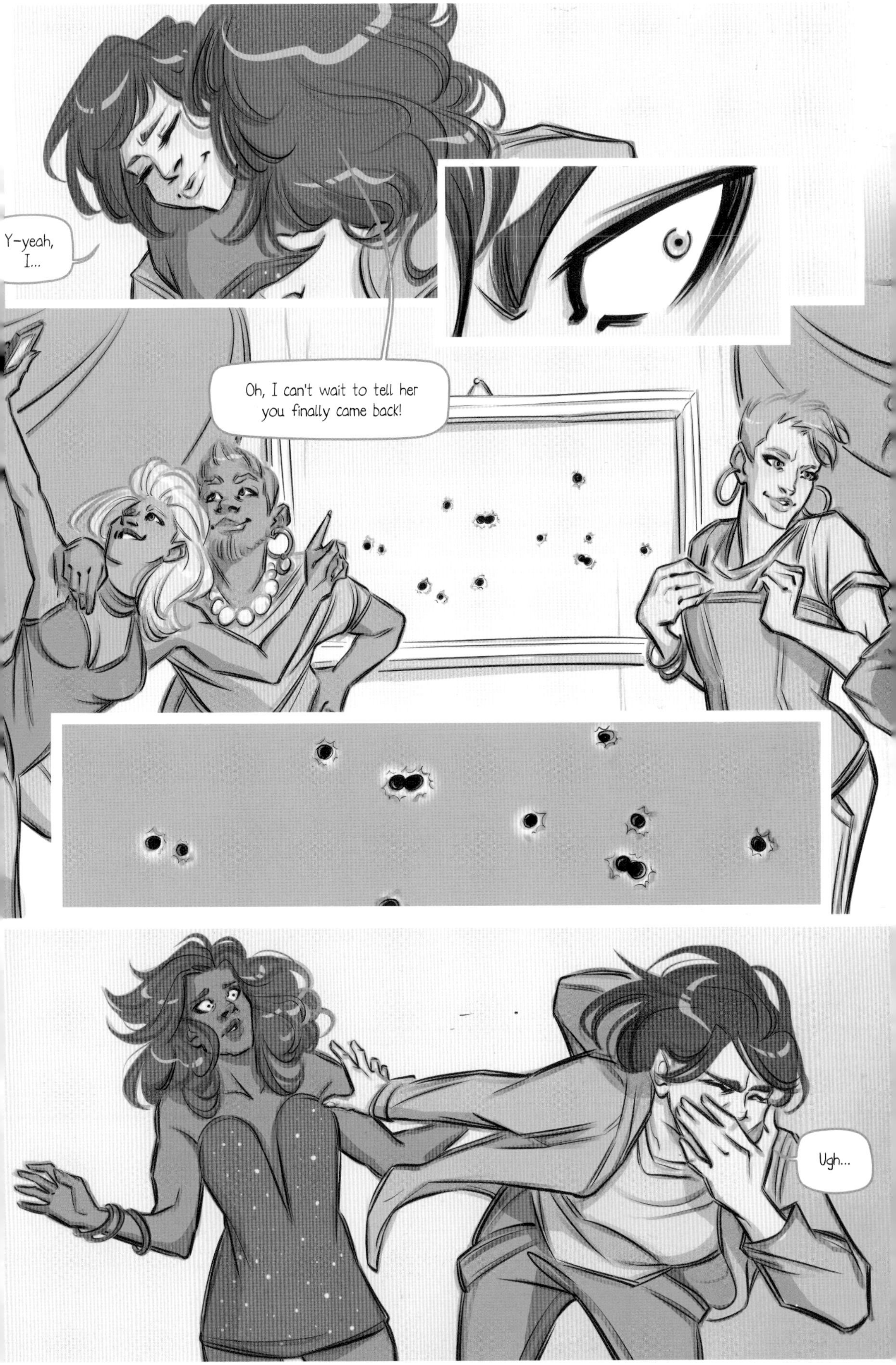
Y-yeah, I...
Oh, I can't wait to tell her you finally came back!
Ugh...

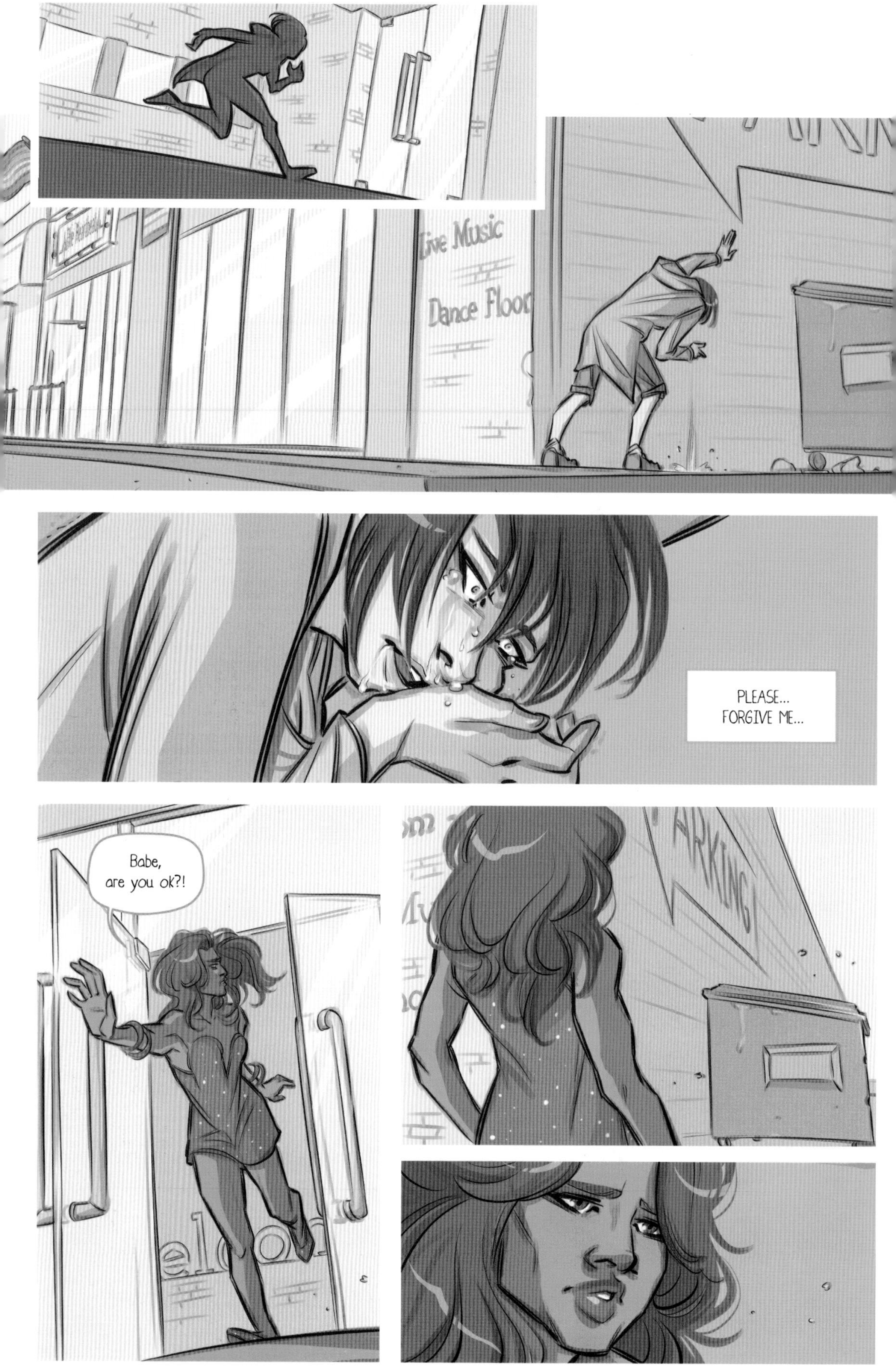
Live Music
Dance Floor
PLEASE...
FORGIVE ME...
Babe,
are you ok?!

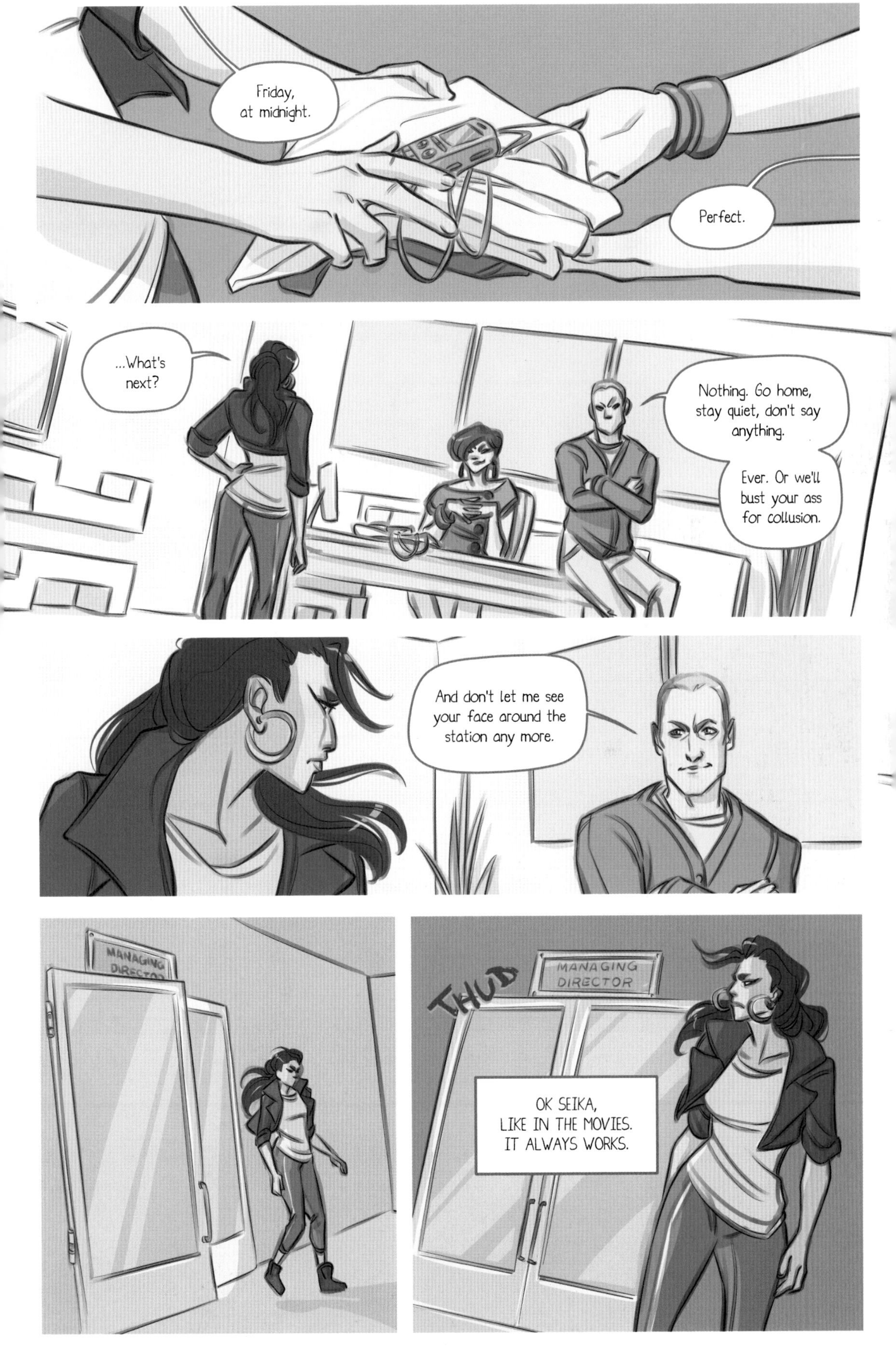
Friday, at midnight.
Perfect.
...What's next?
Nothing. Go home, stay quiet, don't say anything.
Ever. Or we'll bust your ass for collusion.
And don't let me see your face around the station any more.
MANAGING DIRECTOR
THUD
MANAGING DIRECTOR
OK SEIKA, LIKE IN THE MOVIES. IT ALWAYS WORKS.

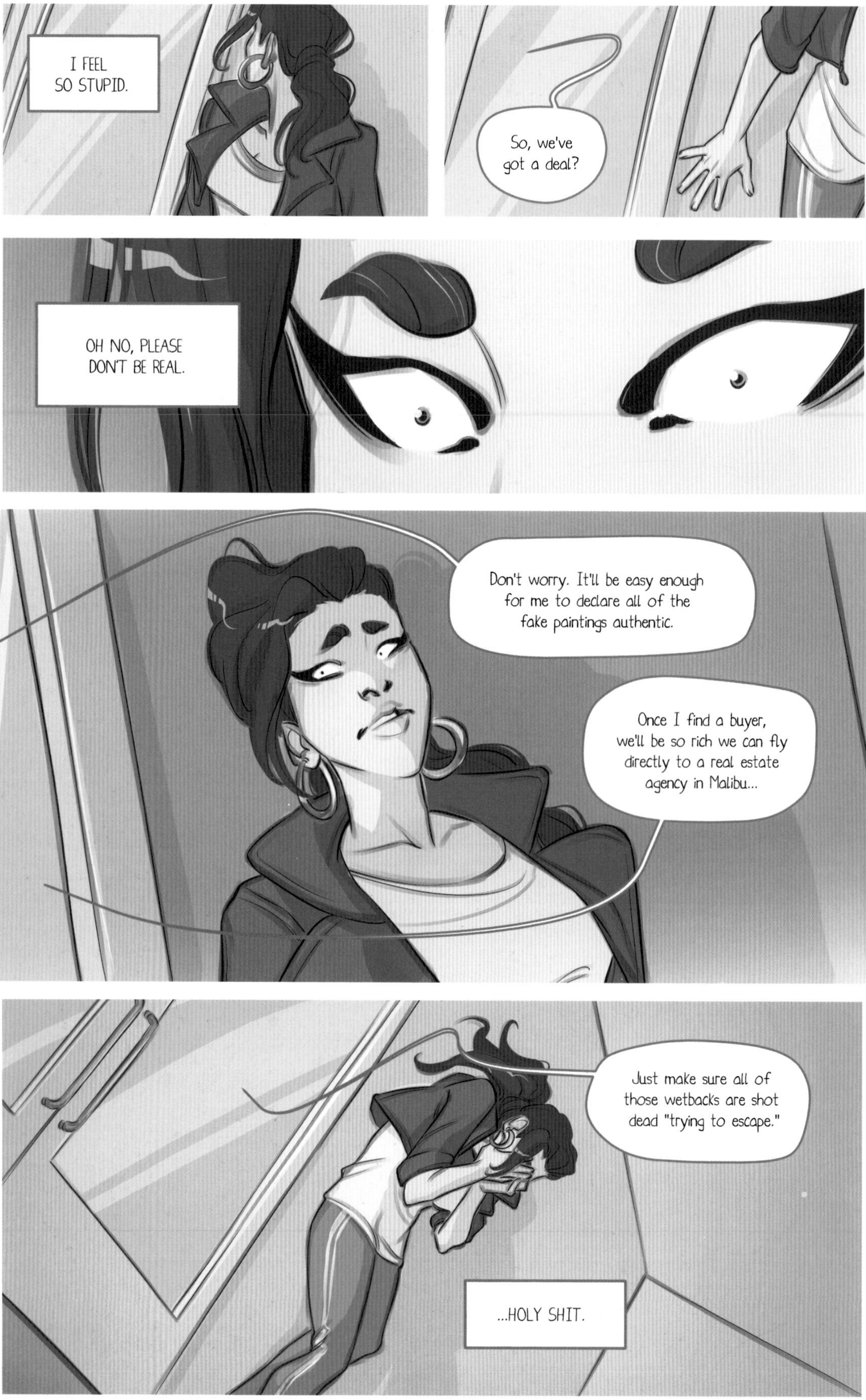
I FEEL SO STUPID.
So, we've got a deal?
OH NO, PLEASE DON'T BE REAL.
Don't worry. It'll be easy enough for me to declare all of the fake paintings authentic.
Once I find a buyer, we'll be so rich we can fly directly to a real estate agency in Malibu...
Just make sure all of those wetbacks are shot dead "trying to escape."
...HOLY SHIT.

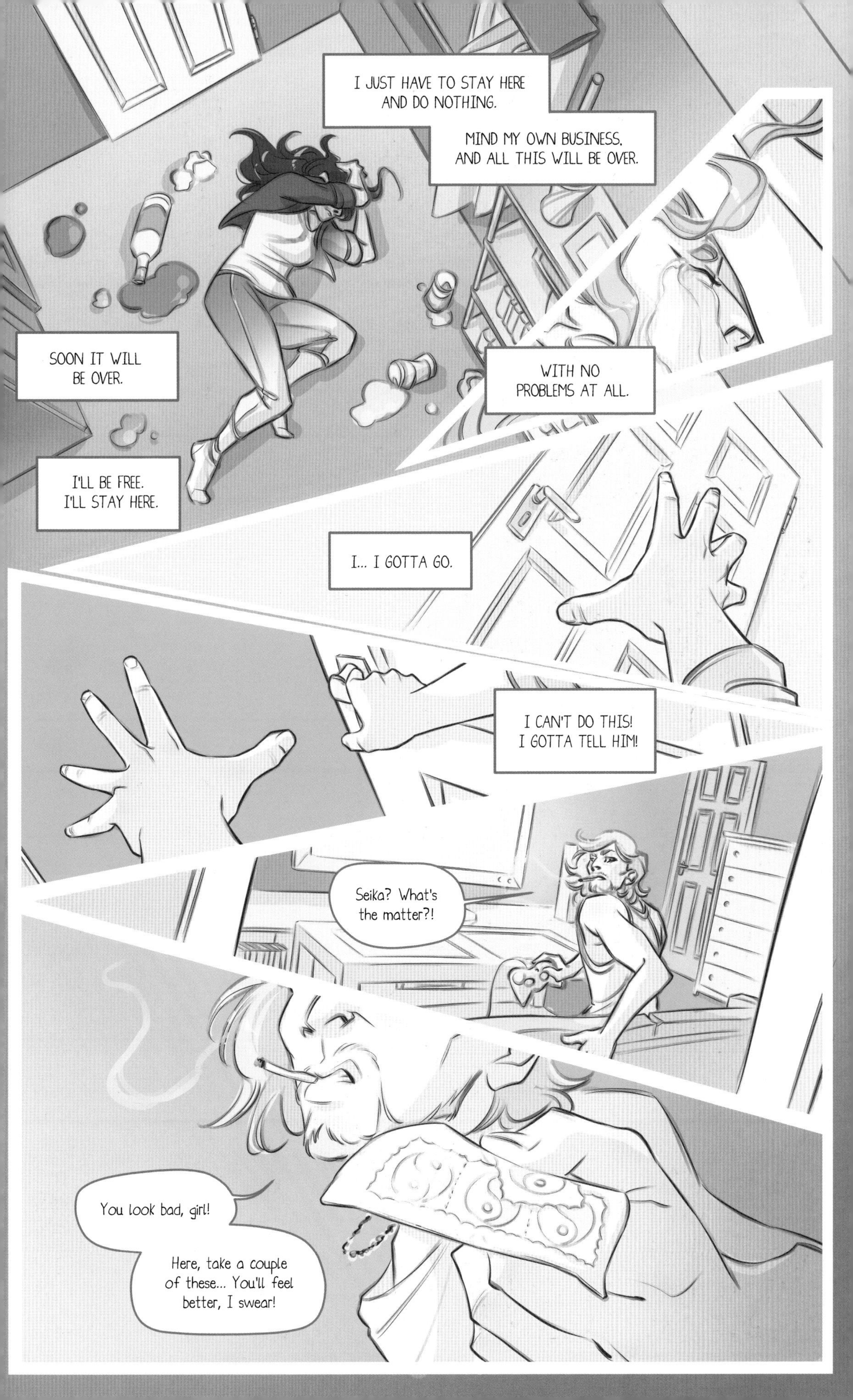
I JUST HAVE TO STAY HERE AND DO NOTHING.
MIND MY OWN BUSINESS, AND ALL THIS WILL BE OVER.
SOON IT WILL BE OVER.
WITH NO PROBLEMS AT ALL.
I'LL BE FREE. I'LL STAY HERE.
I... I GOTTA GO.
I CAN'T DO THIS! I GOTTA TELL HIM!
Seika? What's the matter?!
You look bad, girl!
Here, take a couple of these... You'll feel better, I swear!

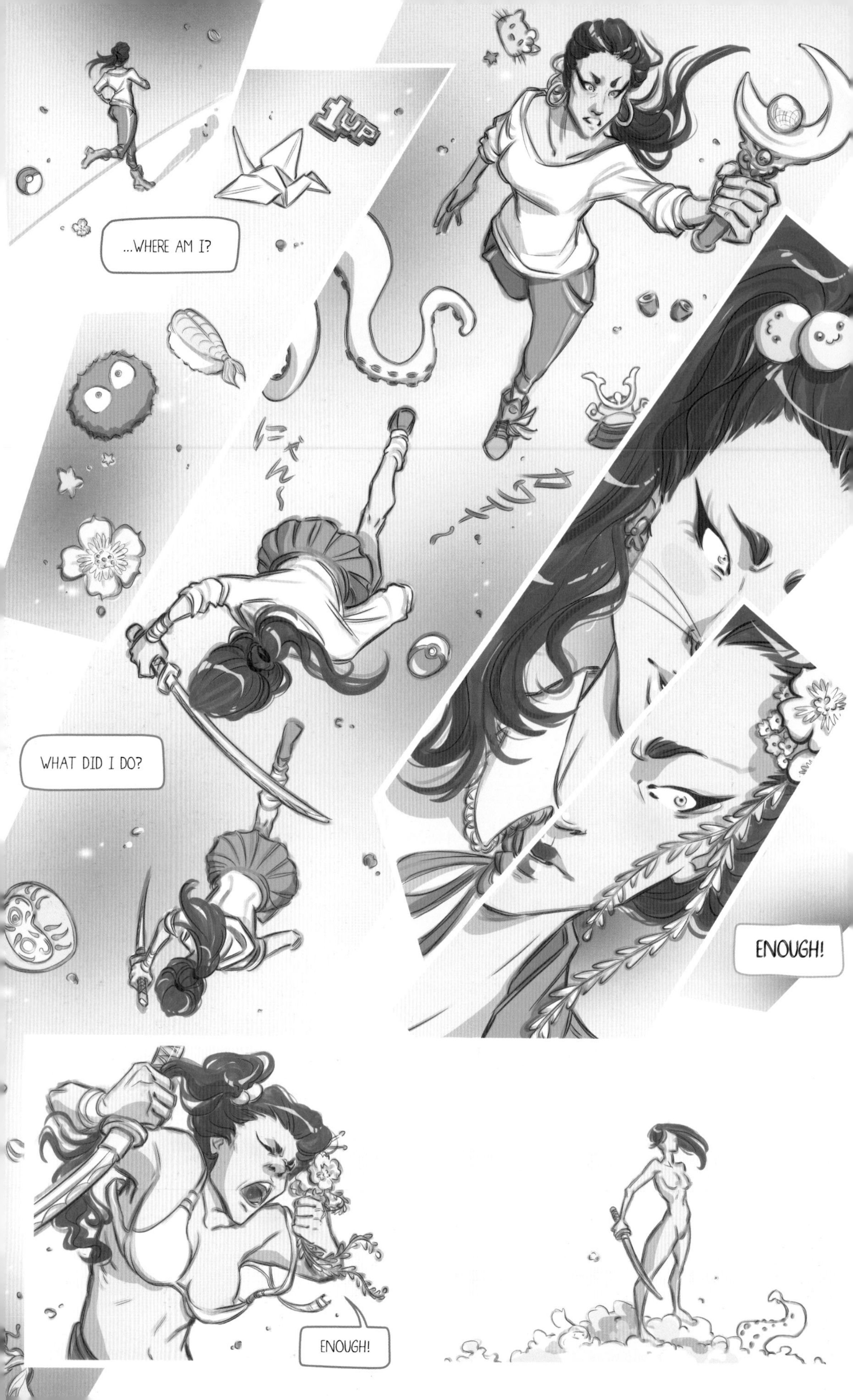
1UP
...WHERE AM I?
にゃん~
WHAT DID I DO?
ENOUGH!
ENOUGH!

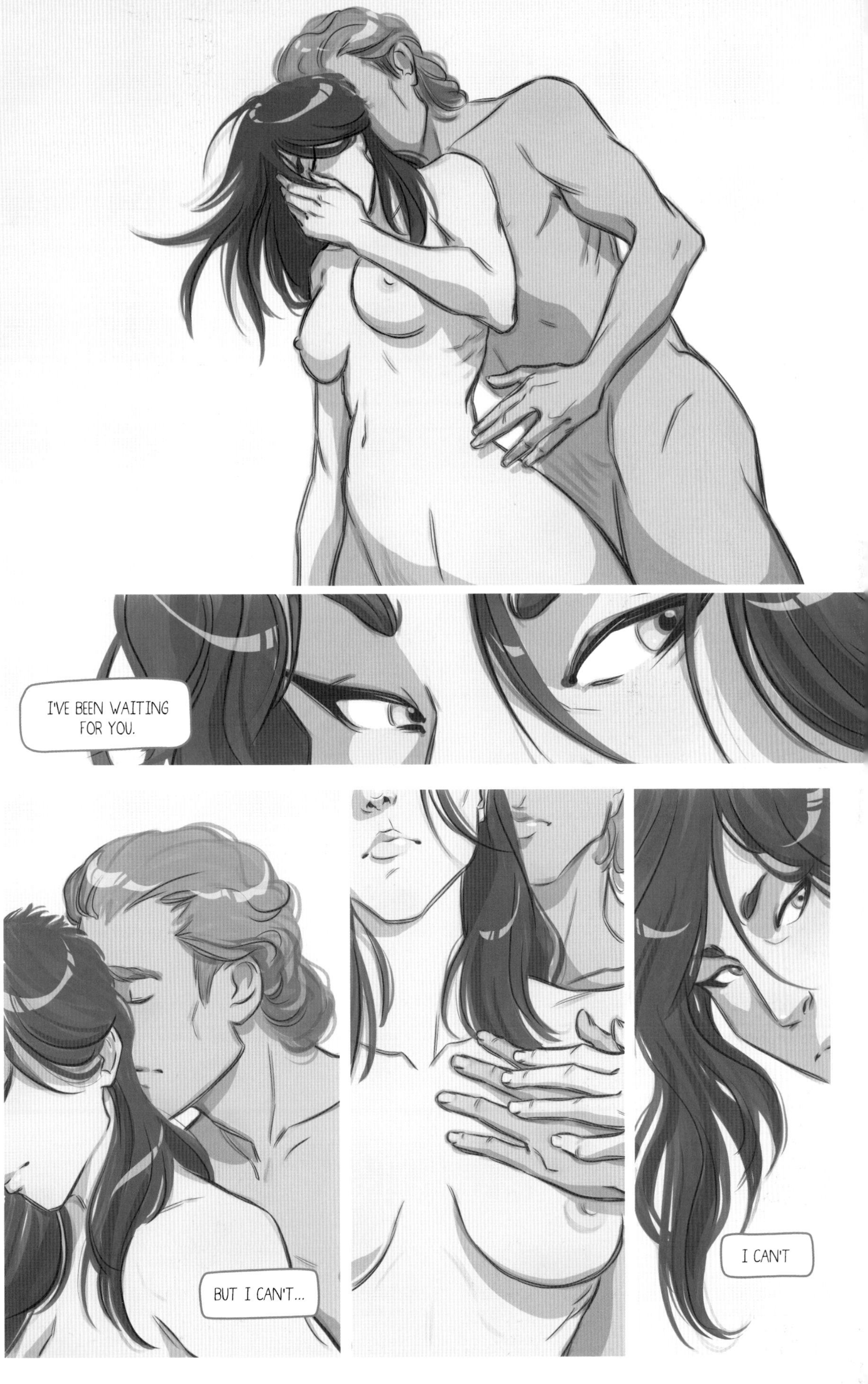
I'VE BEEN WAITING FOR YOU.
BUT I CAN'T...
I CAN'T

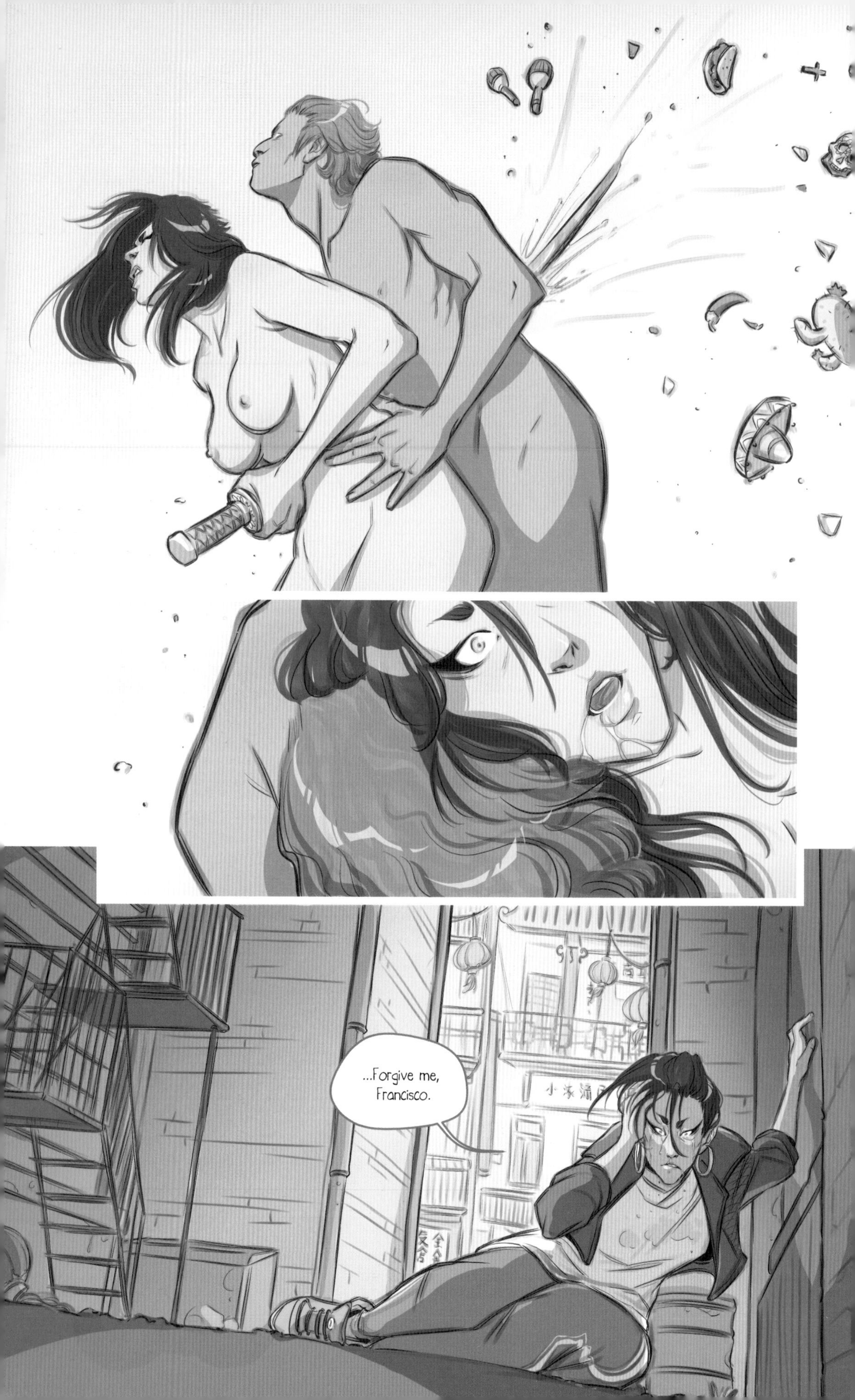
...Forgive me, Francisco.

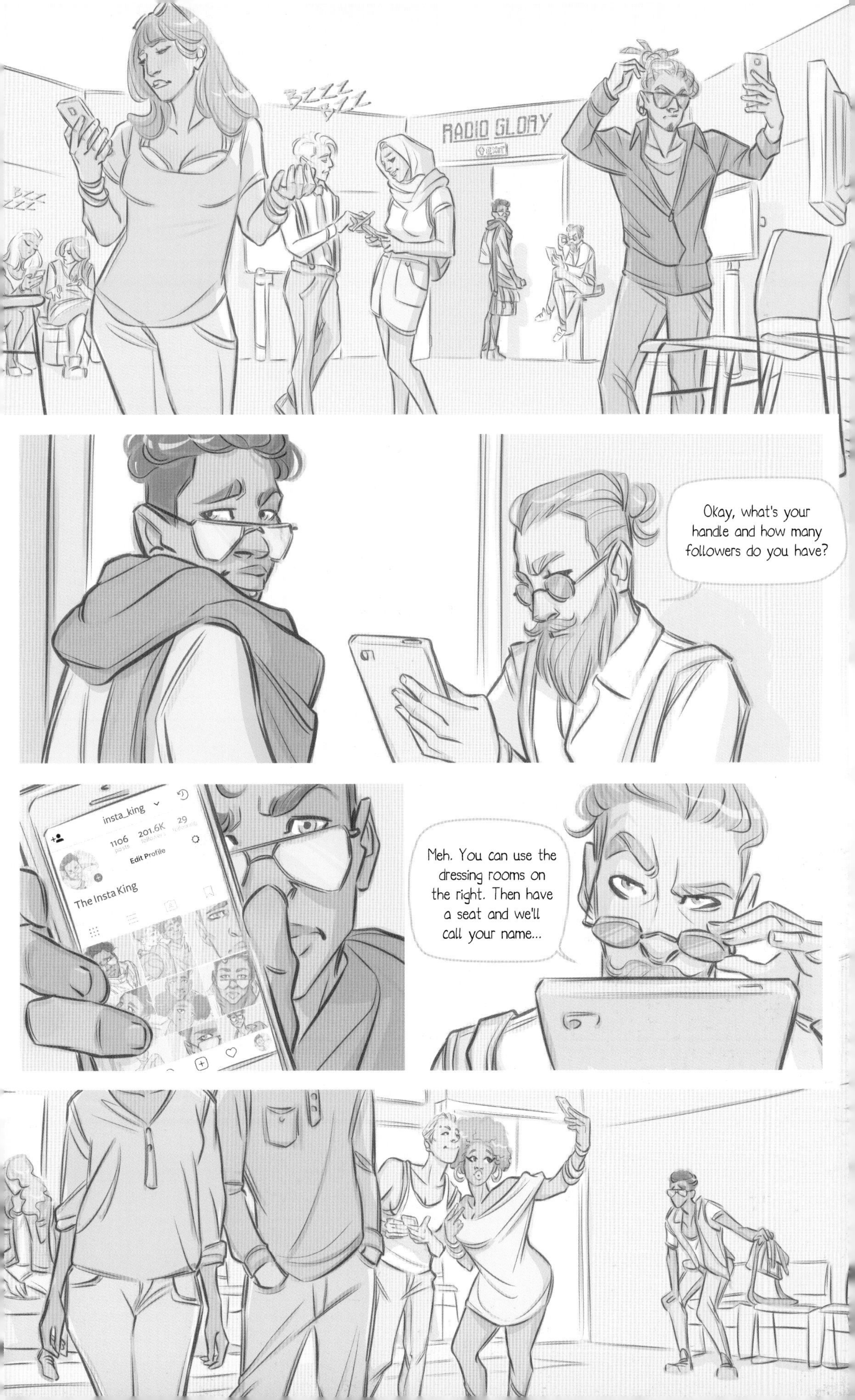
RADIO GLORY
EXIT
Okay, what's your handle and how many followers do you have?
insta_king
1106
201.6K
29
Edit Profile
The Insta King
Meh. You can use the dressing rooms on the right. Then have a seat and we'll call your name...

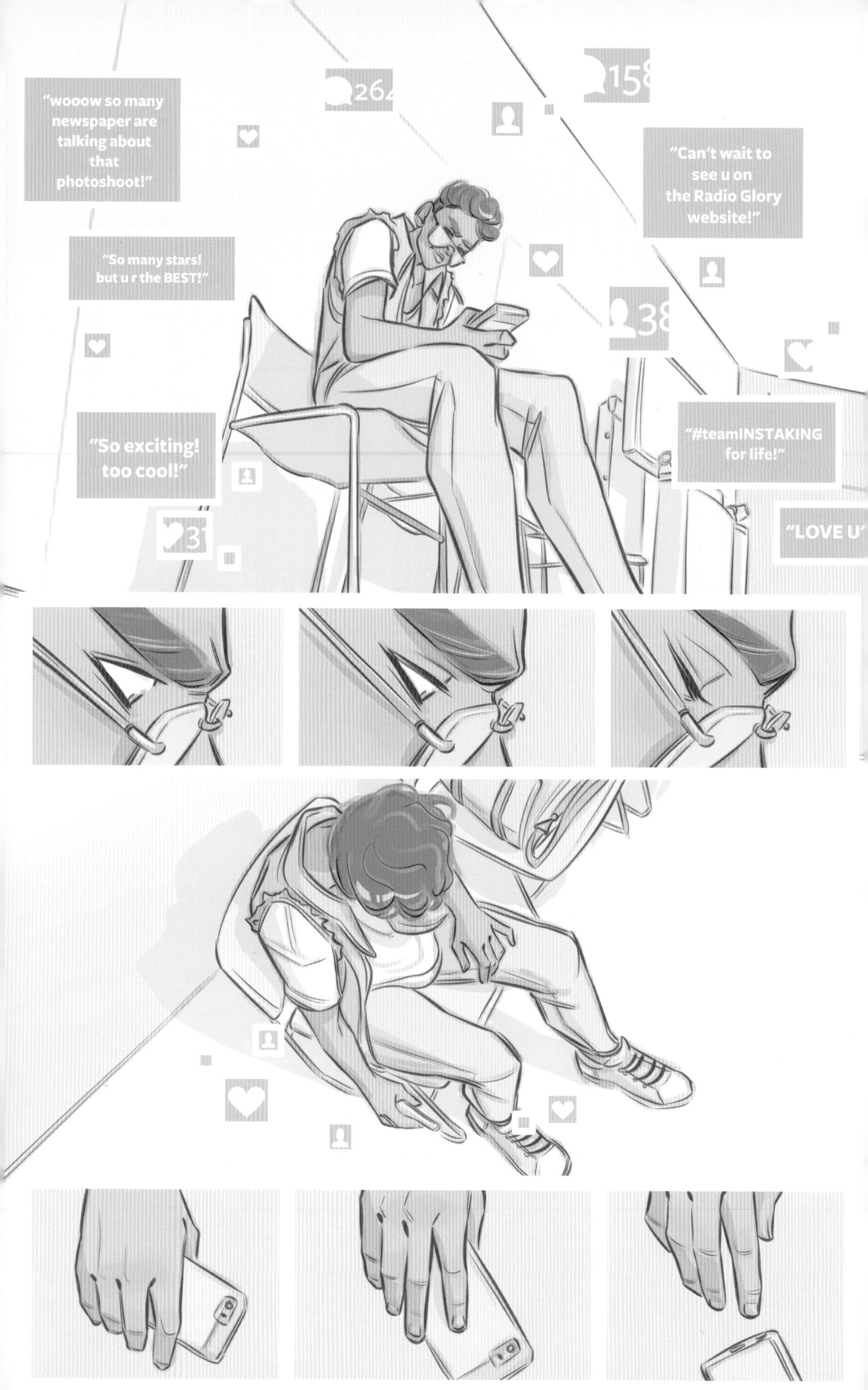

"wooow so many newspaper are talking about that photoshoot!"
264
158
"Can't wait to see u on the Radio Glory website!"
"So many stars! but u r the BEST!"
38
"So exciting! too cool!"
"#teamINSTAKING for life!"
31
"LOVE U"

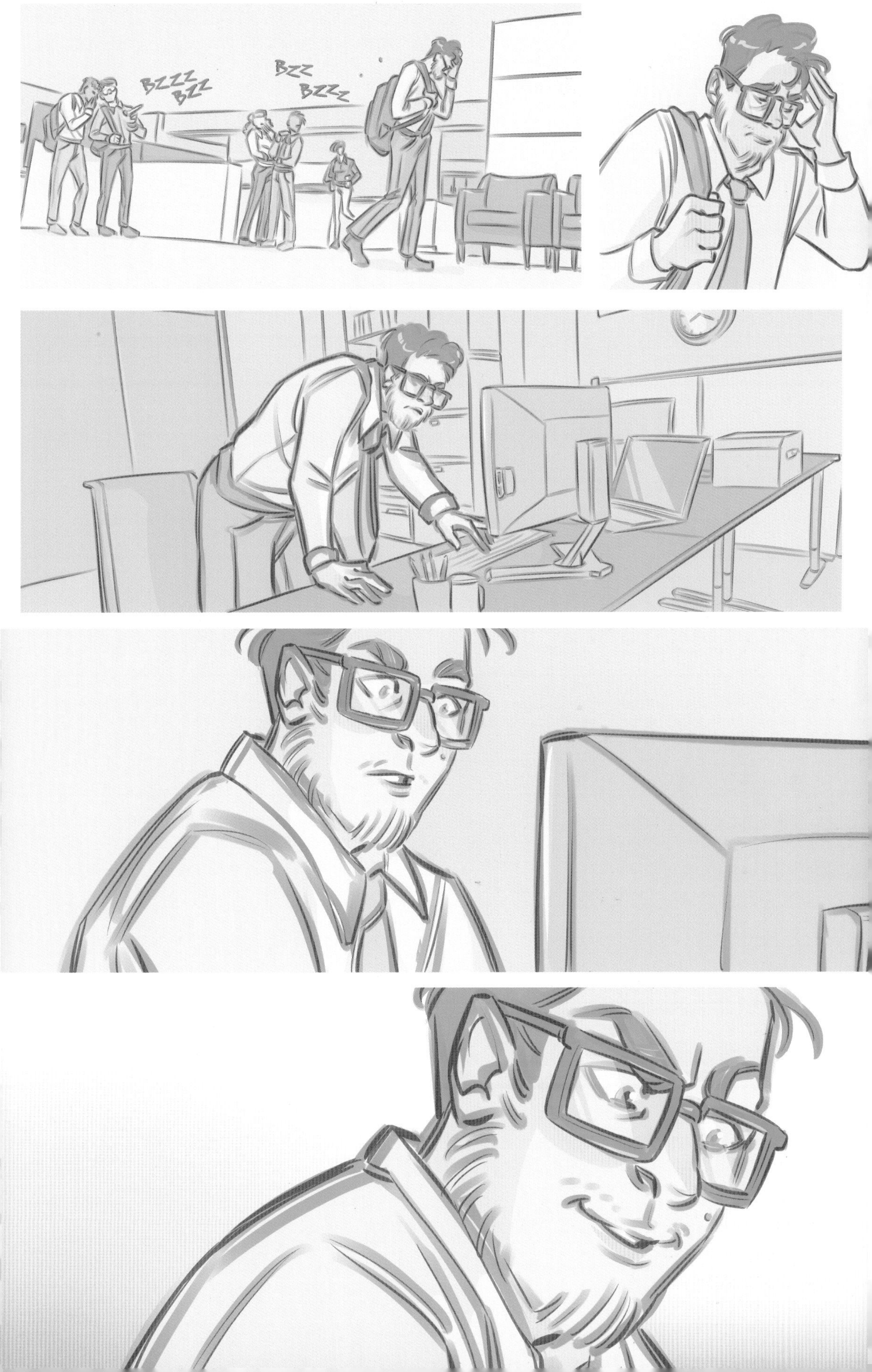
BZZZ
BZZ
BZZ
BZZZ

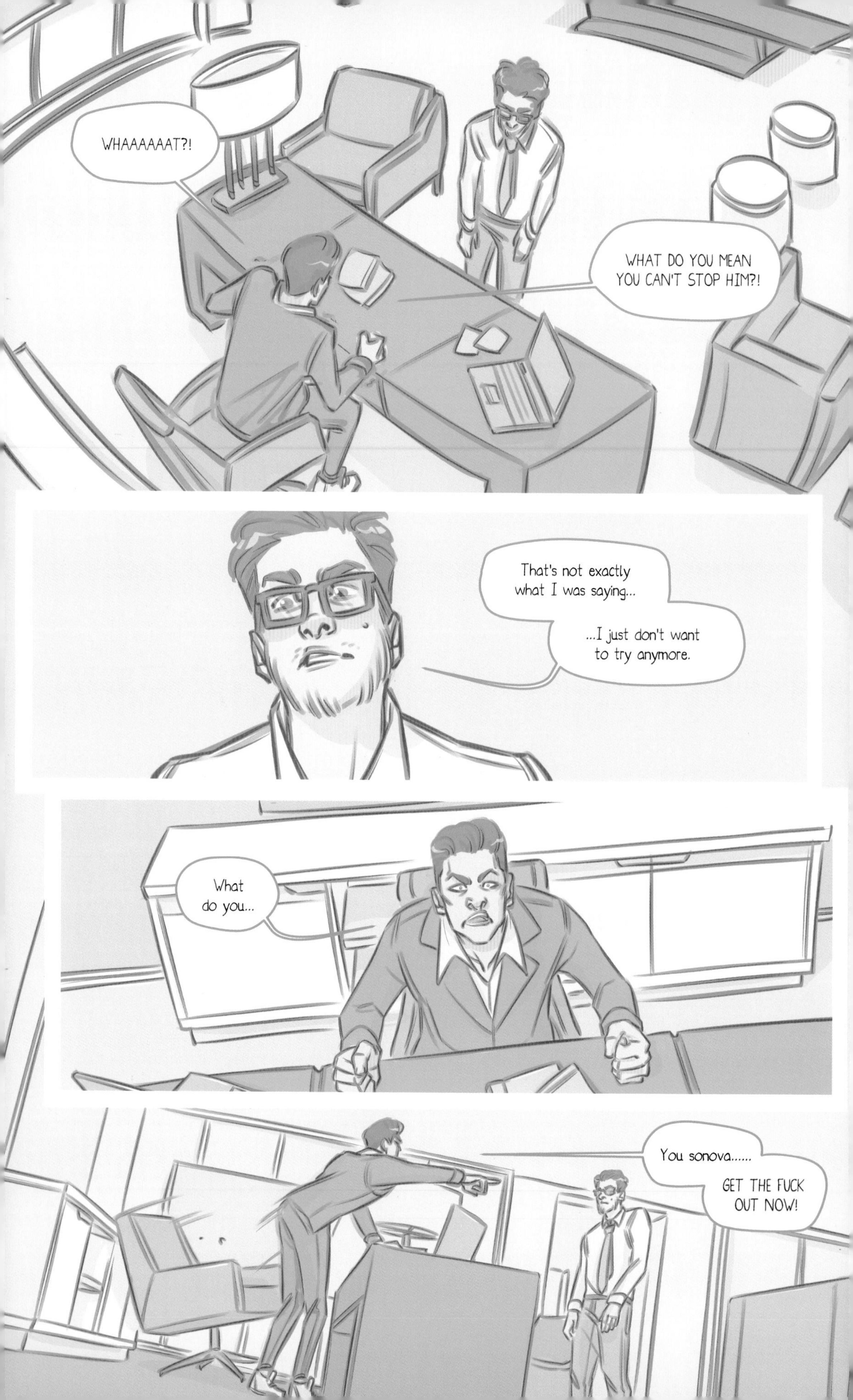
WHAAAAAAT?!
WHAT DO YOU MEAN YOU CAN'T STOP HIM?!
That's not exactly what I was saying...
...I just don't want to try anymore.
What do you...
You sonova......
GET THE FUCK OUT NOW!

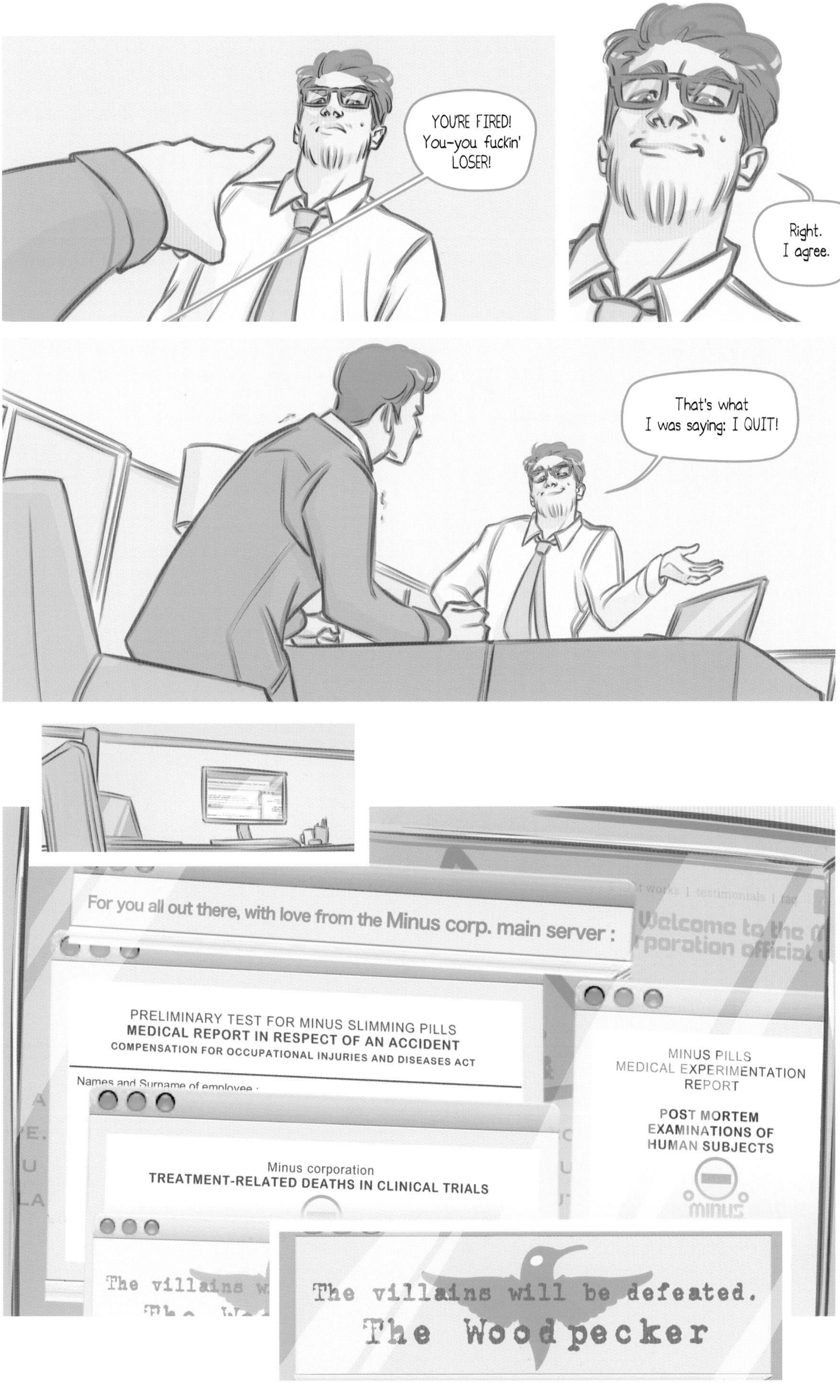
YOU'RE FIRED! You-you fuckin' LOSER!
Right. I agree.
That's what I was saying: I QUIT!
For you all out there, with love from the Minus corp. main server :
PRELIMINARY TEST FOR MINUS SLIMMING PILLS
MEDICAL REPORT IN RESPECT OF AN ACCIDENT
COMPENSATION FOR OCCUPATIONAL INJURIES AND DISEASES ACT
MINUS PILLS
MEDICAL EXPERIMENTATION REPORT
POST MORTEM EXAMINATIONS OF HUMAN SUBJECTS
minus
Minus corporation
TREATMENT-RELATED DEATHS IN CLINICAL TRIALS
The villains will be defeated.
The Woodpecker

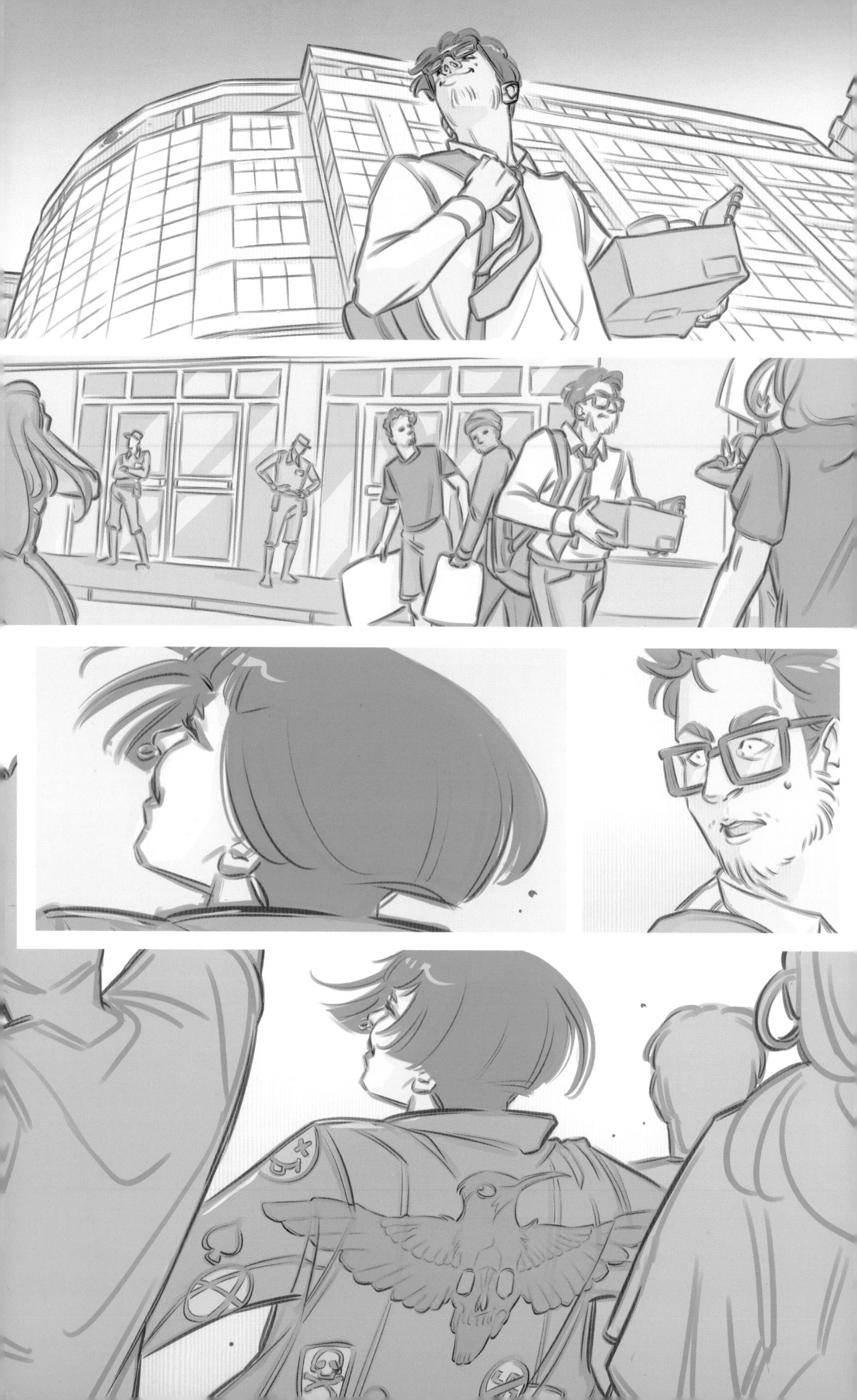

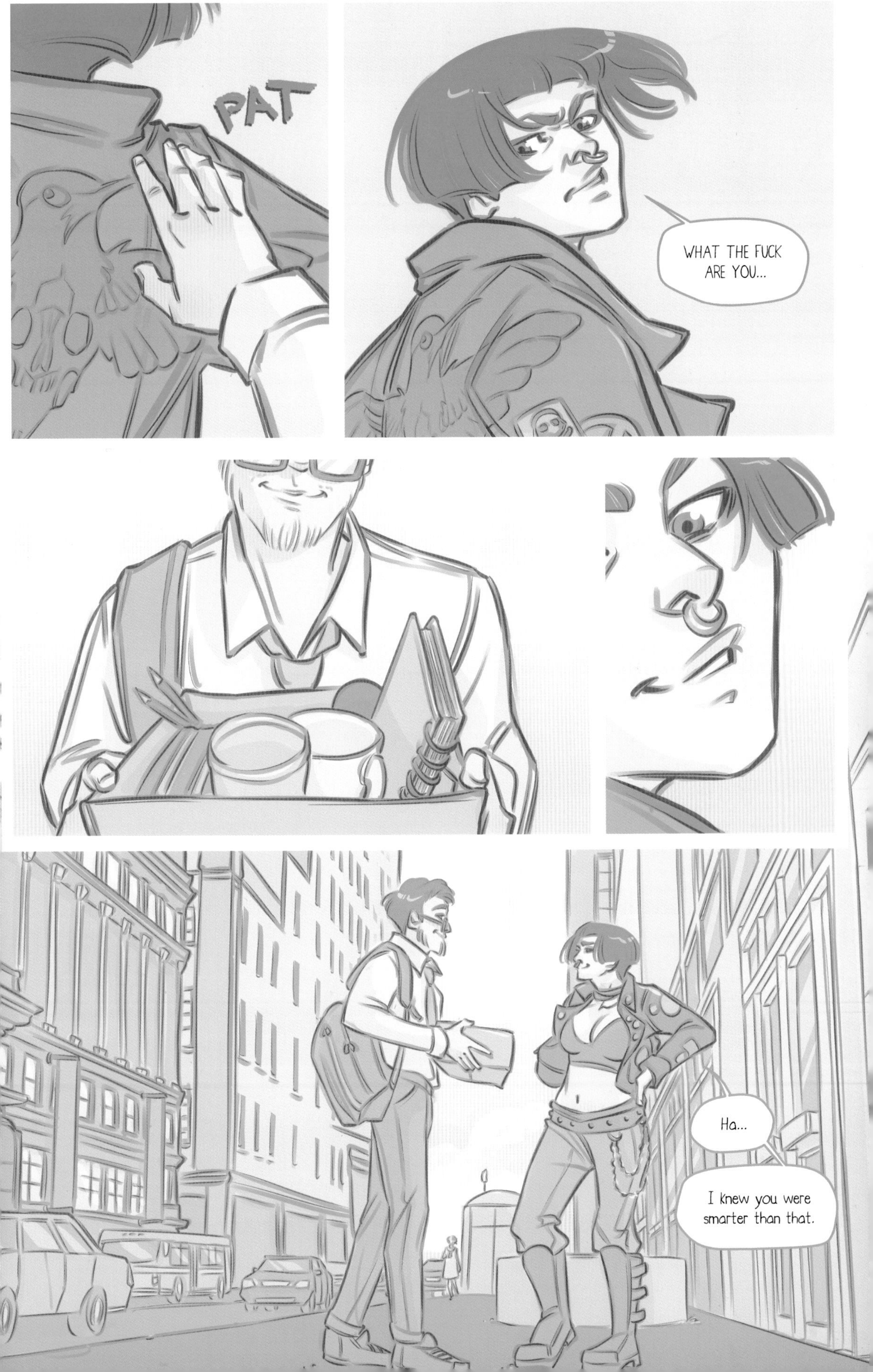
PAT
WHAT THE FUCK ARE YOU...
Ha...
I knew you were smarter than that.

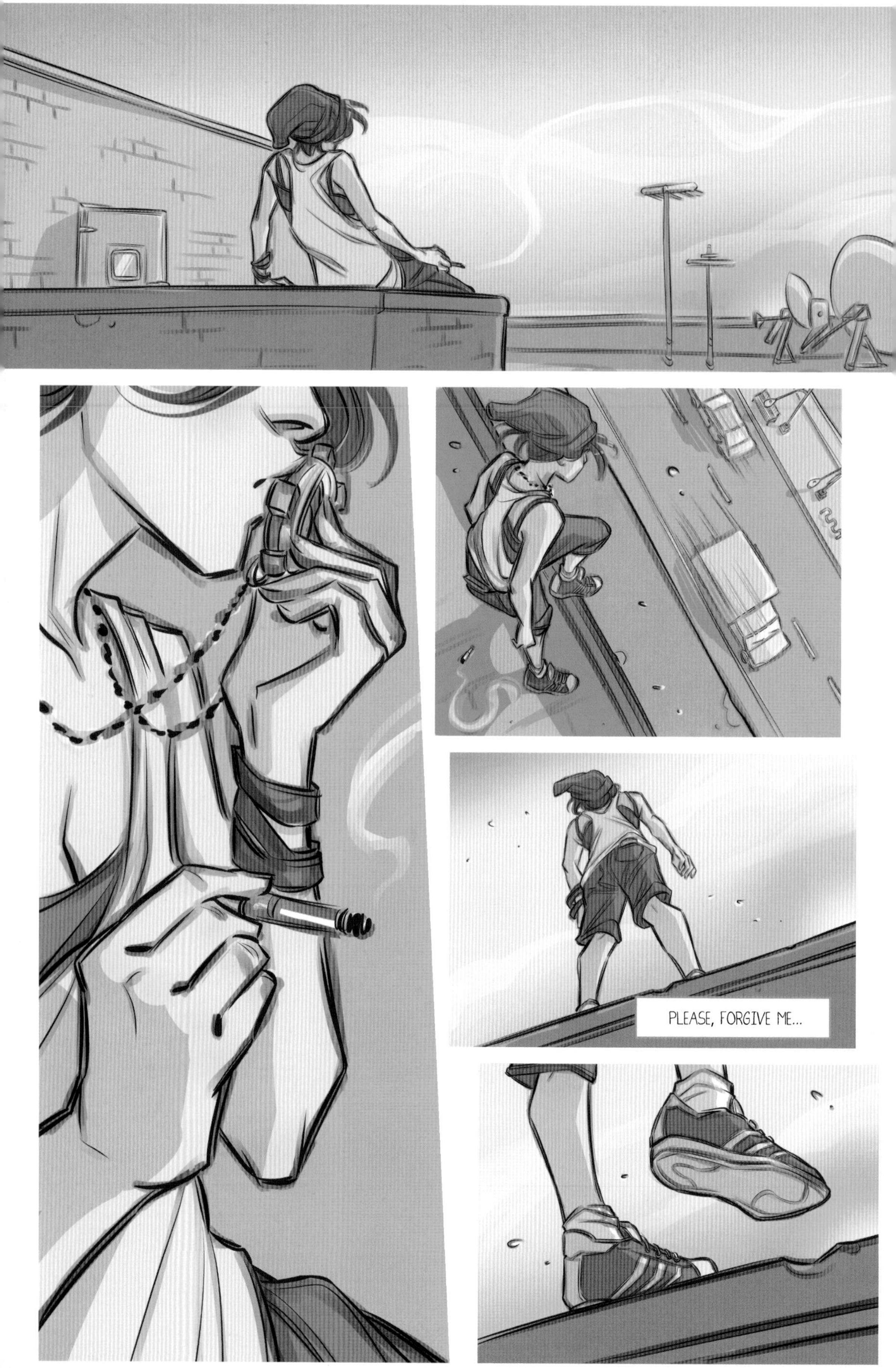
PLEASE, FORGIVE ME...

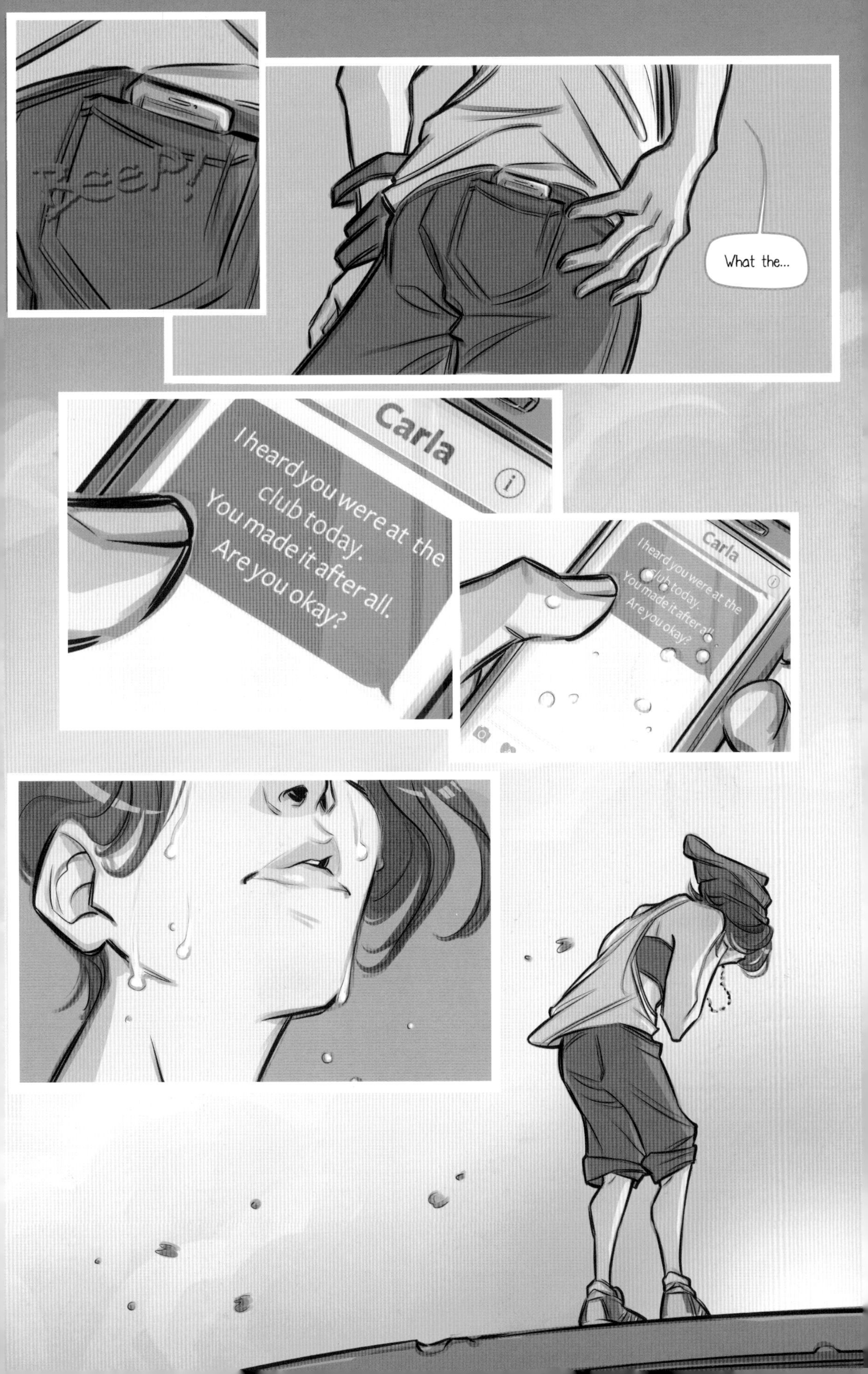
BEEP!
What the...
Carla
I heard you were at the club today. You made it after all. Are you okay?
Carla
I heard you were at the club today. You made it after all. Are you okay?

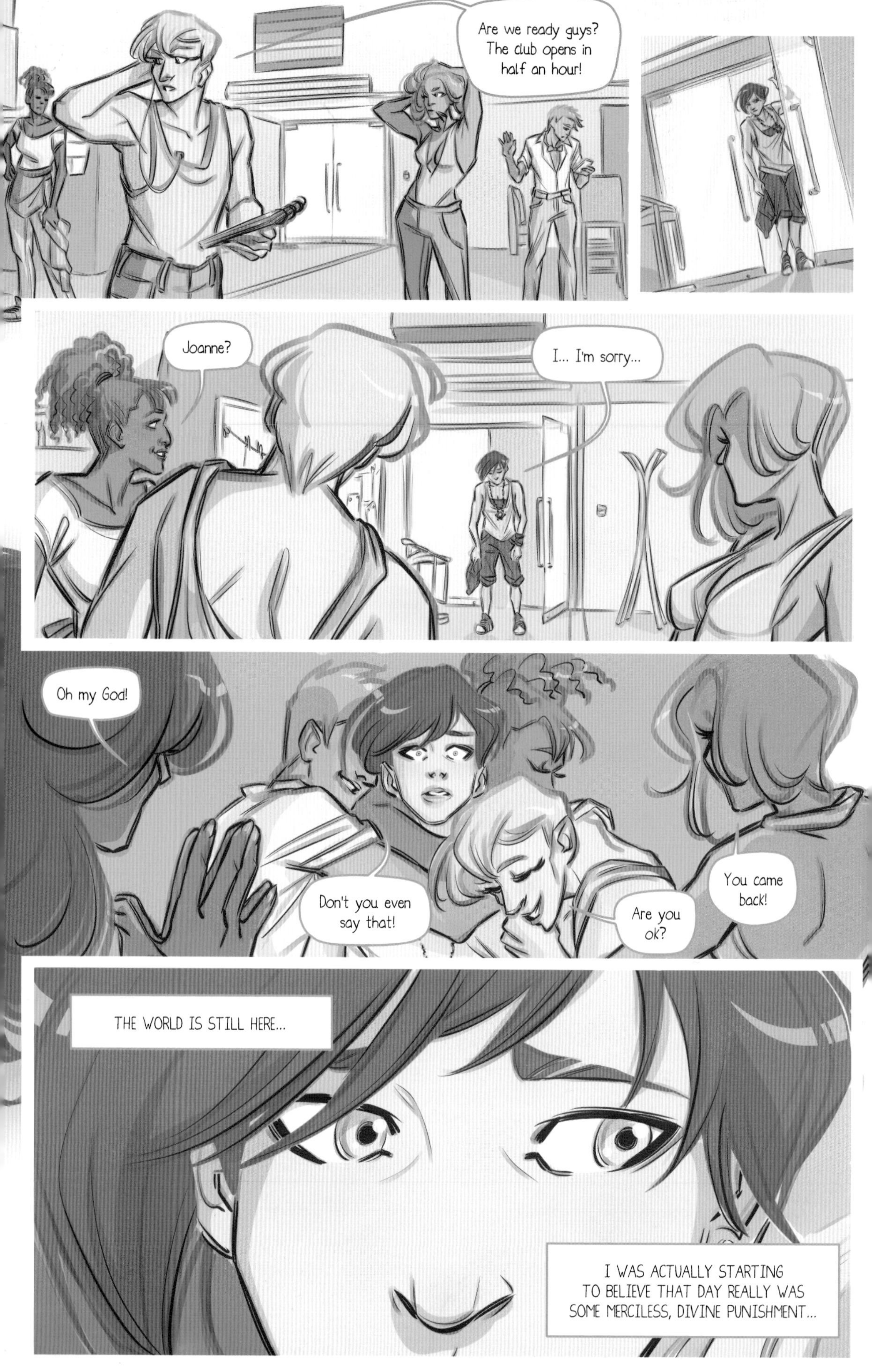
Are we ready guys? The club opens in half an hour!
Joanne?
I... I'm sorry...
Oh my God!
Don't you even say that!
Are you ok?
You came back!
THE WORLD IS STILL HERE...
I WAS ACTUALLY STARTING TO BELIEVE THAT DAY REALLY WAS SOME MERCILESS, DIVINE PUNISHMENT...

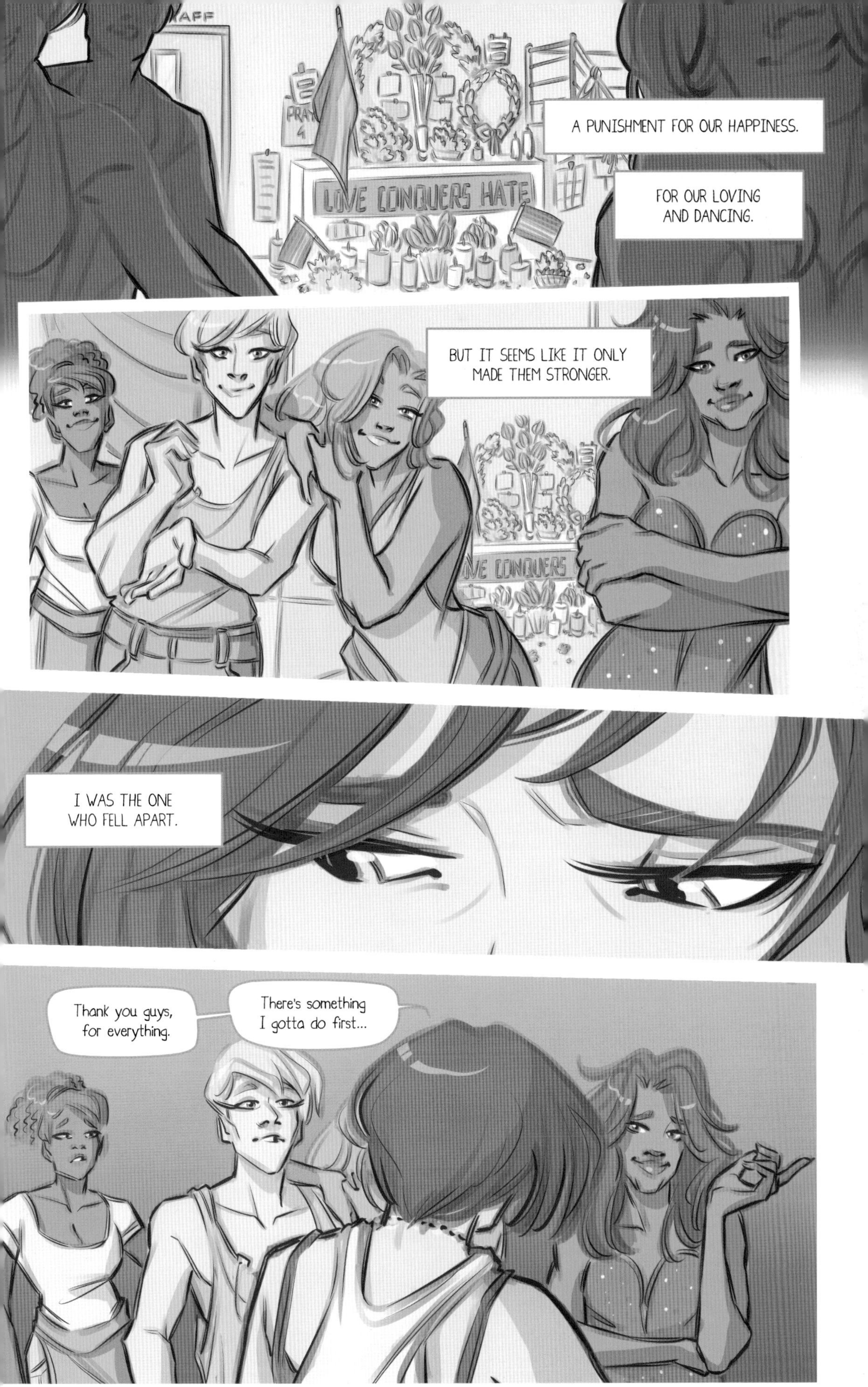

LOVE CONQUERS HATE
A PUNISHMENT FOR OUR HAPPINESS.
FOR OUR LOVING AND DANCING.
BUT IT SEEMS LIKE IT ONLY MADE THEM STRONGER.
I WAS THE ONE WHO FELL APART.
Thank you guys, for everything.
There's something I gotta do first...

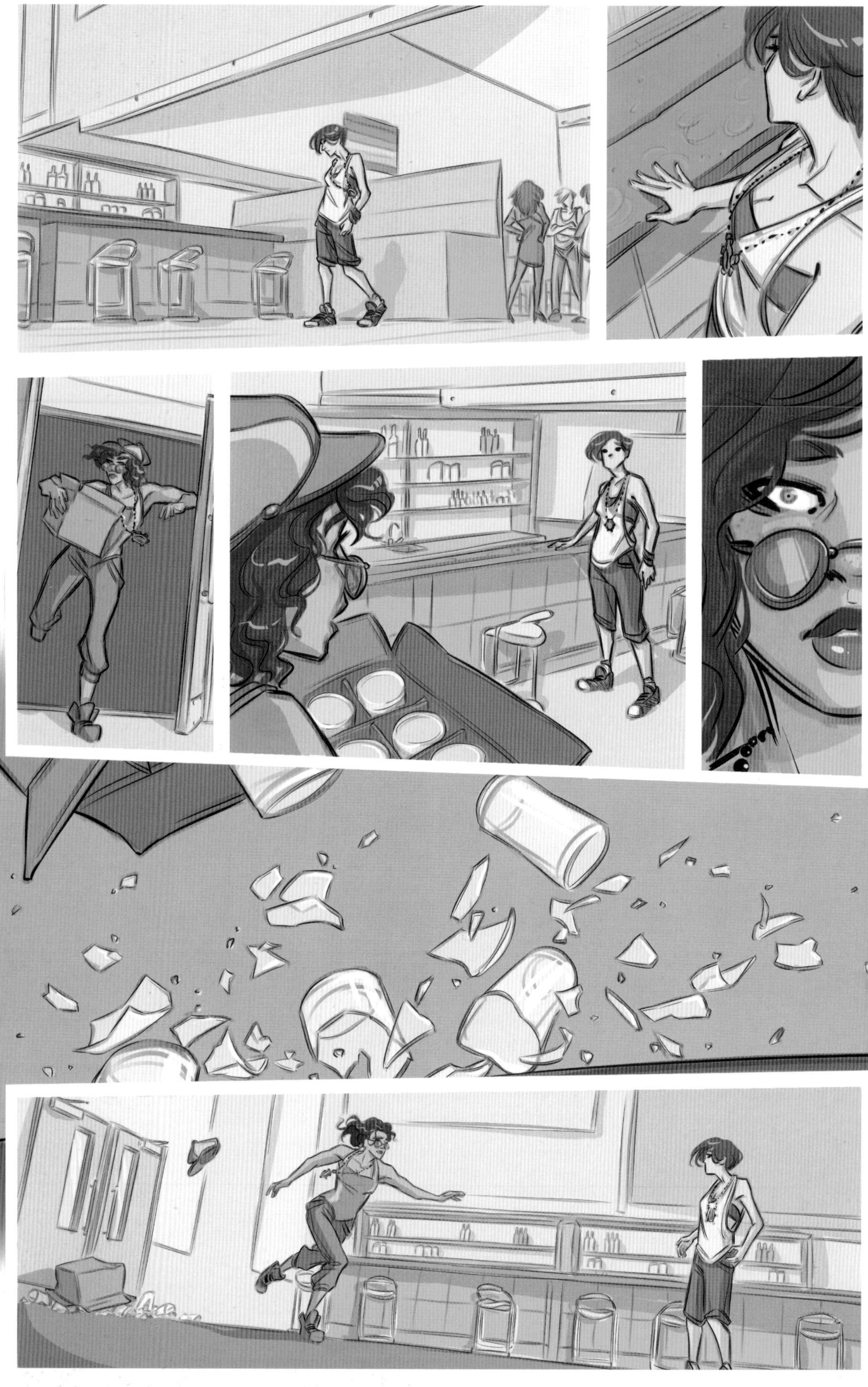

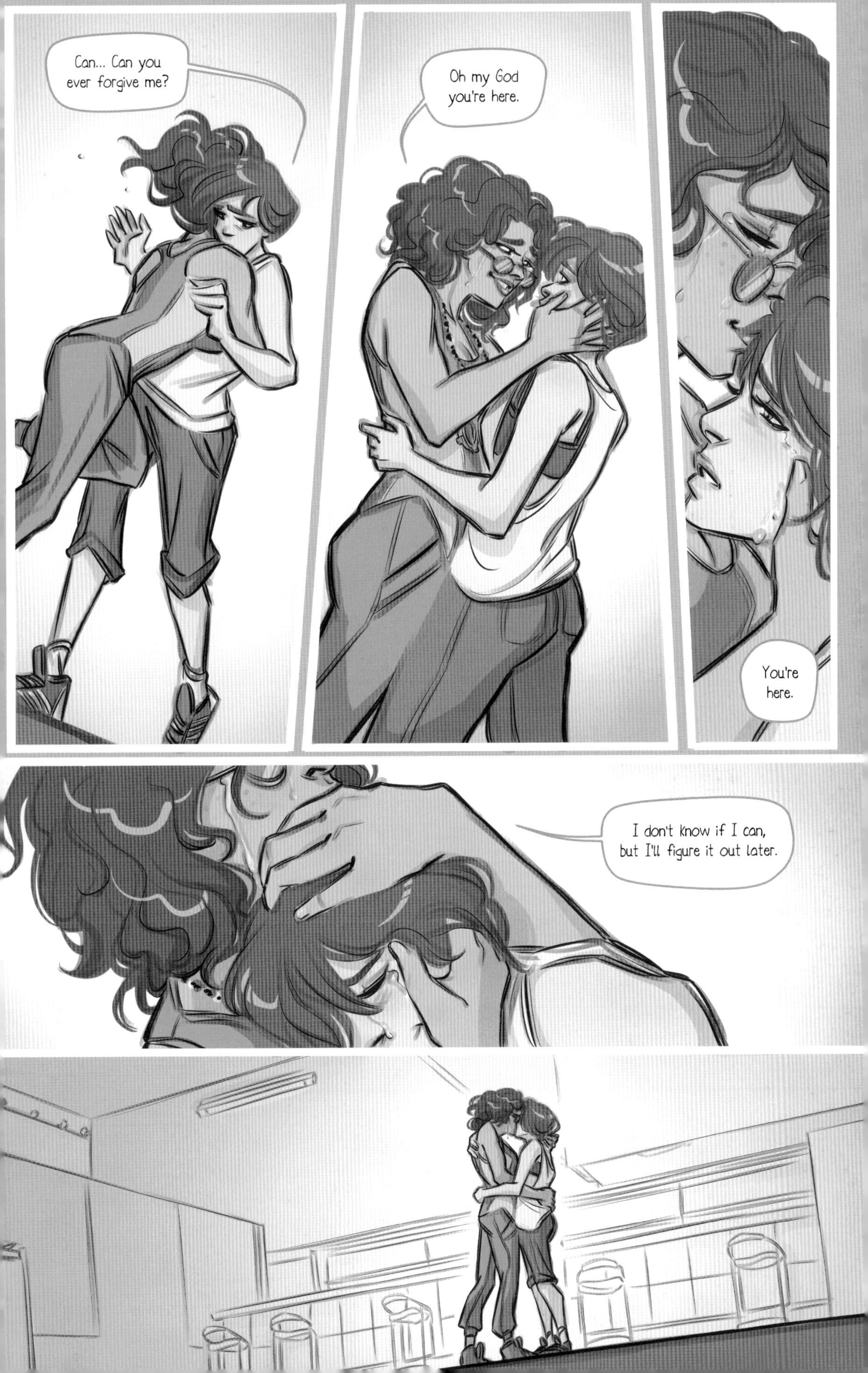
Can... Can you ever forgive me?
Oh my God you're here.
You're here.
I don't know if I can, but I'll figure it out later.

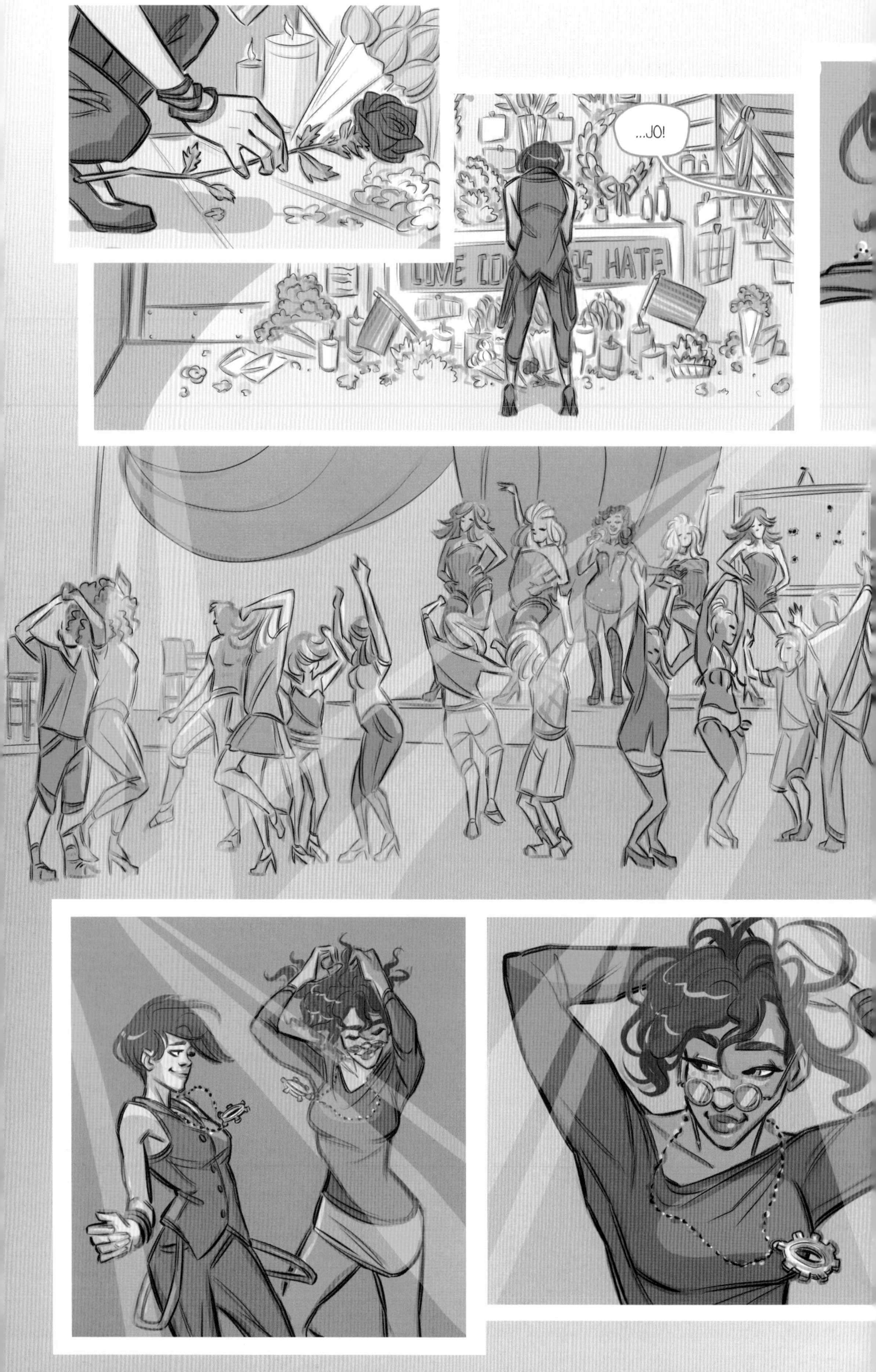

...JO!
LOVE CO RS HATE

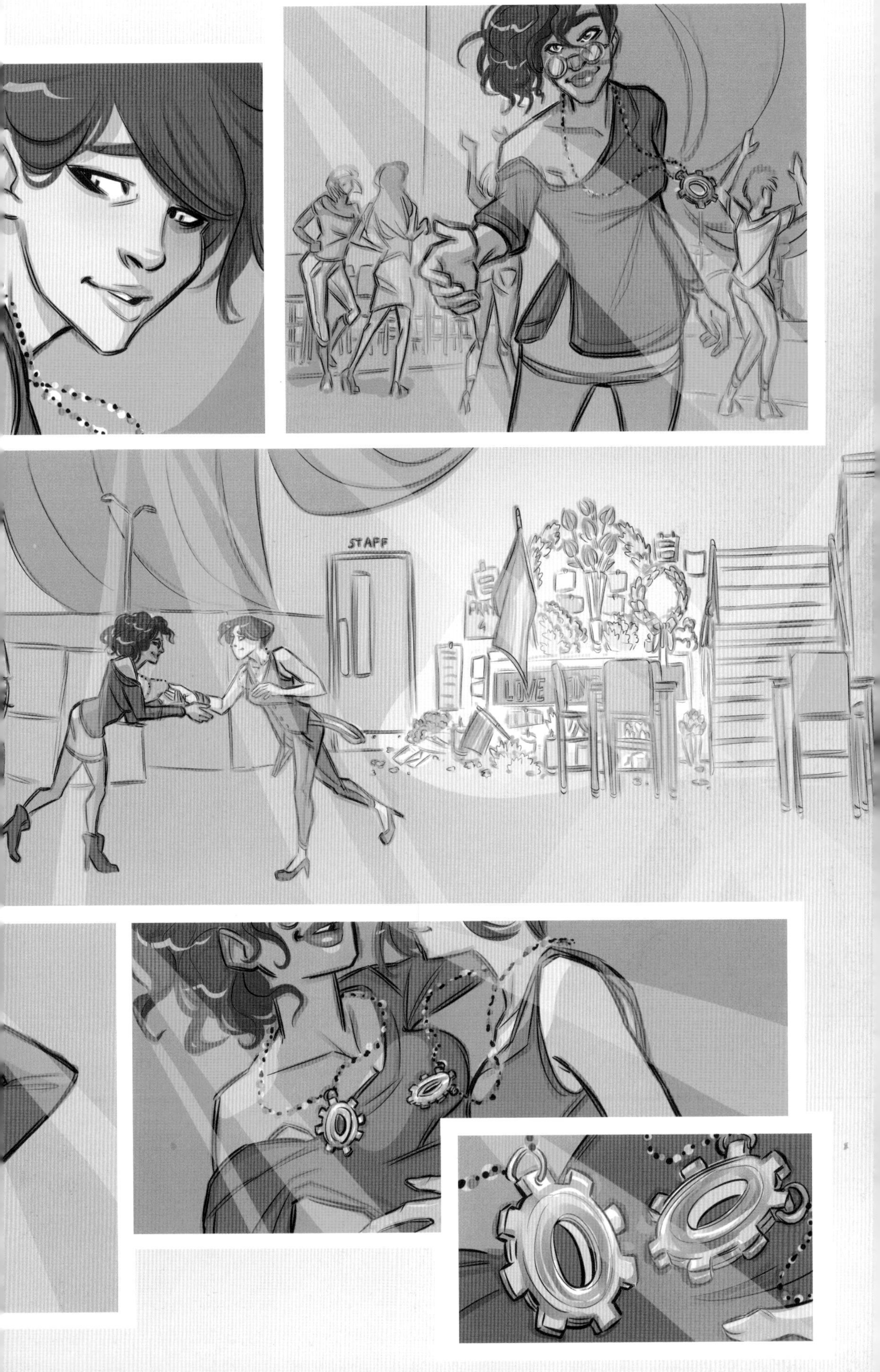
STAFF
LOVE

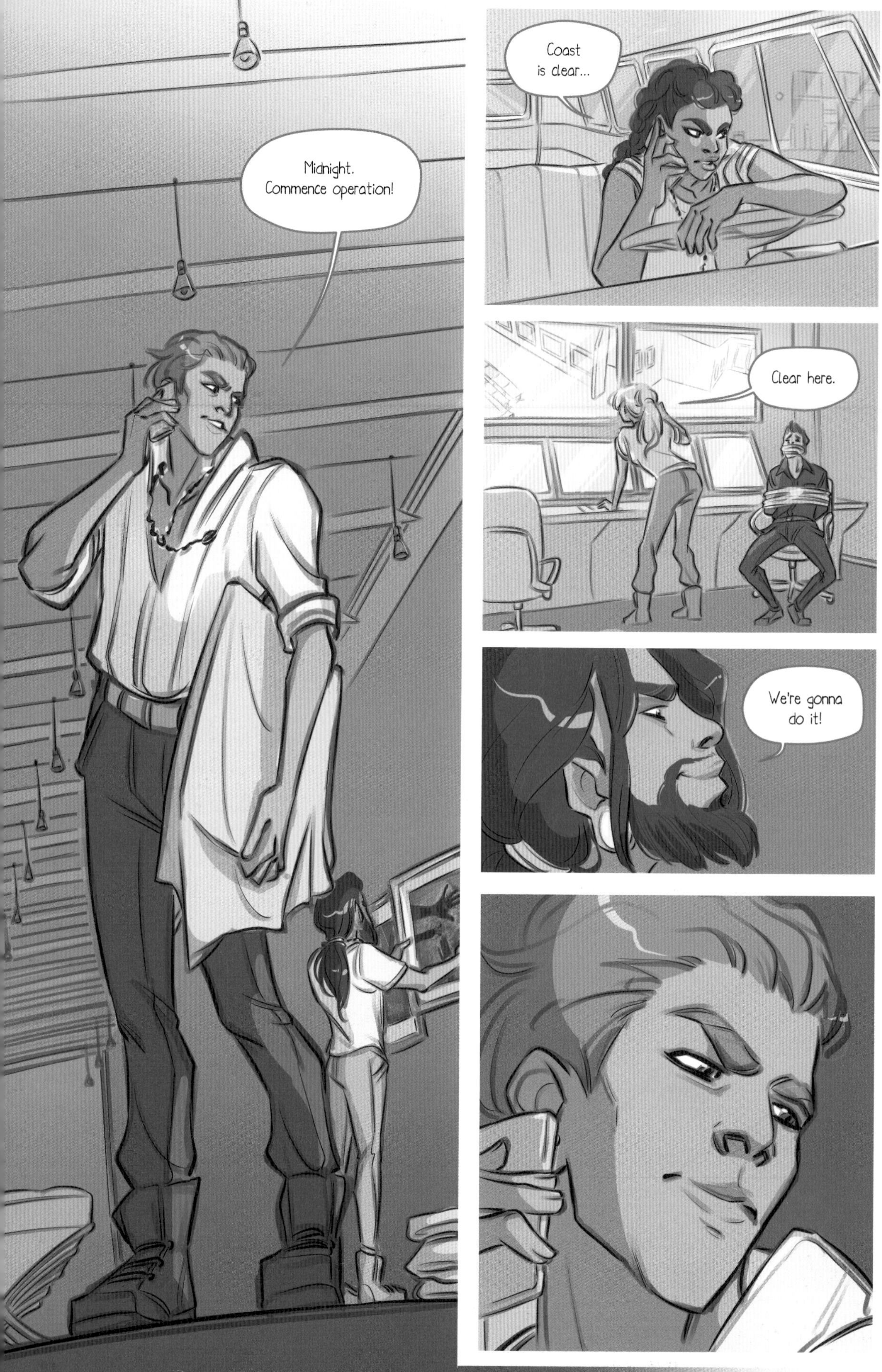
Midnight. Commence operation!
Coast is clear...
Clear here.
We're gonna do it!

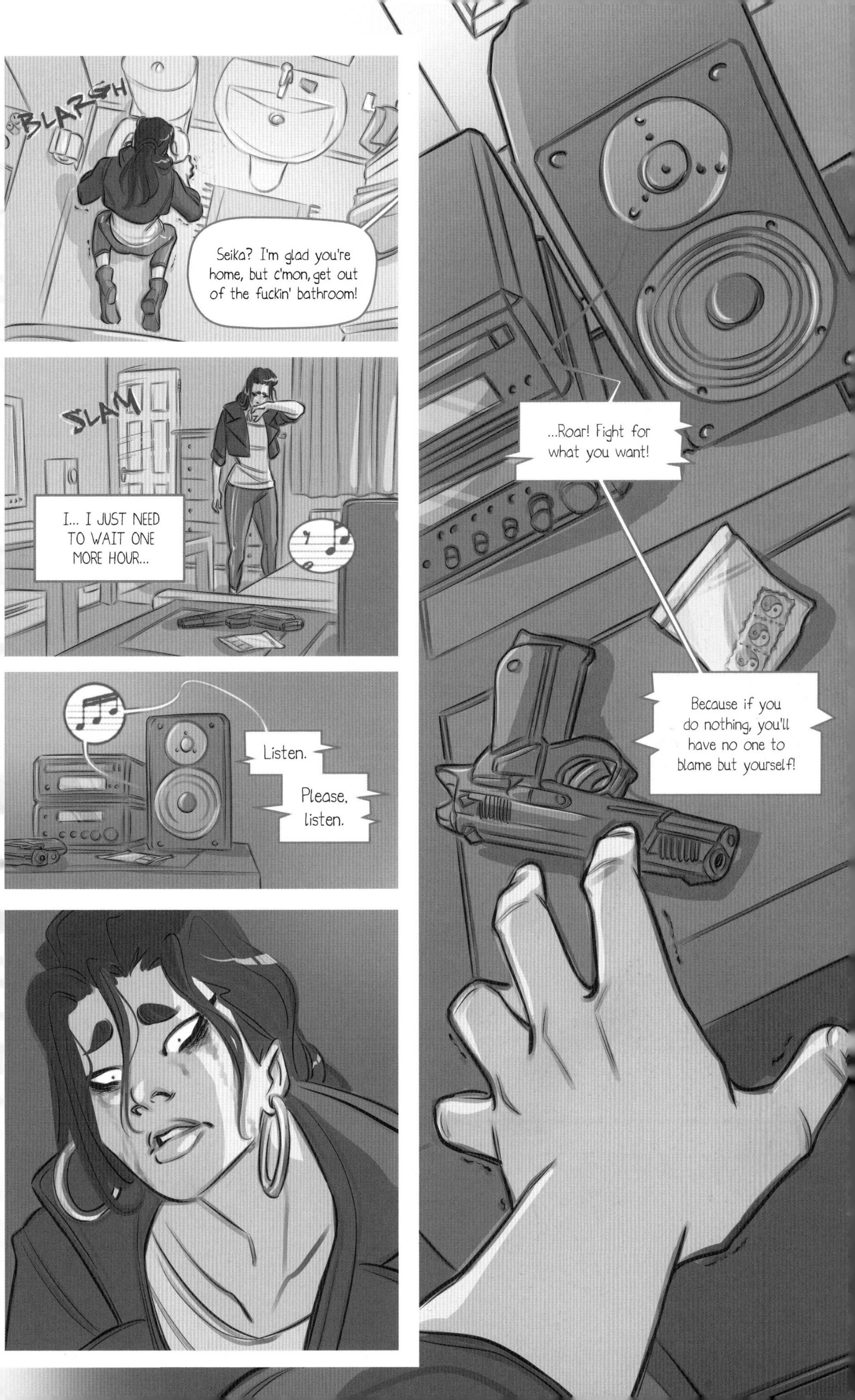
BLARGH
Seika? I'm glad you're home, but c'mon, get out of the fuckin' bathroom!
SLAM
I... I JUST NEED TO WAIT ONE MORE HOUR...
Listen.
Please, listen.
...Roar! Fight for what you want!
Because if you do nothing, you'll have no one to blame but yourself!

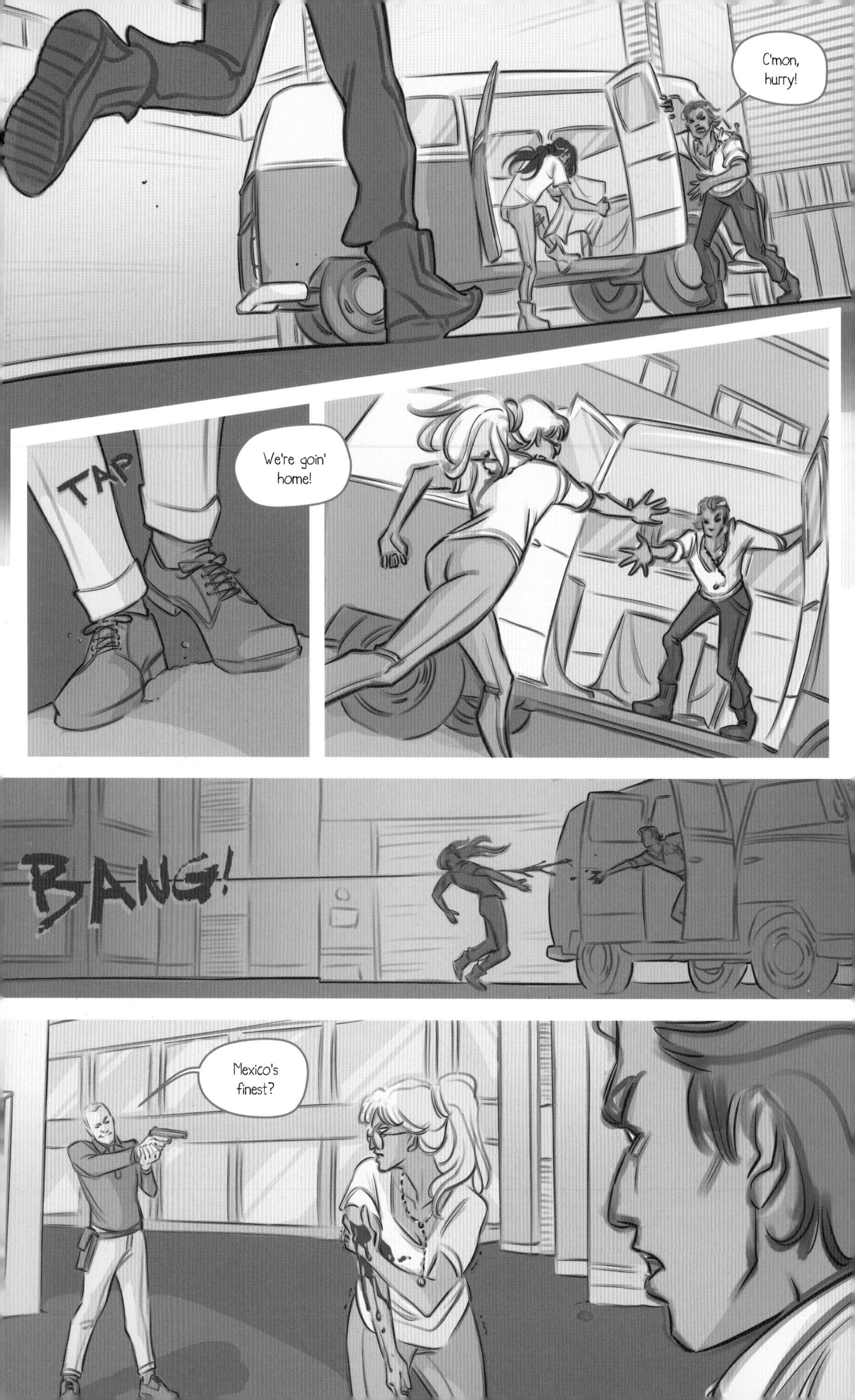
C'mon, hurry!
TAP
We're goin' home!
BANG!
Mexico's finest?

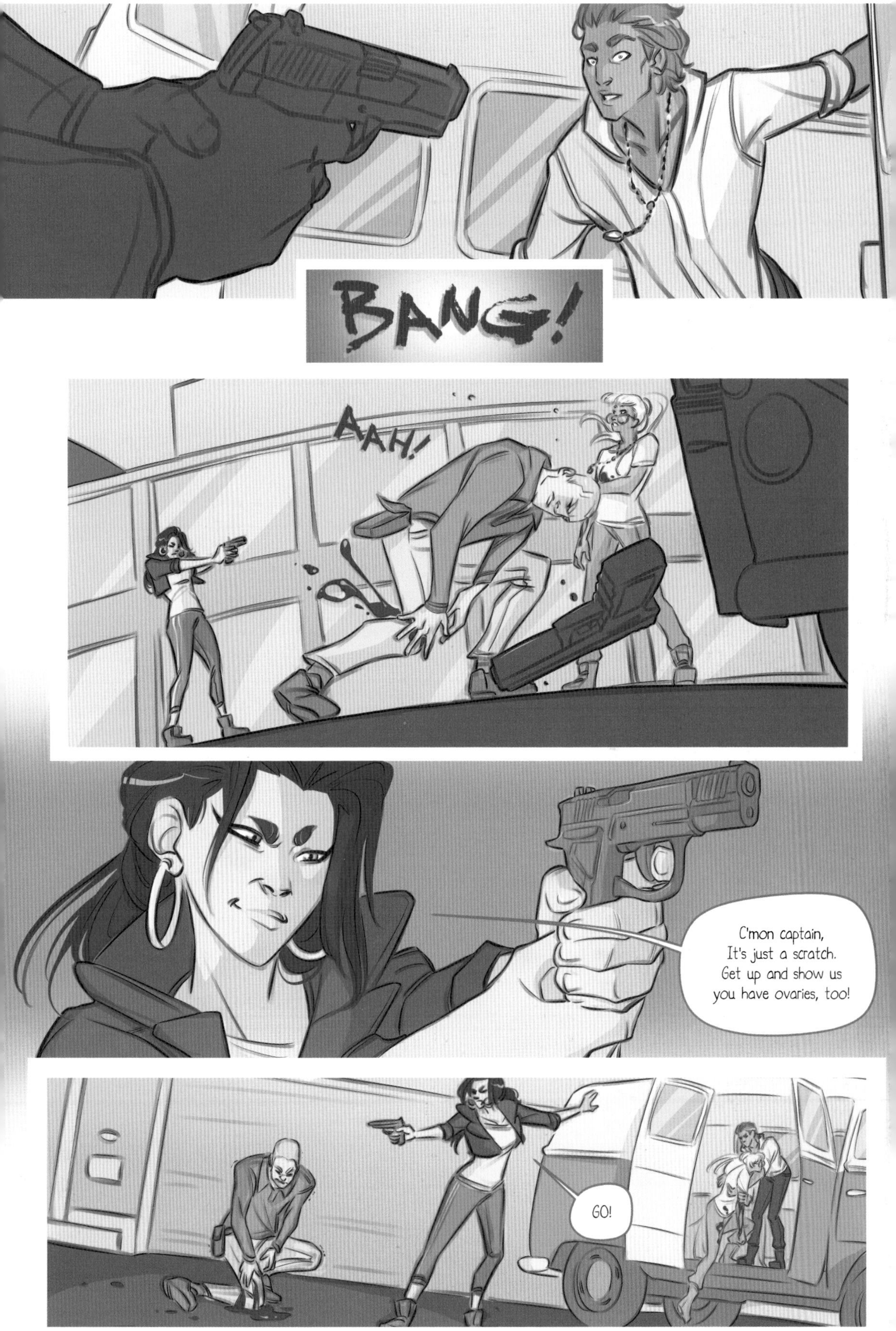
BANG!
AAH!
C'mon captain,
It's just a scratch.
Get up and show us
you have ovaries, too!
GO!

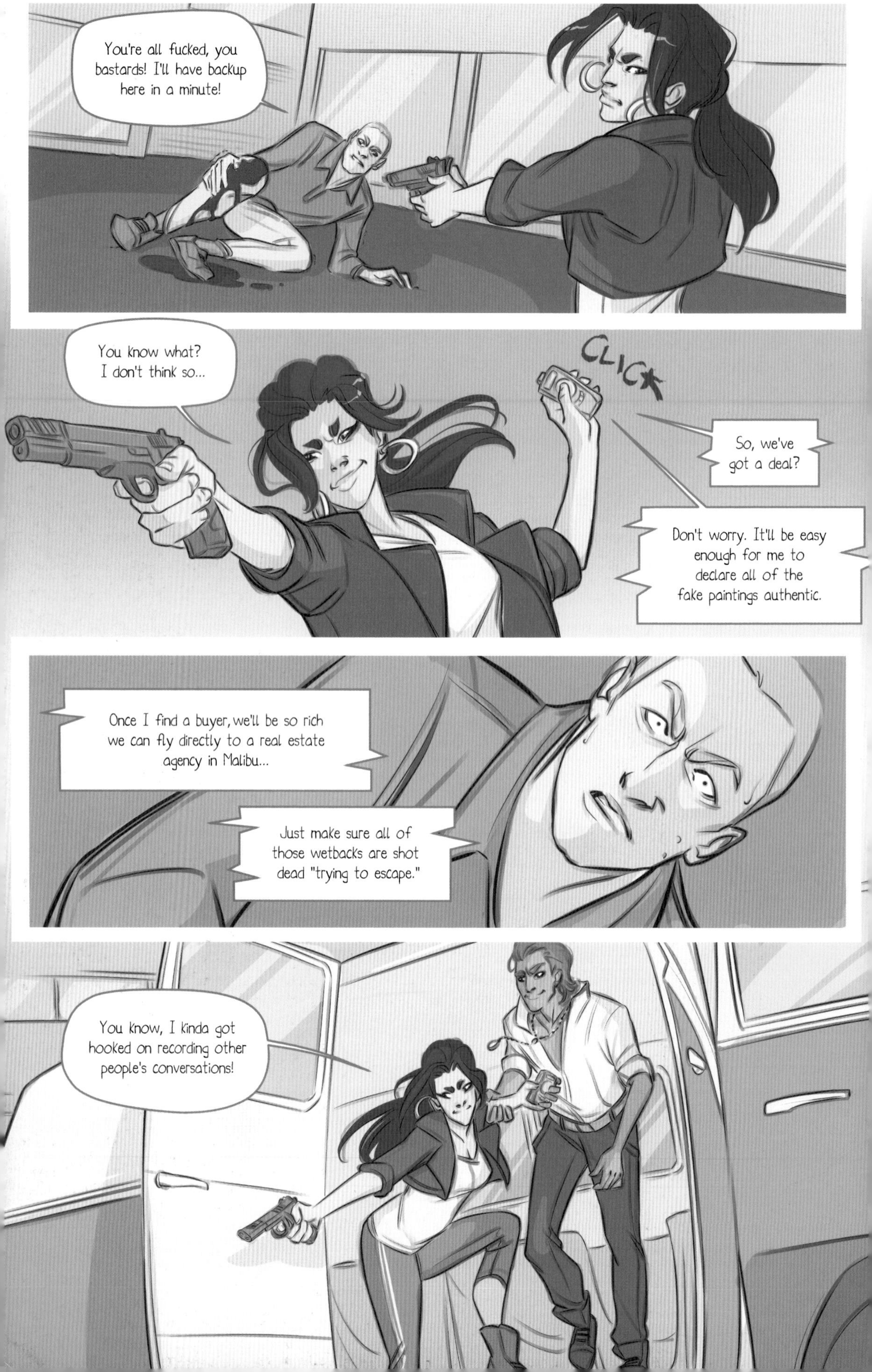
You're all fucked, you bastards! I'll have backup here in a minute!
You know what? I don't think so...
CLICK
So, we've got a deal?
Don't worry. It'll be easy enough for me to declare all of the fake paintings authentic.
Once I find a buyer, we'll be so rich we can fly directly to a real estate agency in Malibu...
Just make sure all of those wetbacks are shot dead "trying to escape."
You know, I kinda got hooked on recording other people's conversations!

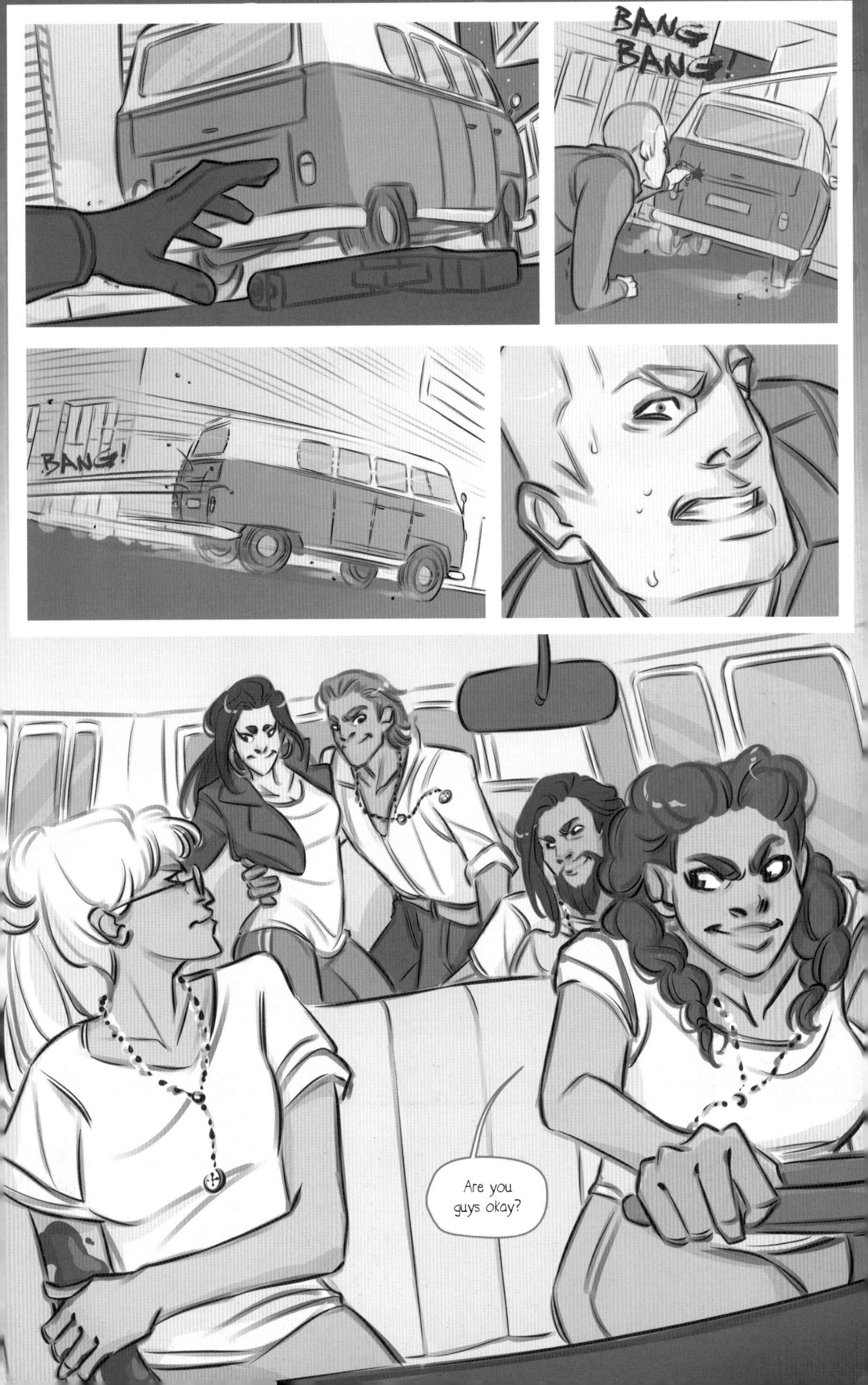
BANG BANG!
BANG!
Are you guys okay?

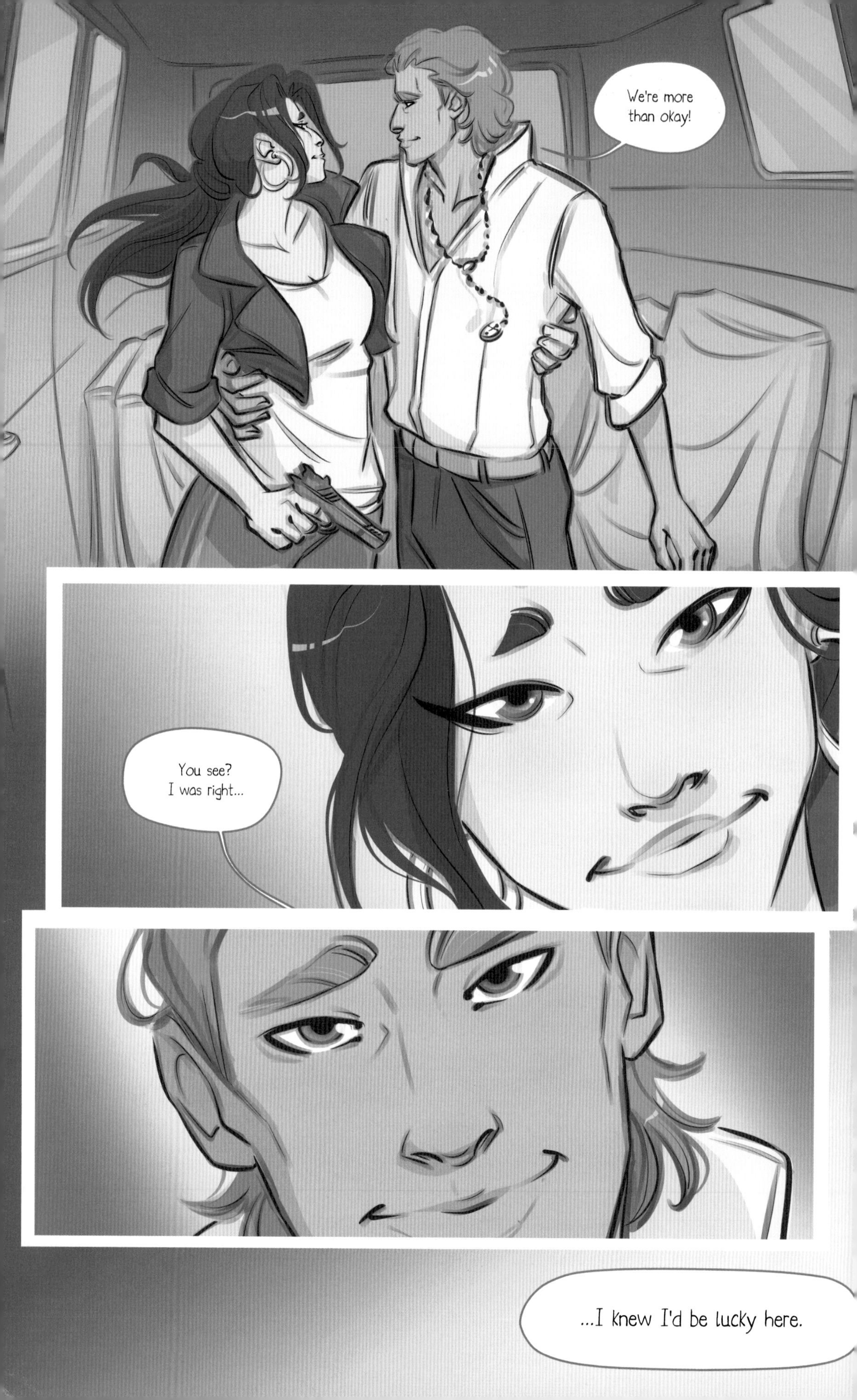
We're more than okay!
You see? I was right...
...I knew I'd be lucky here.

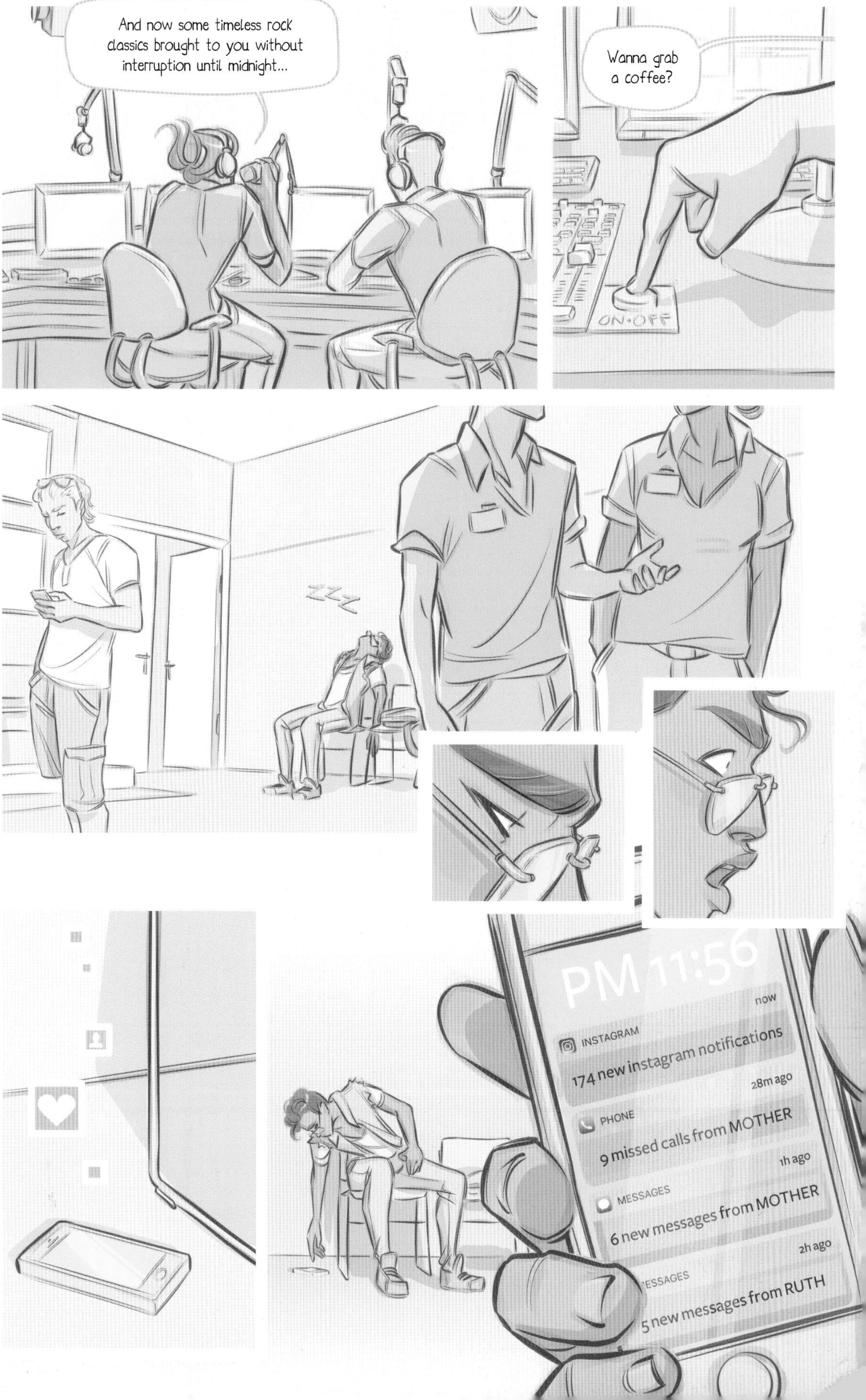
And now some timeless rock classics brought to you without interruption until midnight...
Wanna grab a coffee?
ON•OFF
ZZZ
PM 11:56
now
INSTAGRAM
174 new instagram notifications
28m ago
PHONE
9 missed calls from MOTHER
1h ago
MESSAGES
6 new messages from MOTHER
2h ago
5 new messages from RUTH

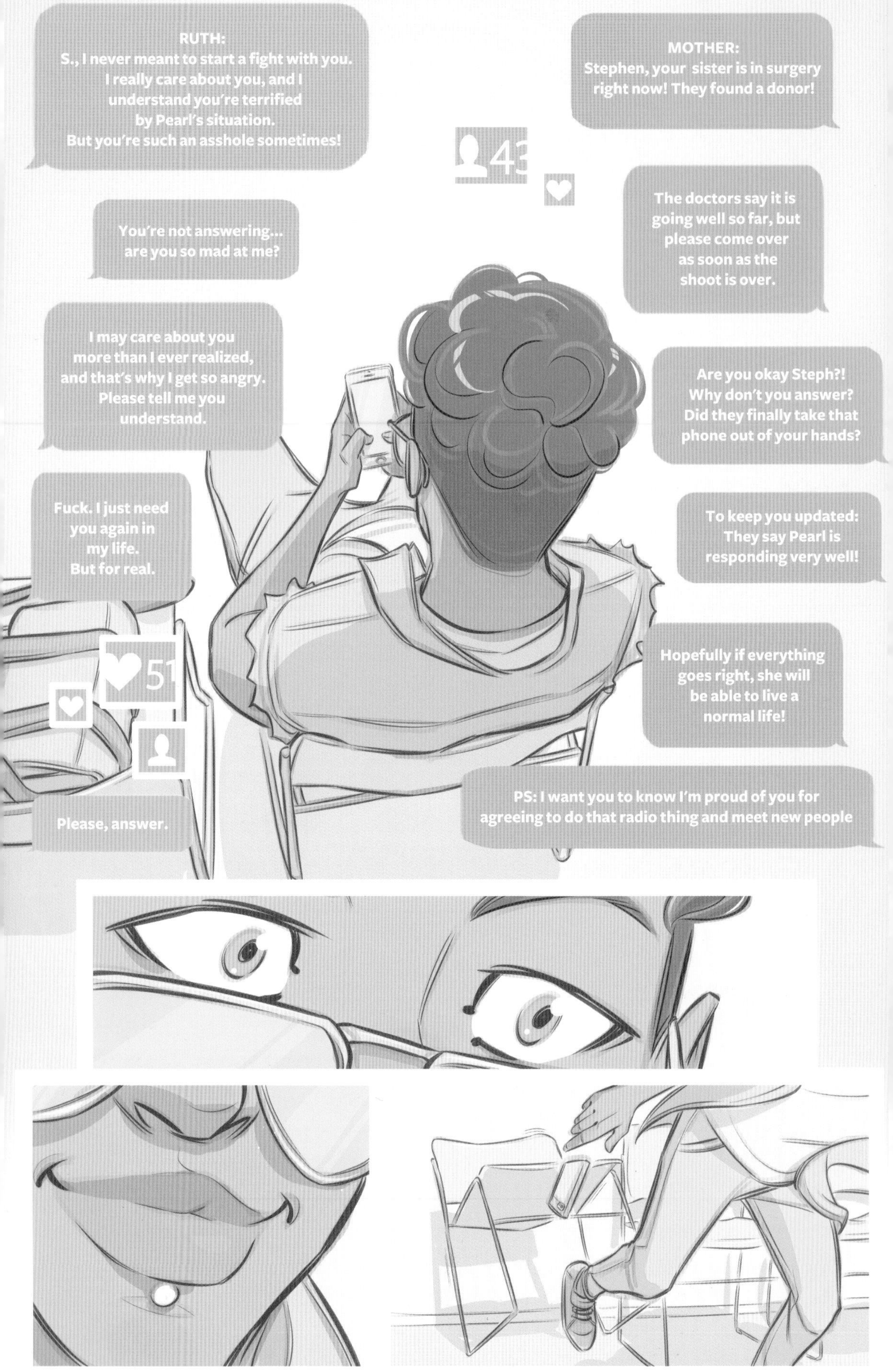
RUTH:
S., I never meant to start a fight with you. I really care about you, and I understand you're terrified by Pearl's situation. But you're such an asshole sometimes!
You're not answering... are you so mad at me?
I may care about you more than I ever realized, and that's why I get so angry. Please tell me you understand.
Fuck. I just need you again in my life. But for real.
Please, answer.
MOTHER:
Stephen, your sister is in surgery right now! They found a donor!
The doctors say it is going well so far, but please come over as soon as the shoot is over.
Are you okay Steph?! Why don't you answer? Did they finally take that phone out of your hands?
To keep you updated: They say Pearl is responding very well!
Hopefully if everything goes right, she will be able to live a normal life!
PS: I want you to know I'm proud of you for agreeing to do that radio thing and meet new people
43
51

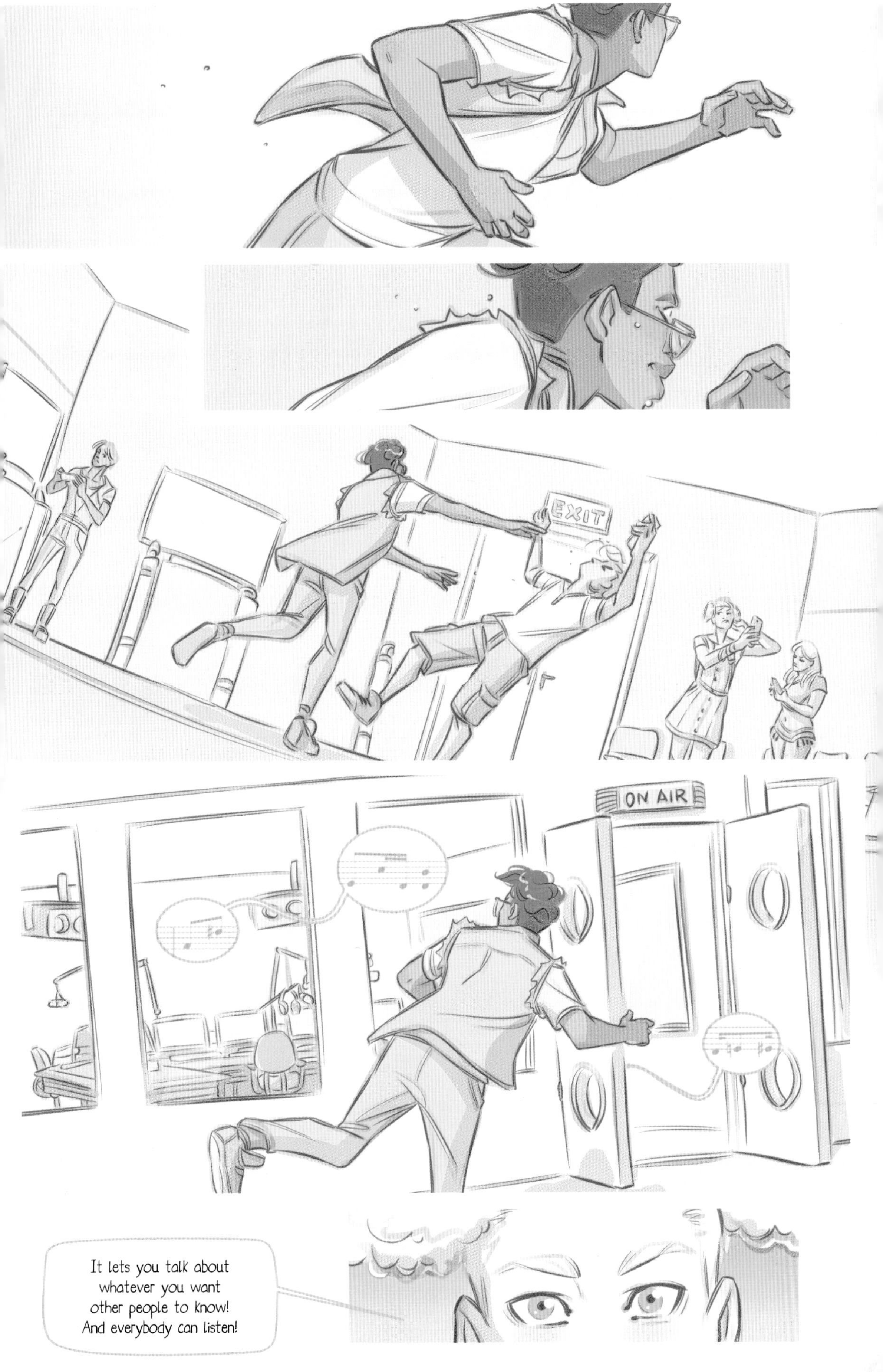
EXIT
ON AIR
It lets you talk about whatever you want other people to know! And everybody can listen!

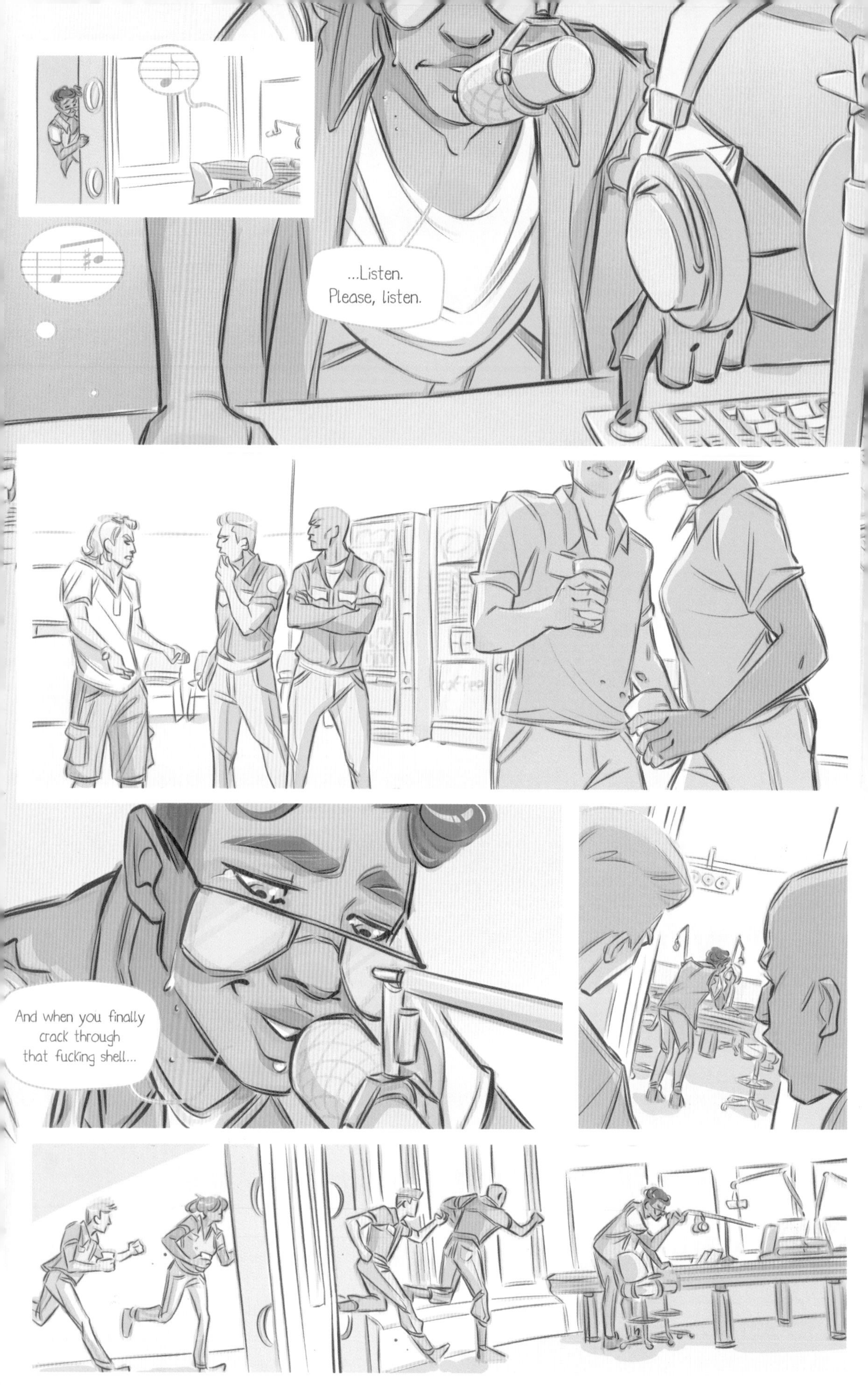
...Listen.
Please, listen.
And when you finally crack through that fucking shell...

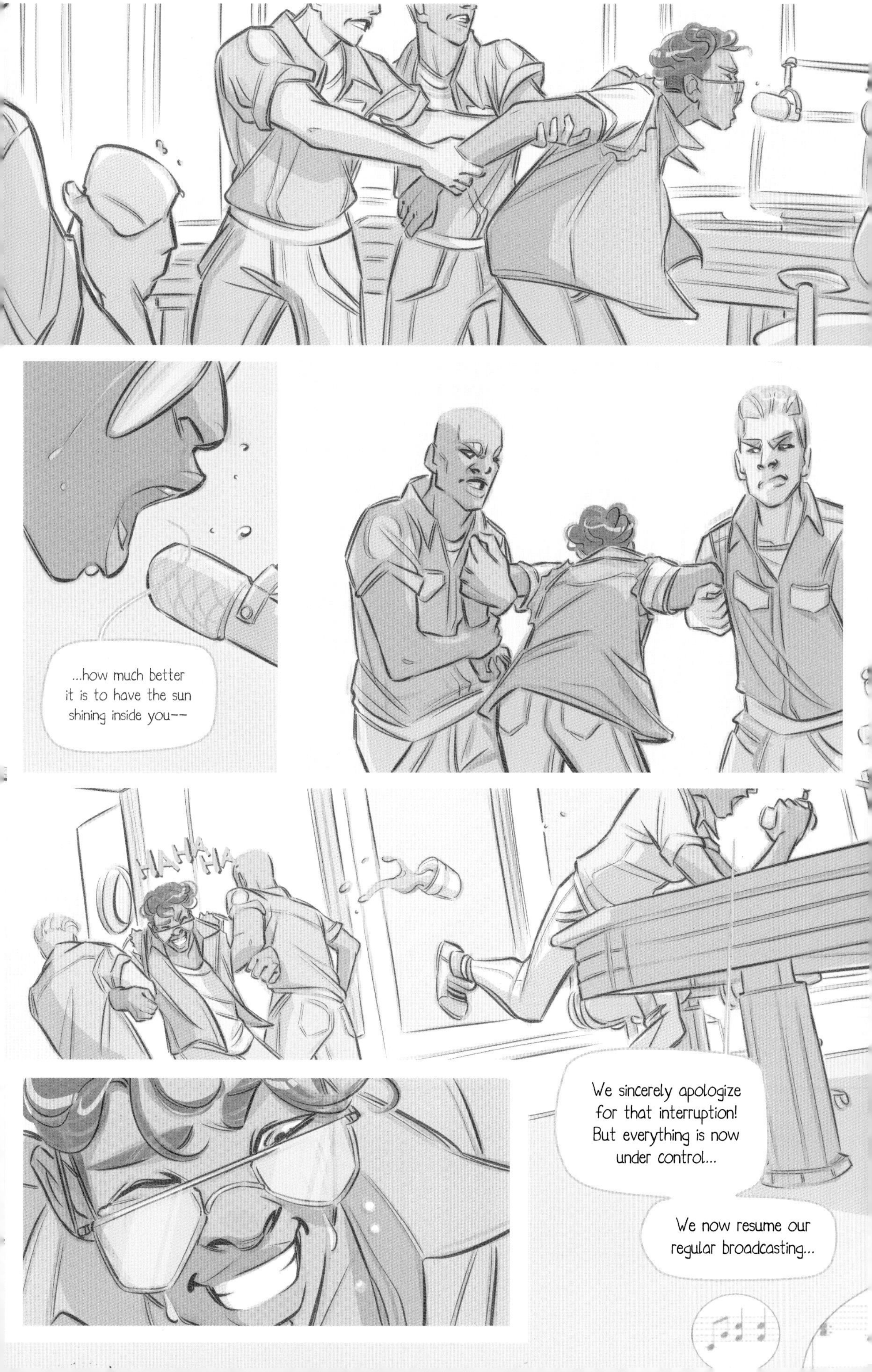
...how much better it is to have the sun shining inside you--
HAHAHA
We sincerely apologize for that interruption! But everything is now under control...
We now resume our regular broadcasting...

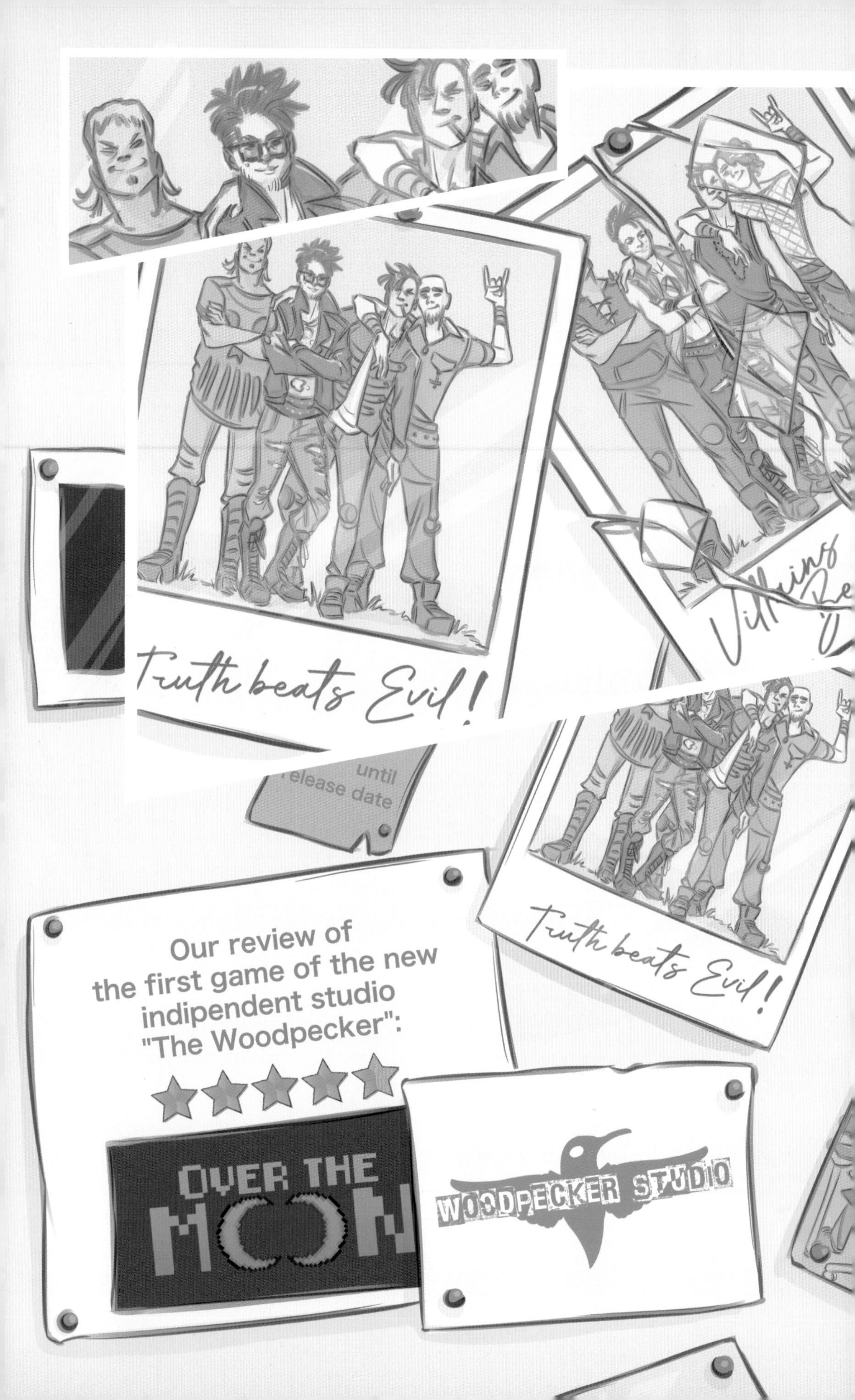
Truth beats Evil!
until
release date
Truth beats Evil!
Our review of
the first game of the new
indipendent studio
"The Woodpecker":
OVER THE
MOON
WOODPECKER STUDIO

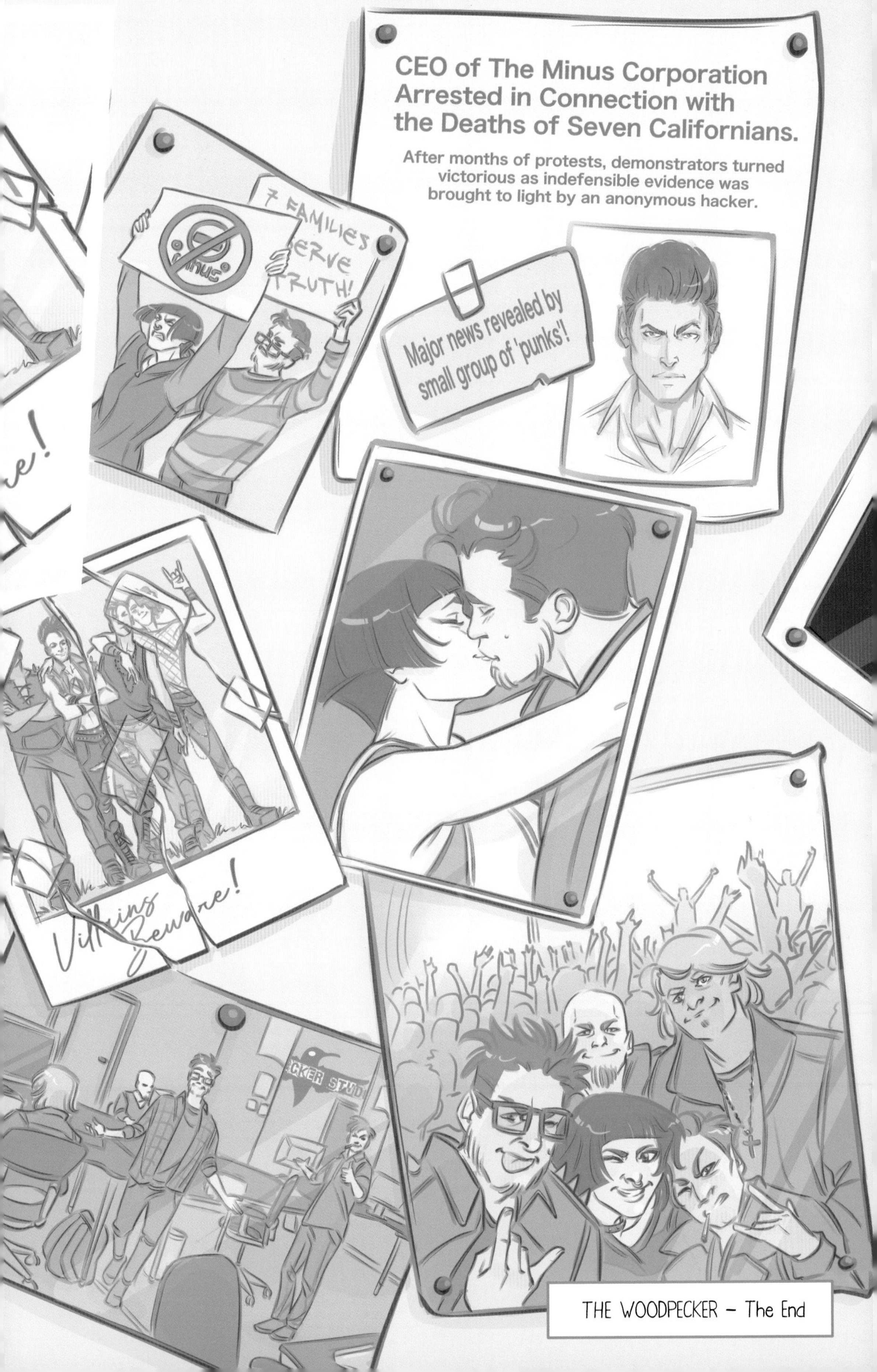
CEO of The Minus Corporation Arrested in Connection with the Deaths of Seven Californians.
After months of protests, demonstrators turned victorious as indefensible evidence was brought to light by an anonymous hacker.
Major news revealed by small group of 'punks'!
7 FAMILIES DESERVE TRUTH!
Villains Beware!
THE WOODPECKER – The End

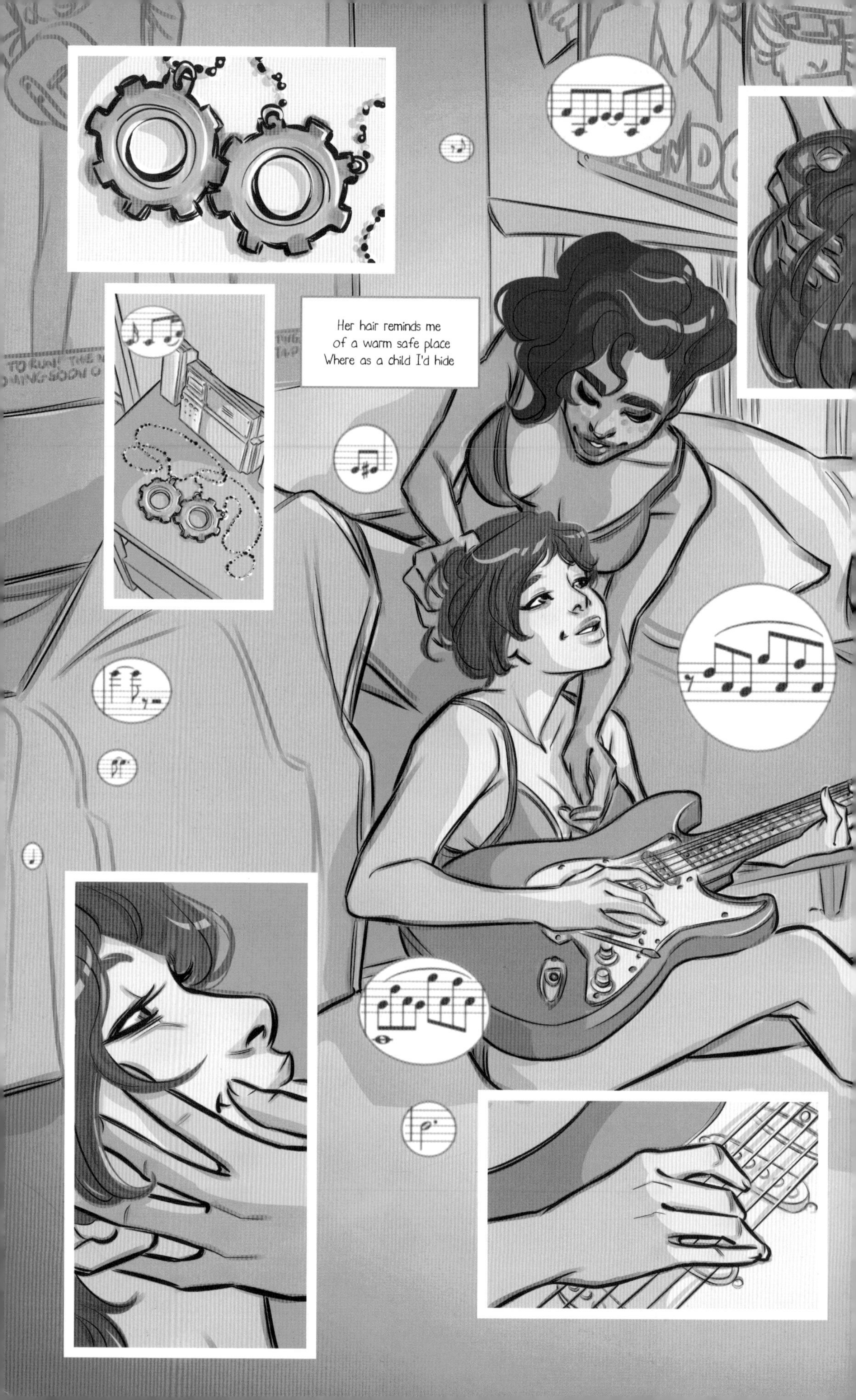
Her hair reminds me
of a warm safe place
Where as a child I'd hide

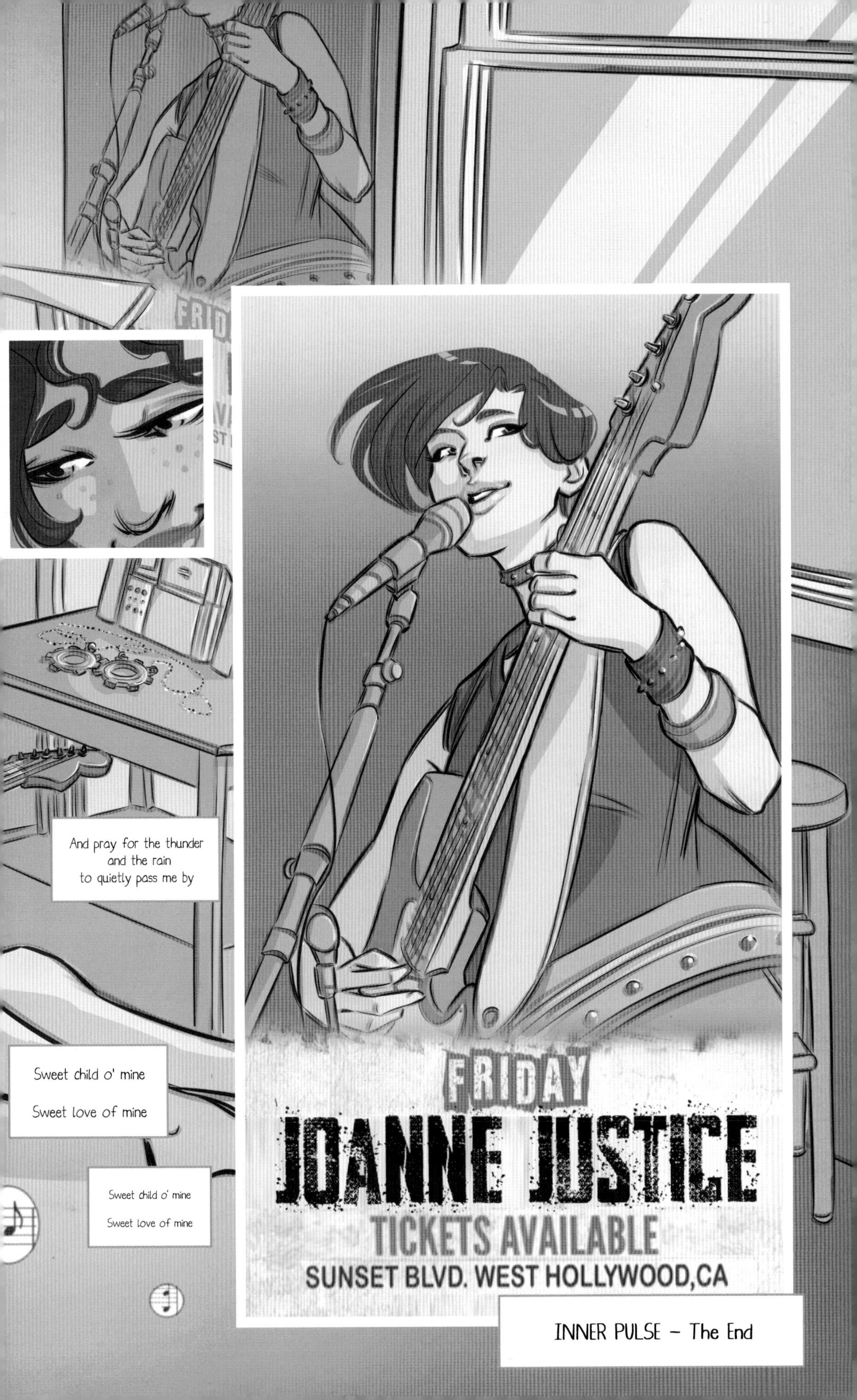

FRIDAY
JOANNE JUSTICE
TICKETS AVAILABLE
SUNSET BLVD. WEST HOLLYWOOD,CA
And pray for the thunder and the rain to quietly pass me by
Sweet child o' mine
Sweet love of mine
Sweet child o' mine
Sweet love of mine
INNER PULSE – The End

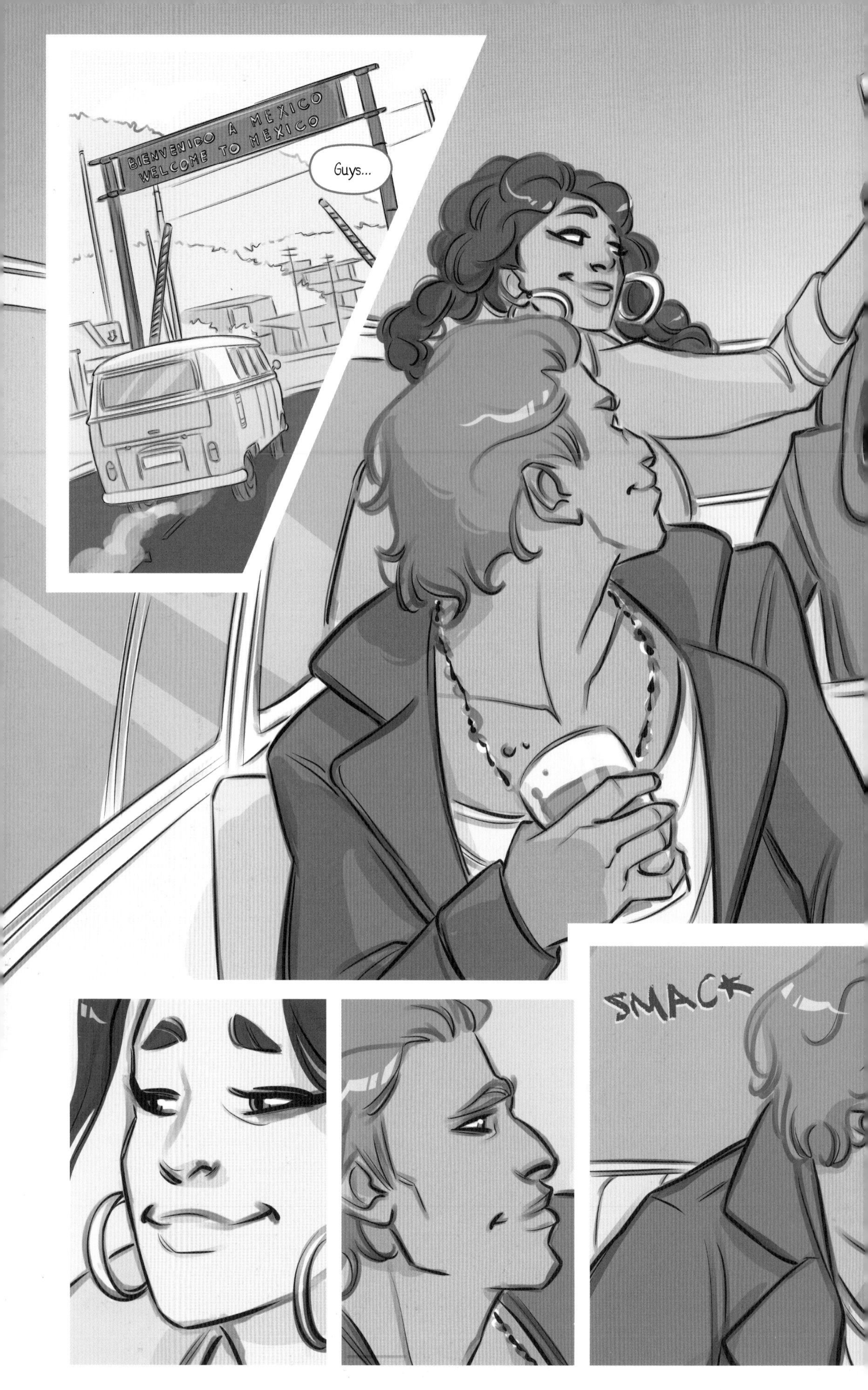
BIENVENIDO A MEXICO
WELCOME TO MEXICO
Guys...
SMACK

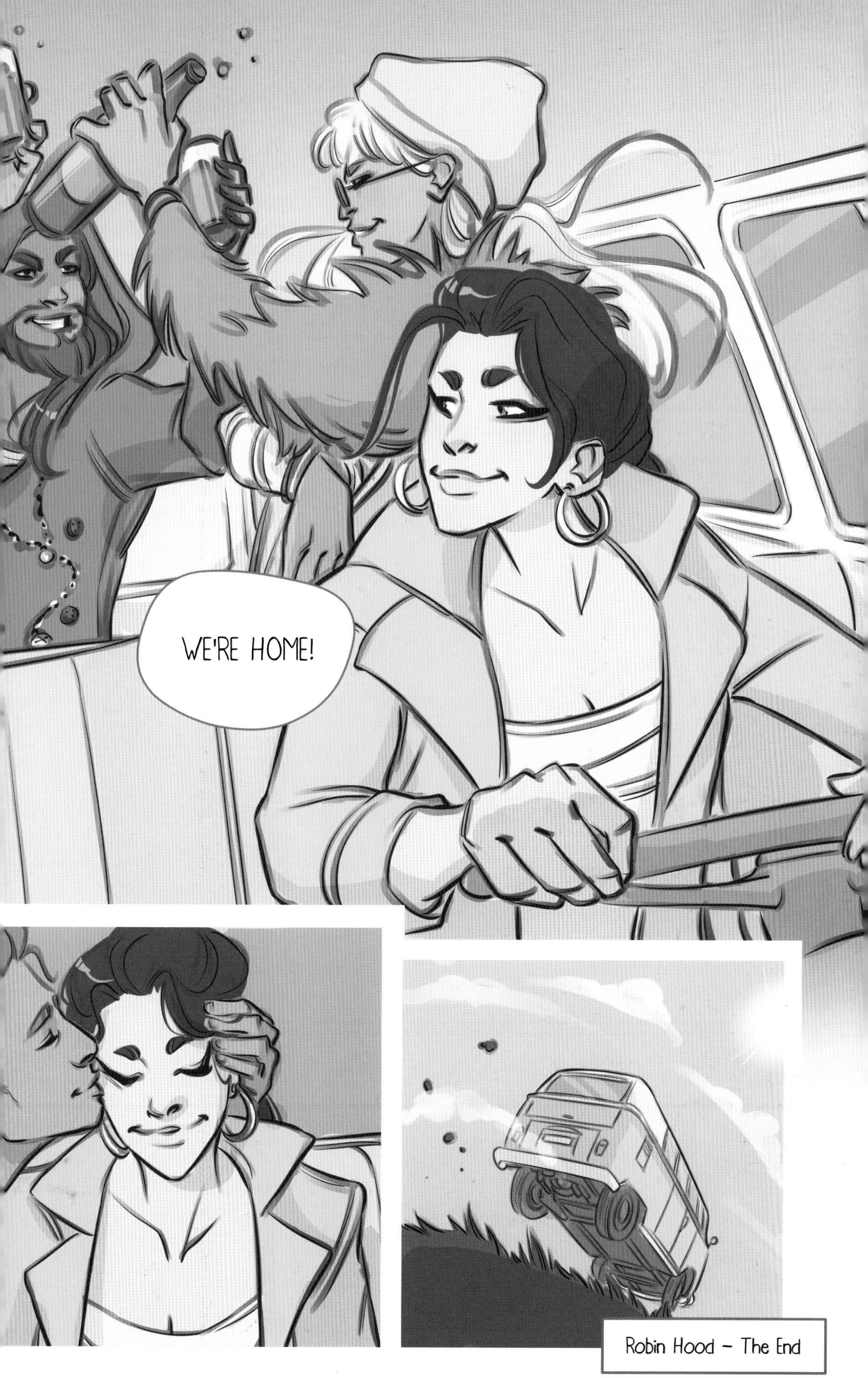
WE'RE HOME!
Robin Hood – The End

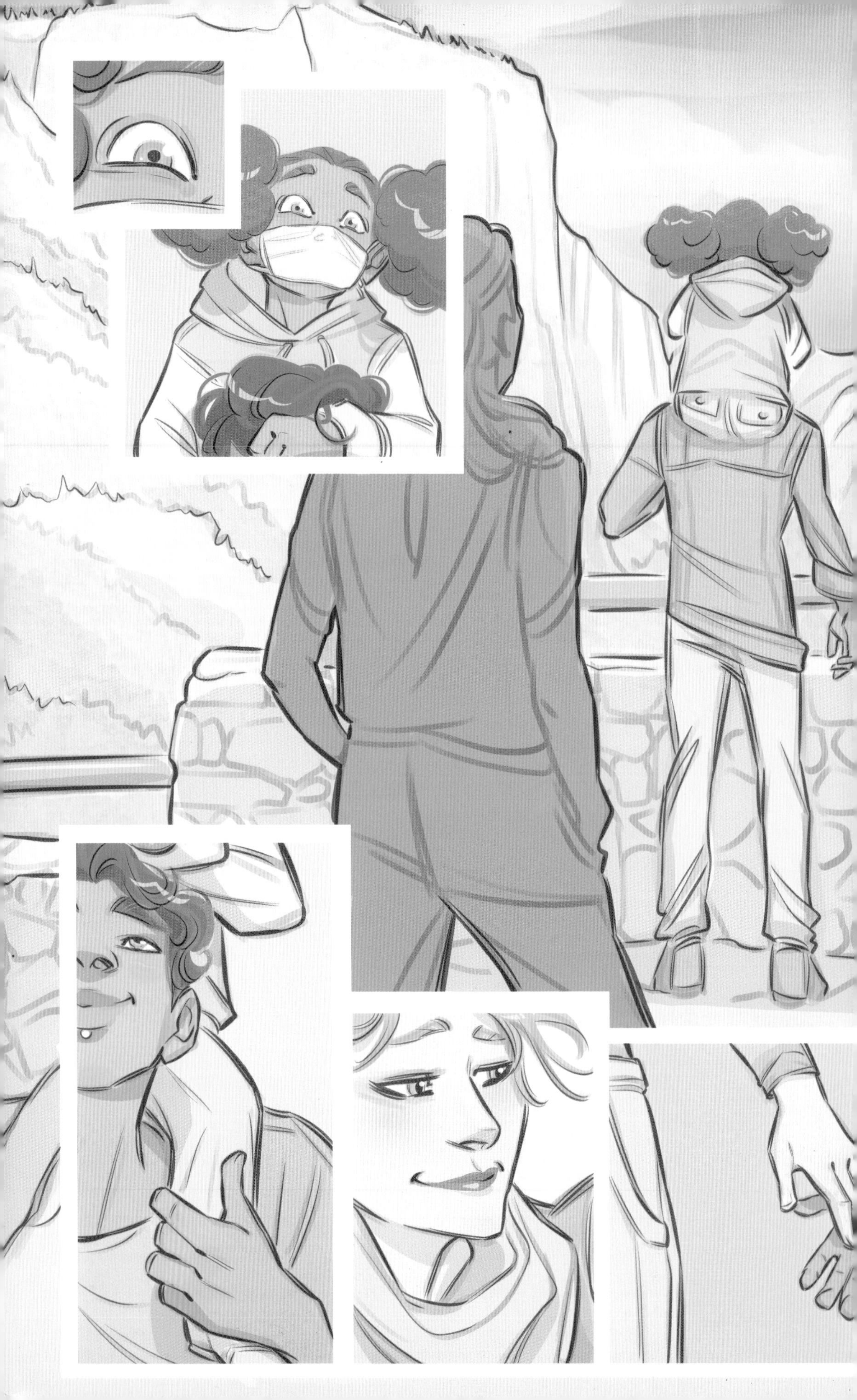

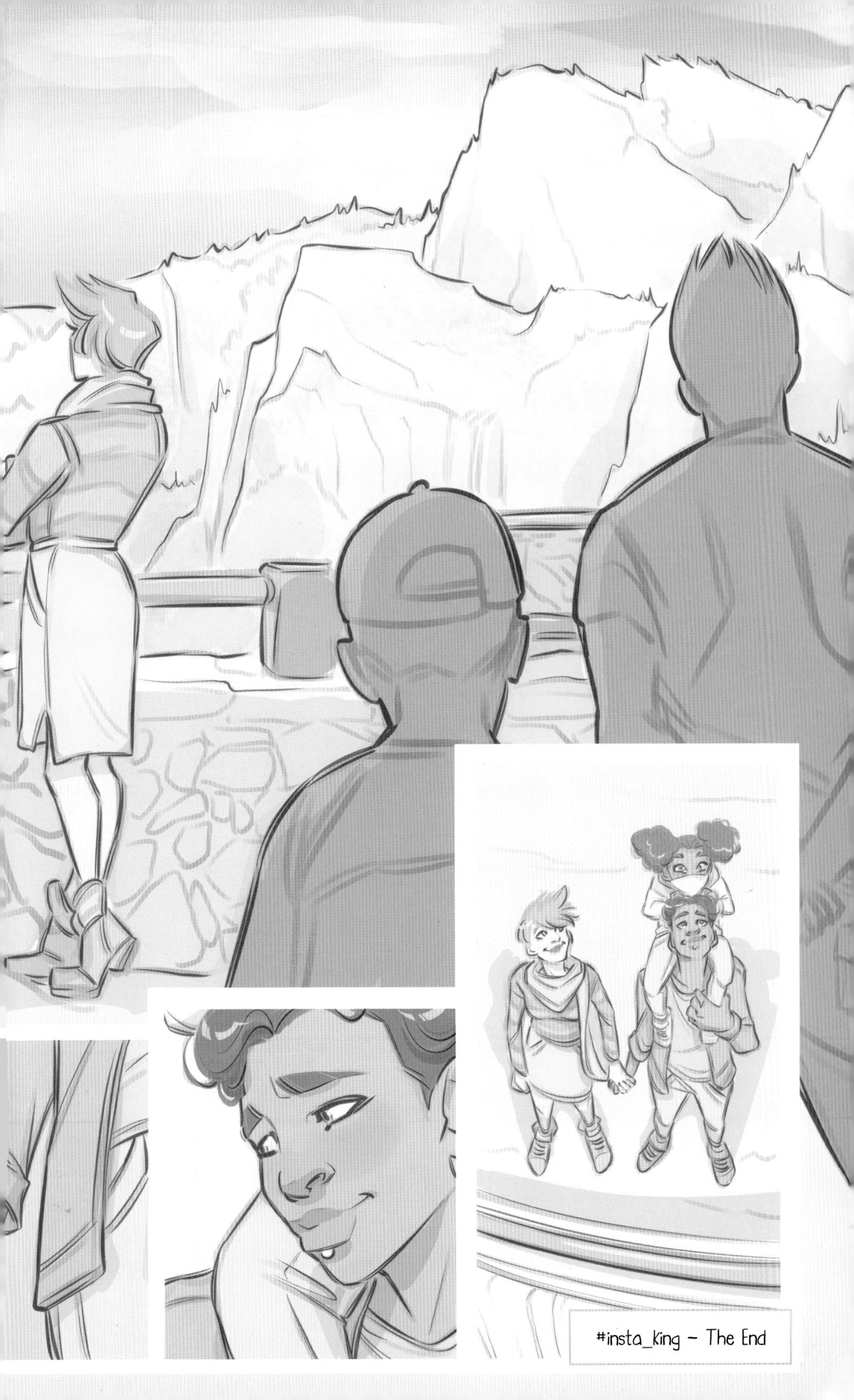
#insta_king – The End

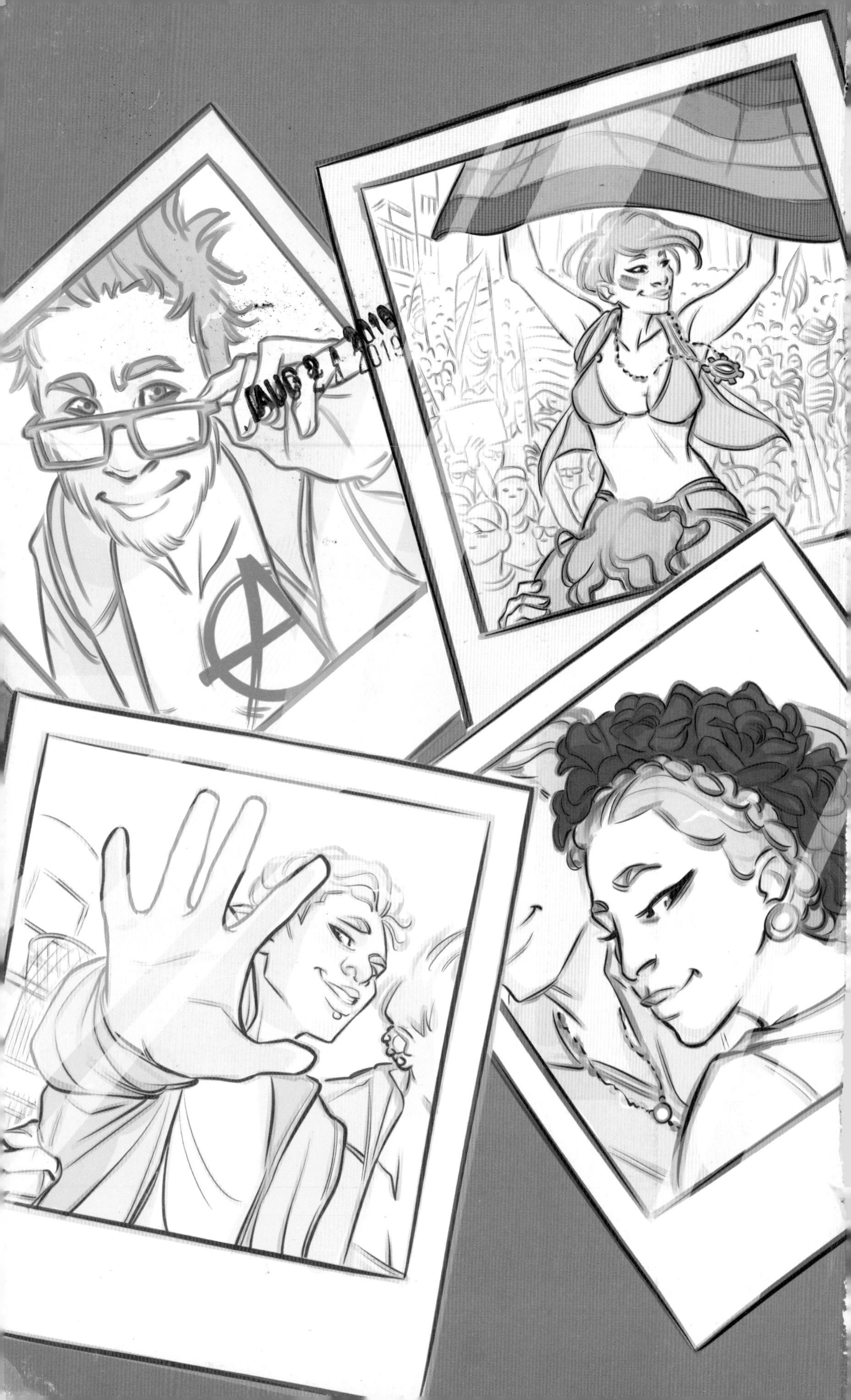